ALDOUS HUXLEY: THE CRITICAL HERITAGE

THE CRITICAL HERITAGE SERIES

GENERAL EDITOR: B. C. SOUTHAM, M.A., B.LITT. (OXON.)
Formerly Department of English, Westfield College, University of London

For a list of books in the series see the back end paper

ALDOUS HUXLEY

THE CRITICAL HERITAGE

Edited by
DONALD WATT
State University College
Geneseo, New York

ROUTLEDGE & KEGAN PAUL: LONDON AND BOSTON

First published in 1975
by Routledge & Kegan Paul Ltd
Broadway House, 68–74 Carter Lane,
London EC4V 5EL and
9 Park Street,
Boston, Mass. 02108, USA
Copyright Donald Watt 1975
No part of this book may be reproduced in
any form without permission from the
publisher, except for the quotation of brief
passages in criticism
ISBN 0 7100 8114 6

Set in 'Monotype' Bembo
and printed in Great Britain by
W & J Mackay Limited, Chatham

General Editor's Preface

The reception given to a writer by his contemporaries and near-contemporaries is evidence of considerable value to the student of literature. On one side we learn a great deal about the state of criticism at large and in particular about the development of critical attitudes towards a single writer; at the same time, through private comments in letters, journals or marginalia, we gain an insight upon the tastes and literary thought of individual readers of the period. Evidence of this kind helps us to understand the writer's historical situation, the nature of his immediate reading-public, and his response to these pressures.

The separate volumes in the *Critical Heritage Series* present a record of this early criticism. Clearly, for many of the highly productive and lengthily reviewed nineteenth- and twentieth-century writers, there exists an enormous body of material; and in these cases the volume editors have made a selection of the most important views, significant for their intrinsic critical worth or for their representative quality—perhaps even registering incomprehension!

For earlier writers, notably pre-eighteenth century, the materials are much scarcer and the historical period has been extended, sometimes far beyond the writer's lifetime, in order to show the inception and growth of critical views which were initially slow to appear.

In each volume the documents are headed by an Introduction, discussing the material assembled and relating the early stages of the author's reception to what we have come to identify as the critical tradition. The volumes will make available much material which would otherwise be difficult of access and it is hoped that the modern reader will be thereby helped towards an informed understanding of the ways in which literature has been read and judged.

B.C.S.

Contents

Antic Hay (1923)

Those Barren Leaves (1925)

Two or Three Graces (1926)

Jesting Pilate (1926)

Point Counter Point (1928)

Do What You Will (1929)

Music at Night (1931)

Brave New World (1932)

Ends and Means (1937)

After Many a Summer (1939)

Grey Eminence (1941)

Time Must Have a Stop (1944)

Preface

My main objective in making the following selection of documents has been to represent in a comprehensive way the dominant critical responses to Huxley's developing art and thought during his lifetime. Comprehensiveness is a commanding factor in making the selection because of the extent of Huxley's career and the range of his productions. Several lengthy essays, especially those in books still widely available, have been omitted in order to assure the necessary breadth. Within the framework of comprehensive representation I have cherished throughout the principle of quality. Huxley's fiction was clearly the central focus of his reputation, so the reception of his novels occupies the bulk of this volume. Nonetheless, I have tried within the limits of the book to indicate as well the important reactions to his major nonfiction. I have included a substantial but by no means exhaustive list of references in Appendix I to give full bibliographical information on materials mentioned in the Introduction.

Editors of books on authors who have provoked such lively and diversified criticism as Aldous Huxley may be advised to bear in mind his remark when introducing *Proper Studies*: 'The best I can do is to warn the reader against my distortion of the facts, and invite him to correct it by means of his own.'

Acknowledgments

I am deeply grateful to all those contributors and publishers who have provided their kind cooperation in the compilation of this volume. I would like to thank as well some of those who have contributed in diverse other ways to the development of this book: Ursula Bender, Thomas M. Donnan, G. W. Field, and Clementine Robert for their translations; Pyke Johnson Jr of Doubleday's and Beulah Hagen of Harper's for information from their files; Gifford Orwen for translating a piece (not reprinted here) by Benedetto Croce; and Sybille Bedford for allowing me to read the typescript of Volume II of her Huxley biography. A special word of thanks goes to Mrs Norah Smallwood of Chatto & Windus for patiently responding to my numerous inquiries.

Every care has been taken to get in touch with holders of copyright for the documents, but I regret that in some few cases this has not been possible. I am glad to acknowledge the permission of the following to reprint copyrighted materials (sources for each of the numbered items appear in detail in the headnotes): Appleton-Century-Crofts for No. 37; the *Atlantic Monthly* for Nos 110 and 119, copyright © (Spencer 1944, R1972) (Rolo 1948) by the Atlantic Monthly Company, Boston, Massachusetts. Reprinted with permission; Michael Ayrton for Nos 22 and 32; Frank Baldanza and the Duke University Press for No. 137, reprinted by permission of the Publisher. Copyright 1959, Duke University Press, Durham, North Carolina; Barrie & Jenkins, Publishers, for No. 73; Mrs Dorothy Cheston Bennett for Nos 29 and 54; Mrs Margaret Bevans for No. 37, reprinted with the permission of the Estate of Carl Van Doren; Professor Louis Bonnerot, 129, Av. du Général de Gaulle, 92170, Vanves, France, for No. 94; No. 36 reprinted by permission of Brandt & Brandt, *Collected Criticism*, Oxford University Press, copyright © 1935, 1939, 1940, 1942, 1951, 1958, by Conrad Aiken; the Estate of Jocelyn Brooke for No. 147b; Sir George Catlin for No. 100; Miss Dorothy E. Collins for No. 74; Commonweal Publishing Co., Inc., for Nos 99 and 111; Contemporary Review Ltd for No. 68; David Daiches and the University of Chicago Press © 1960 for No. 95; G. Duckworth & Co. for No. 6; E. P. Dutton & Co., Inc., and Chapman & Hall Ltd for No. 8, used with their permission;

Mrs Valerie Eliot for No. 43; Martin Green and *Commentary* for No. 138, reprinted from *Commentary*, by permission, copyright © 1959 by the American Jewish Committee; Madame Catherine Guillaume for No. 55; the Estate of L. P. Hartley for Nos 39 and 45; the Executors of the Ernest Hemingway Estate and Charles Scribner's Sons for No. 62; Edgar Johnson for No. 101; Richard S. Kennedy and the *Southwest Review* for No. 148; Frank Kermode for No. 144, copyright © 1962 by *Partisan Review*; Dean Carlyle King and the *Queen's Quarterly* for No. 126; the Estate of the late Mrs Frieda Lawrence and Laurence Pollinger Ltd for No. 53, from *The Letters of D. H. Lawrence*, edited by Aldous Huxley, copyright 1932 by the Estate of D. H. Lawrence, © 1960 by Angelo Ravagli and C. M. Weekley, Executors of the Estate of Frieda Lawrence Ravagli, reprinted by permission of the Viking Press, Inc.; Mrs Q. D. Leavis for No. 80; Mrs Wyndham Lewis and Russell & Russell, Publishers, for No. 76; the *Listener*, and the Society of Authors as the literary representative of the Estate of E. M. Forster, for No. 123; the *London Magazine* for No. 128; the Executors of the Estate of Michael MacCarthy for No. 57; Katharina Mann for Nos 107 and 127; Gabriel Marcel and the Société de Gens de Lettres de France for No. 85; the Literary Executor of the late W. Somerset Maugham for No. 106; Gerald Maurois and the Société de Gens de Lettres de France for No. 58; No. 75 reprinted by permission of the Modern Language Association from *PMLA*, 48 (1933); Raymond Mortimer for No. 13; the *Nation* (New York) for Nos 117 and 145; *Nature*, Macmillan Journals Ltd, for No. 66; Joseph Needham for No. 64; the *New Republic* for Nos 125, 132, and 136, reprinted by permission of the *New Republic*, © 1952, 1955, 1959 by Harrison-Blaine of New Jersey, Inc.; Nos 14 and 25 reprinted by permission of the *New York Post*; the *New York Times* for Nos 23, 33, 41, 51, 61, 84, 114, 118, 122, 129, and 146, © 1923/25/26/28/31/36/45/48/50/55/62 by the New York Times Company. Reprinted by permission; Mrs Sonia Brownell Orwell and Secker & Warburg Ltd for No. 102, excerpted from *The Collected Essays, Journalism and Letters* of George Orwell, Volumes II and IV, edited by Sonia Orwell and Ian Angus, © 1968 by Sonia Brownell Orwell. Reprinted by permission of Harcourt, Brace, Jovanovich, Inc.; *Partisan Review* copyright © May 1942 for No. 105; Nos 63 and 86 reprinted by permission of A. D. Peters & Company; *Philosophy* and the Literary Executors of William Inge for No. 116; Herbert Read and the Saturday Review Publishing Assets Industries, Inc. for No. 140; the Bertrand Russell Estate © 1932 for No. 67; Russell & Russell, for No. 88, from Alexander Henderson,

Aldous Huxley (London: Chatto & Windus, 1936; reprinted New York; Russell & Russell, 1964); *St Paul Dispatch and Pioneer Press* for No. 15; the Saturday Review Publishing Assets Industries, Inc., for No. 130; Charles Scribner's Sons for No. 93; Secker & Warburg Ltd and Alfred A. Knopf, Inc. for No. 59; the *Sewanee Review* and the University of the South for No. 77; the *Spectator* for Nos 10, 20, 42, 46, 60, 65, 78, 91, 103, 133, 139, and 142; the Statesman & Nation Publishing Co. for Nos 4, 5, 21, 31, 47, 79, 97, 113, 115, 120, 121, 124, 134, 135, and 147a; George Stevens for No. 82; Suhrkamp Verlag for No. 72, from Hermann Hesse, *Schriften zur Literatur*, Volume 2, copyright © 1970 by Suhrkamp Verlag. All rights reserved; the *Sunday Express* for No. 19; the *Sunday Times* for Nos 38, 90, and 141; Times Newspapers Ltd for Nos 9, 18, 28, 30, 44, 56, 96, and 112, reproduced from the *Times Literary Supplement* by permission; No. 108 reprinted with the permission of W. H. Allen & Co. Ltd, and Farrar, Straus & Giroux, Inc., from *Classics and Commercials* by Edmund Wilson, copyright 1950 by Edmund Wilson; Virginia Woolf's Literary Estate for Nos 1 and 2; the *Yale Review* for No. 143, copyright Yale University Press; M. B. Yeats, A. P. Watt & Son, Ltd, and the Macmillan Publishing Company for No. 89, from *Letters of William Butler Yeats*, edited by Alan Wade (copyright 1953, 1954 by Anne Butler Yeats).

Abbreviations

B	Sybille Bedford, *Aldous Huxley: A Biography*, 2 vols (London: Chatto & Windus, Collins, 1973–4). References to the second volume apply to the typescript, since the entire biography had not been published when the present edition was compiled.
DNB	*Dictionary of National Biography*
ES	Claire John Eschelbach and Joyce Lee Shober, *Aldous Huxley: A Bibliography* (Berkeley: University of California, 1961)
L	*Letters of Aldous Huxley*, ed. Grover Smith (London: Chatto & Windus, 1969)
MV	*Aldous Huxley 1894–1963: A Memorial Volume*, ed. Julian Huxley (New York: Harper & Row, 1965)
NYHTBR	*New York Herald Tribune Book Review*
NYTBR	*New York Times Book Review*
PR	Interview of Huxley by George Wickes and Ray Frazer, *Writers at Work: The 'Paris Review' Interviews*, Second Series (New York: Viking, 1963)
TLS	*Times Literary Supplement*

A List of Huxley's Major Works

References to Huxley's books, unless otherwise noted, are to the Chatto & Windus Collected Edition. In the following list are given for each major title the original year of publication, and then the year of printing for the Collected Edition copy I have used. For the years in which each title first appeared in a collected format, see Appendix III.

Adonis and the Alphabet (American title, *Tomorrow and Tomorrow and Tomorrow*) 1956*

After Many a Summer (American title, *After Many a Summer Dies the Swan*) 1939, 1968

Along the Road 1925, 1948

Antic Hay 1923, 1949

Ape and Essence 1948, 1971

The Art of Seeing 1942, 1971

Beyond the Mexique Bay 1934, 1950

Brave New World 1932, 1967

Brave New World Revisited 1958, 1972

Brief Candles 1930, 1970

Collected Essays 1959†

Collected Short Stories 1957, 1969

Crome Yellow 1921, 1963

The Devils of Loudun 1952, 1971

Do What You Will 1929, 1970

The Doors of Perception 1954, 1968

Ends and Means 1937, 1969

Eyeless in Gaza 1936, 1969

The Genius and the Goddess 1955*

Grey Eminence 1941, 1956

Heaven and Hell 1956, 1968

Island 1962, 1972

Jesting Pilate 1926, 1957

Limbo 1920, 1962

Literature and Science 1963, 1970

Little Mexican (American title, *Young Archimedes*) 1924, 1968

Mortal Coils 1922, 1958
Music at Night 1931, 1960
The Olive Tree 1936, 1960
On the Margin 1923, 1956
The Perennial Philosophy 1945, 1969
Point Counter Point 1928, 1963
Proper Studies 1927, 1957
Science, Liberty, and Peace 1946, 1970
Texts and Pretexts 1932, 1959
Themes and Variations 1950, 1954
Those Barren Leaves 1925, 1969
Time Must Have a Stop 1944, 1966
Two or Three Graces 1926, 1963
Verses and A Comedy 1946★

★ Has not yet appeared in the collected editions: all references are to the British first edition.
† No collected edition, published only in America.

Introduction

For Aldous Huxley (1894–1963) life and music shared a common quality: they could each be described as a simultaneity of co-existing incompatibles. The same description may be applied to the critical reception of Huxley's work. He was hailed as an emancipator of the modern mind and condemned as an irresponsible free-thinker; celebrated as a leading intelligence of his age and denounced as an erudite show-off; admired as the wittiest man of his generation and dismissed as a clever misanthrope. A few pages of his writing or half a career served equally to evoke the incompatible opinions. Opening the cover of *Point Counter Point*, Wyndham Lewis objected to a 'tone of vulgar complicity with the dreariest of suburban library-readers' (No. 76), while André Maurois discovered in the same opening pages scenes 'worthy of the great Russians' (No. 58). In 1933 C. P. Snow claimed that Huxley 'ought to seem the most significant English novelist of his day' (No. 73a), while G. K. Chesterton quipped: '[He] is ideally witty; but he is at his wit's end' (No. 74).

Huxley's writing, both the fiction and the nonfiction, provoked controversy at almost every stage. Those very features of his work which drew most praise—the scientific contexts, the detached irony, the panoply of startling ideas—provided as often as not evidence which his critics felt could be used against him. The Huxley critical heritage is a history of vigorous contention spurred by not always equal shares of insight and misunderstanding.

At the center of that history was Huxley's own peculiar approach to fiction, what George Catlin (No. 100) called 'that strange mutt of literature,' the 'novel of ideas.' The term provided at most a sketchy description of Huxley's books, but his critics were at a loss to suggest anything better. His attitude toward fiction seemed too casual and iconoclastic. 'There aren't any divinely laid down canons of the novel,' he asserted. 'All you need is to be interesting' (Parmenter, p. 11).[1] Huxley's novels flaunted those conventions of logical realism followed faithfully by older writers, such as John Galsworthy and Arnold Bennett. Accordingly, his younger audience in the 1920s found him refreshing: 'By comparison, most other contemporary writers seemed stuffy, unenlightened, and old-fashioned' (Brooke, p. 6). But at the same time his writing appeared to defy the new authoritative view of fiction as an organic art form which had evolved through the influence of Flaubert and Henry James. Developing standards of criticism in the earlier twentieth century were deeply affected by Jamesian aesthetics, by Bloomsbury's belief in the autonomy of art, and by a severely formalist approach to literature. Huxley's practice of the novel ran counter to these trends: 'From a Jamesian perspective that insisted on rigidly delimiting a fictional world through a filtering consciousness with which the reader was asked to identify but could never wholly rely on, Huxley the novelist was inevitably unsatisfactory' (Firchow, p. 7). To many observers the failure of Huxley's fiction either to adopt a tradi-tional posture or to adhere to a formalist criterion meant that he was stuck in an untenable sort of writing which hovered indecisively be-tween the novel and the essay.

Huxley's critics were slow to realize that he held a different concept of fiction. Like Quarles in *Point Counter Point*, he readily admitted the problems he had in creating conventional plots: 'I don't think of myself as a congenital novelist—no. For example, I have great difficulty in inventing plots. Some people are born with an amazing gift for story-telling; it's a gift which I've never had at all' (*PR*, p. 205). But the telling of stories, for Huxley, was only a small part of what fiction could accomplish. He wrote to Eugene Saxton on 24 May 1933: 'I probably have an entirely erroneous view about fiction. For I feel about fiction as Nurse Cavell felt about patriotism: that it is not enough. Whereas the "born storyteller" obviously feels that it is enough' (*L*, p. 371). The popular style of fiction written by Dumas, Scott, or Stevenson could not satisfy Huxley. Also, as much as he appreciated Arnold Bennett's friendship and advice, he recoiled from the elaborate realism of books like *Riceyman Steps* (*L*, p. 228). Throughout his life Huxley sought to write another kind of fiction. 'My own aim,' he told an early inter-viewer, 'is to arrive, technically, at a perfect fusion of the novel and the essay, a novel in which one can put all one's ideas, a novel like a hold-all' (Maraini, p. 78). The drive to synthesize multifarious attitudes to-wards life moved Huxley to develop an integrative approach to fiction which in its breadth, he hoped, would transcend the limits of purist art. In this radically changed sense Huxley believed that fiction, along with biography and history, 'are *the* forms':

My goodness, Dostoevski is six times as profound as Kierkegaard, because he writes *fiction*. In Kierkegaard you have this Abstract Man going on and on—like

Coleridge—why, it's *nothing* compared with the really profound Fictional Man, who has always to keep these tremendous ideas *alive* in a concrete form. In fiction you have the reconciliation of the absolute and the relative, so to speak, the expression of the general in the particular. And this, it seems to me, is the exciting thing—both in life and in art (*PR*, pp. 213–14).

Huxley at heart cherished the belief that the synthesis of an integrative, not organic fiction, of fiction which would 'bring it all in' as he told Laura (his second wife), would evolve into a comprehensive vision for modern man which could, ultimately, contribute some healing power to a ravished world.[2]

If critical neglect of his positive aims bothered Huxley, he rarely showed it. His responses to his critics were infrequent, oblique, usually private. On occasion he replied in correspondence to a reviewer, such as Henry Seidel Canby on *Point Counter Point* (No. 52), or to a friend, such as Sybille Bedford on *Grey Eminence* (*L*, p. 476). But he told an interviewer near the end of his career that his critics

. . . never had any effect on me, for the simple reason that I've never read them. I've never made a point of writing for any particular person or audience; I've simply tried to do the best job I could and let it go at that. The critics don't interest me because they're concerned with what's past and done, while I'm concerned with what comes next (*PR*, pp. 199–200).

Sybille Bedford confirms the point in her recollection of the Huxleys' home in southern France during the 1930s:

There were no papers. No *Times*, no *New Statesman*; in fact, Aldous took no English newspaper at all, though I remember seeing an occasional copy of the *Continental Mail*. . . . There were, inevitably, stacks of literary reviews sent to him from all over the world. These for the most part remained not only unread but unopened (*MV*, p. 140).

If at all typical those reviews would have included, besides questions about a cavalier attitude toward the art of fiction, three other recurring objections to Huxley's work: indecency, heartlessness, and overproduction. *Limbo* and *Antic Hay* ran into publication difficulties because of their irreverent contents (see below, pp. 7, 9) and *Brave New World* was banned in Australia for four years on grounds of obscenity. Huxley defended himself in part when he spoke, later, of the 'salutary proceeding' of 'sticking pins into episcopal behinds' (*PR*, p. 212). But Huxley's larger purpose surely went beyond the value of shock-for-shock's-sake. Miles Fanning in 'After the Fireworks' reflects Huxley's position when he tells Pamela that the unadulterated truth, however shocking and humiliating, must be told. Pamela writes in her diary:

And M[iles] said it would take a whole generation of being shocked and humiliated and lynching the shockers and humiliators before people could settle down to listening to that sort of truth calmly. . . . And he says that when they can listen to it completely calmly, the world will be quite different from what it is now . . . (*Brief Candles*, p. 261).

To the sometimes comically conflicting charges that his treatment of sex was too libertine or too puritan, Huxley remained quizzically silent.

A related, perhaps more durable charge was that Huxley was too severe with the human weaknesses of his characters. When his novels first appeared, recalls Juliette Huxley, their 'bantering tone, the merciless showing-up of human foibles, an acid undertow, underlay the admirable style and discouraged many readers' (*MV*, p. 42). In 1927 Beverley Nichols complained: '. . . I always feel that he must write with a sharp fountain-pen, filled with ink that has first been clarified and then frozen. . . . [His characters] are the last sort of people whom one would ever wish to visit one in a sick-room' (p. 137). Somerset Maugham later suggested that Huxley's failure to acquire 'the great position as a novelist that his talent seems to authorize' could be attributed to 'his deficient sympathy with human beings' (No. 106). Asked about his alleged heartlessness, Huxley replied with a rare explicit statement on the source of his irony:

I don't feel myself to be extremely heartless. But the impression is partly my fault. I have a literary theory that I must have a two-angled vision of all my characters. You know how closely farce and tragedy are related. That's because the comic and the tragic are the same thing seen from different angles. I try to get a stereoscopic vision, to show my characters from two angles simultaneously. Either I try to show them both as they feel themselves to be and as others feel them to be; or else I try to give two rather similar characters who throw light on each other, two characters who share the same element, but in one it is made grotesque.[3]

Had Huxley stated his position so forthrightly more often, critical misunderstandings would have been reduced, for his 'stereoscopic vision' also explains why his novels never could be expected to maintain a single, Jamesian center of consciousness.

Cyril Connolly was foremost in raising the charge of overproduction, although some reviewers of Huxley's books in the 1930s also questioned what seemed to them too much repetition in the volumes of stories and novels. In *The Condemned Playground* (1936) Connolly proclaimed: 'The first forty years of Aldous Huxley's literary career have been marred by over-production, for which the present economic system is to blame.' Connolly clarified what he meant by 'the present economic system' when he confided, shortly, that Huxley was 'bound to his publisher by golden cords' (p. 115). Connolly continued his attack with a devastating parody of *Eyeless in Gaza* and soon, in a review of *Ends and Means*, he rebuked Huxley for doing 'much harm to literature' (No. 90). Huxley apparently never replied in print to Connolly, but Bedford describes the delicacy of their relationship in the early 1930s (*B*, I, pp. 260–2). It must be noted, too, that Connolly in 1928 had praised Huxley's style in *Point Counter Point* as 'impeccable' (No. 47).

The binding 'golden cords' were in fact a series of three-year contracts which Huxley signed with Chatto & Windus, his British publishers, from 1923 continuously until his death. The first contract, completed in January 1923, called for Huxley to submit 'two new works of fiction per annum (one of which two works shall be a full length novel) written by himself during the next three years,' an arrangement which, Bedford observes, was 'commonplace enough to the Victorians, but what writer of today—of similar talent and literary conscience—would, *could*, take on such an engagement? Yet that kind of contract in those post-war years was by no means rare' (*B*, I, pp. 130–1). As the years went by, the obligation was gradually relaxed. By the time of the signing of the fifth agreement in March 1935, Huxley was asked to do three books of fiction or nonfiction in three years, and after his move to America he worked exclusively on a royalty basis (details of all the agreements are in *B*, I and II, *passim*).

The effects these dealings had on Huxley's work are not easy to assess. Few persons will deny that his was a demanding task. Detractors may well urge that without the pressure of contracts Huxley might have written that one consummate masterpiece his critics always anticipated. The *Letters* and the biography reveal that Huxley often felt the burden of his commitments, and in some of the novellas the interpolating style may seem little more than padding. Connolly refers directly to the early contracts in *Enemies of Promise*:

A contract to produce two books a year forced him to vitiate that keen sense of words with which he started and as he had less to say, so, by a process which we have noticed, he took longer in which to say it. For such a writer who had to turn out two hundred thousand words a year, the Mandarin style was indispensable (p. 60).

The examples Connolly quotes from *Eyeless in Gaza* confirm that Huxley was prone, at times, to a labored and redundant style. But Connolly, possibly, overstates his case. Huxley's publishers, much to their credit, adhered more to the spirit than the letter of their agreements. By the end of the first three-year period, for instance, Chatto's had accepted two novels (*Antic Hay* and *Those Barren Leaves*), two volumes of short stories (*Little Mexican* and *Two or Three Graces*), and two books of nonfiction (*Along the Road* and *Jesting Pilate*) as fulfilling the commitment. When Huxley found it difficult to complete *Point Counter Point* on time, C. H. C. Prentice and Harold Raymond were glad to give him an extension of the deadline (*B*, I, p. 191). Moreover, Huxley would have been a prolific writer whatever his contractual situation. Even before the 1923 agreement he had produced six books and large amounts of occasional journalism. He wrote *Crome Yellow*, for example, in two months. 'I rarely take a complete holiday,' he said, 'as I find that my health begins to break down as soon as I stop working. Holidays are healthful only to those who dislike their work. I happen to find mine tolerably agreeable.'[4] The financial security provided by the contracts went a long way toward releasing Huxley from a Grub Street livelihood. It is unlikely that he would have gained such a large measure of immediate professional autonomy on his own. Though the initial requirements were imposing, Huxley's publishing agreements were markedly to his advantage and probably had, in sum, a quite beneficial effect on his career.[5]

EARLY SUCCESS TO 1928

Soon after the end of World War I an American friend invited Richard Aldington to write an article for the *Outlook* to identify young writers Aldington thought would become known. 'I made a choice which I modestly think wasn't bad for 1919,' says Aldington in *Life for Life's Sake*: 'James Joyce, T. S. Eliot, D. H. Lawrence, Aldous Huxley, H.D., and Marcel Proust. I received a letter from the editor in these terms: "For God's sake, Richard, can't you think of somebody who has been heard of or is ever likely to be heard of?"' Aldington protested; his piece was sent for arbitration to Logan Pearsall Smith, 'who decided that my writers would never be heard of; and the article was rejected' (p. 219).

In 1919 Huxley's reputation was limited. Three years earlier the London *Nation* had published three of his poems, 'but by mistake over the signature of Leonard Huxley, who, Aldous says, received a letter from A. C. Benson congratulating him on the extreme beauty of his verse' (*B*, I, p. 66). Huxley was then well-known in Oxford circles, partly for the unorthodox way he secured his First in English: 'Instead of answering the questions,' L. A. G. Strong told F. W. Bateson, 'Huxley made fun of them; but so cleverly that the examiners could not refuse him his alphas.'[6] Outside of Oxford Huxley did attract some attention with his early poetry. H. W. Massingham wrote to tell Huxley 'how much he liked "Mole" and asked Aldous to send some poems to the new quarterly *Forum*' (*B*, I, p. 62). According to Ford Madox Ford, one of Huxley's poems created a teapot scandal among London's literati (No. 8), while Arthur St John Adcock said Huxley 'made an early sensation with the stark realism of such poems as "Frascatís,"'[7] first published in *Wheels*, 1919.

Two years later Aldington's selection of Huxley for his list was vindicated. With the publication in 1920 of what he called 'my two children—*Limbo* and *Leda*' (*B*, I, p. 109), and with the appearance the following year of *Crome Yellow*, Huxley broke onto the postwar literary scene with some abruptness (see No. 17). The off-beat quality of the 1920 volumes proved fresh and grating. Arnold Bennett thought 'Leda' 'the best modern poem I have read for years' (*Journal*, p. 706), but the *Sunday Times* review contained that blend of qualified praise and admonition which would recur so frequently in coming responses to Huxley's work:

The writer is energetic and voluptuous, without affectation; and in his language as well as in his imagery he shows proof of that intellectual basis which is essential to poetry of a high order. . . . But most of the lyrics are violently ugly, with a determination to shock and astonish, which is highly unpleasing (23 May 1920, p. 5).

The shocking substance of *Limbo*, according to Frank Swinnerton in his autobiography, placed its publication in jeopardy. A senior partner at Chatto's, it was said, having read a set of the proofs, 'refused absolutely to publish anything so appallingly gross, blasphemous, and horrible.' Swinnerton interceded, Huxley agreed to 'three small revisions' in his script, and publication ensued (p. 311). First-year sales in England were only 1,600 copies (*B*, I, p. 108), but the book made an impact. Cyril Connolly remembers borrowing it at school 'from one master only to have it confiscated by another . . .' (*Condemned Playground*, p. 114). Despite reservations about 'youth and cleverness' (No. 2), the general response was expressed in the *NYTBR*'s contention that the reader finishing *Limbo* 'will feel sure of Mr. Huxley as an authentic figure in English letters of the day' (15 August 1920, p. 29).

The publication of Huxley's first novel, *Crome Yellow* (1921), was greeted with widespread cries of delight. 'Almost overnight,' Firchow exclaims, 'Huxley became an internationally famous figure' (p. 62). The book won high praise from F. Scott Fitzgerald (No. 15) and H. L. Mencken:

I have a good deal of confidence in the future of this Mr. Huxley. There is about him an air of unshakable sophistication. . . . The obscene farce about him engages his bludgeon, but also arouses his delight. . . . He sees the intrinsic buffoonery, the vaudevillish bombast and imbecility, and he knows how to present it dramatically and amusingly.[8]

The *New York Tribune* put *Crome Yellow* on its list of recommended books '. . . because it is the latest work of one of the most interesting personalities recently come to the literary front in England' (7 May 1922, sec. vi, p. 6), and three weeks later it had made the paper's 'Six Best Sellers' list. Hart Crane wrote Allen Tate that he liked Huxley's work (*Letters*, p. 90), Max Beerbohm wrote Huxley that he liked *Crome Yellow* (to which Huxley delightedly replied—*L*, p. 206), and Marcel Proust, rather unaccountably, claimed that Huxley 'occupies an unassailable position in the English literary world of to-day.'[9]

The novel nonetheless caused some ill feeling among those who were identifiable models for its characters. As Peter Quennell recalls, several readers were aware that Priscilla Wimbush and Crome 'unmistakably owed a good deal to Lady Ottoline [Morrell] and her Garsington household . . .' (*Sign of the Fish*, p. 120). Huxley's biographer advises that 'Lady Ottoline was offended by *Crome Yellow* and a breach ensued that lasted many years' (*B*, I, p. 123).[10] Dora Carrington, who used to sleep on the roof of Garsington Manor with Huxley, took note of her appearance in the novel as Mary Bracegirdle and concluded 'it's a book which makes one feel very ill' (*Letters*, p. 200). With some justification Frank Swinnerton argued that the 'caricatures annoyed those who were laughed at. By them, Aldous was considered very cheap, and not really at all first class' (*Figures*, p. 188).

The least favorable of *Crome Yellow*'s reviews—which were overwhelmingly positive—urged Huxley to consider the importance of being earnest (No. 13). *Antic Hay* (1923) provoked a more mixed reaction and some graver objections. When it was first published, states Jocelyn Brooke, the novel 'acquired an undeserved reputation for "obscenity", and several of the more respectable libraries refused to stock it' (p. 15). Reports circulated that *Antic Hay* 'was burnt in Cairo (of all places) and banned in the Irish Free State.'[11] Yoi Maraini amused Huxley with the revelation that he had met two American readers who told him they had burnt the book (p. 78). More significantly, George H. Doran recounts in *Chronicles of Barabbas* that when he issued *Antic Hay* in New York the censor was alerted to it 'as a highly immoral book':

He in turn reported it to the District Attorney of New York, who sent for me before taking action; for it had developed that the censor had been more struck by its irreverence than by its plain speech and morals. The District Attorney was rational and understanding. He said to me very frankly that he found the book to be fascinating and artistic, but technically some parts of the book might be misconstrued into the pornographic.

The District Attorney told Doran he would make no protest if the publishers 'did not stress the pornographic aspect' and if they avoided any publicity over threatened seizure (p. 174). Doran of course agreed to the conditions, but not all readers would have agreed with the District Attorney's decision. One of Harvey Curtis Webster's 'old teachers' remarked that 'we'd be much better off if it [*Antic Hay*] had never been written. There is so much disillusionment, so much cynicism . . .' (pp. 196–7). James Douglas added vehemently that if *Antic Hay* 'escapes uncastigated and unpilloried the effect upon English fiction will be disastrous' (No. 19).

Huxley was moved to respond to objections lodged against the book by his father, Leonard Huxley, who, judging by Aldous's letter, must have been emphatic in his strictures:

I am sorry you should have found my book so distasteful. Like you, I have no desire to enter into argument about it . . . I will only point out that it is a book written by a member of what I may call the war-generation for others of his kind; and that it is intended to reflect—fantastically, of course, but none the less faithfully—the life and opinions of an age which has seen the violent disruption of almost all the standards, conventions and values current in the previous epoch.

Huxley went on to identify the artistic impulse which lay behind *Antic Hay* as well as a number of the subsequent novels:

The book is, I may say without fatuity, a good book. It is also a very serious book. Artistically, too, it has a certain novelty, being a work in which all the ordinarily separated categories—tragic, comic, fantastic, realistic—are combined so to say chemically into a single entity, whose unfamiliar character makes it appear at first sight rather repulsive.

I can't say that I expected you would enjoy the book. But on the other hand I expected that my contemporaries would; and so far as I know by what people have written to me, they have (*L*, p. 224).[12]

The reaction of another member of the family, Arnold Ward (son of Huxley's aunt, Mrs Humphrey Ward), was, if less dignified, at least as emphatic as Leonard Huxley's must have been. Osbert Sitwell related an inebriated Ward's comments on his cousin: '". . . If I were to meet him now in Piccadilly I should bloody well take his trousers off and leave him there." "Dear me," said Osbert "and why, may I ask?" "Because," A.W. replies "because I consider (hiccough) that he's disgraced his ancestors"' (*L*, p. 233). Huxley's offense was writing *Antic Hay*.

Among the reviewers, allegations of savagery and misanthropy drowned out the few hesitant acknowledgments of the novel's imaginative power. Joseph Wood Krutch (No. 25) was one of a minority of readers who sensed the underlying seriousness which Huxley claimed for his book in the letter to his father. But *Antic Hay* did achieve a certain distribution (first-year sales in England, 5,000 copies according to *B*, I, p. 142, were double those of *Crome Yellow*), and it appealed, as Huxley wished, to the younger generation of the 1920s. Angus Wilson remembers being given *The Forsyte Saga* and *Antic Hay* at an early age. The Forsyte values 'were what my family paid lip service to, they were what I was in revolt against. But *Antic Hay*! *Antic Hay* was all that I had devoutly hoped for. . . . Aldous Huxley was the god of my adolescence' (p. 73). Isaiah Berlin would later call Huxley 'one of the great culture heroes of our youth' (*MV*, p. 146). Especially for those souls described by Gertrude Stein as the 'lost generation,' *Antic Hay* offered 'the very last word in freedom and self-expression.'[13]

Meanwhile Huxley was publishing more volumes of short stories, which were largely well-received, although there was a strong undercurrent of concern over the random structure of his fiction. Krutch had stated that, 'considering its formlessness, *Crome Yellow* is a novel only by courtesy' (No. 14). Bennett found it difficult to accept Huxley's sketchy treatment of his characters in the long story opening *Little Mexican* (No. 29). Another older novelist, Thomas Hardy, was more puzzled than Bennett by the Huxley manner. Mrs Hardy asked Virginia Woolf if she knew Huxley:

I said I did. They had been reading his book, which she thought 'very clever'. But Hardy could not remember it: said his wife had to read to him—his eyes were now so bad. 'They've changed everything now,' he said. 'We used to think there was a beginning and a middle and an end. We believed in the Aristotelian theory. Now one of those stories [probably 'Nuns at Luncheon,' *Mortal Coils*—ed.] came to an end with a woman going out of the room' (*Writer's Diary*, p. 93).

Other readers were quick to defend Huxley's 'modern' approach to fiction. The *TLS* reviewer of *Little Mexican*, anticipating purist objections to the leisurely opening of 'Uncle Spencer,' proclaimed truculently that he would 'let the purists have their say: we would not lose a word of it' (No. 28). Too, the *NYHTBR* praised the stories in *Two or Three Graces* for 'the endings which strike their last notes with the apparent casualness and the actual carefulness of a Chopin nocturne or a Chopin scherzo' (6 June 1926, p. 6).

The argument over Huxley's disruptive attitude towards conventional notions of fiction was naturally magnified by the publication of his third novel, *Those Barren Leaves* (1925), which sold 8,000 copies in its first year in England (*B*, I, p. 152). Isabel Paterson thought that 'Mr. Huxley's aunt, the late Mrs. Humphrey Ward, would disapprove thoroughly of her nephew's work' (*Bookman*, March 1925, lxi, p. 85), and Lytton Strachey told Lady Ottoline that '*Those Barren Leaves* fluttered from my hand before I had read more than four of them' (Holroyd, p. 515). But the *Sunday Times* summarized both the contending issue and the prevalent attitude of the novel's reviewers:

If there were ever any doubts as to Mr. Aldous Huxley's claims to be considered as an original artist, they must be dispelled by the publication of his new novel, 'Those Barren Leaves'. It is a book which cheerfully breaks every rule devised in the past by lesser men for their own guidance. Its story is unfolded by fits and starts, which must horrify the conventional spinner of yarns. Sometimes, indeed, the story is altogether forgotten and another is introduced. Yet, after reading through these brilliant and fascinating pages, one is conscious of both form and cohesion. . . . The new book may not be a masterpiece, but it is assuredly a stepping-stone to very big things (25 January 1925, p. 9).

Even though Gerald Gould (No. 32) and Conrad Aiken (No. 36) led a protest against the digressive style and the lengthy conversations, *Those Barren Leaves* prompted several other readers to believe that Huxley 'is a very good and very likely will be a great novelist' (No. 30).

By the mid-1920s Huxley was writing with the assurance that he was supported by a substantial reputation. Adcock's estimate of the critical reception of Huxley's work through *Jesting Pilate* (1926) was accurate: '. . . It was greeted with acclamations loud enough to drown the outcries, here and there, of any scandalised dissenters' (p. 136). He had worked extremely hard, to the point where he 'realized that there is a price to pay for writing two books a year' (*B*, I, p. 152). But, as one result, Edwin Muir could declare in 1926 that 'no other writer of our time has built up a serious reputation so rapidly and so surely.'[14] Huxley was bolstering that reputation with the travel essays in *Along the Road*, reviewed most appreciatively by Edmund Gosse (No. 38), and *Jesting Pilate*, which Ernest Boyd in the *Independent* called 'the most arresting and original volume of its kind which has appeared in a generation' (13 November 1926, cxvii, p. 561). A clear sign of Huxley's spreading influence was the effect that he was already having on other writers, such as William Faulkner and Nathanael West (see Tuck, p. 130; Millgate, pp. 73, 75; and Reid, pp. 60–3). Further, Grant Overton reported, in 1924, that prices for first editions of Huxley's books were singularly high: 'A first edition of a new Huxley is something to put aside carefully. The distinction is unusual among living writers and, in the case of a man under thirty, possibly unique' (No. 27).

In spite of recurring critical reservations Huxley's work had generated enough momentum and enthusiasm to justify greater expectations. The characteristic outlook by 1927 was the one which Thomas Wolfe confided to his notebooks: 'The young writer with the highest potentiality—Aldous Huxley' (p. 113).

GROWTH TO FAME 1928–1935

For the large majority of Huxley's readers, the potential discerned by Wolfe was realized in the next two novels, *Point Counter Point* and *Brave New World*. Published in October 1928, *Point Counter Point* sold 10,000 copies in its first year in England (*B*, I, p. 198). The files of Doubleday and Doran indicate that over 40,000 copies were sold in America in the next six years. The novel's distribution was accelerated by its selection as a book-of-the-month by the U.S. Literary Guild, which by itself sold 55,000 copies in 1929. The book 'enjoyed a huge vogue in France and Germany, broadened Aldous's English public and became one of the cornerstones of his international reputation, not to say his fame' (*B*, I, p. 200). Perhaps a measure of the book's status appears in Evelyn Waugh's note, 8 October 1928, on a luncheon companion: 'I detected him talking about "Point Counter Point" before he had read it' (*Observer*, 8 April 1973, p. 19). Gabriel Marcel, then a critic for the *Nouvelle revue française*, was 'most anxious to have it translated at once' (*L*, p. 303). Without question *Point Counter Point* initiated the spread of Huxley's reputation to a hitherto unprecedented degree.

The full reception given the book, however, was by no means uniformly favorable. Wolfe found it 'better than I thought' (*Notebooks*, p. 361), Sinclair Lewis called it 'an admirable novel' (*Letters*, p. 289), and John Cowper Powys (though he disliked the title) said it was 'Huxley's most exciting work' (*Letters*, p. 40). Huxley wrote his brother, Julian: 'I had a very nice note from H. G. Wells about it today, and I gather from the various letters I've had about it that it has pleased' (*L*, p. 303). But Huxley's wife, Maria, was upset by the death of little Phil (*B*, I, p. 207), which Arnold Kettle later described as 'a piece of deliberate masochism' (p. 168). According to his biographer, John Middleton Murry was not especially pleased by the Burlap portrait: 'In fact, he had been more outraged by Burlap than he cared to admit. His first impulse had been to challenge Huxley to a duel . . .' (Lea, p. 249). Two leading Bloomsberries privately expressed disapproval of the novel. Virginia Woolf remembered *Point Counter Point* while she was struggling with the composition of *The Years*:

Not a good novel. All raw, uncooked, protesting. A descendant, oddly enough, of Mrs. H. Ward: interest in ideas; makes people into ideas. . . . I have a horror of the Aldous novel: that must be avoided. But ideas are sticky things: won't coalesce: hold up the creative, subconscious faculty; that's it, I suppose (*Diary*, pp. 238–9).

Perhaps more surprisingly, Lytton Strachey rejected the novel as 'a bad book, in my opinion. The man can't write; his views are rotten; and the total result of his work is a feeling of devitalisation and gloom' (Holroyd, p. 571). André Gide found the novel unreadable (No. 59). D. H. Lawrence told Aldington that 'within a year Huxley would be in a lunatic asylum' (*Portrait*, p. 338). Though Lawrence wrote Huxley, reservedly, that he admired his courage (No. 53), in another context he voiced marked distaste for the book:

An English novel like *Point Counter Point* has gone beyond tragedy into exacerbation, and continuous nervous repulsion. Man is so nervously repulsive to man, so screamingly, nerve-rackingly repulsive! This novel goes one further. Man just *smells*, offensively and unbearably, not to be borne. The human stink! (*Phoenix*, p. 270).

Lawrence's poem 'I am in a Novel' revealed his displeasure with the Rampion portrait, which he rejected more vehemently in a letter to

William Gerhardi: 'No, I refuse to be Rampioned. I am not responsible. Aldous' admiration is only skin-deep, and out of the Mary Mary quite contrary impulse' (Nehls, p. 265).

The reviews of *Point Counter Point*, though, were with few exceptions exceedingly favorable. *TLS* questioned whether the novel was really 'a good example of the craft of fiction' (No. 44), Henry Seidel Canby advised Huxley to write essays (No. 52), and Louis Kronenberger objected to the savagery of his satire (No. 51). But praise far outweighed the adverse criticism. L. P. Hartley said Huxley 'has a power akin to Donne's of investing [scientific fact] with poetry' (No. 45). Cyril Connolly declared him 'admirably gifted for a modern Petronius' (No. 47), while Robert Morss Lovett called the novel 'the modern *Vanity Fair*' (No. 49) and Krutch contended 'it vindicates Mr. Huxley's right to be considered the most able of contemporary satirists' (No. 48).

Point Counter Point concluded Huxley's novels of the 1920s and opened that period in which his critical reputation would reach its zenith for his lifetime. As Clark points out, the novels of the 1920s made Huxley's name: 'The four books established Huxley as a writer who would be listened to' (p. 219).

Yet, as powerful a mark as he had made, in some respects Huxley's serious reputation rested on shaky grounds. According to G. M. A. Grube, for instance, St John Irvine complained of a hatred of existence in nearly everything Huxley wrote. Grube's response was that Irvine 'without any justification' was 'generalizing from Spandrell and his type.' Grube submitted that 'a writer who is so thoroughly misunderstood by an eminent critic has not yet written enough to be understood by the majority of his readers' (*Canadian Forum*, 2 August 1930, x, p. 402). There is indeed much to Charles J. Rolo's contention that the 'twenties painted a false picture of Huxley in their own image' (p. 114). A good deal of his early general popularity, added Harold Watts, 'rested less on a clear view of Huxley's real concern in *Point Counter Point* than on a scandalized and delighted enjoyment of some of the by-products of that concern to be found in the novel' (Introduction, *Point Counter Point*, p. viii). During the 1920s an occasional critic here and there—Krutch, or A. C. Ward—recognized the underlying quest for values in Huxley's work. But Grant Overton's masterly penetration of his contemporaries' oversights was rare, if not unique (No. 27). By far most readers were slow to see beneath the surface of Huxley's concentrated irony.

Such misunderstandings account for some of the attacks on Huxley at the turn of the decade. Desmond MacCarthy said in a 1931 radio broadcast on 'What England Reads' that Shaw, Wells, and Galsworthy had lost some of their vogue. The post-war generation, in its disillusionment, was more 'interested in the cold, discontented cynicism of an Aldous Huxley . . .' (*New York Times*, 7 September 1931, p. 18). The spread of Huxley's reputation beyond leisured intellectual circles into the broader reading public led Hugh Gordon Porteus to warn that 'a writer who takes the trouble, for mercenary reasons, to make his works popularly accessible, should be rather more alive to his responsibilities' (p. 10). A concerted assault came from the citadel of T. S. Eliot, who had earlier called Huxley one who had to write thirty bad novels in order to produce a good one (No. 43). A reviewer of *Music at Night* for Eliot's *New Criterion* dismissed Huxley as 'a literary journalist' who 'has heard of everything and thought about nothing' (January 1932, xi, p. 373). Eliot himself in *Thoughts After Lambeth* (Criterion Miscellany No. 30) charged:

. . . If youth has the spirit of a tomtit or the brain of a goose, it can hardly rally with enthusiasm to these two [Huxley and Bertrand Russell] depressing life-forcers. (Not that Mr. Huxley, who has no philosophy that I can discover, and who succeeds to some extent in elucidating how sordid a world without any philosophy can be, has much in common with Mr. Russell) (p. 9).

But overall Huxley's stock going into the early 1930s was clearly on the rise. Sewell Stokes recalls that during this period John Galsworthy told him 'how greatly he admired' Huxley's work (p. 977). In Maugham's *Cakes and Ale* (1930) Huxley was mentioned as a possible successor of Hardy to the position of Grand Old Man of English Letters. James Joyce, if half-jokingly, advised Nino Frank to translate something by Huxley instead of Eliot or Lawrence for *Bifur* (Ellmann, p. 628). André Maurois (No. 58) and Gabriel Marcel (No. 85), who reviewed *Those Barren Leaves* and *Point Counter Point* for the *Nouvelle revue française*, were eagerly introducing his work to the French reading audience, which, René Lalou soon reported, welcomed it with enthusiasm (No. 94). In spite of a vigorous rebuttal from Ernest Hemingway (No. 62) and Chesterton's lively assault (No. 74), Huxley's influence, now starting to reach the Continent, promised to outgrow that of his contemporaries as a new decade turned increasingly to him for leadership.

Nevertheless, the appearance of *Brave New World* (1932) provoked a bewildered diversity of reactions—incomprehension, resentment, and hostility not the least among them. The book offended the Australian censors (see above, p. 3) and moved H. G. Wells, says Gerald Heard, to write Huxley an angry letter charging treason to science.[15] Derek Patmore recollects that Wells 'said to me savagely: *"Brave New World* was a great disappointment to me. A writer of the standing of Aldous Huxley has no right to betray the future as he did in that book."'[16] Wells was joined by Wyndham Lewis, who referred to the novel as 'an unforgivable offence to Progress and to political uplift of every description' (*Letters*, p. 226). Reviewers were quick to mistake Huxley's satire for a lack of seriousness. H. G. Harwood in the London *Saturday Review* felt the book was 'chiefly intended as a Lark' (6 February 1932, cliii, p. 152), the *New Statesman* called it 'a thin little joke' (6 February 1932, iii [n.s.], p. 172), the *London Mercury* dismissed it as 'poor satire, and half-hearted writing' (March 1932, xxv, p. 493). The American reception was discouragingly cool. Granville Hicks indignantly rebuked Huxley for being 'effectively insulated from the misery of the masses' (No. 71), while Margaret Cheney Dawson rejected his novel as 'a lugubrious and heavy-handed piece of propaganda' (No. 70). Confusion over the book even reached the point, John Hawley Roberts related, where 'some readers have concluded that Huxley approved of his horrible creation' (p. 551).

Joseph Needham's comment that perhaps 'only biologists and philosophers will really appreciate the full force of Mr. Huxley's remarkable book' (No. 64) was largely a correct assessment of the immediate response. Early readers often shared Alan Reynolds Thompson's composed reflection: 'And let him be as savage as he likes, we sit easy in the knowledge that his Utopia is in no danger of materializing; his Utopians are perfectly impossible creatures' (New York *Bookman*, March 1932, lxxix, p. 691). But readers who looked beyond the pale of literary criticism, such as Bertrand Russell (No. 67) and Rebecca West (No. 63), quickly recognized the novel's applicability to the existing world. Hermann Hesse found in Huxley a kindred spirit (No. 72), and it remained for Ralph Straus, then regular fiction reviewer for the *Sunday Times*, to sum up the reactions of a small segment of discerning respondents:

Many people will be terribly shocked by this book. Some who may be rather deeper in their lines than they would care to admit will find in it nothing but the nastiest nonsense. For myself I would regard it not only as a triumph of satirical writing, but as a highly moral tract. Ugly and depressing it may be, but nobody can read it without taking stock of himself, and of how many novels can that be said in this enlightened era of ours? (7 February 1932, p. 9).

Looking backward, Denis Gabor observed with accuracy that *Brave New World* 'had a devastating effect on the intelligentsia of the Western Hemisphere' (p. 10). Coming only four years after the fast-selling *Point Counter Point*, *Brave New World* would gradually develop into Huxley's most popular novel. The book sold 13,000 copies in its first year in England, 10,000 copies the year after (*B*, I, p. 251). In America, according to Doubleday's files, it sold 15,000 copies in 1932–3, and another 18,125 copies during the next five years. The book was eventually translated into nineteen languages; it continues to sell about 2,000 hard-cover copies per year on each side of the Atlantic. Huxley's sophisticated grasp of impending science, his sliding irony and literary horse-play, would intrigue a steady flow of readers finding in the book, with Cyril Connolly, 'a touch of genius' (*Sunday Times*, 22 February 1959, mag.sec., p. 13).

By the mid-1930s Huxley's critical reputation was nearing its peak. Theodore Roethke, writing to Dorothy Gordon on 26 September 1933, could refer to what was still one of the old chestnuts of less appreciative criticism:

I do think he's quite witty and learned. His faults are so obvious that they don't bother me so much. I remember I. A. Richards saying that Huxley was very good second-rate, that he got much of his best stuff from repeating conversations of his brilliant friends (*Selected Letters*, p. 7).

But lingering objections were now being overwhelmed by very high acclaim. C. P. Snow thought 'Huxley is on the way to becoming an English institution' and called him 'the most significant English novelist of his day' (No. 73a). Thomas Mann advised a correspondent, Karl Kerenyi, that he discovered in Huxley's work a splendid expression of the West European spirit (*Briefe*, p. 353). Robert Nichols praised Huxley as 'a genius of European stature' and 'the only living English novelist who at present enjoys and deserves a European reputation' (*Observer*, 8 December 1935, p. 9). In 1935 enough of Huxley's work had crossed the Channel to prompt Dmitri Mirsky, in *The Intelligentsia of Great Britain*, to declare that 'French critics consider him one of the greatest writers of the present age . . .' (p. 129). Positive criticism of some depth was forthcoming from the Continent (No. 75) and the United States (No. 77). Very soon after their arrival in America, an amazed Maria Huxley wrote her sister: 'You have no idea how *famous* Aldous is here' (*B*, I, p. 344).

Fame both abroad and at home was plainly his. In 1928 a friend of C. E. M. Joad's had conducted a survey to see 'which books appeared most frequently on the shelves of contemporary undergraduates at Oxford.' At that time the works of Lawrence were predominant, but a similar survey in 1935 revealed 'a considerable majority of the works of Huxley':

Huxley is read [Joad continues] by undergraduates, dons, teachers, artists, reviewers, critics, even politicians—in a word, by all those who, in the last resort, form the tastes and mould the opinions of their fellow-citizens. He is, indeed, *par excellence*, the novelist's novelist, as Bach is the musician's musician and Spenser the poet's poet.[17]

By 1936, suggests Ronald Clark, 'he was possibly the best-known Huxley of them all . . .' (p. 233). Peter Quennell, echoing Joad, paid tribute to Huxley's impact on other writers, avowing that 'a whole generation of spirited performers is in his debt.' As the troubled 1930s moved closer to a second global conflict, readers waited with growing anticipation to see where Huxley would turn next: 'What course Mr. Huxley's destiny will now assume,' Quennell concluded, 'is one of the most interesting literary problems of the present decade' (*English Novelists*, p. 278).

PERIOD OF NEW TRIAL 1936–1946

P. H. Houston in the *American Review* summarized the position of Huxley's readers in 1934: 'So accurately has he reflected the spirit of his age that now, since the publication of *Point Counter Point* in 1928, his whole emancipated generation seems to have accepted him as their official spokesman before the world' (p. 211). Houston expressed an essential hope of Huxley's international audience as it approached the crucial middle years of the 1930s:

If he chooses to abstract himself from the cynicism and pose and exhibitionism in the midst of which he has lived, and really to study his own nature, he can accomplish something worthy of his brilliant gifts and of paramount value to an age blindly seeking some guide out of the depths of its despair (p. 232).

In the years following *Point Counter Point* Huxley had indeed been struggling to identify some affirmative response to the challenges posed in his own fiction of the 1920s. By 1936 he was ready to take his stance.

The significant results of his stance in terms of his critical heritage were threefold: the explicit message of the later fiction struck most readers as being detrimental to its artistry; criticism of Huxley's craft often became indistinguishable from criticism of his ideas; the popular response to Huxley's work continued to grow, but the critical reception declined.

While they were looking to him for guidance, practically none of Huxley's readers were prepared for the directions he took in coming books. His critics had so consistently overlooked the deeper import of the earlier work that the new outspoken idealism seemed an abrupt reversal, if not a contradiction of attitudes. The net result of the appearance in 1936 of Huxley's pacifist pamphlet, *What Are You Going to Do About It?*, and his 'conversion' novel, *Eyeless in Gaza*, was to leave large groups of his readers feeling baffled and betrayed. George Woodcock in *Dawn and the Darkest Hour* recollects that the 1930s generation was 'disturbed and disappointed at what seemed a retreat into obscurantism on the part of one of the writers we most admired. It seemed another case of the Lost Leader' (p. 16). Stephen Spender in the *Left Review* took vigorous exception to Huxley's plan of appeasement for the emerging power blocks:

What you in fact propose to do with your conference is to sacrifice the freedom and even the lives of oppressed pacifists and socialists in Italy, Germany and Austria on the altar of a dogmatic and correct pacifism, using the militant dictators as priests to perform the human sacrifice (p. 541).

C. Day-Lewis countered Huxley's pamphlet with one of his own, in which he acknowledged Huxley's great talent and achievement but stated ruefully: 'Now it looks as though he is turning his back on us forever' (No. 86). Julian Bell's reaction, expressed privately in a letter on 22 October [1936], was not very uncharacteristic: 'I think Aldous and Gerald Heard must be slightly mad—since I can't believe they are bribed, and that's the only other explanation I can see of their opinions' (p. 165).

The intensity of such remarks indicates the degree of importance which the 1930s had attached to Huxley's contribution to the age. That *Eyeless in Gaza* was awaited with growing interest is attested by its first-year sales in England which, at 26,700 copies (*B*, I, p. 317), were more than double those of *Brave New World*. The reviews of *Eyeless in Gaza* were the fullest and quite often the most analytical of any novel Huxley wrote. Despite grave reservations about the unorthodox time sequence (No. 78), the diary passages (No. 79), and the new ideology (No. 81), the novel did not escape praise. The *Times* reviewer brought up the perennial issue of Huxley's approach to fiction:

The definition of the word 'novel' must be greatly enlarged if it is to take in such a work as Mr. Aldous Huxley's *Eyeless in Gaza*. For it is much less a story or even a psychological analysis than a philosophy—and even when that is said we are left wondering whether it should not rather be called an assemblage of philosophies, a ballet of ideas. . . . We are left fairly astounded at the mental energy and versatility displayed throughout this unflagging narrative of 600-odd pages (19 June 1936, p. 22).

Day-Lewis, his reply to Huxley's pamphlet notwithstanding, thought it 'not, perhaps, his best novel,' but readers 'will be brought up all standing by the exacting morality which the author openly proposes to them at the end,' and he concluded 'this new humanity makes [the novel] by far his most appealing and promising' (*Daily Telegraph*, 19 June 1936, p. 8). The high ideals of the book, of course, elicited severely conflicting opinions from many sources. J. Donald Adams in the *NYTBR* saw *Eyeless in Gaza* as 'a novel which is at least the equal, if not the superior, in intellectual and spiritual content, of any in our time' (No. 84). H[erschel] Brickell, conversely, agreed with the harsher critics of Huxley's ideas: 'There are spots of good writing, as might be expected, but the thinking is either absent or so wholly unrelated to reality that it has no value.'[18]

The appearance in 1937 of *Ends and Means* accelerated the controversy over Huxley's position. '*Ends and Means* became a kind of Bible to the Peace Pledge Union,' says Bedford. 'It greatly affected some young men' (*B*, I, p. 356). As such, the book drew much fire. A spirited debate arose in the pages of the *New English Weekly*, with A. Romney Green classifying Huxley among 'the most dangerous kind of false prophets' and George Orwell replying in Huxley's defense:

The fact that a book like Mr. Huxley's contains a certain amount of self-righteousness (we are all self-righteous in different ways), and is written too much from the standpoint of a middle-class intellectual, is beside the point. Anyone who helps to put peace on the map is doing useful work.[19]

Elsewhere, Reinhold Niebuhr would not allow that Huxley was doing useful work and roundly attacked his 'unrealistic dreaming': 'In its more articulate forms our culture suffers from illusions which weaken its will and its right to survive' (p. 779). The reviewers as a whole gave *Ends and Means* a respectful hearing. With Llewelyn Powys, they admired the clarity of Huxley's style, the force of his argument, and the integrity of his vision, but objected to an aura of aloofness, possibly of *naïveté* in his attitude: 'It is an illuminating book,' Powys wrote a member of his family on 5 January 1938, 'and you should try to get hold of it. It throws light on many matters. I admire the clearness of his mind when not clouded by his new religious views and foolishness about the "non-attached" man' (*Letters*, p. 248).

The reception of *Ends and Means* was emblematic of the response to Huxley at the approach of World War II. It is necessary to dwell on the character of this response because Huxley's pronounced idealism, together with his decision in the late 1930s to remain in America, inevitably colored the critical reception of his later work. High praise was by no means lacking during this period. *After Many a Summer* won the University of Edinburgh's James Tait Black prize as the best novel of the year, and Ernst Kohn-Bramstedt grouped Huxley with Thomas Mann as 'the two greatest literary figures the twentieth century has hitherto produced in England and Germany' (p. 471). But soon after 1936, H. M. Champness recalls, 'ugly rumours began to circulate':

> The master was slipping. His tone and his language were growing more and more theological, the snippets of French and Italian were giving place to Sanskrit, and there were frequent and apparently serious references to the Divine Ground. As a ship will leave a sinking rat he was deserting his *métier*—only to become, of all things, a Hollywood swami. It was too much. From once-devoted adherents the later books received a good deal less than justice. There was applause for their undiminished eloquence of exposition, but there was also regret and laughter (p. 109).

Huxley's 1930s contemporaries felt that a direct confrontation of the problems of war and evil was, in Jules Menken's words, 'a responsibility which he owes to his generation' (*Fortnightly Review*, February 1938, cxliii, p. 247). As Clark observes, Huxley's critics acidly remarked that in *What Are You Going to Do About It?* 'crossing the Atlantic was not among the recommended answers' (p. 242). Once in America, says Bedford, there was 'a curious barrier' between the Huxleys and their friends in England (*B*, I, p. 345). In fact Harold Nicolson records in his diary for 2 April 1940 a dinner with Kenneth Clark, William Somerset Maugham, Mrs Winston Churchill, and Leslie Howard:

> We discuss the position of those English people who have remained in the United States. . . . We all regret bitterly that people like Aldous Huxley, Auden and Isherwood should have absented themselves. They want me to write

a *Spectator* article attacking them. That is all very well but it would lose me the friendship of three people whom I much admire (*Diaries*, p. 165).[20]

The shift of emphasis in Huxley's work introduced during the war years a period of new ferment and trial for his critical reputation. The volume of response never slackened; if anything it increased. At the close of the 1930s, George Woodcock submits, 'a great many young people regarded Huxley not only as one of the finest novelists of the time, but also as a prophet who spoke on their behalf' (*Dawn*, p. 14). Some reviewers had seen *Eyeless in Gaza* as marking the close of an era (Nos 84 and 85). Before long, Huxley came to be regarded as a leader of the new spiritual thought of the 1940s. Charles I. Glicksberg asserted that *Ends and Means* 'marks the beginning of a new ideological current' (p. 175). William Soskin believed Huxley was 'laying the ground for the modern religious renaissance with much fervor and a high idealism' (*NYHTBR*, 28 January 1940, p. 2). The popularity of *Time Must Have a Stop* and *The Perennial Philosophy* would presently verify that Philo M. Buck, Jr, in the early 1940s, was hardly alone in his appraisal of Huxley as 'one of the most significant critics of contemporary life and ideas in Europe, and also one of the best qualified' (p. 170).

But the very thought which placed Huxley in the front ranks of the new romantics was to prove a most grating point with his critics. Buck went on to identify the central issue in Huxley's fiction both at this time and as a whole:

It has repeatedly been said by critics that literature, pure literature if there be such a thing, must not be propaganda. I am not so sure when I think of Dante and *Faust*. It depends on the perfect blending of the author's intellectual or moral purpose with his imagination (p. 181).

Reviewers were quite insistent that Huxley did not achieve such a perfect blending in *After Many a Summer Dies the Swan* (1939). The majority opinion of the novel, voiced by Derek Verschoyle in the *Spectator*, was that Propter's monologues 'occur much too frequently and at infinitely too great length,' making the book 'periodically static' and destroying 'the effect of what has preceded them' (13 October 1939, clxiii, p. 522). Thomas Merton summarily denounced Propter as 'the dullest character in the whole history of the English novel' (No. 98) while, incompatibly, *Time Magazine* praised Propter's speeches as 'some of the firmest, most beautifully articulate essays Huxley has ever written' (29 January 1940, xxxv, p. 72). To most readers Huxley appeared altogether too willing to abandon art for morality. 'His love of pure art has died,' complained Malcolm Cowley in the *New Republic*, 'like the swan of his title. Though he still consents to tell us a story, it is intended primarily as the text and adornment of a moral lesson' (12 February 1940, cii, p. 216). Huxley's own description of *After Many a Summer* reveals that his approach to fiction was basically unchanged from the days of *Antic Hay*: '[It is] a kind of fantasy, at once comic and cautionary, farcical, blood-curdling and reflective' (*L*, p. 441). But the critical audience at large agreed with Frieda Lawrence's feeling that the book 'is queer stuff' (p. 279).

Time Must Have a Stop (1944) was accorded an improved reception despite substantial objections to the 'Epilogue' and some mystification over Huxley's sally via Eustace Barnack into the *Tibetan Book of the Dead*. Huxley told Thomas Barensfeld in 1943 that he thought he had now 'learned the art of embodying the ideas more into the substance of the novel' (p. 2). He later admitted a preference for this over his other novels because 'it seemed to me that I integrated what may be called the essay element with the fiction element better there than in the other novels' (*PR*, p. 206). Edmund Wilson allowed that 'his handling of the religious element' was here better than in the previous novel (No. 108); Theodore Spencer did not (No. 110). Several commentators concurred with Cyril Connolly's judgment that this was 'Mr. Huxley's best novel for a very long time' (No. 113). Thomas Mann wrote that the book 'gave me extraordinary pleasure—it is without doubt an audacious, top-ranking performance in the contemporary novel' (*Story*, p. 96), though in his correspondence he cited some grave reservations about Huxley's thought (No. 107). The didacticism of the book alienated more than one reader, leading for instance the *TLS* reviewer coolly to conclude: 'It seems a little odd that so incommunicable a sense of indwelling superiority should lead him to write a novel about human beings at all' (No. 112).[21] In this vein, George Dangerfield would shortly declare that the way of life advocated in *Time Must Have a Stop* 'put a number of readers into such a fury that they scarcely bothered to find out whether Huxley had succeeded in saying what he had so carefully set out to say' (*New Republic*, 23 August 1948, cxix, p. 21).

In the meantime Huxley's popularity, quite independent of his besieged critical status, had reached such an extent that his 'little book' on visual re-education, *The Art of Seeing* (1943), sold out its British first edition of 10,000 copies in its first few days of publication (*L*, p. 488). Published a year earlier in America, the book by September 1943 had there sold 'about twenty-three thousand' (*L*, p. 493). Gai Eaton estimated that the publication of *The Perennial Philosophy* 'must have doubled, in the course of a few weeks, the number of people in England and the United States who have some slight interest in the Oriental doctrines . . .' (p. 167). According to Philip Thody, over 12,000 copies of *The Perennial Philosophy* were sold before the official publication day (p. 81). In America, says Bedford, the book 'sold 23,000 copies within weeks' (*B*. II, p. 111). *Time Must Have a Stop* in America 'sold at once some 40,000 copies (*B*, II, p. 96) and, publishers' records indicate, the novel there achieved a total hard-cover sale of about 55,000.

But the important nonfiction that Huxley published during the war years, *Grey Eminence* (1941) as well as *The Perennial Philosophy* (1945), noticeably intensified the outcry against his position. *Grey Eminence* won considerable praise in some respects. MacCarthy in the *Sunday Times* said 'Huxley has shown himself an artist in biography' (28 December 1941, p. 3), Crane Brinton said the book was 'a historical work of a very high order' (No. 104). Wyndham Lewis reported from Toronto: '"Grey Eminence" by Huxley has been a wow over here' (p. 316). It is probably a sign of Huxley's still spreading fame that Benedetto Croce was reading *Grey Eminence* a few years later; he disagreed with some of the premises, but pronounced it 'a very penetrating book of history' (*Quaderni Della 'Critica'*, November 1946, ii, p. 85). Adverse criticism, nonetheless, was cutting. In the *New Statesman and Nation* Raymond Mortimer offered that something should be said on Father Joseph's behalf: 'Having decided, however mistakenly, that a particular end was desirable, he was not so spiritually self-centred as to leave the dirty work to other people' (29 November 1941, xxii [n.s.], p. 458). Richard V. Chase regretted the loss of the 'fine strain of biological irony' in the early novels and alluded to Huxley's position as one of 'the current aberrations of the bourgeois mind' (No. 105). Similarly, *The Perennial Philosophy* was pounced upon by Irwin Edman in the *NYHTBR* as 'a symptom of a failure of nerve in both the author and in a whole group of intellectuals of our time' (7 October 1945, p. 3). Although men of the calibre of William Inge (No. 116) and Jacques Maritain[22] would applaud Huxley's efforts, Joad represented the impatience of other readers when he rejected Huxley as a 'sour-faced moralist' (No. 115).

A convergence of two major strains of protest, then, had formed the axis of response to Huxley's work by the mid-1940s. It is one of the persisting ironies of Huxley's career that while he was bringing all his forces to bear on the discovery of a scheme of positive values for the contemporary world, he was most severely criticized for abandoning his kind:

One is tempted to regard the cloistered ecstasies of Huxley's present period as a luxury that should be only sparingly indulged today; indeed they seem something of a betrayal of a humanity sadly in need of teachers for more mundane concerns, chief among them its own survival (H. T. Webster, pp. 380–1).

In addition readers began to feel, with George Orwell, that the later novels 'are much inferior to his earlier ones' (*Collected Essays*, IV, p. 253). On the heels of David Daiches's influential 1939 attack on Huxley as a novelist (No. 95) came a battery of tough synoptic assessments. Edwin Berry Burgum followed Cowley in comparing the dying swan in the 1939 title to 'Huxley's flagging powers as a creative novelist . . .' (*Antioch Review*, p. 62). William York Tindall deplored the effect Huxley's new piety had on his novels and chided him for retreating into the California desert with Gerald Heard. In the most graceful and dispassionate of accounts, Frederick J. Hoffman submitted that the key difference between the earlier and later novels lay in a change from the dramatization to the exposition of ideas. In a variety of ways Huxley's critics had made it plain by 1946 that, if anything, they preferred to be entertained by his wit rather than instructed by his wisdom.

POSTWAR DECLINE 1947–1963

By 1947 Huxley's ideological position, both in itself and in its effects on his fiction, had caused extensive damage to his critical reputation. Cyril Connolly sensed that Huxley had 'made a brilliant recovery' since the later 1930s (*Enemies*, p. 4), but growing incomprehension of his career now impeded any such recovery. An editor of a large-circulation American magazine rejected Huxley's ecologically advanced essay, 'The Double Crisis,' 'with the private comment that its hot air content was high' (*B*, II, p. 142). Joyce Cary, in a private letter on 16 November 1948, claimed Huxley 'is not really very strong in the head': '[His type] are escapists who dodge the troublesome job of moral and political decision by going up a rabbit hole and saying "All is darkness"' (Foster, p. 292). Articles appeared which sounded like premature obituary notices in their assumption that Huxley's productive life was over:

The despair with which he contemplates a world which now seems derelict and whirling toward the final plunge is a projection of his despair of himself. One thinks of Horatio's farewell to Hamlet: 'Now cracks a noble heart. Good night, sweet prince' (Handley-Jones, p. 247).

In America *The World of Aldous Huxley* (1947) sold a disappointing 5,000 copies instead of the expected 15,000 (*L*, p. 581n).

Readers of *Ape and Essence* (1948) frequently criticized the carriage and overlooked the baby. The reviewers recoiled from the horrid forecast of the book, the 'ape,' in many cases without acknowledging its generating idealism, the 'essence.' In his column for the *Sunday Times* MacCarthy speculated that Huxley 'does not care enough what happens to mankind, or he would not describe their degradation in that particular way' (20 February 1949, p. 3). Some readers, such as Teilhard de Chardin, seem entirely to have ignored the novel's concluding sequences:

. . . One cannot escape the feeling, reading the book, that, at the depth of himself, the author believes that science leads primarily to destruction, and sex to corruption. And this is precisely the 'complex' which has, by all means, to be eradicated from the modern mind, both in religious and literary circles! (*Letters*, p. 207).

But *Ape and Essence* clearly was not one of Huxley's better novels and, therefore, it confirmed the belief in many minds that his significant creative career was at an end.

The 1950s witnessed the ebb of Huxley's critical reputation to its lowest point. *Brave New World* now seemed to most critics to be Huxley's only book which would much longer survive. 'There is a good chance,' wrote Andrew Hacker in the *Journal of Politics*, 'that Huxley's work [the book] will be as long remembered as Dostoevsky's [*Brothers Karamazov*]' (November 1955, xvii, p. 600). George Woodcock conceded regretfully that Huxley 'as an artist' has been 'a particularly disappointing failure' (*World Review*, p. 52). In 1950 R. C. Bald thought it well to be grateful for the pleasure and entertainment in Huxley's novels, 'so long as one does not take him too seriously as a novelist' (p. 187). As this most conservative decade wore on, Huxley's status among the critics continued to erode. Sean O'Faolain presently questioned Huxley's intelligence (pp. 21–2), Walter Allen ignored him in his chapter '1914 and After' in *The English Novel* (1955).[23] Arnold Kettle made an influential critique of Huxley's most respected novel as a novel:

It is no good trying to say what is wrong with *Point Counter Point* in terms of construction, style, characterization and the technical weapons of literary analysis because what is wrong is wrong at the very heart. There is no respect for life in this novel and without such fundamental respect words curdle and art cannot come into being (p. 170).

Some of the attacks, for example Roy Campbell's scornful description of Huxley as 'the great Mahatma of all misanthropy' (p. 166), were personal and vindictive. In a remarkably scathing assault, John McCormick called Huxley's later work 'monstrous and horrible' and urged that 'Huxley's own inability to love turned into a hatred of women and of humanity':

In re-reading Huxley the conclusion is inescapable that his vaunted brilliance is the pseudo-brilliance of the precocious schoolboy, the clever undergraduate, written for schoolboys and undergraduates. His erudition is little more than information smacking of the encyclopedia and smatterings of esoterica (p. 286).

The year after Huxley's death the *Year's Work in English Studies* would submit that he 'has been virtually ignored since he was dismissed as a novelist in the early 'fifties' (1964, xlv, p. 344). As recently as in 1971 John Wain wrote: 'There have been times, since about 1955, when I wondered if he was going to disappear altogether' (*New Republic*, 11 September 1971, clxv, p. 27).

But Huxley, generally impervious to the reputation mill, continued to work and to shape anew his career. With the production of *The Devils of Loudun* (1952) and *The Doors of Perception* (1954), he elicited a response similar to the pattern of a decade earlier. *The Devils*, like *Grey Eminence*, commanded much respect; *The Doors*, like *The Perennial Philosophy*, provoked much confusion. The *Spectator* reviewer typified several reactions to *The Devils* in his objection to its 'extremely unpleasant taste': '[This] new book displays a great talent hideously misapplied' (3 October 1952, clxxxix, p. 440). But another reviewer, aptly comparing the book with *Point Counter Point*, recognized that Huxley was still searching for new varieties of literary form (No. 125). The *NYTBR* called *The Devils* the 'peak achievement of Mr. Huxley's career' (5 October 1952, p. 1).

Predictably, *The Doors of Perception* upset large numbers of readers. 'Self-respecting rationalists saw fresh evidence of quackery and intellectual abdication while the serious and religious were bothered by the offer of a shortcut . . .' (*B*, II, p. 280). This book led John O'Hara to speculate on 'mad dogs and Englishmen': 'Well, dear Reader, when a writer starts talking about Not-self and Otherness, your boy slips out quietly to bay at the moon' (p. 50). Alastair Sutherland in the *Twentieth Century* labelled Huxley 'the Witch Doctor of California' (p. 447), prompting Humphrey Osmond to reply good-naturedly that Sutherland was 'a peeping Tom at a knot-hole in the Doors of Perception' ... (p. 522). A variety of disagreements came from such men as Thomas Mann (No. 127), Martin Buber, Arthur Koestler, and R. C. Zaehner.[24] Nonetheless, Huxley's reputation was strong enough in some circles that a few respondents, with J. Z. Young in the *Sunday Times*, 'felt prepared to listen and to learn from his great capacity for exploring the human problem' (14 February 1954, p. 5). The poles of reaction to Huxley's reports of his drug experiences in the 1950s may be represented by the conflicting comments of two other men of letters on *Heaven and Hell*. Kingsley Amis in the *Spectator* thought Huxley's 'present role' is 'that of a crank' (16 March 1956, cxcvi, p. 340); Richard Eberhart in the *Nation* thought this was 'a transporting book' (14 April 1956, clxxxii, p. 309).

What sales figures are available suggest that in the 1950s Huxley's popularity modulated downward from its peak in the earlier two decades. Paperbacks and the printing of Collected Works editions of Huxley's books (see Appendix III) render analyses of trends, even where at all possible, excessively complicated. But, for example, first-year American hard-cover sales of *The Genius and the Goddess* (1955) and *Island* (1962), not much over 20,000 copies apiece, were noticeably less than *Time Must Have a Stop*. And yet the changes in the popular reception seem to have been modest by comparison with the sharp downward curve of Huxley's reputation among the critics.

Like one of Yeats's gyres, though, Huxley's critical reputation at its most reduced moment still had within it an impulse toward recovery. Reviews of *The Genius and the Goddess* displayed that mixture of condescension and *déjà vu* which usually signals the twilight of real interest in a writer's work. But even when the established opinion was at its least flattering there existed along with it a steady undercurrent of tenacious belief that Huxley was a writer of contemporary significance. As Marvin Barrett observed in the *Reporter*:

Huxley's attitude in the last two decades has been to most critics an exasperating one. An intellectual of the deepest dye, he has embraced a violent anti-intellectualism; a prodigious aesthete, he has dismissed art in all its forms as, in the final analysis, worthless. ... He has sawed off the limb he himself is perched on a hundred times, and yet, like some character in an animated cartoon, he refuses to fall (2 March 1954, x, p. 46).

At the same time Floyd W. Matson reflected that earlier critics wrote Huxley off 'as a pathetic divagation from the main stream,' but today 'the critics are less certain': 'Possibly a new age, with a new set of gods, is struggling to be born' (pp. 294–5, 308). Carlyle King (No. 126) and Paul Bloomfield were among a small but decided minority which insisted on the value of Huxley's later work:

Gradually he has revealed himself as one of the few capable makers of a cultural synthesis in our time. . . . His concern for mankind is so obvious that one can only think readers who see nothing in his later fiction but obsessions and bitterness are incapable of appreciating his intentions or his powers (Bloomfield, pp. 140–1).

The *Time Magazine* reviewer of the *Collected Short Stories* revealed that Huxley 'is now so venerable a figure of modern letters that a middle-aged critic—the *Atlantic Monthly*'s Charles J. Rolo—owns a poodle named Aldous' (21 April 1958, lxxi, p. 93).

Recognition of Huxley's achievement was soon forthcoming from more prodigious sources. The American Academy of Arts and Letters gave him its 1959 Award of Merit for the Novel, previous winners of which had been Hemingway, Mann and Dreiser. In 1960 Huxley was nominated for (but did not receive) a Nobel Prize (see Holmes, p. 198). Two years later he was elected a Companion of Literature by the Royal Society of Literature, a position which was 'limited to 10 living persons who had brought special distinction to English letters' (*The Times*, 8 June 1962, p. 8). He joined the company of Winston Churchill, G. M. Trevelyan, Edmund Blunden, Somerset Maugham, John Masefield, and E. M. Forster.

The reception of Huxley's last major work, *Island* (1962), was characteristically divided. The book raised yet again the question of artistry in Huxley's novels. Frank Kermode contended that *Island* was 'one of the worst novels ever written' (No. 144), Wayne C. Booth considered whether standard concepts of the novel were really applicable (No. 143). The outline of a Utopian novel had been gestating in Huxley's mind since the early 1940s. When in 1959 he began its actual composition, the problem of integrating art with idea occurred once more:

I am working away on my Utopian novel, wrestling with the problem of getting an enormous amount of diversified material into the book without becoming merely expository or didactic. It may be that the job is one which cannot be accomplished with complete success. In point of fact, it hasn't been accomplished in the past. For most Utopian books have been exceedingly didactic and expository. I am trying to lighten up the exposition by putting it into dialogue form, which I make as lively as possible. But meanwhile I am always haunted by the feeling that, if only I had enough talent, I could somehow poetize and dramatize all the intellectual material and create a work which would be simultaneously funny, tragic, lyrical and profound (*L*, pp. 875–6).

The aesthetic ideal of *Antic Hay* remained a constant in Huxley's approach to fiction. When *Island* was finished, however, he was not entirely satisfied with the result: 'The weakness of the book consists in a disbalance between fable and exposition. The story has too much weight, in the way of ideas and reflections, to carry. Alas, I didn't know how to remedy this defect' (*L*, p. 930). Connolly thought that Huxley had handled the problem quite well (No. 141), but the *Times* reviewer found the book boring: 'His new book, *Island*, is about as interesting as a prolonged session of fishing during which the fisherman fails to tickle the nose of a single trout, bass or even pike' (29 March 1962, p. 15).

Huxley, for once, says Bedford, 'felt not indifferent' to reviews (*B*, II, p. 513). While he might have conceded that the bulk of exposition could become oppressive, he 'was saddened and upset,' according to Julian Huxley, 'by the incomprehension' of some responses (*MV*, p. 24). Longtime admirer Rolo painfully reported that the 'blueprint for the sane society is a disconcerting mish-mash of mystical doctrine and a variety of Huxleyan fads' (*NYHTBR*, 25 March 1962, p. 4). William Barrett in the *Atlantic Monthly* went so far as to suggest 'there is the outside chance' that Huxley may have intended the book 'as a satire on his own most cherished values' (April 1962, ccix, p. 155). Yet other readers, such as Chad Walsh, welcomed *Island* as a significant contribution to Utopian literature (No. 146), and D. H. Stewart would shortly hail it as 'symptomatic of a new spirit in the world' (p. 334).

At the time of his death in 1963 Huxley's critical reputation was at best quite tentative. As Richard S. Kennedy observed, 'Critic and commentator had adopted a rather patronizing tone' (No. 148). The opinion widely held, especially in formalist circles, was that Huxley had achieved little as a creative artist and could be dispatched in a footnote to the history of modern letters. The obituaries, at times graceful, at times dismissive, engaged in noncommittal generalities and personal compliments to accommodate the diminished state of his critical reputation. *The Times* mentioned only in passing Huxley's different approach to fiction:

His death brings to an end a literary career of outstanding versatility and brilliance. His first novel, *Crome Yellow* (1921), made him famous, and was the precursor of a whole body of fiction devoted in the main to the violent demolition of Victorian and Edwardian values. The whole system of a logically developing plot was jettisoned (25 November 1963, p. 14).

In the minds of a majority of critics Huxley was fixed as an entertaining recorder of the frenetic 1920s who later recoiled into an aesthetically suicidal mysticism. An alternative view, offered by those who continued to admire his work, was offered by Frank Swinnerton just before Huxley's death:

To him, as to Shaw, 'the golden rule is that there is no golden rule.' He was always an original, not a systematizer. He is still an original, aloof from current ideas, following thought into uncharted regions for which the 'traditionalists', who need dogma, express contempt (*Figures*, p. 186).

TOWARD REASSESSMENT 1964–1973

Swinnerton's allusion to Shaw was doubly appropriate. Shaw, the so-called 'dramatist of ideas,' had experienced with Huxley sustained difficulty among the critics because of the expository style of his work. Like Shaw's, the sum of Huxley's work at the end appeared to the critical establishment to amount to little more than a scintillating showpiece for a bygone period of cultural history. '. . . Even before the long drawl of his body is cold,' lamented Robert Craft over the announcement of Huxley's death,

the reputation industry will have attended to the summing-up—which is obituarese for hatcheting down, the denigrating epithet being so much easier to find than the epithet for the value quality. . . . Aldous Huxley, a man gentle and good and a writer better than any who will literarily bury him, dear Aldous will be patted on the head and put away as an era (p. 16).

To be 'put away as an era' certainly seemed to be Huxley's critical destiny in the early 1960s. Some signs of genuine critical interest in Huxley's literary achievement had appeared in the last years of his life—John Atkins's book in 1956 (the first, since Henderson's, in twenty years), A. E. Dyson's long essay on Huxley's irony in the *Critical Quarterly*, and a handful of analytical articles on single novels (see No. 137). But J. B. Priestley presented the received argument against

Huxley's work as a subject for serious critical study when he declared that 'his novels are made, not really created,' and that 'he is concerned with ideas and not with persons' (p. 427).

The dearth of critical recognition near the end of his life was, however, no measure of his popular success. Bedford relates the enthusiastic response to the several lecturing engagements Huxley accepted in his last years (B, II, *passim*). The rise in Huxley's royalties income since World War II indicates that his reading public over the long run was substantial. His income from English book sales rose from £970 in 1936 to £3,300 in 1948 and to £7,239 in 1959. 'In 1962 Aldous's gross income from book royalties came to £6,496 and 26,646 dollars respectively [in England and America]. *Island* had been doing well financially' (B, II, p. 525). Moreover his works had achieved a sizeable international popularity. The files of his British publishers reveal well over 350 translations of Huxley titles into some twenty-five foreign languages (see Appendix II). Plainly, the critical boycott of Huxley's writings had not done that much to discourage his reading audience.

The process of critical reassessment commenced in the later 1960s with an unprecedented burst of activity. '. . . If one feels that academic criticism has been less than fair to him,' Dyson had reflected in 1961, '. . . Time will bring the Ph.D. thesis along with the worm' (*Critical Quarterly*, p. 293). The Ph.D. thesis and considerably more, in fact, have materialized in the decade since Huxley's death. Since 1968 eleven major book-length studies of Huxley (including Clark's *The Huxleys*) have been published, as compared with three during his life. In 1969 Grover Smith presented a scholarly edition of Huxley's letters. The authorized two-volume biography was being done by Sybille Bedford in 1973-4. At this writing, an entry on contemporary Huxley criticism in Prentice-Hall's 'Twentieth Century Views' series was in press. And several serious investigations of his writing have appeared in recent years in important scholarly and critical journals, such as the *Philological Quarterly*, *Modern Language Review*, *Sewanee Review*, *Modern Language Quarterly*, and the *Yale Review*.

The quality of the recent critical work has been, in large measure, encouragingly high. The best studies of Huxley's developing thought, those by Charles M. Holmes and George Woodcock, achieve an informed, realistic overview of his career as an intellectual. They track Huxley's quest for that 'synthesis for free human beings' (L, p. 408) which he always hoped to create. Even more promising is the arrival of a group of critics willing to examine fresh approaches to Huxley's fiction as its own kind of creative art. Most notable among these critics, perhaps, are Peter Bowering, Peter E. Firchow, Keith M. May, and Jerome Meckier. Meckier's is a contention which illustrates the renewal of interest in Huxley's work as literature: 'As a serious literary crafts-man, Huxley has done something new and original with the novel and one cannot explain this away by pointing to his antecedents' (*Aldous Huxley*, p. 6).

The intensity and achievement of this new work suggest that critical interest in Huxley, at least in America, has already gone beyond the predictable flurry of activity which follows an author's demise. What Huxley's London publisher used to tell Gerald Heard applies to the posthumous critical response to his canon: 'Aldous shoots in front of his public flock. In a couple of years they have flown into his shot' (p. 56). Certainly a part of the new receptivity is due to a current swing in some academies away from the influence of modern formalist criticism and back toward the classical moral realism of Sidney, Johnson, and Ruskin. The willingness of the 1960s to admit Shaw, and Lawrence, at least somewhere into the company of James and Joyce surely lends fresh impetus to a revaluation of Huxley. An equally important factor, though, is the greater objectivity which time generously bestows on critical pursuits. A major accomplishment of the Huxley revival over the past decade has been the pronounced refutation of the view that he was merely a popularizer of ideas. Keith M. May's argument, for instance, signals the reversal of an attitude prevalent during Huxley's career: '. . . It is an exaggeration, if not a downright error, to see Huxley as a thinker who happened, for accidental or tactical reasons, to take up the writing of fiction' (p. 224). How far James Sutherland was right in forecasting that not many of Huxley's novels 'will survive the century' (p. 132) of course remains to be seen. But whatever posterity's ultimate judgment may be—if indeed there are such things as 'ultimate judgments'—the best Huxley criticism of the later 1960s and early 1970s offers the assurance that responsible analysts cannot complacently 'pat him on the head and put him away as an era.'

One can neither compile a volume on Huxley's 'critical heritage' nor speculate upon the brave new world of his critical future without being reminded of his own response when confronted by the typescript of a bibliography of his own writings from 1916–59. 'Literary fame,' he reflected, 'is a function of fossilizability.' A writer's works, 'transformed by time into the equivalents of ammonites or petrified saurians,' become 'museum pieces upon which the learned geologists of Criticism make their comments and erect their towering socio-aesthetic theories' (*ES*, p. v). The cautionary value of so much of Huxley's work, it is to be hoped, will be borne in mind by critics seeking further to assess the flora and fauna of his career. The best motto for such endeavors may be that one which Huxley so admired by Goya: 'Aún aprendo—I am still learning.'

NOTES

1 For full information on materials cited, consult the Bibliography and Appendix I.
2 *This Timeless Moment*, p. 207. Huxley's 1931 interview with J. W. N. Sullivan contains a modest projection of his ambitions, and the *Letters* include key revelations about his goals for *Antic Hay*, *Point Counter Point*, *Time Must Have a Stop*, and *Island*.
3 Parmenter, p. 10. Bedford suggests Huxley may have responded to similar criticism of *Crome Yellow* via Dolphin and Hutton in his next book, *Mortal Coils* (*B*, I, p. 122). See also Huxley's description of English literary criticism in 1930 as 'all for being nice and gentlemanly and public-schooly' (*L*, p. 337), possibly a response to the *New Statesman* review of *Brief Candles* as 'very cheap, and too often very nasty . . .' (24 May 1930, xxxv, p. 218).
4 *New York Times*, 24 November 1963, p. 22. 'Aldous used to complain of himself as a fairly slow writer in terms of Arnold Bennett's daily thousand. Actually, he must have averaged 500 words a day, and that with very great regularity. Every day that Aldous was at home, every day he was not on a journey, he worked. He worked on Sundays. There was never any question of doing otherwise' (Bedford, *MV*, p. 142). Huxley told his daughter-in-law in 1955 'that he became physically ill if he didn't work a good part of every day' (*B*, II, p. 334).
5 Some other general reasons for critical attacks on Huxley will be found in the *Memorial Volume* and in recent books on him—for example, André Maurois: 'For all the excellence of the thought and writing of Huxley's books, one thing is missing: the ordinary man' (*MV*, p. 63), Leonard Woolf: 'His curiosity was so intense and his intellect so strong and subtle that his imagination never entirely broke loose from the reasoning part of his mind. That is why, I think, his novels, with all their merits, are never in the highest class' (*MV*, pp. 37-8); Philip Thody: 'It may be that they [Huxley's literary critics] cannot forgive him the knowledge of science which they lack, and they may find it hard to admire an author who wears his intellect so obviously on his sleeve' (p. 75).

6 *Essays in Criticism*, January 1965, xv, p. 5. See Strong's more detailed account in *Green Memory*, p. 180.

7 *The Glory That Was Grub Street*, p. 143. Harold Acton recalls how, each time he passed through Spottiswoode's shop, he read a poem from the display copy of *The Defeat of Youth*, 'and finally bought the volume' (*Memoirs of an Aesthete*, p. 76).

8 From press clippings cited in Weaver, p. 63, I, together with Mencken's American publishers and the editor of *Menckeniana*, have been unable to locate the original source of this statement.

9 *Cities of the Plain*, p. 52. Forty years later Huxley said: 'I never met Proust and have no idea how he came to know about me—as it was far from being truc that . . . I occupied a preponderant position in English literature at that time' (*B*, I, p. 121).

10 Cf. Clark's claim that Lady Ottoline 'did not object to the way in which she scandalously dominated some of his pages' (p. 223). Clark discusses other subjects of Huxley's portraits in fiction (pp. 223–5).

11 Hodson, p. 257. Henderson insisted that the report that '*Antic Hay* had been burned by the Public Librarian in Alexandria because it "smelled too strongly of the goat"' was 'a piece of journalistic licence' (No. 88).

12 Bennett records a visit by Huxley on 23 September 1924: 'We agreed on nearly all literary questions except the value of his *Antic Hay*. He likes that book, thinks it has a point to it' (*Journal*, p. 790).

13 *Book Review Digest* (New York; Wilson, 1924), p. 256. John Lehmann described himself as 'a devotee of *Crome Yellow* and *Antic Hay*' (p. 123), but Edward Marsh entered a dissenting view: 'Aldous Huxley's *Antic Hay* is having a bad press. I must say the first six chapters or so amused me quite enormously, but it tails off into a rather nauseating caricature of X and her surroundings which I think he might have left to Michael Arlen' (Hassall, pp. 515–16).

14 'Aldous Huxley,' p. 144. Alec Waugh wrote in 1924 that it is 'doubtful if there is, with the exception of Mr. Aldous Huxley, a single Neo-Georgian who stands as high in popular and critical esteem as he did six years ago. . . . No one has revealed more to the modern mind than he has' (pp. 126, 132).

15 *Kenyon Review*, p. 57. Huxley wrote Harold Raymond on 19 March 1932: 'I'm glad the book still does so well. In Cannes, we saw H. G. Wells who, I fear, wasn't pleased with it. On the contrary (surprisingly enough) Edith Wharton is enthusiastic!' (*L*, pp. 358–9).

16 *Private History*, p. 154. 'Wells's old friend, Moura Budberg, said "H.G. was very cross, he said it was *defeatist*"' (*B*, I, p. 253). Huxley later said his novel 'started out as a parody of H. G. Wells' *Men Like Gods*, but gradually it got out of hand and turned into something quite different from what I'd originally intended' (*PR*, p. 198).

17 *Outline*, p. 597. Robert Kee recalled: 'For those who made their first contacts with contemporary literature in the mid 1930s it is still difficult to take a dispassionate critical view of Mr. Huxley. He was the greatest English novelist—the greatest at any rate who consistently wrote novels—who had appeared in one's life-time (*Spectator*, 20 August 1948, clxxxi, p. 248).

18 *Review of Reviews,* September 1936, xciv, p. 13. Only recently has the novel received any sustained examination as an important work. See for example the books by Meckier, pp. 144–60, and Woodcock, pp. 195–206.

19 12 May 1938, p. 99, and 26 May 1938, p. 136. See Kingsley Martin's balanced argument, 'The Pacifist's Dilemma To-Day,' *Political Quarterly*, April–June 1938, ix, pp. 155–72. Clark writes of *Ends and Means* that 'it was natural that Huxley's philosophy should be badly received on the Left, which felt that one of its more important potential supporters was engaged in pulling the rug smartly from beneath its feet at a crucial moment' (p. 289). Clark gives a very full analysis of the response to this book (pp. 288–92). Notably, *Ends and Means* has sold more copies in the Collected Edition than any of Huxley's books except *Point Counter Point* and *Brave New World* (see Appendix III).

20 Nicolson did a famous series of articles, 'Marginal Comment,' in the *Spectator* from 1938–52. Cf. John Lehmann's comment that Isherwood's pacifism 'wrote the epitaph to our friendship as we had known it . . .' (p. 223).

21 Desmond MacCarthy raised a perennial objection to Huxley's work when he wrote that the background of mundane folly 'becomes more arresting than the goodness it was meant to throw into relief. Thus, judged as a whole, the novel fails in intention, much as a tract on chastity might fail which dwelt too infectiously on lust' (*Sunday Times*, 25 March 1945, p. 3).

22 Maritain shared Huxley's sensed need for a re-awakening of spiritual values in the contemporary world, said his 'testimony is important and significant', and urged the spread of the perennial philosophy by the large-scale establishment of spiritual centers. See *The Range of Reason*, p. 49.

23 In contrast, Pelham Edgar in his 1933 study, *The Art of the Novel from 1700 to the Present Time*, had devoted a sixteen-page chapter to Huxley.

24 See Buber, *The Knowledge of Man*, pp. 42–5, 99–102; Koestler, *The Ghost in the Machine*, pp. 335–6; and Zaehner, *Mysticism Sacred and Profane, passim*. Two samples of the continuation of the controversy are the articles by Arthur N. Gilbert and A. W. Sadler.

Note on the Text

The text reproduces the documents in the yearly order of their first publication. Exceptions occur where comments by one person over different years are conveniently brought together (e.g. Orwell, No. 102), or where one review among several grouped under a single title is a year out of sequence (e.g. Marcel, No. 85). Within a single year appropriateness of grouping has been followed rather than monthly chronological order. In all particulars the text follows that printed version of each document cited in its heading. Substantial excisions from the documents are explained in bracketed editorial remarks, minor ones indicated by ellipses. Longer quotations from Huxley not essential to contributors' arguments have been replaced by bracketed references to their sources in the Collected Edition (see A List of Huxley's Major Works, pp. xxiii–xxiv). Occasional misprints and a few factual errors in dates, names, and titles have been silently amended.

1. Virginia Woolf, unsigned notice of *The Defeat of Youth* in *TLS*

10 October 1918, p. 477

Among the earliest notices of Huxley's work were those in *TLS*, which said his first book, *The Burning Wheel*, revealed 'considerable literary talent,' but advised he should give up 'grinding dark brooding thoughts into tortured expression' (5 October 1916, p. 479). Huxley found the *TLS* review of this first book 'pleasantly offensive,' and the one in the *Morning Post* quite pleasing: 'They make me out very distinguished. Don't they?' (*B*, I, p. 68).

ES (Item 1242) attributes the present notice to Virginia Woolf (see No. 2 for a biographical note). Woolf has here been discussing Muriel Stuart's *The Cockpit of Idols*, which she reviews along with Huxley's book, Edith Sitwell's *Clowns' Houses*, and an anthology of recent poetry.

The connexion between Miss Stuart and Mr. Huxley is the obvious one that they have nothing in common. The one is strong precisely where the other is weak. Miss Stuart has too many ideas and emotions, and is too careless as to what she does with them. But after reading the first few poems in Mr. Huxley's little book it is clear that any idea or emotion that comes to him has the best possible chance of surviving beautifully. The criticism implied is, of course, that he is better equipped with the vocabulary of a poet than with the inspiration of a poet. He writes about the things he has thought and seen rather than about things he has felt, and in rendering them he shows a facility which begins by charming, but ends, as verse that relies so much upon happy adjectives is always apt to end, by running fluently to waste. The advice that one is inclined to give to an urbane and cultivated writer of his quality is to cease to use poetry in the serious, traditional manner, and to use it instead to explore those fantastic, amusing, or ironical aspects of life which can only be expressed by people of high technical skill and great sensibility.

[Refers to 'Social Amenities,' 'Topiary,' and 'On the 'Bus' as 'quite capable of doing this']

LIMBO

February 1920

---

2. Virginia Woolf, unsigned review in *TLS*

5 February 1920, p. 83

Virginia Woolf (1882–1941), novelist and critic in the first rank of
English women authors, wife of Leonard Woolf (see No. 31), and
a central figure of the Bloomsbury Group. In her *Writer's Diary*
Woolf expresses a distinct aversion to Huxley's fiction (Introduction, p. 13). For Huxley's views of Woolf's works, see *PR*, p. 208.

ES attributes the review to Woolf (Item 1258). The title of the
review, 'Cleverness and Youth,' suggests an ambivalence, in com-
plimenting Huxley for his cleverness, which recurs often in later
responses to his writing. See Introduction, p. 7.

We know for ourselves that Mr. Huxley is very clever; and his
publisher informs us that he is young. For both these reasons his
reviewers may pay him the compliment, and give themselves the
pleasure, of taking him seriously. Instead, that is, of saying that there
are seven short stories in *Limbo* which are all clever, amusing, and well
written, and recommending the public to read them, as we can conscientiously do, we are tempted to state, what it is so seldom necessary
to state, that short stories can be a great deal more than clever, amusing,
and well written. There is another adjective—'interesting'; that is the
adjective we should like to bestow upon Mr. Huxley's short stories, for
it is the best worth having.

The difficulty is that in order to be interesting, as we define the word,
Mr. Huxley would have to forgo, or go beyond, many of the gifts
which nature and fortune have put in his way.

[Discusses Huxley's wide reading and intellectualism]

We hold no brief for the simple peasant. Yet we cannot help thinking that it is well to leave a mind under a counterpane of moderate ignorance; it grows more slowly, but being more slowly exposed it avoids that excessive surface sensibility which wastes the strength of the precocious. Again, to be aware too soon of sophisticated society makes it tempting for a young writer to use his first darts in attack and derision. If he is as dexterous and as straightforward as Mr. Huxley the attack is an inspiriting spectacle. Humbug seems to collapse, pretension to be pricked.

[Cites examples of Huxley's ability to entertain: the description of Mr Glottenham, pp. 40-1, and the dinner with Mr Crawister, p. 18]

It is amusing; it is perhaps true; and yet as one reads one cannot help exclaiming that English society is making it impossible to produce English literature. Write about boots, one is inclined to say, about coins, sea anemones, crayfish—but, as you value your life, steer clear of the English upper middle classes. They lie, apparently, so open to attack, they are undoubtedly such an obstacle to vision; but their openness is the openness of the tiger's jaw which ends by swallowing you whole and leaving no trace. 'Happily Ever After' is but another proof of their rapacity. Mr. Huxley sets out to kill a great many despicable conventions, and to attack a large and disgusting schoolmaster. But having laughed at the conventions and the schoolmaster, they suddenly turn the tables on him. Now, they seem to say, talk about something that you do believe in—and behold, Mr. Huxley can only stammer. Love and death, like damp fireworks, refuse to flare up in such an atmosphere, and as usual the upper middle classes escape unhurt.

But with Mr. Huxley it is only necessary to wait a little longer; and we can wait without anxiety. He is not merely clever, well read, and honest, but when he forgets himself he discovers very charming things.

[Quotes the descriptions of fashion plates and the piano from 'The Bookshop,' pp. 261-2]

Emboldened by our pleasure in such good writing as this, we would admonish Mr. Huxley to leave social satire alone, to delete the word 'incredibly' from his pages, and to write about interesting things that he likes. Nobody ever takes advice; even so, we hazard the opinion that Mr. Huxley's next book will be not only clever, amusing, and well written, but interesting into the bargain.

3. Herbert S. Gorman, review in
New Republic

13 October 1920, xxiv, pp. 172–3

Signed 'H.S.G.', quite likely Herbert [Sherman] Gorman (1893–1954), journalist, critic, biographer and editor. Gorman's review characterizes the enthusiastic American reception of *Limbo*.

Mr. Aldous Huxley, a new and extremely prepossessing English writer, has just been introduced to America with two volumes, *Limbo*, a collection of prose sketches written in a vein that is, to say the least, individual, and *Leda and Other Poems*, containing verse that smacks mightily of Mr. T. S. Eliot, and yet has an intriguing appeal quite its own. It was, I believe, in 1916 that Mr. Huxley's first book, *The Burning Wheel*, was published. A slender volume of verse, bound in paper covers and forming a link in Blackwell's Adventurers All Series, it hardly awakened more than a passing curiosity. But there was more in it than dexterous rhyming. The influence of Jules Laforgue was faintly manifesting itself; a precocious sophistication made itself dimly evident. Mr. Huxley has progressed as a poet since those days.

But it is the prose of Mr. Huxley that has suddenly projected him into the English periodicals and induced an American publisher[1] to bring him out over here. The seven pieces that make up the book (not all of them may be defined by the term 'stories') form a delectable ensemble. Mr. Huxley possesses the insolence of youth and a sprightly sophistication that can hardly be called disillusioned, although it approaches cynicism with frequency. It is a fastidious cynicism, though. If he suggests the pessimist at times we may be very sure that it is not the false pessimism of youth. He does not fly to extremes. He has not suddenly discovered that art is short and time is fleeting or that there

---

[1] George Doran in New York. Frank Swinnerton called *Limbo* to Doran's attention: '. . . I suggested to Doran that if he wanted to cultivate young talent, as he did, he should take the American rights.' *Figures in the Foreground*, p. 188.

are more people in the world intent upon bread and cheese than lyrics and lilies. Mr. Huxley is well-bred, without suggesting it. He is debonair without any flamboyant swashbuckling. He is precise in his prose and irresistible with his epigrams. Above all, he is the City. It is the sophistication of Hyde Park that he emanates.

So I come to the one English writer with whom he appears to have a certain kinship. Behind the pages of *Limbo* (at least for me) glimmers the nonchalant phantom of Max Beerbohm. The incomparable Max, a trifle weary, yawning a bit obviously, swings a gallant cane behind the 'Farcical History of Richard Greenow' and 'Happily Ever After.' He even appears, perhaps, a trifle more poetical than his wont, in 'Cynthia' and 'The Bookshop.' This may be doing a grave injustice to both Max Beerbohm and Mr. Huxley, and perhaps it is wise to insist that I am not attempting to postulate that the younger writer is at all aping his elders. It is merely a kinship of mood, a likeness of general attributes. 'The Farcical History of Richard Greenow' might have fitted into Max Beerbohm's *Seven Men* without disordering that adorable volume in the least, but it is equally native to *Limbo*. Both writers are of the City. Both of them draw their characters with smartness and with individuality. Both of them display a sophistication that is beyond their years. Alas, we may not say this of Max now, but when we consider Max Beerbohm collecting his half dozen essays into a slender volume, writing a farewell preface to them, and publishing them as his *Collected Works*, while he was still in his early twenties, we smile and attribute his gesture to the insolence of youth. The same insolence hovers over *Limbo*. If anything Mr. Huxley is a bit more poetic. He is urbane but not to the extent of Max Beerbohm. Neither is his gift of humor so magical, so consistent. Mr. Huxley likes to be serious at times. His sophistication does not suggest the playfulness that is evident in Mr. Beerbohm's work.

The two pieces in *Limbo* that appear to stand out most startlingly are 'The Farcical History of Richard Greenow' and 'Happily Ever After.' Both of them are animated by a worldliness that is more implicit than expressed. Richard Greenow possesses a dual mind. Mentally he is an hermaphrodite. The figure of this man changes rapidly from light comedy to tragic implications. The crashing down of the war upon England eventually destroys him. When we consider Richard, part of whose time is taken up living the life of a radical editor of a paper opposing the war and the rest of it existing as a lady novelist writing the most obvious patriotic war-mush, we must smile, but behind the incongruous theme is a passionate and heart-rending situation. Even in his death-throes Richard's dual nature is fighting against itself.

'Happily Ever After' is obviously cynical. It is satire handled with a deftness that is admirable. There is a truthfulness about the figure of Marjorie that ought to hurt. Perhaps this story is the best in point of character drawing, for there is a roundness about all the figures that move through its action. They suggest reality in a vivid and startling fashion. If we are to consider Marjorie being comforted in the arms of George when she hears of Guy's death in battle too seriously, we are apt to grow a bit cynical about the durability of love.

[Quotes pp. 190–1]

While 'Cynthia' and 'The Bookshop' and 'Eupompus Gave Splendour to Art by Numbers' may be merely mentioned as delicious trifles or tours de force, two other sketches in the book must be especially noted. 'Happy Families,' written in dialogue form, possesses a symbolical significance that sets it a bit apart from the other efforts. By means of certain figures the hidden traits of the two principal personages are presented. Thus a slobbering Negro who keeps interjecting himself into the action personifies the man's primitive instincts.

'The Death of Lully,' which concludes the book, may be suspected of being an old legend or at least having its derivative inspiration in some old story. It is not Raimon Lully, the contemporary of Molière that is meant, but a religiast of the Mediterranean. Here again there is symbolism, and a surprisingly obvious symbolism for Mr. Huxley.

Limbo, taken as a whole, suggests a fine maturity in a writer so young. Mr. Huxley has fulfilled the promise that he intimated in his earlier books to the few who knew him, and demonstrated that he is one of the finest writers of prose in England today. He is finished and fastidious, sophisticated and diverting, an authentic figure of some actual importance and with many potentialities. That he must take a decided place among the younger contemporary writers in England is without doubt.

LEDA

May 1920

4. Desmond MacCarthy, review in
New Statesman

4 September 1920, xv, pp. 595-7

For a biographical note see No. 57.

Mr. Aldous Huxley is one of the most interesting of the new poets, partly because he has already written good poetry, but chiefly because he is a finer, richer poet in the making. But the emotional and intellectual elements in him have not yet been fused together into a malleable compound fit for the handling of the subjects which most often attract him. It naturally follows that it is the expression of an emotional or intellectual discord that he is most often prompted to express in verse. This is a characteristic common to many of the new poets. They can point to examples in past literature in which discords of that kind have flowered in poems of high excellence; the immense admiration which Donne's poems excite today springs from the need to point out to the world that the thing can indeed be done.

[Discusses Donne and modern poetry]

To return to Mr. Huxley. He has science in the blood. He is often preoccupied, as a poet, with experience as it may be felt in the light of science. This alone would make his work interesting; but, alas, it does not also make it beautiful. The fundamental reason why the ban has been removed from the expression of 'ugliness' in literature, is that artists have so much new unconsecrated material to assimilate. But the poet with the imaginative digestion of a Lucretius has not yet emerged.

Mr. Huxley, when he handles experience from this point of view, creates merely the grotesque or the curious; he is interested and excited himself, he takes a morose delectation in paining himself and his reader, but he is homesick all the time for the old mythological world. When he makes intellect the starting point of his inspiration, he allows his nerves (oh! fatal weakness!) to have the controlling influence on the result; he never rises to the peaks of contemplation. There is pathos in this failure; but it is a pathos that is interesting rather than satisfying. He relapses, after flutterings, upon the half-way ledge of irony, where he can perch and utter those mordant reflections which may be a relief to the poet himself, but can never raise the minds of others. Contrast his poem 'Leda' with the series of poems in this volume called 'Philosophers' Songs'. In 'Leda' he is back in the old smooth, mythological world, consecrated by a thousand poets. He pays occasional tribute to ugly fact in the course of this poem, but he is at home while describing Leda with her maids bathing in Eurotas, her shining body and the clear deep pools! The modern terror of the too-perfect world makes him dwell longer, and more humorously, than his predecessors would have done, upon Jove tossing on his Olympian couch, tortured by his continence, and sending the searchlight of his glowing eye travelling over the earth below to find some object worthy of his god-like lust.

> Over the world his focused passion flies
> Quicker than chasing sunlight on a day
> Of storm and golden April.

There is imaginative intensity in the poet's description of the effects of that burning, searching eye-beam, travelling over the world; and listen, the verse, too, is fine:

[Quotes the effects Jove's passing glances have upon country maids]

But the beings that beam reveals are far from pleasing to the god, until it lights on Leda; other disgusting or insipid creatures offer the poet opportunities for paying passing homage to the ugly; for descriptions in which his morose delectation can revel, not only of scenes in which

> Dryads with star-flowers in their woolly hair
> Dance to the flaccid clapping of their own
> Black dangling dugs through forests overgrown,

but descriptions of flowers, carrying suggestions, in the manner of Huysmans, of loathsome, terrifying, fleshly diseases. Then the clouds of morbid morphology clear away and the blue heaven of Lemprière,

Keats and Chapman is once more above us. The description of Jove's descent as a swan from heaven, pursued in sport by Venus in the form of an eagle, is magnificent in movement.

[Quotes the eagle's assault on the swan and Leda's reaction]

The sailing, swift approach of the swan towards her is equally fine, and the close of the poem, which reminds one of 'Hero and Leander' in its sensual rapture:

[Quotes last twenty lines of 'Leda']

Thus Mr. Huxley writes when he is on the old ground; no emotional incoherence or lack of balance here, either in diction or in mood. But turn to the other poems, where he attempts to absorb material as yet unconsecrated, to use as themes, memories, facts, images and ideas which are neither simple nor sensuous, and if capable of rousing passion, only a cold self-regarding passion in the poet himself. Having little space to quote I refer the reader—to the rest of the book. Does one regret these experiments? The answer is an emphatic 'No'. Who does not seek will never find. But are they successful? The answer is an equally emphatic negative.

In the centre of the book the reader will come across a preface, composed of separate reflections, in which the poet's aims and perplexities are obscurely set forth; where by means of an irritatingly allusive and imaged prose, for which Mallarmé's *Divagations* are a precedent, he asks himself what the task of the poet is. The first answer is: 'Let us abandon ourselves to Time, which is beauty's essence'—that is to say, dwell pensively on the imperfection and the passing of happiness and all beautiful things. He brushes aside this answer: 'If I have said "Mortality is beauty", it was a weakness.' . . . [sic] If he has set up death and nothingness as an ideal (and in some of his poems his bitterness comes near to doing so), it is only his desperate mind that has desired it: 'never my blood, whose pulse is a rhythm of the world'. On the other hand, the pure imaginative ideal is equally unsatisfactory: 'Beatrice lacks solidity, is as unresponsive to your kisses as mathematics' (Personally, I consider this a silly pronouncement); 'she, too, is an oubliette, not a way of life.' What, then, is the common measure, he asks? What is true poetry? He replies in a series of metaphors: 'It is not the far-fetched, dear-bought gem; no pomander to be smelt only when the crowd becomes too stinkingly insistent.' He wants poets to be 'Rather a rosy Brotherhood of Common Life, eating, drinking; marrying and giving in marriage; taking and taken in adultery; reading, thinking, and when thinking fails, feeling immeasurably more subtly, sometimes perhaps creating . . . *Ventre à terre*,[1] head in the air—your centaurs are your only poets. Their hoofs strike sparks from the flints and they see both very near and immensely far.'

Now, this is a robust poet's creed, and Mr. Huxley is not a robust poet—perhaps that is why this creed attracts him. True, he can not only waive away the pomander, but hold his nose and our noses, too, over the most complex and stenchful exhalations; he can keep his eyes without blenching on the most hideous sights and the most grating disappointments. But the poetry that results? Those poems are the turnings and churnings of a queasy stomach. The last quotation from 'Leda' showed him as a renaissance-classic poet revelling exquisitely in a delicious sensuality. Now read him as a modern poet on the same theme; the poem is called 'A Morning Scene':

[Quotes last eight lines]

That is an admirable piece of description, but not a poem. However, the interesting point about it is, that the author is now disgusted at what he idealised before. Turn to the verses on Simon Stylites, while using the vocabulary of asceticism to abuse sensuality he despises the ascetic. This is an example of the emotional disequilibrium I mentioned above. Again, when science has suggested to him a theme on the prodigality of life ('The Fifth Philosopher's Song'), it is not to rejoice that he uses it, like one of 'the rosy Brotherhood', but to lead up to a melancholy little quip that it was such a germ as produced himself by chance among a million that might have fertilised his mother's womb; instead, perchance, that of another Shakespeare, Newton, Donne. The mention of Donne brings me back to the point from which I started. Like Donne, like his centaur-poets, he would strike fire from flints (cutting facts), but as I pointed out, while the rebound from painful fact made Donne soar into a scholastic empyrean full of mystical conceits, it makes our modern poets dive instead into the dim confused underworld of the semi-conscious. That is the true 'oubliette', not Dante's Heaven; and then—farewell, poet! But I have said enough to show that Mr. Aldous Huxley is a poet always interesting to the intellect and sometimes superbly satisfying to the aesthetic sense.

[1] 'At full speed.'

5. John Middleton Murry, review in
Athenaeum

28 May 1920, pp. 699–700

John Middleton Murry (1889–1957), husband of Katherine Mansfield and editor of the *Athenaeum* 1919–21, was an important figure in the post-war literary generation, with books on Shakespeare, Swift, Keats, Lawrence, and others. According to the *DNB*, a friendly critic described Murry as 'the best-hated man of letters in the country.'

At the time of this review, Huxley was working as a member of Murry's *Athenaeum* staff. Murry is generally recognized as the original for the corrosive portrait of Burlap in *Point Counter Point* (Introduction, p. 13).

The opening of Murry's review, here omitted, contains a discussion of Huxley's prose poem 'Beauty.'

. . . The Beauty that Mr. Huxley has glimpsed would justify—more, give a value to—the most intimate diary of the journey towards it, when once it has been achieved. What makes us uneasy is a suspicion that Mr. Huxley, who is clever and sensitive and learned and knows this, must believe that he has attained the object of his search and struggle. We feel that he puts his long poem 'Leda' before us as the evidence of victory.

We cannot accept it. The elements that Mr. Huxley has desired to combine, the precious esoteric beauty and the ugliness which were to be blended into a new comprehensive beauty in whose light nothing should appear common or unclean, are still as unmixed as oil and vinegar. The beauty that the poem has—and it has not a little—is the old beauty of elimination; the ugliness that it has—and it has a passage of surpassing ugliness—is the old ugliness of repulsion, naked, unresolved. Mr. Huxley has, we think, deceived himself. His reconciliation of opposites is unreal; and the reason why, being so clever, he has deceived himself is precisely that he is so clever. He has chosen his ground too adroitly, for the myth of Leda and the swan is one of the few that permit ugliness to assume the vesture of beauty.

In other words, it is a conjuring trick played with the incidentals of poetry. It has the air of being an advance upon the early Keats; it is in reality a long step backwards from him. It looks for a moment as though it were a kind of classical perfection of modern poetry, whereas it is an evasion of the problems that modern poetry, with all its stupid and intelligent hesitations, is trying to face. Were it another than Mr. Huxley, we should accuse him of playing to the gallery. A man of a little less than complete sincerity may, however, play to the gallery of his own mind.

'Leda' is a retrogression from 'Endymion', from which it outwardly derives, because the beauty at which it aims is purely external. Nothing could be more 'richly apart'; it is emphatically not 'an ethic, a way of belief and of practice',[1] as was the beauty which Keats sought with groping confusion and flashes of insight in 'Endymion'. Like the classicism of M. Pierre Louÿs,[2] of whom it continually reminds us, it is without significance. A classicism without spiritual significance, as Mr. Huxley himself in the passage we have quoted clearly sees, comes near perversity. On the other hand, 'Leda' is an evasion of the problem which the most authentic modern poetry is endeavouring to solve, which is to give beauty a fuller content by exploring unfamiliar paths of sensation and perception. At present the issue is obscured by the importunities of the rank and file whose only notion of poetry is that they themselves want to be advanced, but the most original spirits of our time leave the discerning in no doubt that their aim is a new acceptance, a new comprehension and, paradoxical though it may sound, a new asceticism. 'Leda' seems to us, both in form and content, a self-indulgence rather than a self-discipline.

If Mr. Huxley wishes to be judged, he should elect to be judged, not by 'Leda', nor by any of the shorter poems in this book, but by 'Soles Occidere et Redire Possunt', which we hope and believe was written after 'Leda'. It is fragmentary, unrealized, and chiefly it lacks an essential austerity in the use of rhythm and language; but it is definitely

[1] In 'Beauty' Huxley writes that beauty is 'not a thing richly apart, but an ethic, a way of belief and of practice, of faith and works, medieval in its implication with the very threads of life' (Leda [London: Chatto & Windus, 1920], p. 54).

[2] Louÿs, French novelist and poet (1870–1925) who sought to express pagan sensuality with stylistic perfection.

in the main stream of modern poetry. In it Mr. Huxley has had no more than glimpses of what he wishes to express; the emotional music has been only half-heard. But whereas 'Leda' is a backsliding, 'Soles' is an advance. As for two-thirds of the shorter pieces, we think he would have been well advised never to print them. They might have their place in an *oeuvre*; in the present condition of their author's achievement they will not only make the ignorant blaspheme, but cause even the well-intentioned to stumble.

6. Harold Monro on Huxley's Poems

1920

Harold Monro (1879–1932), poet, editor, bookseller, founded *Poetry Review* (1911) and the *Chapbook* (1919), and started the famous Poetry Bookshop in 1913.

From *Some Contemporary Poets* (London: Leonard Parsons, 1920), pp. 124–30.

Aldous Huxley is among the most promising of the youngest generation of contemporary poets. He has a brilliant intellect, rare force of imagination, command of language, subtle penetration, irony and style; and the progress of his development has been rapid from the beginning. Keats has influenced him slightly: otherwise he owes little to any particular dead or living English poet. But his debt to French literature is unmistakable, and we do also notice an occasional hint of German influence. Some of the earlier poems, such as 'The Canal' in *The Burning Wheel*, read more like translations than originals, so effectually has the style of the best kind of French sonnet imposed itself on his temperament.

The gloomy or sarcastic impatience of these first poems is gradually modified in later ones.

> I had been sitting alone with books,
> Till doubt was a black disease....

We can sympathise with that. It is one kind of trouble. Another kind is expressed in 'The Ideal Found Wanting'. He shouts, 'Damn the whole crowd of you! I hate you all!' and 'I'll break a window through my prison!' but, true child of his time, he finds there is nothing much to be done; that he must tolerate more or less; that making a fuss is generally equivalent to looking ridiculous:—

> Is it escape? No, the laugh's turned on me!
> I kicked at cardboard, gaped at red limelight;
> You laughed and cheered my latest knockabout.

His third trouble is that he can't control his feelings: 'And oh, the pains of sentiment!' It seems not quite decent, and truly not pleasant, to give way to natural feeling in the disgusting surroundings of the present world.

On the verge of becoming a lover he suddenly calls in scholarship to provide him with an analogy:—

> And when I kissed or felt her fingers press,
> I envied not Demosthenes his Greek,
> Nor Tully for his Latin eloquence.

Creating an imaginary garden he exclaims: 'I insist on cypresses', and adds quickly: 'I'm terribly romantic.' In the forest he notes the following:—

> And on the beech-bole, smooth and grey,
> Some lover of an older day
> Has carved in time-blurred lettering
> One word only:—'Alas.'

He takes Amoret with him to 'live free', but she, as might have been expected, prefers the town, and tells him so.

On the civilised mind he passes the following comment:—

> We're German scholars poring over life,
> As over a Greek manuscript that's torn
> And stained beyond repair. Our eyes of horn
> Read one or two poor letters; and what strife,
> What books on books begotten for their sake!

'The Walk' is a brilliant poem. Though not without indications of its writer's youthfulness, it introduces a new style into English literature.

'The Defeat of Youth', the title poem of the second work, was apparently intended to form a narrative, but it is not more than a loosely united sonnet sequence. The fifth sonnet may be quoted in its entirety. In spite of a Wordsworthian flavour, it is a model of clarity and condensation.

[Quotes fifth stanza of 'The Defeat of Youth']

He is not now so afraid of giving Beauty (figuratively) a big B, nor so shy in the presence of trees, flowers and the other conventional properties of nature-poetry. He need not fear to fall into the ordinary tricks of the poetaster. Much thought has rendered him proof against them. He can even use the words 'illimitable', 'imperishable', 'inscrutable', 'reverberated', 'methinks' and 'imperturbable' without much detriment to the force of his own style. Now he indulges in some pleasant free verse jottings. He also renders Mallarmé and Rimbaud into his own language.

'Leda' is the most finished poem that Huxley has yet written; a sensual and brightly coloured representation of the episode from mythology.

[Quotes two long passages from 'Leda']

The art of Aldous Huxley is developing in three directions. The verse of 'Leda' is orthodox, but the style of the poem is new, its diction original, and its language personal. Then he writes poetry of a very modern type: style and content both 'shocking'. Lastly he is using a condensed prose, intricately and cleverly fashioned; far more satisfactory than the free verse of most of his contemporaries.

7. Early opinions

1920

An anonymous review-summary entitled 'A New Satirist of Life's Hypocrisies' in *Current Opinion* (June 1920), lxviii, pp. 830–1.

There can be no doubt that Aldous Huxley, one of the youngest and cleverest of England's new generation of writers, has introduced a new spirit in literature. His first volume *Limbo*, a collection of stories, sketches and plays, has aroused more interesting critical reactions than have been aroused by any other first volume of the last year or two. His subject-matter is new, but a writer signing himself 'Affable Hawk,'[1] notes in the *New Statesman* that the originality of the new author does not preclude one from comparing him with Jules Laforgue, because of his ironic attitude toward sentiment, and with the bitter J. K. Huysmans, because he writes 'like a man with a queasy stomach for life.' Like Huysmans, we are told, he uses his nerves too much as a writer, and 'too often he uses them as a touchstone of values, mistaking a shiver of repulsion for a deep intuition.' Further:

He is in a cold rage with the body, because it is often ugly, often smells, is prone to diseases, gets worn out and will go its own way in spite of reason and the claims of the imagination. The trouble of a man who, having tried to put impulse in its place by understanding the mechanism of instinct, finds himself nevertheless no nearer being on good terms with life, is the subject Mr. Huxley treats best. His great defect as a describer of human nature is lack of sympathy. He despises human nature; this, if he could admire and love as much some traits and characters as he despises others, would be very well; but in this book he has not shown that he can.

It is the satirical aspect of the young writer's work that most appeals to the critic of the London *Nation*. In 'Happy Families,' a brilliant one-act play which has been published in this country by the *Little Review*, we watch a young man in a conservatory proposing in a manner which

[1] Probably Desmond MacCarthy.

shows his ancestors taking part in the job, his arboreal as well as his knightly forbears.

[Quotes stage directions, p. 211]

In the dialog of this curious burlesque, Freud jostles Mendel.[1] The plants snap and bite the humans. 'Happy Families,' says the London *Nation*, is Rabelaisian, and 'The Death of Lully,' the literary gem of the set, is worthy of Anatole France. At the back of all the stories in *Limbo* there is 'the homesickness of the soul born in an age that is dying in squalor for the clarity and coherence of some age of faith—at which, for very hunger, it needs must mock.'

Aldous Huxley is at his best in satirizing the double-faced humanity of our day. In this sense 'The History of Richard Greenow' is acclaimed by the *Nation* a masterpiece:

Greenow, who in waking life is a critical objector to the folly of war, makes his money, unknown to one of his selves, by writing, under the name of Heartsease Fitzroy, fulsome articles on sacrifice, national honor, and all the wordy stock-in-trade of the war-monger. Here, in fact, are vulgarity and sensitiveness, cynicism and illusion, brought under one hatbrim till the wearer of the hat awakes in the hell of lunacy. . . . The air of life-likeness is derived from intensely physical imagery and the figures of the caricature are so vivid in detail that one must believe in them. And for those who have lived through the war with open eyes no literary device can be too strong to represent the awful contrast between the facts of war and the travesty of them created by sentimental art and religion in the deepest blasphemy of all, that against truth.

[Summarizes the reaction of the *TLS* reviewer (No. 2) and refers to the narrator of 'The Bookshop']

When he sees a piano—'the yellow keys grinned at me in the darkness like the teeth of an ancient horse.' The *Times* critic, emboldened by his pleasure in such good writing as this, admonishes Mr. Huxley to give us more of it and to leave social satire alone. Perhaps it is evidence of the new writer's versatility that he has won high praise for his efforts in fiction, verse and criticism. Like other youngsters in art and literature, he is a member of the Clarté[2] group of England.

[1] Gregor Johann Mendel, nineteenth-century Austrian biologist, experimented with heredity factors in plants.

[2] 'The Clarté movement as it developed in France between 1919 and 1921 was a significant manifestation of the revival of the internationalist ideal after the first world war.' See Nicole Racine, 'The Clarté Movement in France, 1919–1921,' *Literature and Politics in the Twentieth Century*, ed. Walter Laqueur and George L. Mosse (New York: Harper & Row, 1967), pp. 187–200. Reprinted from the *Journal of Contemporary History*, 2 (1967).

8. Ford Madox Hueffer [Ford] on a Huxley poem

1921

Ford Madox Hueffer [Ford] (1873–1939), author, critic, collaborator with Joseph Conrad, is known especially for his four-volume cycle of novels collected under the title *Parade's End*.

The extract is from *Thus to Revisit: Some Reminiscences* (New York: Dutton, 1921), p. 144. See Introduction, p. 7.

The least instructed of readers is probably sensible of the fact that for, let us say, eighty years or so, there has been in existence in these Islands a peculiar jargon which we may as well agree to call the Poetic Vernacular. This provincial dialect has nothing to do with any living, practicable or spoken speech. It is not necessarily meant to convey anything connected with life; it is a sort of blended product of industry and pruriency. Perhaps its nature is best expressed in this way: There is now a poet—I think it is Mr. Aldous Huxley, and in that case I may as well say that I have a respect for his achievements and still greater expectations for his future—who, I am told, had occasion to state in the course of one of his poems that after a convivial meal in familiar society he sometimes undid his collar stud, or his waistcoat button—something like that. Again, I am told—for I have this story from hearsay alone—that this poem caused more than a ten days' scandal amongst the literati of London. It is, in short, not to be thought of that a collar-stud should make its appearance in verse.

CROME YELLOW

November 1921

9. Unsigned review in *TLS*

10 November 1921, p. 733

'I am tired of seeing the human mind bogged in a social plenum; I prefer to paint it in a vacuum, freely and sportively bombinating.' The plan was ascribed to a fabulous author in *Crome Yellow*, by Mr. Aldous Huxley: and it is the manner of Mr. Huxley himself. A vacuum is suggested by the rarefied seclusion of his fantastic country house, where a small group of human beings reveal their amusingly simplified traits. But this void is, judiciously, not quite complete. The tone of Mr. Huxley's story matches the title and the covers; it is a rich, full yellow, which suggests the exhilarating glow of summer and the answering temperature of mind. In this atmosphere the characters bombinate, so far as the heat allows. On the high towers of Crome by starlight (Mr. Huxley will explain in whimsical fashion why they were so absurdly tall), in the cool shadows of the granary, along the deep yew alleys by the swimming pool, the transitory action passes; while the things that are not done (so often more important than those that are) bubble in the mind, betray themselves in spontaneous gestures, or float down the stream of talk.

Mr. Huxley's personages are drawn with an extreme verve of crispness; in fact the merit of his comedy is that it becomes always more amusing as it grows. Little Mary Bracegirdle, with the earnest blue eyes and bell of short gold hair, would be very tiresome if she talked much of her 'repressions'; so she is confined, for the most part, to simple and fatal acts. Mr. Scogan, on the other hand, whose forte is a dry, racy monologue which drones at intervals beneath the bombination, is enlivening for just so long as he would naturally be; only near the end is he revealed in the full colours of a bore. The way in which Mr. Huxley manoeuvres his party, displaying them by adroitly contrasted little scenes, has a good deal of Anatole France's touch; and it is quite in the manner of that master to stay the narrative with a choice extract from the family records or a fuliginous sermon on the Second Advent by the vicar. Mr. Huxley suggests the same tone, too, by his rich converse with books, and by the 'direct action' of the younger members of the party, which puts ideas to rout. But then the master himself, though he is steeped in knowledge and plays with contemporary follies, never leaves us with a notion that he is limited by fashions or by culture. Of Mr. Huxley we do not feel quite so sure; like his Henry Wimbush, who remarks at a village dance that 'if all these people were dead this festivity would be extremely agreeable'—for then one could simply romantically read about them—he almost invites us to believe that the proper study of mankind is books. Almost; but not quite; for in Denis, the hero of this little story, through whose eyes we see most of it, the tragi-comedy of adolescence becomes really poignant at the end. The stroke which ruined Denis's hopes and chances was something that went deeper than his love-affair; it was the discovery, in a humiliating form, that there was a real world of remorseless and self-centred persons which impinged on his own crystal world of illusions and ideas. This shock gives the point to Mr. Huxley's fantasy, which is so engaging that we hardly wish it other than it is; all we miss is a certain feeling of assurance that he is using his imagination freely for himself.

10. Unsigned review in *Spectator*

3 December 1921, cxxvii, p. 750

Identified in *Spectator*'s files as Lady (Amabel Strachey) Williams-Ellis, b. 1894, the paper's literary editor 1922–3, and now a widely published writer.

The affinities between *Crome Yellow* and the fiction of Thomas Love Peacock, mentioned in this review, were widely observed. Huxley himself called his book 'a Peacockian novel' (*L*, pp. 198, 202).

In *Crome Yellow* Mr. Aldous Huxley appears before his readers in the character of a Cubist Peacock. It would be pleasing to elaborate the double meanings, ornithological and metaphorical, which this phrase would carry with it; it would be possible to contrive half a dozen appropriate comparisons—pleasant, but alas! not practical within the limits of a review. We must come to the point at once by saying that it is not the gaudy bird nor the type of vanity, but Thomas Love Peacock who comes into our minds as we turn Mr. Huxley's pages. Here is the same delightful talk, but here is also much more suavity and none of the exaggeration which, Peacock's greatest admirers must admit, often mar the pages of *Headlong Hall* or *Nightmare Abbey*. Here, as in Peacock, are characters floating suspended in a medium of house party, and enjellied in the same bland and succulent matrix are—to complete the early nineteenth-century atmosphere—several detached sermons and short stories. Like a work of Peacock's again, the novel is entirely static. Henry Wimbush, whose handsome face is so like the pale grey bowler hat which he always wears, is left at the end of the book much where he was found at its beginning. Mary, the serious, innocent girl of twenty-three, with hair that hangs 'in a bell of elastic gold about her moonlike cheeks,' discusses Malthusianism, divorce reform, psycho-analysis, and the more serious aspects of Cubism as single-mindedly in the last as she does in the opening chapters, and remains all through the book what we found her at first—a charming donkey. Nor does Mr. Scogan, the rationalist, who is 'so like one of the extinct bird lizards of the Tertiary', change. Nor does Gombauld, the Byronic painter; nor Anne, the graceful charmer with her doll-like face and acute mind. Mrs. Wimbush, with her deep voice, her square, middle-aged face, and coiffure 'of a curiously improbable shade of orange', like Wilkie Bard declaring that he is going to 'sing in op-pop-pop-pop-popera', stands unshaken by the events of the book. The only person whose character seems to be at all modified by the things that happened at Crome—that beautiful Elizabethan country house—is Denis, a perfectly drawn specimen of the modern Oxford under-graduate, who is also a poet. He leaves Crome decidedly a little wiser than he was when he arrived, but he is at a stage of such rapid mental and emotional development that three weeks passed anywhere where he was not in complete solitude might have done as much for him. The chapter in which we are in the most proper and regular manner introduced to the house party sitting at tea in the shade of one of the summer-houses is charming:

[Quotes from Chapter III, pp. 16–17]

. . . Incidentally, Denis is revealed as writing poetry which, not un-naturally, as it is from the pen of the author of *Leda*, is rather good.

At the end of the book there is a really brilliant treatment of the question of 'human contacts'—a question which is, of course, at the moment, really agitating just the sort of people about whom Mr. Huxley writes. But here we come to the great strength of the book. Not only is it intrinsically amusing and ingenious, but if due allowance is made for the slight formalization, concentration and exaggeration which are the right of the novelist, the book is a completely accurate piece of observation. Just so do such young people talk, and their re-actions with various types of older people are capitally portrayed. *Crome Yellow* is a delightful book.

11. Review in *Nation* (New York)

22 March 1922, cxiv, p. 349

Signed 'L.L.' and entitled 'Yellow for Green,' the review was by Ludwig Lewisohn, at that time Associate Editor of the *Nation*.

The youngest of the Georgians recalls the last of the Victorians; *Crome Yellow* is *The Green Carnation*[1] after thirty years. There is the same week-end party in an English country house, the same eddying of brilliant conversation, the same weary, ultra-civilized mockery, the same touch which is so sure without ever being innocent, the same phosphorescence which we shall let someone else call the phosphorescence of decay. There is even a young poet who, like Dorian Grey, admires his mirrored image. But the eroticism has changed in character and now centers about a young person named Mary who is desperately afraid of developing complexes through repression and wears her hair 'clipped like a page's in a bell of elastic gold about her cheeks.' The types, in a word, have been brought up to the minute; the mood is the same—an intensified Alexandrianism, enormously clever, amusing, learned, futile.

The party that is assembled in *Crome Yellow* is representative if not very inclusive. Priscilla recalls the dowagers of Oscar Wilde; Mary belongs to the Freudian moment; Anne is vague. The men are more expressively defined. Mr. Scogan is a Wellsian and discourses with more wit and eloquence than belief on the Rational State; Henry Wimbush lives in the past and seems the least empty of them all; Mr. Barbecue-Smith and the Reverend Mr. Bodiham are two varieties of the species pure fool—the inspirational uplift monger and the monger in prophecy. There remain the two young poets—Denis Stone and Ivor Lombard. To anyone whose chief contacts with contemporary verse are American these two will seem subtly archaic. They are as passionately concerned with the luscious bloom of words as the most

[1] By the late-Victorian writer, Robert S. Hichens.

heavily decorative of the Victorians; they have not yet the slightest feeling for the sober or the stripped in poetic diction and scatter verses freighted with perfume and orotund vowels. In the orthodox way, too, they sit waiting for lyrics to be wafted to them out of the common sentimental moods of dawn or dusk and institute no research into such fresh perceptions and observations as may create new forms by virtue of a force within them.

It is clear, then, that Mr. Aldous Huxley has, in his work, none of those specifically new notes or tendencies which one commonly associates with the work of the instinctive or consciously militant post-Victorians. He lives in a different world from that of D. H. Lawrence or James Joyce or Dorothy Richardson. He cultivates a firm tradition and will seem original only to those ultra-modern youngsters—their number increases daily—who have read no books but those written in the present century. What Mr. Huxley has, however, is a literary skill which only sound learning coupled with ripe talent could produce. He strikes no note of his own; he does the accepted but in the heat of this literary moment almost forgotten thing superbly. His Henry Wimbush is supposed to be writing a history of the House of Crome and from that history he reads two episodes to his assembled guests. These passages, the story of Sir Hercules Lapith and the story of the Three Lovely Lapiths are magnificent exercises in an all but forgotten manner. The prose is the firm, sound, syntactically vigorous prose of the eighteenth century, shapely and elastic, felicitous without strain and eloquent or striking at the bidding of the occasion alone. In such writing Mr. Huxley shows a type of scholarship and appreciation that is becoming more precious as it becomes rarer. The same qualities shine less brilliantly in his exercises in parody—the sermon of the Reverend Mr. Bodiham and the paragraphs that introduce Ivor Lombard into the narrative. These, too, however, are excellent and confirm the observation that the talent exhibited in *Crome Yellow* has little or nothing to do with the urge and spontaneity of creation but is allied to the gifts that produced the Latin verses of Marvell and Johnson, the Italian sonnets of Milton, and the French odes and songs of Swinburne.

12. Notice in *Bookman* (New York)

April 1922, lv, p. 191

Signed 'J.F.' and entitled 'Fooling Between Yellow Covers.' *ES* (Item 1241) identifies the author as John Farrar.

Mr. Huxley showed his unusual powers of invention in his earlier *Limbo*, a collection of sketches; but in *Crome Yellow* his satirical abilities have developed remarkably. With his punning title and his style, confessedly imitative of Peacock, he sets the note of preciosity; but the human quality of his characters, all of whom are a trifle mad, gives a far wider appeal to his story than you are led to expect. These strange house-party guests so over-conscious of sexoddity (the word seems to me a good one) are so pungently drawn that I suspect them of being caricatures. Denis, the hero, is a strange bird, as mad as a hatter, as ineffectual as a Dodo, and yet with a definite appeal. The women are less real. The high spot in the book seems to me to be the story of two midgets destroyed by their children, who revert to type and by their normality break the hearts of their parents. This is fine satirical writing. *Crome Yellow* is determinedly eccentric and unflaggingly delightful.

13. Raymond Mortimer, review in *Dial*

June 1922, lxxii, pp. 630–3

According to Clive Bell, Mortimer, b. 1895, was introduced to Bloomsbury by Huxley (*Old Friends*, London, 1956, p. 131n). Mortimer, author of *Channel Packet* (1942) and others, later became a regular reviewer for the *Sunday Times*.

He perhaps echoes Virginia Woolf's review of *Limbo* (No. 2) when he calls *Crome Yellow* 'desperately clever.' Will Cuppy argues against Mortimer's position (No. 16). Peter Firchow says of this review that 'instead of asking Huxley to be more serious, Mortimer might have acted more wisely by taking himself less seriously' (*Aldous Huxley*, p. 63).

Mortimer entitled his review 'Bombination.' See Introduction, p. 8.

The name of Huxley is suggestive. The eminent sceptics of the Victorian age remained the children of an earlier time. While they destroyed traditional opinions and beliefs, they retained themselves traditional habits of mind and of feeling. They remained as earnest, serious, and moral, as their religious opponents.

Now their work is producing fruit. We have a generation sceptical and sophisticated beyond the dreams of the destructive Giants. It has carried the work of its grandfathers to its logical end, and welcomes the psychological determinism of Freud as the confirmation of its deductions. Taking a particular and detached view of things, it is remarkable for intelligence rather than for intellect. The centre of interest has shifted. Instead of a division into good and evil, or fit and unfit, or beautiful and ugly, we have a new standard and a new dichotomy.

We say that a thing is or is not 'amusing'. That does not mean that it is comic, or even that it is bizarre. A picture by a Primitive, a sermon by Donne, the music of Rossini, the character of Gladstone—these are all 'amusing'. If the meaning of the word could be successfully analysed and defined, it would contribute something to the critical understanding of much modern work and feeling.

I fancy that the taste for the 'amusing' consists largely of an intense and intellectualized appreciation of things for their own sake, of their *ipseity*; of what is characteristic in them, and peculiar to them; of the differentia which makes it possible to label them. Thus the actions of historical personages are 'amusing' just in so far as they are 'mannered', 'of the period', and appear to us to be antics. It is by reason of the difference between them and ourselves, that we find people 'amusing'.

When the 'amusing' becomes the principal interest, and the only criterion, all capacity and inclination for moral judgement naturally disappears. Its place is taken by a dilettante attitude which seems eventually to be rather sentimental; it seeks by this intelligent appreciation of things to compensate for an absence of emotion.

The beginnings of this attitude are, I think, perceptible in the *Correspondence* of Flaubert, and the Goncourt *Journal*. It is strong in Laforgue, and now there are several English writers who in their different ways are remarkable for it, Lytton Strachey, Norman Douglas, and Pearsall Smith eminent among them. But Mr. Huxley is perhaps the furthest gone. The one thing impossible to him is any sort of earnestness. To him the world is a vast aquarium peopled by fantastic goggling creatures; and only in so far as they goggle, do they interest him.

Mr. Huxley has produced a number of poems and a book of short stories called *Limbo*. We are now given a desperately clever discursive novel. Crome is an English country-house complete with farmyard and village. In it Henry Wimbush and his viraginous wife, the gorgeous Lady Priscilla, entertain a house-party of some eight persons. They spend their time chiefly in conversation; and what they chiefly talk and think about, and dabble in, is venery. (The word is not used in the sense of *la chasse*;[1] never was a house-party less sporting.) The party includes a modern painter, a modern poet, a New Thought philosopher, and a real philosopher, Mr. Scogan, who is a cross between Cannan's Adrian Stokes and Norman Douglas's Mr. Keith; there are also several cultured and nubile young women. It might be called Foible Farm, you suggest? Mr. Huxley will admit Peacock in his genealogy. Rather like *South Wind*, someone else will murmur. It is certainly collateral; not that Mr. Huxley imitates Mr. Douglas. But their subject is similar, though the scene is different. Characters could wander from one book to the other

---

[1] 'The chase, the hunt.'

without doing much damage, and some of the Cromians will certainly end in the Bay of Naples. But for the present they are in the country. The War is responsible for that. Those who did not object to it were often billeted on farms: those who did, performed Work of National Importance on the land. This return to Nature is very different from that sought by Rousseau and the makers of the Petit Trianon. 'Farming seems to be mostly cruelty or indecency,' the Cromians declare; not that they have much objection to either.

They are disaffected to a degree rarely achieved except by certain English types who chiefly appear in French fiction, and from whom they must be descended:

[Quotes Scogan on English aristocrats, Chapter XI, p. 71]

They are futile and sterile and ironical and delightful. The name of Crome might after all be Heartbreak House; Shaw would find them far more heart-breaking than his own characters. He could not create people so alien to his temperament. Brain has become an illness, a parasitic growth: in Mr. Huxley's own words, it 'bombinates in the void', like the Chimaera in Rabelais. It is a machine that races, having nothing to propel.

But the inhabitants of Crome are not alive; they are *fantoches*,[1] with gutta-percha entrails, and behind them is always the enigmatic figure of Mr. Huxley. Listen to him speaking through Mr. Scogan's mouth:

[Quotes Scogan on the future, Chapter V, pp. 31–2]

There is no criticism of Mr. Huxley that he does not forestall you by making himself. You complain that he is too literary. He admits, and deplores, it. He reckons the books he has read by their weight in tons. He demands 'a mental carminative'. His favourite subject is the young man so clever and well-read and sophisticated that he is incapable of action. You can divine behind all this ingenuity and *dandysme* and *pirotecnia*, a certain bitterness, a suffering from the inability to be simple, a deep-rooted feeling of what the French think we call spleen.

To divert him he has the engaging religion of words. They are for him as for Villiers, almost miraculous. Ekbatana and Pompanazzi are objects of his hyperdulia, and he is even in danger of repeating his phrases, so piously does he consider them. He is a master of the just epithet, but when he wants to describe direct and simple beauty, he is at a loss, self-conscious, blushing, and he generally fails.

[1] 'Puppets, insignificant men.'

I doubt if he is a story-writer at all. He does not care to concentrate, to dig. All the time his fancy, which is monstrously alive, meanders into attractive side-paths, in pursuit of the 'amusing'. His sensitiveness to the atmosphere of a period or *milieu* would make him an admirable critic. But Mr. Huxley takes nothing seriously: least of all his own talents. In Mr. Douglas and Mr. Pearsall Smith this attitude is the not unbecoming cynicism of men who were young in the Nineties. In Mr. Huxley it is a sort of precocity, and in one who has published three or four books, precocity is no longer decent. At the risk of feeling, as well as of appearing, ridiculous, I must insist to him upon the importance of being earnest.

14. Joseph Wood Krutch, review in *Literary Review*

4 March 1922, ii, p. 464

Joseph Wood Krutch (1893–1970), a widely-published essayist and critic, a founder of the Literary Guild of America, author of *The Modern Temper* (1929) and *The Measure of Man* (1956).

His reviews of Huxley's work through *Point Counter Point* are among the most perceptive of early American responses. See Nos 25, 34, 40, and 48.

This review is entitled 'An Elegant Futilitarian.'

The author of *Limbo* and *Leda* is again running true to form. *Crome Yellow* is another exercise in graceful diabolism, this time again in prose. Like *Leda*, it consists chiefly of the random reflections of a somewhat over-cultivated and self-conscious young man upon the futility of society, and it is again executed with amazing if somewhat trivial virtuosity. It is rumored that the book is not merely autobiographical, but also biographical of well-known English contemporaries. Mr. Huxley, indeed, may stand as an excellent representative of the elegant-naughty division of Insurgent Youth. He yields to no one in disillusion, but he is far too smart socially to go in for forward-looking à la Wells. For him is rather elegant despair and the ancient fine art of shocking, practiced according to the latest technique, with Freudianism introduced into the drawing room. He is the æsthete brought up to date—Oscar Wilde scientifically analyzing the sunflower in his buttonhole.

In considering his three testaments one is reminded of *A Young Girl's Diary*. When the charming author of that work became aware of certain physiological facts, she resolved that she would never, never, never——. Hers was the typical youthful reaction to the discovery of the surprising foundations of our existence, and in a somewhat more complex form this reaction is the substance of Mr. Huxley's satires. By nature he is a 'super-poetical hyper-æsthetical' young man, but he is keenly aware of that mass of unromantic fact which science has gradually accumulated. One imagines him as having read Havelock Ellis in the nursery, and at first he was profoundly shocked by the fundamental discrepancy between the truths, let us say, of the *Vita Nuova* and the *General Introduction to Psychoanalysis*. His 'defence re-action' took the form of humor, and since the contrast between man the son of God and man the son of primordial slime was inexpressibly painful to him, he has reminded himself of it as often as possible, laughing scornfully all of the time. Sex, as the most striking and piquant instance of the universal irony, concerns him much, and one might sum up the substance of his plaint thus: The tragedy of life is this—one seeks romance and only succeeds in committing adultery. Physiological references abound, and he addressed a biological poem to the sperm-atozoön which dared to develop into himself. In *Limbo* his youth and maiden in the first ecstasy of love sit 'quietly sweating palm to palm,' and so enamoured was he of this contrast that he repeated the phrase exactly in *Leda*. The idea is at the basis of most of his situations, and once at least he gave it almost classical expression. Carried away by admiration for the sub-limits of man's mind, he brought himself thumpingly to earth and sang:

> But oh, the sound of simian mirth!
> Mind, issued from the monkey's womb,
> Is still umbilical to earth,
> Earth its home and earth its tomb.

There is not much more to be said upon that subject.

Considering its formlessness, *Crome Yellow* is a novel only by courtesy. Its scene is the familiar but mythical English country house where anything may happen and its hero is Mr. Huxley's latest avatar, Denis, who may be best described as a young man who has taken seriously Pater's advice to live ecstatically by seizing the one perfect form in each moment of flux, but who is finding it extremely hard to find any perfect forms. In so far as any plot disengages itself from the amusing discussions of things in general, it may be described in one sentence: A young man falls in love with a girl, but, being extremely timid, he does nothing about it. Indeed, he does nothing about anything, for his mental sophistication is so far in advance of his experience that his life is reduced to a blank because he can think of nothing worth the while of so remarkable a young man. Thus, in an agony of envy he pretends to read while another jazzes with his beloved, because dancing is one of the many things which he analyzes and despises but has by no means enough courage to do. Moreover, life is to him a perpetual *non sequitur*. When his hostess is discussing the vanity of riches when compared with the things which happen in the heart, he cannot help speculating whether her hair, which is of a 'curiously improbable shade of orange,' is 'the real thing and henna' or only 'one of those complete transformations one sees in the advertisements,' and when a young girl demands his choice for the three most promising poets he cannot help answering her banality by repeating from the agricultural catechism which he is reading: 'Blight, Mildew, and Smut.'

Undoubtedly Mr. Huxley is consistently diverting and self-mockery keeps his self-consciousness sweet, for he is perfectly aware of the fact that he is writing youth's satire upon itself. In a short story which he contributed recently to a popular magazine his hero finds that the street lamps reflected upon the wet asphalt look like strips of bronze, and he resolves to use the comparison in a story. Here are three levels of self-consciousness. One layer invents an image, the next resolves to make use of it, and a third sees the absurdity of the whole business. Of course all are Mr. Huxley himself, and he consistently endows his characters with the two layers and reserves the third for himself as commentator. In *Crome Yellow* Denis struggles desperately to find the *mot juste*[1] for the gentle heaving of the landscape. 'Dinted, Dimpled, Wimpled—his mind wandered down echoing corridors of assonance and alliteration ever further and further from the point. He was enamoured with the beauty

1 'Precise word.'

of words.' Mr. Huxley's heroes are always admiring their own complexity and taking a certain satisfaction in their futility. They float gracefully through the world and are not completely sorry to realize that they will never be crude enough to accomplish anything.

Whatever disappointment Mr. Huxley's admirers may feel in *Crome Yellow* will not be due to any failure to amuse. Every page is sparkling and the preciosity of the style is always successful, but it opens no new field and it strikes no deeper than his former books. Indeed, it strikes hardly so deep. *Leda* was a really remarkable volume of poems, for underneath all the smartness there was a genuine sting. One felt, as was said before, that his laughter was a defence reaction and that when he wrote

> While happier mortals take to drink,
> A dolorous dipsomaniac,
> Fuddled with grief I sit and think,
> Looking upon the bile when it is black,

there was an actual residuum of gall. But now it seems as though he had been a little spoiled by the tribute which was paid to his cleverness and that he is a little too complacent in his cynicism, so that he is not so much indignant at things as he is glad that they offer so excellent an opportunity for agreeable satire. The gestures of his cynicism have begun to be somewhat stereotyped and the adventures of his soul to lack variety. *Crome Yellow* is really the third description of the first phase of his spiritual autobiography. The question which his admirers will now ask anxiously is: 'Will there be a second phase?'

15. F. Scott Fitzgerald on Huxley

St. Paul Daily News, 26 February 1922, Feature section, p. 6

Francis Scott Key Fitzgerald (1896–1940) was one of the most famous American novelists to emerge after the War: *This Side of Paradise* (1920), *The Great Gatsby* (1925), *Tender is the Night* (1934).

H. L. Mencken shared Fitzgerald's admiration for the early Huxley (see Introduction, p. 8). But Fitzgerald later wrote to Maxwell Perkins (c. 15 July 1928) of Huxley's 'total collapse' (*The Letters of F. Scott Fitzgerald*, ed. Andrew Turnbull (New York: Scribner's, 1963), p. 211).

Now this man is a wit. He is the grandson of the famous Huxley who, besides being one of the two great scientists of his time, wrote clear and beautiful prose—prose better than Stevenson could ever master.

This is young Huxley's third book—his first one, *Limbo*, was a collection of sketches—his second, *Leda*, which I have never read, contained one long poem and, I believe, a few lyrics.

To begin with, Huxley, though he is more like Max Beerbohm than any other living writer (an ambiguity which I shall let stand, as it works either way), belongs as distinctly to the present day as does Beerbohm to the '90's. He has an utterly ruthless habit of building up an elaborate and sometimes almost romantic structure and then blowing it down with something too ironic to be called satire and too scornful to be called irony. And yet he is quite willing to withhold this withering breath from certain fabulous enormities of his own fancy—and thus we have in *Crome Yellow* the really exquisite fable of the two little dwarfs which is almost, if not quite, as well done as the milkmaid incident in Beerbohm's *Zuleika Dobson*.

In fact I have wanted a book such as *Crome Yellow* for some time. It is what I thought I was getting when I began Norman Douglas' *South Wind*. It is something less serious, less humorous and yet infinitely wittier than either *Jurgen* or *The Revolt of the Angels*. It is—but by telling you all the books it resembles I will get you no nearer to knowing whether or not you will want to buy it.

Crome Yellow is a loosely knit (but not loosely written) satirical novel concerning the gay doings of a house party at an English country place known as Crome. The book is yellow within and without—and I do not mean yellow in the slangy sense. A sort of yellow haze of mellow laughter plays over it. The people are now like great awkward canaries trying to swim in saffron pools, now like bright yellow leaves blown along a rusty path under a yellow sky. Placid, impoignant, Nordic, the satire scorns to burn deeper than a pale yellow sun, but only glints with a desperate golden mockery upon the fair hair of the strollers on the lawn; upon those caught by dawn in the towers; upon those climbing into the hearse at the last—beaten by the spirit of yellow mockery.

This is the sort of book that will infuriate those who take anything seriously, even themselves. This is a book that mocks at mockery. This is the highest point so far attained by Anglo-Saxon sophistication. It is written by a man who has responded, I imagine, much more to the lyric loves of lovers' long dust than to the contemporary seductions of contemporary British flappers. His protagonist—what a word for Denis, the mocked-at mocker—is lifted from his own book, *Limbo*. So is Mr. Scogan, but I don't care. Neither do I care that it 'fails to mirror life'; that it is 'not a novel'—these things will be said of it, never fear. I find Huxley, after Beerbohm, the wittiest man now writing in English.

The scene where Denis was unable to carry Anne amused me beyond measure.

And listen to this, when Huxley confesses to a but second-hand knowledge of the human heart:

[Quotes Chapter XXVIII, p. 204]

Huxley is just 30, I believe. He is said to know more about French, German, Latin and medieval Italian literature than any man alive. I refuse to make the fatuous remark that he should know less about books and more about people. I wish to heaven that Christopher Morley would read him and find that the kittenish need not transgress upon the whimsical.

I expect the following addenda to appear on the green jacket of *Crome Yellow* at any moment:

Drop everything and read *Crome Yellow*.
— H-yw-d Br-n.

Places Huxley definitely in the first rank of American (sic!) novelists.
— General Chorus.

(The 'sic' is mine. It is not harsh as in 'sic 'im!' but silent as in 'sick room'.)

It may be I'm old—it may be I'm mellow,
But I cannot fall for Huxley's *Crome Yellow*.
— F.P.A.

Exquisite. Places Huxley among the few snobs of English literature.
— G-tr-de Ath-r-t-n.

16. Huxley as a serious writer

New York Sunday Tribune, 25 June 1922, Section 5, p. 5

A letter by 'Will Cuppy' which the editor printed as a review of *Mortal Coils* under the title, 'Seriousness of Aldous Huxley.'

William Jacob Cuppy (1884–1949), journalist and author, wrote, for example, *How to Tell Your Friends from the Apes* (1931) and *The Decline and Fall of Everybody* (1948).

In the *Dial* for June Mr. Raymond Mortimer opines that the principal end and aim of Aldous Huxley is to be 'amusing,' and insists to the author of *Crome Yellow* upon the importance of being earnest [No. 13].

On May 27 Mr. Burton Rascoe, having lunched, allowed in the Doran offices as to how Aldous Huxley, 'undoubtedly the most adroit and amusing' of the clever young Englishmen, 'deals in superficies, but with a gay, satirical touch.'

On June 13 Mr. Ben Ray Redman, having dined, announced at Mr. Louis Untermeyer's that Aldous Huxley 'was like Oscar Wilde in the '90's, the clever young froth writer of his day.'

If this sort of thing goes on I don't want to.

And it's almost sure to go on, for *Mortal Coils*, which has just followed

Crome Yellow, is a book of shorter pieces almost as clever and amusing as the novel. I want to point out, with due respect, that *Mortal Coils* is also just as deeply serious, purposeful, holy, flaming and passionately true and wise as is so certainly *Crome Yellow*.

Aldous Huxley deals in both books (with a gay, satirical touch, truly) with the inevitable cruces of this, our mortal, life, with the sickening, blasting ironies of this vale of tears, with the beautiful poisonous snares of this utterly marvellous world, with the mere emotions and ideas, such as they are, of us human creatures; with the resistless desires and shattering half-truths by which we live and die. Are these superficies? Is this froth?

I should hate to see Aldous Huxley tagged as superficial. Nobody is superficial anyway. There is no such thing. (Least of all Huxley, or Wilde either, for that matter). The author of *Mortal Coils* is a direct and lineal descendant, a true son and disciple of the authentic and sacred philosophers of the above-mentioned world. Wisdom has bloomed in him as an orchid, not as a cabbage. That is all.

Does Mr. Huxley deal in half-truths? Is that the charge against him? Do I? Does Nietzsche? Are there any whole-truths? Perhaps not. Surely then, I may insist that Aldous Huxley is a serious and an earnest writer, since I but point to the reverse of the medal. And by way of harmonizing my views with those of one critic I may mention that even superficies may seem to be, if rightly considered, as deep as hell itself, and just as true and important.

'The Gioconda Smile,' the first piece in the new book, sets forth in a fantastically ironic framework the expert and authentic anatomy of the libido of a Mr. Hutton, who was either just an old fool or Everyman, and of the fabulous face of Janet Spence, a homicidal virgin of thirty-six who thought she was by Leonardo. (It is Mrs. Hutton who shuffles off.) Poor old Hutton. One shrinks from the picture. 'And actually, really, he was what?—Who knows.' Absolutely true and beautifully done, except for one dubious page where the author jumps out of Mr. Hutton's skin omnisciently, but awkwardly, to administer the arsenic.

'Nuns at Luncheon' is a tale told by a sob-sister, full of sound without the least fury, signifying everything. Two writers jesting hideously over the seduction of Sister Agatha and discussing how to turn it into salable fiction. Out of heartless comments and brutally callous jokes this Huxley fashions something so piteous and so terrible that few will dare reread it. A masterpiece? Perhaps. The art that produced 'Nuns at Luncheon' is something to admire.

'Green Tunnels' is a mildly interesting thing about a young girl sur-
rounded by some of those middle-aged grubs that Huxley sometimes
digs up. 'The Tillotson Banquet' is an anecdote—more irony. 'Permuta-
tions Among the Nightingales' contains a woman who is steatopygous,
whatever that is.

Several things in *Mortal Coils* look like studies for *Crome Yellow*. In
fact, *Mortal Coils* is the stuff from which *Crome Yellow*s are made. But
froth? Well, why not? And now I placate Mr. Redman. I bethink me of
what Lytton Strachey says apropos another work not so dissimilar as
some might think, the *Lettres Philosophiques* of Voltaire:

He offers one an exquisite dish of whipped cream; one swallows down the un-
substantial trifle, and asks impatiently if that is all? At any rate, it is enough.
Into that frothy sweetness his subtle hand has insinuated a single drop of some
strange liquor—is it a poison or is it an elixir of life?—whose penetrating influence will spread and spread until the remotest fibres of the system have felt
its power.

And this mysterious drop, which I cannot bear to have undervalued
or misunderstood, is in the case of *Crome Yellow* and *Mortal Coils*
simply the immortal soul of the artist who wrote those books.

17. Trans-Atlantic responses

The Literary Digest, 5 August 1922, lxxiv, p. 37

An unsigned review-summary entitled 'The Pantaloon in Contemporary English Letters.' See Introduction, p. 7.

The young are having a terrible to-do about Aldous Huxley; they
flutter and buzz about his candle, without so much danger of singeing
their wings as of beating each other down. His greatest endowment,
says one of his appraisers, is 'a gift of satire and a sort of cosmic irony
super-imposed upon a genuine poetic gift and a superb technique.' He

has caught on splendidly for a young man of twenty-five. He has four or five little books to his credit. *Leda: and other Poems* has called forth a critic's praise as 'a glorious stretch of color in Keats's most luscious vein.' Then there are collections of short stories such as *Limbo, Crome Yellow*, and finally *Mortal Coils*, which puts him almost with the angels. The critics use up all their highest praises before he turns twenty-seven. Perhaps it is because of the twin names of Matthew Arnold and Thomas Henry Huxley, from whom he descends, that have [sic] blinded them. They take him a little more calmly at home. 'At first sight Mr. Aldous Huxley seems to be distinguished from our other young writers chiefly by his lack of earnestness,' says a writer in the London *Times*.[1] 'He has the rest of their qualities—on the positive side a sound knowledge of literary tradition, and on the negative, a certain short-windedness. But he appears to be the least serious of a very serious group.' And the writer seems to find him a relief to his more serious brethren:

In a generation of writers who are, above all, acutely conscious of their responsibilities toward the mind of the age, Mr. Huxley alone seems content merely to amuse us. . . . A recurrent problem of Mr. Huxley's young men is whether they shall choose a literary career or become social reformers. Mr. Huxley has chosen a literary career—chiefly, we suspect, because he felt he would be ineffectual as a social reformer. And, having chosen, he does not mix the roles. He does not write novels to reform the world—perhaps he does not believe that novels ever do reform the world. No, the choice, in Mr. Huxley's mind, is a definite one. Literature means something bright, amusing, fantastic. Its cardinal virtue is to be *readable*. It is not, in short, one of the serious activities of life.

Over here the excitement seems to reach the pitch of a quarrel. Will Cuppy in the New York *Tribune* takes several of his contemporaneous appraisers to task for shortsightedness:

[Quotes extensively from Cuppy's objections (No. 16) to the view that Huxley is merely an amusing writer]

[1] *The Times*, 22 May 1922, p. 16. The article was called, 'Mr. Aldous Huxley, A Juggler of Ideas.'

ANTIC HAY

November 1923

---

18. Unsigned review in *TLS*

8 November 1923, p. 749

It is usually in their 'teens or their early twenties that sensitive boys are smitten with a physical disgust by the consciousness of their own and other people's bodies. By a sudden, possibly recurrent and almost always very brief, fall from romance they find themselves filled with loathing. All life seems stercorous, and nothing in it more so than passion. The several defences against this disgust are pretty well known. There is the defence that makes all life a jest; it is disgusting, but we can laugh at it. There is the defence of making the worst of it, of wallowing ostentatiously in 'sin', in the fashion that was showily cultivated in the eighteen-nineties. There is the defence of exquisite self-indulgence, which tries not to notice the grossness of its own substance. There is the defence of aggressive denial, which tries to drown the still small voice of loathing in shouts that life is lovely, real and earnest. There is, too, the surrender: the weary question which the music-hall comedian asked and answered once for all—'What's the good of anything? Why, nothing!' Each of these defences against the imminent nausea has its representative in Mr. Aldous Huxley's *Antic Hay*. Theodore Gumbril is the jester. He is what schoolboys would call a mean toad, because he, perhaps alone among them all, sees and touches the other side of truth and then betrays it to make a jest for his fellow-sufferers. A brute called Coleman, snapped up quite frankly from Russian fiction and called the Cossack, is the wallower in sin. Mercaptan is the exquisite sensualist— the aesthete. Lypiatt is the self-deluding idealist, and Myra Viveash's die-away voice is the very tone of the surrender.

When we think of *Mortal Coils* and then watch the goat-feet of this

78

book's men and women like satyrs dancing the antic hay, we wonder what has happened to cause in Mr. Huxley this reversion to the adolescent. Adolescent the subject and the people are, no matter how adult in knowledge of the world and mature in craft is this violent story. Now and then we are tempted to think it all a joke. We smile with a relief when, after a disgusting scene, Mr. Huxley rings down the curtain on a chapter as smartly as an experienced writer of farce on an act:

'My name is Porteous,' murmured the young man.
'Good Lord!' cried Gumbril, letting himself fall on to the couch beside Mrs. Viveash. 'That's the last straw!'

Who the young man was matters so little to the story that we jump at Mr. Huxley's hint that he is only trying to make us laugh all the time. But that cannot be. If he wanted to make us laugh, and that only, he would have kept out of his brutal story two things: Mrs. Viveash's not altogether despicable regret for her boy lover who was killed in the war, and the simple beauty of the woman called Emily. It takes a little courage, perhaps, to stand up to Mr. Huxley's blows and to see, through the jesting and the wallowing and the nausea, that Emily and her *nuit blanche*[1] with Theodore Gumbril was sacred and beautiful, and that Gumbril's betrayal of them was worse than the messy niceties of Mr. Mercaptan and the lasciviousness of Rosie Shearwater and the stercorous lusts of Coleman. The Mr. Huxley who wrote *Antic Hay* was not in the temper to look fairly at Emily and her gift. He uses them, in effect, only to strengthen his display of the foulness of life and of those that live it.

Fortunately, he has faced his disgust. He has made a clean breast of it. It is not likely, therefore, to stay in him and accumulate poison. And when he has worked it off and has come to the point whence he can see that truth has two sides, that the beautiful is no more a lie than the hideous, what a novel, with the power of expression that he here shows, he will be able to write! In spite of its savagery it is a book that shows great power of imagination and method; and for one thing in particular we like it—its thoroughness. Mr. Huxley himself would use here a medical metaphor. Let us say that, if you wish to purge your bosom of much perilous stuff, it is as well to do it thoroughly, as he has done here.

[1] Sleepless night, lit. 'white night.'

19. James Douglas, review in *Sunday Express*

25 November 1923, p. 7

James Douglas (1867–1940), journalist, editor, novelist, Director of the London *Express* Newspapers, edited the *Sunday Express* 1920–31, and wrote, for example, *The Man in the Pulpit* (1905), *Adventures in London* (1909), and *Down Shoe Lane* (1930).

The review is entitled 'Ordure and Blasphemy.' See Introduction, p. 9. In his article 'In Praise of Intolerance,' Huxley discusses Douglas's famous attack on Miss Hall's novel, *The Well of Loneliness*, in which Douglas had declared that he would rather give a healthy boy or girl a phial of prussic acid than this novel. Huxley makes Douglas 'a sporting offer' of providing a child, some acid, and a copy of the novel: '. . . And if he keeps his word and gives the boy the prussic acid I undertake to pay all the expenses of his defence at the ensuing murder trial and to erect a monument to his memory after he has been hanged.' To Douglas's position on Huxley, Huxley offers the following rejoinder: 'Mr. Douglas is that rare and, to the newspaper proprietor, extremely valuable person—a writer of Sunday articles who really believes in his own sermons. He has the great and precious gift of hysteria. He can work himself up almost instantaneously into a state of rhapsodic fury or raving admiration. I myself, for example, have been the subject both of his indignation and his praise. He has denounced me as a limb of Satan and extolled me as the Ibsen, the Homer, the goodness knows who else of my age' (*Vanity Fair*, February 1929, xxxi, p. 49). The point of Huxley's essay is that rigid intolerance causes an opposite reaction and is therefore self-defeating.

Which is the more despicable—witless smut or witty smut? Which is the more pestiferous—dirty dulness or dirty brilliancy? Which is the more poisonous—stupid indecency or intellectual lubricity? Which is the more dangerous—the swinish dullard or the hog of genius? There can be little doubt about the answer to these questions. Dulness is rarely

perilous. It terrifies the sedulous ape. But wit dazzles the young imagination and coruscates in coteries and cenacles. There is pardon for the
blockhead who lacks light to sin against. There is no pardon for the
artist who bedaubs his own visions and befouls his own dreams. Where
much is given much is required.

Mr. Aldous Huxley is beyond question a diabolically clever young
man. He is the Sacha Guitry[1] of English letters. His foible is audacity.
He delights in the rather cheap pastime of shocking Mudiedom,
Bootsdom and Smithdom. He likes to jar the sensitive nerve of piety
and puritanism. He specialises in blasphemy and impropriety. He does
not risk the brazen outrages of James Joyce, but he can knead words
into cunning and crafty hints of the unutterable and the unspeakable.
And there is a brainless school ready to cackle and chuckle over his
fescennine acrobatics. In *Antic Hay* [line missing in original] but has
gone too far. It is a witty novel, but its wit compels the reader to hold
his nose.

The motto on the title page is this couplet from Marlowe's play,
Edward the Second:

> My men like satyrs grazing on the lawns
> Shall with their goat-feet dance the antic hay.

Most of his men are satyrs with goat feet. And so are his women.
Gumbril, Coleman, Mercaptan, Mrs. Viveash, Zoe, and Rosie are all
sexual maniacs and degenerates. Some of them resemble certain living
persons. Coleman is carefully, ingeniously, and persistently blasphemous. He has a blonde beard. ' "This beard," says Gumbril,
"Why, may I ask?" "For religious reasons," said Coleman, and made
a sign of the cross.

> Christlike in my behaviour,
> Like every good believer,
> I imitate the Saviour,
> And cultivate a beaver.

There be beavers which have made themselves beavers for the kingdom
of heaven's sake. But there are some beavers,' etc. These and similar
wanton blasphemies are, I submit, vulgar without being funny.

Another specimen of Coleman's blasphemy I do not care to quote.
One expects to find these expectorations in Willy, but not in Mr.

---

[1] Sacha Guitry (1885–1957), Russian-born French actor and dramatist, a brilliant
improviser and prolific writer.

Huxley. The English novel has not yet boxed the compass of blasphemy or travelled through all the signs of the zodiac of innuendo. But there is a scene in the thirteenth chapter which vies with the most reckless flights of Gallic licence. The sixteenth chapter is almost Ulyssean in its nauseous horror. But in the twentieth chapter blasphemy culminates in an appalling infamy of outrage. Coleman actually parodies the agony and anguish of the Crucifixion. And the abomination ends in an ecstasy of Sadism.

It may be said that Mr. Huxley is a satirist as well as satyrist. It may be pleaded that his blasphemies and indecencies are but the salted thongs of a cat-o'-nine-tails. Shearwater sweating on his stationary bicycle may be acclaimed as a moral symbol. Gumbril senior, his architectural dreams, and his starlings, may be represented as the true moral antithesis of all the muck-wallowers in the story. Mrs. Viveash may be justified as a picture of the noisome ashes of a weary sensualist. These extenuations and palliations are as old as the hills. They could be employed to excuse any horror and any desecration. But if *Antic Hay* escapes uncastigated and unpilloried the effect upon English fiction will be disastrous.

I can predict the consequences. Mr. Huxley will have shoals of imitators. His licence will provoke clever young men and clever young women to out-Aldous Aldous. We shall have herds of literary rats exploring every sewer. The craft of letters will be debased and degraded until literature becomes a synonym for bad smells and bad drains.

The cloacre of vice will be dredged for fresh infamies. There will be a popular cult of blasphemy and a profitable school of nameless innuendo. The novel will creep and crawl with the vermin of diseased imaginations. There are few turpitudes which cannot be limned by the expert juggler with words. Literary subtlety can adumbrate moral cancers and leprosies that make even the pathologist shudder in his consulting-room. There is no limit to the resources of wordcraft when it is prostituted to the abysses of baseness.

And what is the remedy for this empoisoning of our literature? Not the police. Oh, no! They are a clumsy defence against the delicate arts of the connoisseur in innuendo. There is no moral outrage which a master of phrase cannot perpetrate without tumbling into the meshes of the law! No! The true cure is public opinion based upon the high conscience of the great lords of letters. Literature has its own laws and its own lawgivers. It is to those laws and to those lawgivers that I appeal. They are the same in all ages and all languages. The great artists are pure and austere. The great poets are as clean as the east wind. The great novelists are as sane as Dartmoor or Exmoor, as Snowdon or Mont Blanc. The blowflies shrivel in the flame of literature. Mr. Huxley is a blowfly. But if he chose he could be a fairy dragonfly shimmering in the holy sunlight over running water.

20. L. P. Hartley, review in *Spectator*

22 December 1923, cxxxi, p. 998

Leslie Poles Hartley (1895–1972), novelist and critic, author of *The Go-Between* (1953), *The Novelist's Responsibility* (1967), and many others, was a literary commentator for British weekly reviews for nearly forty years.

It is a more grateful task to praise Mr. Huxley than not to praise him. For our sakes he has ransacked the ages and despoiled the climes; he has made us familiar with the figures and fashions of several centuries, including our own; he has provided us with ancient and modern jokes, in every style and suited to every taste. He has recovered that sense of the exciting strangeness, the decorative quality of scientific phenomena which has been so rare since the Elizabethans. If only for fear of the censure of specialists or pedants, few writers of the present day would dare to be so heroically encyclopaedic, such ardent gleaners of the gossip and table-talk—as well as the profounder reveries—of literature, history, science and religion.

Mr. Huxley's efforts to find a new figure in what he evidently considers the threadbare carpet of the novelist's art do not end with antiquarianism, or with the exposure of vulgar errors and the establishment of esoteric truths. He strives, perhaps less successfully, to adopt the spacious, liberal, carefree attitude of Rabelais; to take for granted, even to make regular, all whimsicality and irregularity in social

83

behaviour, especially irregularity in sexual relationships. He goes about this heavy task not sympathetically, nor yet in a spirit of mere buffoonery, but conscientiously. His fantasy has a better wind than his high spirits, and runs on when they are tired; satire, too, keeps gaining on them, and sentimentalism is not far behind. So far as its subject-matter goes, *Antic Hay* gains rather than loses from its cheerful promiscuity, its vivid contrasts and unexpected juxtapositions, all of which serve Mr. Huxley's wit and cluster round it. But the effect of his alternations of mood is bound to be centrifugal and disintegrating. The picture is clear enough while his satyrs are 'dancing the antic hay'; decidedly blurred when they stop to weep over their sins, or bite each other, or wonder where the next meal is to come from. Nor is Theodore Gumbril, ingenious inventor of the Patent Smallclothes, quite callous or lighthearted enough to be comfortable in his deliberate licentiousness. It sits awkwardly on him, like the false beard he wore to allure his victims.

Indeed, *Antic Hay* offers a wide field for criticism. In respect of unity and completeness it falls short of Mr. Huxley's earlier novel, *Crome Yellow*, for its action is spread loosely over years, not condensed into days; its many love affairs are always provisional and anticipatory, never conclusive. There are passages, too, in which coarseness, that quality dear to the full-blooded, cannot be held to redeem indecency. The impermanence and fluctuation of aesthetic standards, a disquieting thought never to be wantonly indulged, occupies Mr. Huxley continually. An established reputation exasperates his characters. Their preoccupation with the paradoxical and the trivial—a preoccupation not always reproved by satire—runs through the book like a refrain, sometimes with an agreeable effect of languor, sometimes with a devastating effect of devitalization and sterility.

[Quotes Mercaptan, Chapter V, p. 56]

It would be unreasonable to identify Mr. Huxley with Mr. Mercaptan: but it is not unreasonable to search the pages of *Antic Hay* for tokens of a consistent attitude, a recognizable identity. And that, precisely, is what Mr. Huxley does not or will not provide. We may deny that his heart is not in the right place; we cannot deny that it has no fixed abode. But when all this is said, there remains the extraordinary vigour and gusto which he brings to every page that he writes—a liveliness not always inherent in the subject but imposed upon it. How promptly and powerfully he focuses his interest, as though that interest, like a searchlight, were independent of its object's attractiveness. He has a genius for elucidation, but it feeds upon complexity, not upon subtlety; and that is why his characters, even Lypiatt and Mrs. Viveash, are less successful than the treatises on architecture and advertisement, and the abstract and mechanical properties of the book.

21. Raymond Mortimer, review in *New Statesman*

10 November 1923, xxii, p. 146

For a biographical note see No. 13.

Mr. Aldous Huxley is an intensely clever young man. Such a description would in most cases, for reasons that it would be impolite to specify, signify extreme disapproval. It seems to me a superlative compliment. One cannot, alas, remain young very long, and a comparison of the first books of our most successful authors with their last ones reveals that cleverness also is a flower that all too quickly fades. Our gratitude, then, to Mr. Huxley for gathering, while he may, his roses and making them up into such frequent and astonishing bouquets. They are hardly the flowers that made fragrant the gardens of our grand-mothers, and there will be some to complain that they are positively malodorous; but modern science has brought into fashion strange sports, and Mr. Huxley's decorations are nothing if not voguish. Ephemeral, too? Well, it is we for whom they are destined and not our possible posterity. It will be a sad Future if it cannot produce Mr. Huxleys of its own.

Antic Hay is a full-length novel. It is even better than *Limbo*; that is to say, it is its author's best book. *Crome Yellow* disappointed. Indeed, it seemed doubtful whether Mr. Huxley had not mistaken his vocation. For the gift most necessary, perhaps, of all for a novelist is the power to make human beings whose reality, on no matter how fantastic a plane of existence, one can believe in. And the Cromians lacked ichor; only the constant wit of the ventriloquist could preserve the reader's interest in such obvious mannikins. In *Antic Hay* this disability is more ingeniously concealed, but I doubt if Mr. Huxley has it in him to overcome it. He seems to doubt it himself, for he continues to borrow his characters from real life. It is a pity that he has recourse to this dangerous practice, but evidently he finds it a necessity. The only characters even in his new book which seem at all real are those that I recognise as portraits. These I can clothe with the flesh which I know them to possess, and I suspect that some of the characters whose reality escapes me would take on life if I had the honour to know their originals. But an author cannot rely on his readers to do this part of his work for him. The other great weakness of Mr. Huxley as a novelist was one less easy to define. For a comic writer to lack seriousness may not at first appear a matter of importance. No sensible person would now want Mr. Huxley to flagellate the vices: our conception of satire has changed. But a writer of fiction, no matter whether it be tragic or comic, does need to have some emotional relation to his characters; and this was lacking. Mr. Huxley felt no affection or pity, or even contempt. He just did not care, and his indifference was naturally infectious. In *Antic Hay* the needful seriousness appears. Mr. Huxley is wittier than ever, and the most Ninetyish æsthete could hardly accuse him of moralising; but his work has taken on a much deeper resonance. There is a scene at a coffee-stall where the characteristic personages of Mr. Huxley's fancy are suddenly confronted with the material miseries of the poor. A few years ago he would himself have dismissed it as sentimental, and probably many of his admirers will still so dismiss it. Sentimental it certainly is, but not, I think, therefore to be dismissed. Such use of *chiaroscuro* marks an improvement in his art, particularly noticeable in the tragic history of Lypiatt, a very painful and pitiful study of that inferiority-complex to whose workings most of the silly things we all do are attributable. Still more interesting is the replacement of the old carelessness by a more active, a more ferocious, emotion.

Novelists have a way of describing with admiration the wittiness of their heroes and heroines, and then omitting to give them anything witty to say. Mr. Huxley has a different method. He despises, he even detests his puppets, and fills his books with their conversation, which is quite admirable. This intense bitterness on the author's part gives *Antic Hay* a character and a reality which its predecessors lacked. There have been few writers whose view of life at its best is so thickly mildewed as

Mr. Huxley's. He has had experience of every good thing that civilised society has to offer, and he has not a good word to say for it. The only things that excite his admiration are the two most abstract arts, music and architecture. (The odd thing is that his passion for Wren does not induce him to take more pains with the architecture of his book, which is unnecessarily formless.) Otherwise he can only interest himself in things that strike him as repulsive enough to be amusing, often quite harmless things, but for some reason stimulants of his hatred. He is on the way to become the complete misanthrope: he revels in his own disgust. He has tried all the pleasures, enjoys none of them, and cannot bear that others should. His distaste for life resembles at moments that of a Falsetto in face of a Casanova. This new intensity of emotion gives a new savour to the wit which is, after all, what we read Mr. Huxley for. But if, as I think, *Antic Hay* is more entertaining than any novel that has appeared this year in England, I also feel somehow that Mr. Huxley is capable of writing a book a lot more entertaining than *Antic Hay*.

22. Gerald Gould, review in *Saturday Review* (London)

17 November 1923, cxxxvi, p. 550

Gerald Gould (1885–1936), poet, essayist, editor, was complimented by the *Sunday Times* as 'one of the greatest contemporary critics of fiction' (5 October 1924, p. 8).

Modernity! Is it a disease, or only a disease of the imagination? Is it a state peculiar to the twentieth century, or the perpetual and incurable state of all centuries? It is at any rate the favourite theme of twentieth-century authors.

[A paragraph on other novels being reviewed is omitted]

Gumbril's Patent Small Clothes, a sort of trouser which enables the leanest to sit with comfort on the hardest seat: such is the basis of Mr. Huxley's fantasy. It is, if the inept metaphor may pass, his standing joke. He returns to it at intervals, with the gusto of Artemus Ward's[1] tiger, who was seen 'with a large and well selected assortment of seats of trowsis in his mouth'. Why the sedentary position should be considered comic is a mystery. It is the position of judges and other awful and intimidating figures. What, according to the poet, did 'the haughty and the strong' do in 'the high places'? They sat in them. There is no Professor without his Chair. The life sedentary is the life thoughtful and debonair. But Mr. Huxley will have his little joke, and it must be one that, however inexplicably, every schoolboy shares. Presumably that is why he is still playing 'Beaver', a game which for the rest of the world ceased to be amusing some twelve months ago. That is why he thinks it worth while to print blasphemous rhymes which the crudest undergraduate would scarcely repeat in a tipsy conversation. That is why he presents us with a young lady whose eyes to the idealist look 'plumbless with thought' when she is actually thinking: 'If I wait till the summer sale, the crêpe de Chine will be reduced by at least two shillings a yard.' The fact is that the cheap, the obvious, the popular, has a fatal fascination for Mr. Huxley. It is his Dark Angel, struggling with the Muse for possession of what is, when all's said on the other side, one of the rarest and most promising intelligences of our time. There are passages in *Antic Hay* of a pure and rhythmic beauty: passages so fine, so just, that they move one like good music. Casimir Lypiatt, the would-be genius, trying to drown the still small voice of self-knowledge in the violence of self-praise: Emily, the gentle lover— Mr. Huxley has drawn, in these, pictures of a really exquisite truth. He has tragic moments. His general reflections, when they are serious, are profound. His best descriptive passages are too long to quote; and if I praise them as I think they deserve to be praised, but without quotation, I can scarcely hope to be believed. Their beauty and wisdom are such as to make moderate laudation seem skimpy and grotesque. They are real: they flow and sing: they could not be other than they are. And then—plump!—on the next page we are back again in a painful un-reality: in a dirty, trivial world of the constant effort—and failure—to be clever; of aimless, pointless, seductions at sight. There may exist such worlds, but they certainly do not exist in the light in which Mr. Huxley portrays them.

[1] Artemus Ward, pen name of Charles Farrar Browne (1834–67), one of the best and most popular nineteenth-century U.S. humorists.

His title he explains by a quotation from Marlowe:

> My men like satyrs grazing on the lawns
> Shall with their goat-feet dance the antic hay.

'Satyrs' in the modern sense most of his men are, but the reference is inappropriate all the same. For the real satyrs were at least lusty and vigorous, whereas Mr. Huxley is preoccupied with creatures decadently squirming and fainting. Perhaps he agrees with the king in *Alice*— 'There's nothing like hay when you're faint.'

23. Unsigned review in *NYTBR*

25 November 1923, pp. 8–9

Aldous Huxley's latest novel is apt to leave the first impression that it is a somewhat belated 'cry for madder music and for stronger wine.' There is in it a delirium of sense enjoyment, with the ever-present, listless certainty that boredom is sure to follow. An after taste of bitterness comes with reflection upon the book. It would almost seem to belong to the twilight of the Jacobins: ardent humanitarianism in politics, and new form for truth in art, and an intoxication of order, proportion, beauty in architecture and music are wearily waved away as 'really pathetic' or quaintly old-fashioned. The end of the world is at hand; why worry?

T. S. Eliot's *The Waste Land* is recalled by the casual allusions to classical lore, the devilishly clever garbling of familiar quotations and the total effect of dissolution. Mr. Huxley has the American poet's flair for topical wit of a distinctly metropolitan flavor. London of the theatres and electric billboards, the smart cabarets and dancing places, the parks and the dingy suburbs, is evoked with the skill of a sleight-of-hand performer. It is, perhaps, a little higher in the social scale than Mr. Eliot's city, with a little more money to spend. But its point of view is much the same.

Antic Hay is satirical light literature, done with a deft, sure touch. The portraits, or rather travesties, of the characters are the most delightful features. Gumbril, Junior, escaped pedagogue and inventor of the patent small clothes; Gumbril, Senior, architect, dreamer of a truly lovely city, which he builds in little plaster casts; Shearwater, the physiologist, engrossed in the kidneys; Lypiatt, the overemphatic, too-protesting artist; Mercaptan, his critic, and Myra Viveash, the incomparable, the beautiful, the calculatingly impulsive Myra, are all of them joyously and maliciously portrayed.

The plot is as inconsequential as that of a musical comedy. The reader never does find out whether the British public adopted the patent small clothes, and sat thenceforward on 'pneumatic bliss,' instead of hard, cold benches. It does not matter. There is the poor young wife who longs to be a great lady and is constantly afraid that she is doing things 'in other people's taste.' There is the idyl of the twosome over the week-end in the country, in a governess cart behind a fat pony—spoiled by the caprice of Myra Viveash. There is, eternally, the immediate and tangible thing pushing out of sight the reasoned, forward-looking plan. Accident, it would appear, is the new high god and fortuitous circumstance the successor of that doughty purposefulness which the older writers celebrated. Mr. Huxley is at least having his revenge upon his forebear, the biologist, and his kinsman, Matthew Arnold, the apostle of law and order, 'sweetness and light,' in art. And Gumbril, Senior, crying: 'Proportion, proportion!' and condemned to designing model workmen's cottages, is somehow the strongest figure, for all his son hogs the centre of the stage. It is a brilliant, entertaining satire, with a faint suggestion of 'ungestured sadness.'

24. Kurt Daniels, review in *New Republic*

12 December 1923, xxxvii, pp. 71-2

Daniels's contention that the interior play occurs for 'no reason at all' may be compared with Frederick R. Karl's article on the play's importance (See Appendix I, p. 473).

The title of Daniels's review is 'Shadow Boxing.'

The most entertaining book I ever knew was a three-pounder called *The Popular Handbook of Curious Information, Familiar Allusions and 10,000 Foreign Words and Phrases* which, read through story-wise, bore me through a siege of convalescence and conferred a most discursive and elegant education. *Antic Hay* comes close to matching the charm of that volume, perhaps because it might be its very novelization. It has the literary delights of the intelligence questionnaire, characters who don't talk in conversations but in charades, with satire japing sophistication as well as the more obvious targets, engaging naughtiness narrated for its own sake, rising and falling in broad comedy and in episodes deliciously strange and tender. Out of a storage-house of second-hand conventions, tri-lingual expressions, and classical allusions inserted much as in the book I first mention, evolves something which is new; which makes it humour on its own terms; which uses devices, but not stale ones; allusions but not clichés; allying erudition and craftsmanship with a philosophy usually contrasted with those moral virtues, much as Anatole France sometimes shocks the church-going by his superior familiarity with the lives of the saints and the fathers.

High school English classes studying the art of writing won't learn very much from *Antic Hay*. It might be one of those facile essays of *On the Margin* which stretched the word-limit of a middle article and expanded in three or four directions until it filled a book. A writer finds himself much like a gardener tending a rose-bush. To grow a perfect flower he must trim off the buds and shoots that draw life from the stalk, prune away ideas which, though fresh and lovely, are taking the growth away from the master rose. For a book like *Ethan Frome* or *My Antonia* there must have been sacrificed a hundred ideas, variations and footnotes which budded while the main branch grew. Huxley, however, is so interested in watching the profusion of his flowers that having them—ramblers and tea roses, red, white and (for experiment) orange or blue—growing on the same bush only amuses him and doesn't disturb.

[Summarizes the book's opening and mentions the main characters]

Gumbril buys a false beard, because it is a talisman for confidence and because the cries of 'Beaver!' it raises offer a brilliant opening for conversation with pretty girls otherwise inaccessible. It startingly alters the proportions of his face:

[Quotes Chapter IX, p. 94]

With this splendid equipment he sallies forth. Successful in his first venture with anonymous prey, he finds it is Shearwater's wife who has yielded to the lure of the Complete Man—'the sheep in beaver's clothing.' A situation suavely worked out. Emily follows, in chapters different in tone and content, where the real strength of Huxley's prose exhibits itself. After a Mozart concert, Gumbril, now unbeavered, finds himself in the rarest and tenderest of moods.

[Quotes Chapter XIII, p. 154]

But Emily, four years married, leaves the book still virginal, untaken although won. For diversion, Huxley contrives to circulate his women in this small company like bright pennies among school-boys. Mrs. Viveash is successfully loved by Gumbril, Lypiatt, and Shearwater. Rosie, successively by Shearwater, Gumbril, Mr. Mercaptan, and Coleman, the originator of the beaver stratagem, but whose beard—and Cossack nastiness—isn't, like Gumbril's, attached with spirit-gum. For no reason at all we have a morality, a Christmas mummery (revised version) like an O'Neill play in twelve pages, inserted near the end, an end which is not a finality, and, though untheatrical, is adroit rather than inevitable.

Longer than *Crome Yellow*, but made of the same material, *Antic Hay* doesn't carry Huxley along a new road of departure. He continues to be willing, along with other possessors of classical educations, non-utilitarian Latin, and bright notions, to turn them into profitable Georgian literature.

25. Joseph Wood Krutch, review in *Literary Review*

29 December 1923, iv, p. 403

For a biographical note see No. 14. The title of Krutch's review is 'Antic Horror.' Krutch was among the earliest of critics to observe the scientific impulse behind Huxley's writing. See Introduction, p. 10.

As everyone knows, youth experiences no keener joy than the discovery of sorrow, and the young man never feels more exultingly alive than when, having hit upon pessimism all by himself, he can prove that life is not worth the living. Now, Mr. Aldous Huxley, though a superlatively clever young man, was no exception to the general rule, and so when he discovered the rich possibilities of despair he took his pen in hand and wrote with such ingenuity and zest that the nothingness of life, the brutality of love, and the disgustingness of that filthy animal man were never more delightfully set forth. Yet no one ever suspected that either his cynicism or his wickedness was more than a very clever intellectual exercise.

One thing alone set him off from other wits and that was the fact that he was the first to exploit thoroughly the cynical possibilities of science. Our forefathers knew in a general way that man was dust, and some of the saints stated in no uncertain terms that love was merely a form of lust; but thanks to the laboratory we have really a much more accurate knowledge of the details of these truths than any one ever had before. The theory of evolution itself, for example, is a splendid joke; all our psychologists, physiologists, and anthropologists are excellent if slightly cynical wags, who love to confront our exalted imaginings with disillusioning truths; and of all these facts Huxley was amusedly conscious. Two hundred years ago, it is true, Congreve remarked that he could never watch a cage of monkeys without a certain embarrassment, but his feeling was only very vague, whereas we, with more knowledge at our command, are compelled to take the thing more seriously and confess with Huxley:

> Mind issued from the monkey's womb
> Is still umbilical to earth,
> Earth its home and earth its tomb.

Nor do we stop even there without further elaboration of the idea. If Congreve was embarrassed by a few natural monkeys, what would he have felt if conducted into the laboratory which we are shown in *Antic Hay*?

[Quotes description of Shearwater's experiments, Chapter XXII, pp. 252-3]

Really, if the exquisite feminine modesty and charm which have inspired all of our poets is to be explained as merely the result of gland actions, and if those traits of character which seemed to Jonathan Edwards the blessed signs of divine election are due simply to the fortunate presence of the correct hormones in the correct numbers, why should we take the whole thing so seriously?

To some people such arguments are genuinely disturbing; others dismiss them with a reference to the 'fallacy of origins.' But the young Huxley did neither, for he found delight in his own cleverness so much more than an adequate recompense for disillusion that he was merely delighted with the joke and the discovery of a new kind of dandyism. Such at least was the impression given by his first book. But in his latest work a change seems to be coming over his spirit and he shows signs of going over definitely to the ranks of those who feel, quite seriously, that it is hard for the human spirit to make itself a home in the world which science has revealed to it. The despair which he wantonly created seems in danger of becoming something of a Frankenstein, and he is appalled by the ugliness which he has searched out. His new hero, like all of his former heroes, starts out with a mind disorganized by too much miscellaneous and very modern knowledge. 'Good,' he meditates; 'good! It was a word people only used nowadays with a kind of deprecating humorousness. Good! Beyond good and evil? We are all that nowadays. Or merely below them, like earwigs? I glory in the name of earwig.' But when he starts out to live his life by this philosophy he plunges into dissipation, boredom soon appears, and he ends in a disgust which is not at all funny.

The book, a farrago of burlesque and bitterness, is too confused to be described, but it inevitably suggests the *Satyricon* and is, literally, nearly as obscene. Yet the obscenity is felt as such, and some of the pictures, as, for example, that of the midnight dance restaurant, are so genuinely savage that Huxley, who began as a harmless *enfant terrible*, begins to assume a Juvenalian tone. The man who could write, for instance, the following passage has ceased to be merely a joker:

[Quotes Gumbril on 'quiet places in the mind,' Chapter XIII, pp. 146–7]

When *Crome Yellow* appeared the present reviewer felt that Mr. Huxley had about exhausted his vein, but the present book obviously opens up another. Half low comedy and half a genuine cry of despair, it is in one way not so good as some of the author's previous works because it is not so perfect an expression of what he is trying to say; but it proves that he has not ceased to grow. What he can do with his new manner remains to be seen, but he will not go on doing the same thing over again. He is ceasing to play with ideas and beginning to feel them. Perhaps a new Huysmans[1] is impending.

[1] Joris-Karl Huysmans (1848–1907), a French writer whose work tells the story of a protracted, agonized odyssey towards human values.

26. H. W. Boynton, review in *Independent*

8 December 1923, cxi, pp. 287–8

Henry Walcott Boynton (1869–1947), journalist, essayist, educator, with books on Bret Harte and James Fenimore Cooper.

Boynton here groups *Antic Hay* with Stephen Vincent Benêt's *Jean Huguenot* and Edith Summers Kelley's *Weeds*. He describes these books as displaying 'the after-war mood of youth—and the restlessness and recklessness, the ardor for change, the exaltation of the lesser self, the scorn of precedent and authority, the hysteric pursuit of joy, and the brooding unhappiness of a generation vainly striving to forget its racial and secular inheritance.'

One of the most brilliant and 'provocative' of the young after-war novelists is Aldous Huxley. With *Crome Yellow* he threw his individual top hat into the ring of militant satire. In *Antic Hay* he continues his fretful and ingenious gambols, which yield much laughter, on a rather shrill pitch. If his were really 'goat-feet dancing the antic hay,' if the blood of a satyr urged him instead of the mind of a satirist, we should have had a bigger book out of him. But he has the usual scunner of his generation against everything else, before or outside his generation. He affects an utter contempt for all persons in authority, all the fogies and hypocrites and respectable ones—and is totally unable to ignore them. It is to this gallery that he continually plays—a gallery which he pictures to himself as listening with fascinated horror to his audacities and irreverences; the chances being that it listens, if at all, with the indulgent smile which greets the newly-culled cussword of a small boy who is somewhat over-proud of his acquisition.

For the discouraging thing about all this 'new' and immensely smart fiction is that it is so patently derivative. Whatever is indigenous in it is Wells; and the four-fifths that is not indigenous, is of French or German or Russian origin. Aldous Huxley, I should say, is a joint product of

96

Wells and Anatole France. He has the brisk 'reportorial' curiosity of the one, and the elegant and elaborate diabolism of the other. He revels in clever blasphemies, and if his men are satyrs of the antic hay, his women are fit companions for them—willing nymphs of (let us discreetly put it) the wanton bower.

Antic Hay, to come down to the case, is the airy record of a year or two in the life of one Theodore Gumbril, Jr., B.A. Oxon. On our first glimpse of him he is usher in a boys' school. We behold his escape from that absurd past-and-parson-ridden prison (cf. Hugh Walpole's *The Gods and Mr. Perrin*). We stray with him into an artistic and sporting circle in London, which is full of wild talk, alcohol, and episodic sexuality. The after-war mood of weariness and unrest is upon these young people. They believe in nothing, care for nothing but the sensation (which includes any variety of excited mental image) of the moment. There is Coleman, laboriously blasphemous and animal; there is Mercaptan, mincing æsthete, an embodied sneer at philistine matters like honor and duty and generous love. There is Shearwater the scientist, so easily gulled by his wife and his friends, though more of a person than any of them. There is the pompous and piteous failure Lypiatt, who represents the empty tradition of the Past. There is Gumbril himself, who represents the complacent and fatuous 'quest' of the Present. And there are Mrs. Viveash and Rosie Shearwater, the two women who are more or less literally handed about among these males, according to the turn of the cards. It is all very amusing from a continental or, let us say, early eighteenth century point of view. You may find analogues for these types, for this fleeting humor, in the comedies of Congreve and Wycherley, with their rakes and boobies and powdered wantons. And it is extremely 'well-written,' now in the truncated manner of the period, now with an individual lilt that gives many of its descriptive passages real charm: 'Floating she seemed to go, with a little spring at every step and the skirt of her summery dress— white it was, with a florid pattern printed in black all over it—blowing airily out around her swaying march. . . .'

Apart from its readability, and its brilliant satirical portraiture, the book contains an abundance of clever dialogue, in which all sorts of ideas are touched on and played about from various angles. And it should be admitted that reckless as is his mockery of all things cherished (or at least publicly upheld) by persons in authority, it by no means spares his own generation. If there is any moral hero of the piece, it is the creative-souled Gumbril Senior, who sells his own most cherished treasure to win back the lost treasure of his friend. There, if you like, is a situation almost unique in our 'young' fiction—the son, not the father, is the ass!

27. Grant Overton on Huxley

1923, 1924

Grant Overton (1887–1930), American critic and editor, author of *The Philosophy of Fiction* (1928) and *The American Novel* (1929). The first two paragraphs below are from Overton's *American Nights Entertainment* (New York: Appleton, 1923), pp. 34–5. The rest of the selection is an extract from an essay entitled 'The Twentieth Century Gothic of Aldous Huxley' in Overton's *Cargoes for Crusoes* (New York: Appleton, 1924), pp. 97–113.

Overton's essay was among the first responses to recognize, with Will Cuppy (No. 16), Huxley's fundamentally serious aim. In fact, Overton's foresight in identifying so surely the mystical character of Huxley's mind was quite remarkable. See Introduction, pp. 12, 14.

Aldous Huxley has been known to us hitherto as a poet and a writer of fiction. Both his poetry and his fiction have been marked with a graceful artifice and that simplicity which comes only from a completed sophistication. His new book, a collection of essays, is distinguished by those qualities. There is something about Huxley's writing—I don't know what it is and those who know what it is, can't tell—which brings a gleam to the eyes of all who love literature for its own sake. In *On the Margin* Huxley the satirist walks comfortably with Huxley the student. For Aldous Huxley is a very studious young man.

[Describes Huxley's physical appearance]

. . . Intimates know him as one of the most learned men in England, though devoid of poses and devoted to finding pleasure in the works of Charles Dickens. His scholarliness shows itself in *On the Margin*, where Chaucer, Ben Jonson, and the devilish biographer, Mr. Strachey, divide attention with the question of love as practised in France and England, the justice of Margot Asquith's strictures on modern feminine beauty, and the evolution of ennui.

[Overton opens his essay in *Cargoes for Crusoes* with an extensive excerpt from the 'strong light dome' passage in the last chapter of *Antic Hay*, p. 254]

This is not the Aldous Huxley, you will say, of *Limbo*, or of *Crome Yellow*, nor even of the collection of tales called *Mortal Coils*. No, it isn't. The intelligent child, the studious Oxford youth, the young man in maiden meditation fancy free, have gone somewhere. (We need not mind where.) The person that emerges in their place has a mind vaulted and full of pointed arches. His thoughts are lighted through stained glass, glass that singularly resembles the colored microscopic slides with which Grandfather Huxley was intently preoccupied. It is a Gothic mind with a special twentieth century illumination through the windows of applied science; the lighting is not very satisfactory nor is the source entirely congruous; but this mind-place is one of many and singular pleasures. A sense of airy spaciousness exists, and there is a comfortable feeling that one is not too closely observed, except by God. The delight of sanctuary would be perfect if one were not forced to go outside, now and then. However, there is the sense of escaping, of having escaped—from Grandfather, with his courage and his science and his controversies; from Aunt Humphrey Ward with her formula for writing novels; from Laforgue and the French school; from Oxford and the English school; from Applied Religion; and this goes some way to compensate for the necessity of living in London and struggling to build up a strong light dome of life with stories, critiques, poems, books, essays, *feuilletons*.[1]

[Reviews Huxley's heritage]

. . . And it is due to the shape of Huxley's head, not the outer shape but the shape inside—as we have said, all curious vaultings, pointed arches, mediæval, constructed for all the rites of a ceremonious mysticism but constrained by the circumstances of his era and the exigencies

[1] 'Articles and *belles lettres*.'

of daily living to be used rather as a laboratory than a cathedral. One must eat. When Grandfather Huxley gave over eating meat, he was unable to think, and his grandson, obliged to use a beautiful brain in journalism and letters, can hardly dedicate it to worship.

'Worship.' The word may seem strange to be used in speaking of the author of *Antic Hay*, in which there is much genial blasphemy; but what the careless reader may not see is the bitter cry beneath the surface of a stony contempt. The cry is there, nor is it always embittered. . . .Those familiar with the story of the two dwarfs, Sir Hercules and Filomena, in *Crome Yellow*, know what pathos and tenderness Huxley can command in a narrative of entire simplicity undisturbed by the self-conscious tendency of much of his work. . . . Of the several attitudes assumed in the world to-day by gifted writers whose core of feeling is mystical, Huxley's, I think, has the most courage to commend it. . . . Huxley, however, has learned from Dickens the art of caricature. As he draws, his really vast erudition comes crowding through the aisles of his strange and beautiful mind. Like little imps, like twisted gargoyles come to life, figures of the past fling themselves on the haft of his pen, to move it this way and that. A heavier stroke here, to show the semblance of a satyr; this curve a little thinned by pity; a blot here for the spirit made flesh. . . . [sic] So you have gradually assembled his company, grotesque, exaggerated, wretched, bizarre, inhuman-human, like drawings by Cruikshank or Phiz, like illustrations to a new *Nicholas Nickleby*, or *Pickwick*, repulsively true, their meaninglessness carrying their deepest meaning. That meaning is so significant that only a mystic can be expected to grasp it. It goes back to the struggle between paganism and Christianity which led into what we call the Dark Ages. Mr. Huxley has looked at his world and seen with disgust—but also with anguish and pity—how the wheel has come full circle, how for the mystical mind a Dark Age is again come upon us. . . .

This young man has been everywhere and seen everything. He writes, not that he who runs may read, but that he who reads may run. He subtly, but more and more urgently, invites us to flee—the wrath to come? No, the madness already here. Does his generation fancy itself as pagans and revel in its paganism? He will show them their precedents and quote for them their texts—which they may ponder before passing out to the vomitorium. One might divide Aldous Huxley's work to date into two classes: and if one class is juvenilia, most certainly the other division, led by *Antic Hay*, is Juvenalia. The Goth laid waste, even as this young Goth from Oxford is laying waste; and then the Goth built churches. They are the incomparable, those edifices. The son of the Arnolds and the Huxleys, the Oxford scholar, the pupil of London, is preparing for us his twentieth century Gothic.

[Reviews Huxley's young career and then quotes a letter in which Samuel Roth discusses Huxley (dated 28 June 1922). Roth's last sentence follows]

'But it should interest you to know that at a luncheon of young Oxford poets to which I was invited he was referred to several times as the most learned man in England.'

Huxley's personal appearance and agreeable manner have been frequently described and his conversational gift is not aptly epitomized by that very famous English novelist who recently said of him: 'He looks clever. He says nothing—he has no need to say anything. It suffices for him to sit silent, looking clever.' The same novelist, a very penetrating analyst of literary powers, added: 'But this young man is almost the only "white hope" in English literature at present.'[1] Huxley is at his best, conversationally, in a small company. One of his close friends is Frank Swinnerton whose judgment of Huxley's gift as a writer strongly confirms the novelist's estimate just quoted.

The Burning Wheel (1916) and *The Defeat of Youth* (1918) were volumes of poems, as was *Leda* (1920). Only *Leda* has been published in America. Although it is not ten years since the appearance of Mr. Huxley's first book, the first (London) editions of all of them are held at a premium by dealers and collectors. One may pay, for a particular item, anywhere from ten to fifteen pounds in some instances—or certainly not less than $60 or $75 in New York. A first edition of a new Huxley is something to put aside carefully. The distinction is unusual among living writers and, in the case of a man under thirty, possibly unique.

Much unwisdom has been uttered concerning Huxley's prose. The applausive enthusiasm of the ordinary Huxley devotee may be dismissed without comment; superficiality (not to say shallowness) may call for pity but certainly not for censure. A misapprehension of what the author was doing in *Antic Hay*, though common enough and a more serious matter, will rectify with time. A comparison of such poetry as 'Leda' to Keats is better ignored than made the subject of delicate differentiation; but what shall we say of these? 'The wittiest man, after Beerbohm, now writing in English' [Fitzgerald, No. 15]. 'His humor

---

[1] This novelist, regrettably, remains unidentified.

is hot as well as shining' [Mencken]. 'He is finished and fastidious, sophisticated and diverting' [*New Republic*]. 'There's no doubt about it. Huxley is brilliant' [John V. A. Weaver]. Mr. Clement K. Shorter, in the London *Sphere*, pronouncing *Mortal Coils* the best book Huxley had yet written, said: 'There's a great deal of brilliancy in it, although one or two of the stories are too chaotic for my taste, and one, "Nuns at Luncheon," is too morbid. The best are "The Gioconda Smile" and "The Tillotson Banquet". . . . [sic] Mrs. T. H. Huxley had distinct gifts as a poet, and I have a volume of her verse I highly value. The son, Mr. Leonard Huxley, is a man of varied talent and the editor of the *Cornhill Magazine*. Mr. Aldous Huxley's talents have taken a widely different turn, but they should carry him far.' If they are to carry him much farther, one grieves for Mr. Shorter, already lagging a little. It was commonly remarked that *Crome Yellow* derived from Peacock—a modernized *Headlong Hall* with the slapstick eliminated and the addition of overtones on the (then) current sex motif.

[Examines a few of the short stories to 'test some of these characterizations']

The novels, *Crome Yellow* and *Antic Hay* exhibit the same characteristics and underlying intention as the shorter pieces; they have the added value of unity of form (in *Crome Yellow*, of time and place as well). *Crome Yellow* is more varied in its emotional presentation as well as lenient; *Antic Hay* is sterner, more peremptory—the rapier driven home. But where is the likeness in all this or in any of this, to Max Beerbohm? Mr. Huxley is witty—incidentally. His humor, described as 'hot as well as shining,' is no more humor than the work of Mark Twain in *The Mysterious Stranger*. No doubt his prose is a 'finished' prose; but 'fastidious, sophisticated and diverting'! The picture conjured up by such adjectives is one of an elegant trifler. Yet hardly a man writing can use such uncompromising, Old-Testamentary speech; and if the bulk of Huxleyana is diversion, then Savonarola should be considered with reference to his possibilities as a vaudeville entertainer. And 'brilliant'. It is a word from the outermost darkness, spreading darkness around.

Perhaps as a result of these singular misapprehensions, the remark was general, when Huxley's book of essays, *On the Margin*, appeared, that here was a volume which might be the work of any gifted young man. Not quite. The display of learning was rather too great for gifted young men to manage, as it were, without parade. Yet the very ones who made the comment—and this writer must number himself among them—could have learned more concerning what a conventional biographer would love calling 'the real Aldous Huxley' from a re-perusal of On the Margin than from any other of his books. . . . In fact, the essay on 'Sir Christopher Wren' in On the Margin is the single most self-illuminatory bit of writing Mr. Huxley has offered us. Like the great architect of London, Aldous Huxley is a designer who prizes in his work a quality peculiar and individualizing; and as with Wren, the quality is not æsthetic but moral.

It is explicit, for all its unobtrusiveness, in the title story of his new collection, Young Archimedes and Other Stories. Comedy and irony in various proportions are the material of five of the six tales, but the principal story, in length a novelette, is a charming narrative of a child in Italy, a child with a beautiful forehead and eyes that could flash ripples like the sunshine on clear pale lakes. The young Guido showed an extraordinary penchant for music; but when he was a little older, like Archimedes, his mind turned to the theorems of mathematics; it was evident that his genius was larger. The tragedy of his life in the hands of a grasping woman is told with an affectionate sadness. Un-doubtedly this piece of his fiction, austere and tender, will give to thousands of readers a new conception of Aldous Huxley. They will perhaps see that the mind of the child, Guido, is a miniature of the mind of the one who writes about him; and that there is even a profound likeness between both those minds and the one of which Emerson wrote:

> The hand that rounded Peter's dome,
> And groined the walls of Christian Rome,
> Wrought in a sad sincerity. . . .

28. Huxley's elasticity

Unsigned review of *Little Mexican*, *TLS*, 22 May 1924, p. 318

See Introduction, p. 11.

About Mr. Aldous Huxley there is an elasticity that keeps his work interesting and even exciting. His last novel, *Antic Hay*, was as rigidly constructed and tightly compacted as a novel could well be: technically (we are speaking only of technique), a firm piece of carpentry. The book of fiction before that was *Mortal Coils*, in which he was so consciously literary that nearly every one of the stories was offered as an exercise in method. Now comes another book of stories, *Little Mexican*, in which none of the six displays its method, and only two are at all firmly carpentered. One of these two is 'Hubert and Minnie', a common-place of fiction so far as its subject goes, but as well told on its own lines as any story that we know. From the touch about the ferrets to the afternoon light in the mill-garden the story is a little masterpiece of suggestion, contrast, shading-off, so finely contrived that in the first reading one only feels how actual the story is. 'Fard' is equally well told; but by comparison with 'Hubert and Minnie' it seems made-up, not real. The contrast between the opulent mistress and her worn-out old servant-woman is a shallow theme that needed either intensifying in incident or studying at one remove in the manner of some of the stories in *Mortal Coils*, if it were not to seem bare. To that manner of seeing things at one remove Mr. Huxley returns with great effect in 'The Portrait'. Told by a fraudulent picture dealer about a sham old master portrait of a woman, this tale of eighteenth-century Venice, master, jewels, elopements, and what not, takes on a double fantasy; but we wish that Mr. Huxley had not underlined the cheat by showing us the 'devil' employed to paint Venetian old masters. He might as well have told us what happened to Minnie after Hubert left her at the mill.

In the other three stories we come upon what is truly exciting in Mr.

Huxley's new book. They are longer than the usual short story, and it looks as if he had determined to challenge any rules there may be about compactness, suggestion, and so forth. 'Uncle Spencer' begins on the first page of the book: we get to the story on page 80, when the war breaks out, and Uncle Spencer, sugar refiner in Longres, is imprisoned in Brussels with Emmy Wendle, a Cockney 'male impersonator' of the music-halls. Every page of the first eighty, telling of Uncle Spencer's nephew's boyhood in the Belgian town, is delightful. In the end every page helps us to know that fascinating mixture of Mr. Shandy and Sir Roger de Coverley which was my Uncle Spencer. But the purists will certainly tell Mr. Huxley that not a word of it, from his most Proustian sentence to his sharpest, was necessary. Let the purists have their say: we would not lose a word of it, nor a word of the descriptions of Italian scenery which lead us, ever so leisurely, into the tragedy of an Italian peasant-boy and a vulgar woman who adopted him. In a less degree Mr. Huxley lays himself open to the same charge of disproportion in the deliciously wicked tale which gives its title to the book ('Little Mexican', by the way, is a hat, not a film heroine): a tale of an Italian nobleman, who is 'old and gay' like the fairies in Mr. Yeats's poem, the prodigal father of a conscientious and very safely married son. In these cases, either Mr. Huxley is not sure of the worth of his story as a story, or he is so sure of it that he is resolved to indulge himself to the top of his bent in the writing. The result is in each case good enough to warrant him in doing what he pleases and us in pleasantly wondering what he is going to do next.

29. Arnold Bennett on *Little Mexican*

1924

(Enoch) Arnold Bennett (1867–1931), best known for his novels
The Old Wives' Tale (1908) and *Clayhanger* (1910), often ranked
with H. G. Wells and John Galsworthy as occupying a dominant
place in Edwardian literature.

Bennett's comments may be compared with Thomas Hardy's
(Introduction, pp. 10–11). Huxley and Bennett visited each other
frequently in the 1920s, and Huxley expressed his indebtedness
to Bennett for his advice in a glowing obituary in *The Times*, 31
March 1931, p. 16. But Huxley confessed in an interview that he
could not emulate Bennett's method of writing (*New York Times*,
6 May 1933, p. 14). Also, the *Letters* (p. 228) reveal Huxley's
disagreement with Bennett's realism in fiction. See Introduction,
pp. 2, 10, and No. 54.

The excerpt is dated 15 September 1924 in *The Journal of Arnold
Bennett* (New York: Literary Guild, 1933), p. 789.

About 'Uncle Spencer'. This is the first book of Aldous Huxley's that I
have really liked. Character drawing in it, for the first time in his books.
Uncle Spencer is *drawn*, emphatically. But technically the story is
clumsy. The story nearly ends artistically. Aldous doesn't finish; he
ceases. But another perfect page and the end would have been good.
He shirks the final difficulty and so there is no end. Same with the next
best story 'Little Mexican'. No end to it. But the character drawing of
the N. Count is good. 'Fard' is a Chekhov story. But the feelings of the
maid when the mistress tells her to rouge herself to hide her tiredness
are shirked.

More about novel writing and character drawing. You couldn't fill
in a whole character except in a book of enormous length. The young
ones don't seem to me to 'select'. They shove in pell-mell whatever

happens to strike them. They don't construct even a character. Then they think they are truer to life: but they aren't. Description of faces is futile. Waste of time. Give the reader something to hold on to, and then let him fill in for himself.

THOSE BARREN LEAVES

January 1925

30. Unsigned review in *TLS*

22 January 1925, p. 53

See Introduction, p. 11.

Mr. Aldous Huxley is forging ahead. We saw him very lately, in *Antic Hay*, down in the trough of the misery and rage which seize on sensitive souls at odds with the reality that they know. In the new novel he is trying his course towards a more real reality. The sea is still pretty rough, but the ship is carrying sail and the steering gear is at work again.

Cardan, Chelifer, and Calamy are the three voices in which he says most of what he has to say in *Those Barren Leaves*. If we may confuse for a moment music and morals, we should describe Cardan as a low, indeed as a base, C. Elderly sensualist turned parasite, he looks forward dismally to a dismal and penurious old age, and with horror to the worms and the corruption of death. He makes us think of the last years of Casanova; but he more richly deserves an end like Casanova's because his intellectual powers were far higher, and he has used them only to pamper his appetites. And nothing about him is more disgusting than his frustrated attempt to provide for his last years by marrying a wealthy half-wit. Chelifer is middle C. He is as middle-class as he can be. There is in him a little of the Mr. Aldous Huxley who wrote *Antic Hay*, but he lacks the noble rage which inflamed that fiery young man. He is, as Calamy called him, an inverted sentimentalist. He is at odds with reality as he sees it, because it does not adapt itself to his tastes; and he uses his clever, shallow little mind to convince himself of the general futility, and protects himself against his distaste for his middle-class reality by wallowing in it. He lives in a boarding-house, and edits a paper about rabbits. Calamy starts at the octave. When we leave him, there is at least a chance of his rising to be C *in alt*. He has some sort of faith in a reality outside women and sport and travel. He goes away alone to learn whether or not, by contemplation (omphaloskepsis is old Cardan's juicy name for it), he can discover that reality. Cardan tells him that he will fail. Even in those remote Italian hills some woman will come by, and Calamy will fall again. It may be so. But, should he succeed, the reality that he finds will not be the reality to which thought led the immortals in *Back to Methuselah*. It will be more like the kind which was discovered under the Bo-tree, or in forty days in the wilderness.

The women in the story make up the harmonies and discords, and indulge the artist in fine comedy who is strong in Mr. Aldous Huxley. We regard Mrs. Aldwinkle as a very good work in fine comedy indeed. She is the hostess of this miscellaneous, almost Peacockian or Mallockian, party of talkative guests in her Italian castle; and from her toneless voice with its unrelated notes to her miserable, middle-aged passion for Chelifer, she is a masterpiece. Miss Thriplow, the novelist, was easier to do; but she is very well done. She is the self-conscious machine for producing 'copy'. Without a thought or a feeling of her own, she is incessantly acting novels to herself and to everyone else. These two are parts of the sort of reality—false, clumsy, unfinished, truly only half-existent—with which the three men in their different ways are at odds; and they provide also the occasions for the comedy with which Mr. Aldous Huxley at once choicely and lavishly delights us. And we must not forget little Irene, Mrs. Aldwinkle's niece. One cannot help liking Irene, partly because she is so pretty and 'such a dear', and partly because she is so reassuring. It seems to be true that the modern young girl can say (and understand) the most appalling things and yet remain genuinely innocent.

We wish, indeed, that Irene and her companion innocent, young Lord Hovenden, could have had a more important share in the story. Their mere presence in it, and especially such simple fun as Lord Hovenden's manner of proposing marriage, are grateful because they help to mark off the Mr. Aldous Huxley of this book from him of *Antic Hay*. The time may come when he will give them consciousness, will develop them, and see the place of them, conscious and developed, in what used to be called the 'idea-plot' of a novel. The subject of the whole book is the relation of man to reality; yet these two children are the only people in it who have hit on one notion of that relation: a notion that has occurred to minds as different from each other as those of Blake and Browning and Meredith—the notion that one way to more real reality is through simple acceptance of the reality to hand, the faithful following of the path which an eye heedful of the positive in life will discern leading from the easily to the less easily known. These two children had that notion, but they did not know that they had it; and living only by instinct, they will feel no need to search beyond the easily known.

From the self-torturing negatives of *Antic Hay* we have passed to a more or less hopeful, at any rate an adventurous, positive; and the effect on Mr. Huxley's literature is very marked. The pattern of the book is rather odd; Mr. Chelifer has too much space in it, Calamy too little. Once, at least, it swings wide of dramatic fitness. We might commit an unseemliness in giving detail here of a situation which in Mr. Huxley's text is not indecent (his 'impropriety' is always a genuine expression of what he feels he must say); so we will only hint that the circumstances in which Calamy philosophized about his hand seem to us utterly improbable: men do not thus speak their deepest thoughts. But the many-toned wit of the book, the beauty and shrewdness of its descriptions, the learning, the thought, the richness of character, the intellectual and artistic honesty of it, show that Mr. Huxley is a very good and very likely will be a great novelist.

31. Leonard Woolf, review in
Nation and Athenaeum

24 January 1925, xxxvi, p. 584

Leonard Stanley Woolf (1880–1969), editor, historian, political scientist, was the husband of Virginia Woolf (see Nos 1, 2). He founded the Hogarth Press in 1917 and was literary editor of the London *Nation* 1923–30.

Messrs. Constable have published Mr. Shaw's four novels, *An Unsocial Socialist*, *The Irrational Knot*, *Love Among the Artists*, and *Cashel Byron's Profession*, in a cheap edition at 3s. 6d. I read *An Unsocial Socialist* and *Love Among the Artists* with a vague idea that it might be possible to write something about Mr. Shaw as a novelist. But I have been diverted from my original intention by the publication of Mr. Aldous Huxley's new novel, *Those Barren Leaves*. I was lured into reading it through, and then into comparing it with Mr. Shaw's novels, and finally into some inconclusive reflections upon novels generally.

Mr. Shaw's novels were written over forty years ago; Mr. Huxley is among the most distinguished of our younger and most modern novelists. It is customary to say that Mr. Shaw is a writer with a purpose, and nowhere more obviously than in his novels; to say that Mr. Huxley writes 'novels with a purpose' would seem at first sight to be absurdly paradoxical. The disparity between the two ought to be striking, and yet reading them consecutively I found it difficult to see that they belonged to different ages, except in the unimportant superficialities which are without significance, or that the form, conception, use of the novel have changed materially in the last forty years.

Those Barren Leaves is the best novel by Mr. Huxley that I have read. The ordinary reviewer's adjectives write themselves almost automatically upon the well-used typewriter—it is brilliant and daring, admirably written, humorous, witty, clever, cultured. The characters have length and breadth; they are curious, sometimes interesting, people whose portraits are drawn distinctly, with assurance and firmness of line, upon the printed page; occasionally they even have a depth which is more than that of the printed page. These are the book's obvious merits; it has some equally obvious defects. Mr. Huxley tends to take his characters too literally and too photographically from the life. One becomes a little tired of Mrs. Aldwinkle, whose prototype shows too crudely through the disguise of the 'character', and who, unless I am mistaken, has appeared before as a model in Mr. Huxley's novels. The objection to a novelist 'drawing from the life' is, of course, absurd; but he does so at his peril, and the nearer he keeps to reality, the more perilous is his method. Mr. Huxley is much too skilful and sensitive a writer to give us 'life' crudely and undigested, as the realist does, in his novels; but it is just as bad art to set before the reader real characters who have not been properly absorbed and digested by the writer, and this Mr. Huxley, I think, does too often.

A more serious criticism of Mr. Huxley is that he does not seem to be quite certain of what he is aiming at. His book is on a different level from the ordinary novel, and he must be criticized from a much higher standard. In writing his book, he clearly has a purpose other than that of merely writing a seven-and-sixpenny novel of 400 pages. He would probably say himself that his purpose was artistic and quite different from the purpose of Mr. Shaw in his novels. But I am not sure that there is not a good deal of confusion in the use of the term 'novel with a purpose'.

[Discusses some 'purposes' in Shaw's novels]

. . . Now Mr. Shaw sometimes forgot completely that his object was to write a sermon, and then we are given simply and solely, for page after page, a most amusing cross-section of life; sometimes he remembers that he ought to be writing a sermon, and then, being a man of simple and direct methods, he stops his novel and makes one of his characters, Trefusis usually, spout the sermon. There is something, too, in Mr. Huxley's book which answers to Mr. Shaw's sermon, for, if you try to define it, to dissect it out of the fabric of the book, it can quite naturally fall into the form of a 'lesson'. It is neither so simple nor definite as Mr. Shaw's purpose. The nearest that I can get to it in a few words is to call it a philosophy of life. All the talk of Cardan and Mrs. Aldwinkle, the contrast of character between Chelifer and Calamy, and the final scene in which Calamy leaves the 'indoor sport' of love-making in order to contemplate on a hill-top are, in a sense, meaningless except in so far as they are informed by this central idea of a philosophy of life. As a mere work of art, Mr. Huxley's novel fails very much as Mr. Shaw's novels fail by vacillating between photography, didacticism, and art. Mr. Shaw thinks that he is didactic, but gets so interested in his story and characters that he suddenly remembers that he has forgotten the moral; Mr. Huxley thinks that he is writing a modern novel without a purpose, and every now and then gets so interested in his purpose that he forgets the story and characters.

Where Mr. Huxley fails, he fails in company with practically all novelists who are now writing. They do not know exactly what they are after. Is it to tell a story, 'delineate character', or give a cross-section of life? None of these things, by themselves, are going to produce a first-rate novel, and clever writers like Mr. Huxley recognize this, and attempt to overcome the difficulty by superimposing on the typical novel, with its characters and story, a philosophy of life. But superimposition is always fatal in art. To superimpose a philosophy of life upon a story does not produce a work of art any more than to superimpose a story upon a sermon. But a great novel might be—probably has been—produced by allowing a story to grow out of a sermon or a philosophy of life to grow out of a story.

32. Gerald Gould, review in *Saturday Review* (London)

31 January 1925, cxxxix, p. 108

For a biographical note see No. 22. See Introduction, p. 11.

Mr. Aldous Huxley continues to go up and down like the line on a temperature chart. He is often brilliant and very seldom less than entertaining; he continues obstinately to be promising; but he is getting to a state at which to be promising is to be disappointing. *Antic Hay* contained some delicious things, amid a great deal that was not delicious;

one began to hope that the strong vein of poetry would outvie the strong vein of facetiousness in the author's talent; *Little Mexican* followed, and two of the stories in it seemed like a fulfilment of that hope, so sane, clear and adult were they; it seemed that Mr. Huxley had but to shed his more obvious weaknesses and his next volume must be a masterpiece. But, instead of that new leaf, we get *Those Barren Leaves*. It is a remarkably readable book; but it puts the prospect of a masterpiece further off instead of nearer. It is clever—O so clever!—just when one had hoped that Mr. Huxley was outgrowing cleverness. It is satirical—O so satirical—but it employs the easiest devices of parody for its satire. The plot, which faintly recalls that of *The New Republic* ('The little less, and what worlds away!'), is broken by the introduction of the autobiographical form. There is a gathering of the usual people—the wealthy lion-hunter, the *blasé* man-of-the-world, the lady-novelist, the labour-leader, and so forth: to them enters a young intellectual, and the narrative is interrupted so that he may give the story of his life. Not that the hero inserts his narrative as an episode into the main story, like Odysseus or Aeneas: there is no such reconciliation of forms: the 'Fragments from the Autobiography of Francis Chelifer' are just simply presented as a different medium for the telling of the story, and, after a little while, we are with equal abruptness switched back to the third person. From then on, the characters talk and make love. Most of them do both: all do one or the other. One of the most persistent talkers, however, being somewhat advanced in years, and terrified by the prospect of an impoverished old age, diversifies the general atmosphere of amorousness by taking severely practical steps towards marriage with an imbecile who has some money: he is frustrated by her death. The long and numerous conversations show an astonishingly wide range of acquaintance with fact and theory, but few of them go deep. Indeed, it would not be possible for any human brain to be deeply familiar with all the subjects on which Mr. Huxley touches. One is left wondering why he touches on so many. He attempts to give some of his speculations a factitious interest by making his characters utter them in unusual circumstances—circumstances, I mean, unusual as a setting for such speculations. Thus a young man, being alone in the dark with a young woman, says:

[Quotes Calamy to Mary on 'an almost inconceivable number of atoms', Part V, Chapter I, p. 344]

I suppose that sort of thing can be taken from an up-to-date text-book of physics: in a text-book it would be interesting enough: but I do not find it highly amusing in a novel. Surely any novelist could make any of his characters expound any technical matter at any moment; and if all that is required, to turn the dull into the delightful, is the introduction of unexpected physical concomitants, why should not everybody be a brilliant novelist? As thus: 'He took her in his arms and pressed his lips passionately to hers. "Darling," he murmured; "an adjective agrees with its noun in number, gender and case."'—'Strange love-talk, is it not?' And the set-pieces of metaphysical discussion are crude. They would pass for bright among undergraduates—at any rate they would have done so when I was an undergraduate—but the discussers are supposed to be, not undergraduates, but mature men of culture and experience. Of course, Mr. Huxley says some good things; but he seems to be content with effects curiously unworthy of the power and beauty of his own mind. 'The upper hem of his trousers followed an ample geodesic.' Is not that simply bad writing? It fails as description: it fails as facetiousness. And I could quote scores of parallels to it from these pages. On the other hand, it is really witty to say: 'She pictured to herself a Calamy who was one of Nature's Guardsmen'—though even that is much less successful than Mr. Bernard Shaw's description of the man at the bottom of the poll as one of 'Nature's M.P.s.'

I pay Mr. Huxley the compliment of serious and detailed adverse criticism, because I am convinced that he is, in natural capacity, one of the best among the younger writers. I believe he has gifts which, properly cultivated, would assure him a permanent place in English literature. But he will not achieve that place by books such as this— though even here there are some lovely things. The sketch of Francis Chelifer's mother and her pre-war home in Oxford is drawn with the tenderness—and therefore with the truth—which Mr. Huxley so rarely allows himself: and, for some of the natural descriptions, I must revert to the word 'brilliant'. For instance:

[Quotes the description of Hovenden's approach to Volterra, Part IV, Chapter I, pp. 275–6]

Certainly, 'brilliant' is not too strong. But all the more does one feel that a man who can write like that ought not to be content to give us the distinctly less admirable stuff which makes up the bulk of *Those Barren Leaves*.

33. Unsigned review in *NYTBR*

25 January 1925, p. 9

The review is characteristic of several which were already identifying Huxley as a spokesman for his generation. The hope that Huxley would lead his generation out of its post-war frustration would be expressed with growing volume and intensity during the coming decade.

Mr. Huxley has disappointed us. His progress from the light-hearted ideas of *Crome Yellow* to the deft caricatures of *Antic Hay* and the drift from character to action that was presaged in 'Young Archimedes' has led nowhere. It is the tragedy of the 'young English intellectuals' who have hailed Huxley as their chieftain that this leader has preyed upon and exploited their shallow shams and solemn absurdities with the apposite skill of Satan rebuking vice; it is Aldous Huxley's misfortune that, to date, he has not been able to rise above his source and that his work, for all its sparkling charm, should have made no more progress toward fruition than has his generation.

Those Barren Leaves is clever, extremely clever, with the metallic brilliance that we have learned to associate with this author. But we fancy that he is more than a little weary of these cul-de-sac adjectives; 'brilliant' and 'clever' admit no thoroughfare; they are pigeon holes; and Mr. Huxley will have to retrace a considerable distance before he emerges from his maze. Sterile, static, devoid of action and crammed with desultory, irresponsible ideas, *Those Barren Leaves* is almost a description of itself; even as the autumnal glory of the falling leaf owes its chief beauty to dissolution, so we find here an iridescence akin to decay. The narrative staggers elaborately along, beautiful in its articulations, but invertebrate in its effect, without arriving anywhere, much like a drunken man circling a lamp-post. Here and there we find a flashing phrase that lights up the surrounding verbiage with an effect of heat-lightning and which is about as serviceable as heat-lightning as a guide unto our feet. Now and again we find a trace of that precocious smartness which has damned the work of most of his contemporaries, and occasionally we stumble upon a jewel-like sentence which reverses the Shakespearean analogy and which contains within it some toadlike thought.

The chief literary merit of this book is in its characterizations. . . . [T]hese are presented in a whirl of scintillant conversation, aborted epigram and scarifying analysis. The plot is about as conclusive as the operation of a merry-go-round: the semblance of motion is there—staked out much as a surveyor marks the site of a projected structure—but there is little relative change, no progression of action or of character, merely a gyration to tinny music, which is entertaining to observe, but one remembers that the only prize in store for those who win the brass rings by reaching from the backs of Mr. Huxley's wooden horses is the privilege of another ride. Getting nowhere, proving nothing, talking self-consciously, analyzing interminably, these characters are the lay figures of a biting satire on a rather inane set of people, who indeed are barren leaves. Unfortunately their barrenness has proved infectious to the detriment of a writer whose talent for description and exposition of sophisticated character is rather perfect.

Perhaps, after all, it is the fault of the times rather than of the man. Mr. Cardan expounds this attractive thesis with a charming cynicism:

[Quotes Cardan, Part I, Chapter III, p. 35]

Nevertheless, to the average man it seems rather stultifying to devote 400 pages of beautiful language to demonstrate the futility of the concededly futile.

However, the amateurs of the vogue for examining their friends under a microscope, the adepts in the art of breaking beetles on a wheel, will not be deterred from their enjoyment of Aldous Huxley's youthful zest for pulling the legs off flies. And perhaps he is right when he says that he has no patience with 'the jolly optimistic fellows who assure us that humanity is all right, because mothers love their children, poor folk pity and help one another and soldiers die for a flag,' who are comforting us on the grounds that 'we resemble the whales, the elephants and the bees.' Life for this generation has not been edifying, and the greatest tragedy of the war is the spectacle of slain and mutilated ideals. If ideals seem illusions to men like Huxley, it is because he chose the wrong time to be born rather than because he is that sort of man. And much must be forgiven him because of his genuine reverence for those aspects of beauty which are changeless, and because this latest, smartest, bitterest exponent of the de-idealized generation whom he represents and which imposes its own limitations upon his writing can still lift up his eyes unto the hills of natural beauty and draw from them a strength of style which cannot be destroyed by the vacuity of his literary structure and which may, in the end, lift him from the pit into which he and his generation have fallen.

34. Joseph Wood Krutch, review in *Nation* (New York)

18 February 1925, cxx, pp. 190–1

For a biographical note see No. 14. The title of Krutch's review is 'Divine Philosophy.'

The English house-party is conducted upon a broadly tolerant principle. Anyone with the slightest modicum of individuality—even if it be merely enough to make him a recognizably distinct variety of the general class of bores—is considered eligible; and while one man is invited because he has won a great battle another is likely to find himself asked merely because he happens to be mad upon some unhackneyed subject, like trousers for women or the cross-breeding of white rats. The result is not only a delightful social institution which offers the opportunity to study more different varieties of the human animal than can be found in any other similarly restricted area, but also a perfect framework for the satirical novel. In *Those Barren Leaves*, as in a previous work, Mr. Huxley takes advantage of it and is able, without the slightest apparent lack of verisimilitude, to bring together in the Italian villa of an English lady a marvelous menagerie which includes among others, a lady novelist, an aging parasite, a gilded youth interested in love and the other arts, and the impecunious editor (lately down from Oxford) of the *Rabbit Fanciers' Gazette* as well as a variety of minor personages who are all sufficiently distinguished by some virtue or defect to be regarded by their eclectic hostess as 'interesting.' Of each he draws an unforgettable satiric portrait, and in their company he continues his search, long ago begun, for that which, lacking a better word, we must still call his soul.

Incidentally, and lest these remarks should seem, by their flippancy, to imply the contrary, it may be said that Mr. Huxley has never written a richer book or one in which clearer or more cogent thought lay behind the superficial extravagance of his manner. Perhaps because he himself revolted in horror from his own hideous masterpiece, *Antic Hay*, he has returned to the manner of *Crome Yellow*, delicately pinning and neatly labeling his butterflies instead of breaking them upon the wheel of his scorn; but behind it all is clearly visible a desperately lucid mind which has sought in vain for some unmistakable reality, moral, philosophical, or scientific, but which has found nothing which could, with any assurance, be called more than appearance. Tentatively and with a disarming smile of self-mockery he puts into the mouths of his editor or his amorist the speculations of his own astoundingly detached intelligence; but they lead him nowhere. The collapse of the religio-philosophical attempt to find a meaning in life and the impotence of science to say more than that life lives and reproduces itself seems to him to leave no rational course open except the ancient pursuit of wine, women, and song. The second is the essential member of that trinity, and one need take only a single look at the mechanical amorist to realize that love, unless it be made resplendent by some mysticism or at least fascinating by some prohibition, is no passion great enough to fill a life. The oratorical enthusiasm of Mr. Falx, who perceives the promise of life fulfilled in the imaginary contemplation of millions of laborers housed in model tenements, he cannot share; but the aesthete and the Don Juan bore him no less. He is not content to dismiss St. Peter's as no more than the tangible evidence of the existence of a past age of oppression. Yet when he turns to beauty for consolation he finds Mrs. Aldwinkle, with her 'large and inarticulate enthusiasm' for all works of art, the type of those who are willing to worship the beautiful without trying to discover in it the meaning which he has never been able to find; and in Mrs. Aldwinkle's especial admiration for Filippo Lippi—who 'though but a friar had the strength of mind to run off with a young girl at a convent school'—he suspects not unnaturally that he has discovered the source of her aesthetic appreciation, namely, a gentle titillation of those amorous passions of which he is already weary. The circle is, it seems, closed. We live to love or we love to live, and whichever way we choose to take it the one seems no adequate justification of the other.

It is Mr. Huxley's ill-fortune as a man and his good-fortune as a writer that he happens to be possessed of an absolutely detached mind which, however much it may share the natural human longing for certitude and fixity, never deludes itself into believing that it has found them. Given any premise he can elaborate it with clarity, logic, and force into a world-philosophy; but he always chooses to put this philosophy into the mouth of another because he knows perfectly well that, given another premise, he can produce another system quite as logical as the first. In *Those Barren Leaves* we have presented the thinker, the aesthete, the sociologist, and the epicurean, and we can take our choice; but we know as Mr. Huxley knows that none is good or satisfactory. Once, when he was just emerging from the Victorian belief in rational progress as an adequate substitute for Providence, he tried to believe in science; but science showed him, in *Antic Hay*, only a hen which was trying to crow because male organs had been grafted on her, and the only implication was the insistent suggestion that character, personality, and the soul were no more than the result of some obscure chemistry. Today in *Those Barren Leaves* he has come to say:

How charming is divine philosophy! . . . Gall and Mesmer have given place to Freud. . . . Can we doubt that human intelligence progresses and grows greater? Fifty years hence, what will be the current explanation of Filippo Lippi? Something profounder, something more fundamental even than faeces and infantile incestuousness; of that we may be certain. But what, precisely what, God alone knows. How charming is divine philosophy!

35. T. K. Whipple, review in
Saturday Review of Literature

7 March 1925, i, p. 576

Thomas King Whipple (1890–1939) wrote books on *Martial and the English Epigram* (1925) and modern American life (*Spokesmen*, 1928), and he contributed to *New Republic*, *Yale Review*, *Nation*, and others.

His alert judgment that Huxley expresses his own concept of fiction via the mocking portrait of Miss Thriplow is verified in the *Letters*. His review is entitled 'Brilliance and Brilliants.'

In *Those Barren Leaves* Mr. Huxley has closely followed the formula he used for *Crome Yellow*. He has shifted the scene from an English to an Italian country-house, but otherwise little is changed. Like its predecessor, the present novel is a record of a house-party, in which is gathered a group of diverting eccentrics who make love in what time they can spare from their perpetual conversation. And, as one of them exclaims, 'what a classy conversation!'—ranging over all topics from love and death and art to the Etruscan language and the breeding of mice and rabbits. As in *Crome Yellow* there was the pathetic episode of the dwarfs, so in *Those Barren Leaves* there is the pathetic episode of the half-witted Miss Elver. And it is all clever and amusing and well written—that is, suavely and somewhat ornately written. The performance is fully up to Mr. Huxley's reputation as a lavish entertainer, brilliant and sparkling; and even if some of the sparklers are not genuine stones, the stage-effect is as good as ever. Mr. Huxley has never assembled a better cast of characters. Mrs. Aldwinkle, rich, romantic, sentimental, and middle-aged; the ingenuous pair of young folk, Irene and Lord Hovenden; Mr. Cardan, the cynical epicure and indefatigable talker; Miss Thriplow the novelist, so much the victim of her own poses that one never learns what, if anything, she is really like; Chelifer, the poet who fled all the amenities in search of 'reality', which he thinks he has found in editing *The Rabbit Fanciers' Gazette* and in living at Miss Carruthers's boarding-house in Chelsea; Calamy, whose natural bent toward love-making and whose predilection for mystical contemplation ill agree—and so on. *Those Barren Leaves* is an excellent example of the smart, sophisticated novel, and very post-war.

They like my books (Miss Thriplow is speaking) because they're smart and unexpected and rather paradoxical and cynical and elegantly brutal. They don't see how serious it all is. They don't see the tragedy and the tenderness underneath. You see . . . I'm trying to do something new—a chemical compound of all the categories. Lightness and tragedy and loveliness and wit and fantasy and realism and irony and sentiment all combined. People seem to find it merely amusing, that's all.

Surely Mr. Huxley could not have written that passage without thinking of his own works. Nor is his protest altogether without justification, for, impossible as it seems, many readers seem to have missed the marked tragic theme in *Antic Hay*—a theme which is still more marked in *Those Barren Leaves*. From the beginning Mr. Huxley has shown a fondness for the role of the broken-hearted buffoon, and has given us many variations on the theme of *Pagliacci*; in his last two novels, he has depicted a Dance of Death, has grown more and more macabre.

His tragedy might be called the tragedy of incongruity. He is nothing if not ironical. He has a keen eye for inconsistencies of all sorts—for the disagreement between circumstances and human wishes, between facts and human beliefs, between flesh and spirit, between action and purpose, between emotion and intelligence. By a process of disintegration, he reduces human life and human beings to a chaos of warring elements. He likes to blow little bubbles of sentiment in order that he may prick them, especially he likes to mix the categories of the mental and the mechanical. For instance: 'The greatest tragedy of the spirit is that sooner or later it succumbs to the flesh. . . . The tragedies of the spirit are mere struttings and posturings on the margin of life, and the spirit itself is only an accidental exuberance, the product of spare vital energy, like the feathers on the head of a hoopoo or the innumerable populations of useless and foredoomed spermatozoa.'

Mr. Huxley's tragedy is also the tragedy of freedom. Most of his people are sceptics who have emancipated themselves from belief in anything, have freed themselves from the last scruple, restraint, or prejudice—'religion, patriotism, the moral order, humanitarianism, social reform'—says Chelifer—'we have all of us, I imagine, dropped all those overboard long ago.' The result is boredom and futility. Nothing matters; what can one do save seek oblivion in the distraction of the senses, in ever cruder and stronger sensations? Thus in the end Mr. Huxley's is a tragedy of nervous exacerbation, beneath which always beats the refrain of Ecclesiastes. His work is a treatise, in twentieth-century terms *de contemptu mundi,* or perhaps *de contemptu vitae.*[1] But at the end of *Those Barren Leaves* is heard a note which heretofore has been absent from his writing; in the best mediaeval manner, Calamy forsakes the world to try to lead the meditative or contemplative life. Perhaps this action is merely another of those vagaries to which Mr. Huxley's characters are given, such as Chelifer's editing of *The Rabbit Fanciers' Gazette*; but I think not. For one thing, throughout the final discussions as to the nature of reality there runs an almost H. G. Wellsian solemnity. For another thing, it is natural that nowadays disillusion should continue to lead where it has always led, to mysticism, and that scepticism should still lose itself finally, as it has always lost itself at last, in an O Altitudo. Not, of course, that Mr. Huxley commits himself; but he seems to suggest, with somewhat more seriousness than is usual with him, that in mystical contemplation there might possibly be an escape from the inanity of life.

I do not wish, however, unduly to moralize Mr. Huxley's fantasies. They remain, when all is said, chiefly means of amusement—amusement for those who enjoy sophistication. Mr. Huxley may complain if he likes that his readers don't see the tragedy and the tenderness underneath, and we readily grant that the tragic element is there—but we may retort that it is no more than a spice which adds piquancy to the entertainment, like the doleful melodies, which are jazzed in the 'blues.' It is true that Mr. Huxley's theme is 'All is vanity and vexation of spirit'; nevertheless, what matters is less the theme than the treatment of it. To talk of mixing lightness and tragedy and wit and irony and sentiment is all very well—but the result of the mixture turns out to be merely amusing. How could it turn out otherwise? To write tragedy in terms of burlesque is, after all, to write burlesque; to write romance in terms of farce is to write farce; to speak flippantly of pathetic matters, or of anything else, is to be flippant. When Mr. Huxley puts his fantastic puppets through their antics, the spectacle is diverting, but it cannot well be moving; and those of Mr. Cardan's persuasion who say, 'True, I like to be amused. But I demand from my art the added luxury

[1] 'In contempt of the world,' 'in contempt of life.'

of being moved,' will necessarily care less for Mr. Huxley than for more single-hearted and simple-minded writers who are unsophisticated enough to afford them that luxury.

36. Conrad Aiken on Huxley's conversational style

1925

Conrad Potter Aiken, b. 1889, poet, novelist, critic, recipient of a Pulitzer Prize and a National Book Award for his poetry, as well as the Bollingen Prize (1956) and the National Medal for Literature (1969).

The text of Aiken's essay is from *Criterion*, April 1925, ii, pp. 449–53. The essay also appeared in *A Reviewer's ABC* (New York: Meridian, 1958), pp. 225–30. See Introduction, p. 11.

Mr. Aldous Huxley has acquired a remarkable position among the younger novelists; and there can be no question that he is—to use advisedly a term perhaps a little invidious—a very accomplished writer. It has been freely suggested that he is brilliant; it has been taken for granted that his position is unique. Of his three novels, and three volumes of tales, it has been urged that they witness to the evolution of an 'artist' in fiction: it has even been suggested that the artist thus posited may, ultimately, prove to be great. If this attitude is a trifle solemn, nevertheless one willingly enough subscribes to a part of it. Mr. Huxley *is* exceptionally accomplished; his talent *is*, in the contemporary medley, conspicuous; and it is not for nothing that critics have so unanimously pronounced him to be ophidianly clever. The latter quality, indeed, has occasioned a particularly loud chorus of encomium. The critics, and Mr. Huxley's audience, have been pleased to dwell on something a little sinister in it, and a little naughty. It has been seen as a peculiarly delicious blend of the best wit and most ingenious *morbidezza*[1] of the 'nineties' with the very latest fashions (and modern improvements) in morals and ideas from Paris and Vienna. There is also, it is pointed out, his erudition. How astonishing his ease and copiousness of allusion! And what could be more appropriate, in this post-war world of sad, gay disillusionment and scientific luxury, than Mr. Huxley's macaronic *mélange*[2] of the classical and the up-to-date, of Peacock and the *fin-de-siècle*, of Folengo[3] and Freud? Mr. Huxley's affinities, in this respect, are easy to find. During the last decade there has been what one might almost call a macaronic 'school'—an international school concerned with satire, with burlesque, and, in the absence of any stable convictions concerning art or morals, with the breakdown of forms and the extensive use of reference and quotation. If Mr. Huxley does not go as far as some in the direction of the *cento*,[4] he at any rate shares in that tendency.

It is this absence of conviction that most impresses one in his work; it is in this that his cleverness, his wit, his queer, uncomfortable ingenuity of fancy seem to strike their somewhat shallow roots; and one begins to wonder, after reading his sixth book of fiction, how likely it is that a basis so insubstantial can make of Mr. Huxley the writer one would like to see him become. Mr. Huxley seems himself to be in some doubt about this. He has steered a somewhat uncertain course. He has always had a little the air of one who could not quite decide how serious he dared to be, or to what extent the act of being serious is a kind of naive confession of credulity, a lack of sophistication which might be too maliciously enjoyed in drawing-rooms. This ambiguity was pretty clear in his first book, *Limbo*. The beginning of a serious attempt at seriousness can be seen there in such stories as 'Happily Ever After' and 'Richard Greenow'; but in both of these the impulse to be clever, to be sophisticated, finally triumphed, with the result that they were not successful either as satire or as credible fiction; neither very amusing nor wholly true. In *Crome Yellow*, his next book, it was natural that, taking so frankly the Peacockian model, Mr. Huxley should also take a step backward, a step further away from the actual. *Crome Yellow* is as artificial, as flimsy, and, alas, as unreadable as a clever book can be. The

---

[1] 'Softness, delicacy.'
[2] 'Mixture.'
[3] Teofilo Folengo (1491–1544), the most important of the Italian macaronic poets.
[4] 'A piece of writing composed wholly of quotations from the works of other authors.'

occasional note of sincerity, of verisimilitude, of feeling, of seriousness, which now and then almost brought his characters alive in *Limbo*, has here been deliberately exorcised; and in its place Mr. Huxley abandons himself to his terrible passion, a passion positively narcissistic, for conversation. His *personæ*, totally lifeless and indistinguishable one from another, are merely ventriloquist's puppets, the device by which he can indulge himself, as often and as long as he likes, in witty talk. Has Mr. Huxley a frustrated desire to be a great conversationalist? The question is an impertinence, but it is one that it is difficult to refrain from asking; for, despite its ingenuities, *Crome Yellow* is simply an apotheosis of talk, talk in the most exasperating drawing-room style. One sees, of course, what Mr. Huxley was after—he indeed tells us himself, describing the 'great Knockespotch, who delivered us from the tyranny of the realistic novel. . . .'

[Quotes Chapter XIV, p. 102]

There, of course, but for the grace of God, goes Mr. Huxley. He, too, has a passion for the superlatively and purely articulate, for intelligences (but not emotions) relieved of imbecile preoccupations, for immense erudition, immense fancy, incessant wit, and a verbal surface richly semined (to borrow his method) with oddities that smell of camphor. He shares, also, with the great Knockespotch, his passion for ideas. One imagines him sitting with Bartlett in one hand and *The Times* in the other, compiling thus his *omnium gatherum*[1] of the antique and the quotidian, and turning it all into airy talk: setting it in motion with his easy and skilful rhetoric; giving it the accomplished twist that imparts a sparkle. One is aware that he regards this purely as a kind of boring game; he wishes to give the impression of employing his skill automatically, as if without too much lending to the performance either mind or heart; but one also perceives, as noted above, a secondary Mr. Huxley who wants, a little timidly, to do something else.

For in *Mortal Coils*, *Antic Hay*, *Little Mexican*, and now in *Those Barren Leaves*, it is perhaps not altogether fanciful to guess a growing doubt in Mr. Huxley's mind, a doubt as to whether the great Knockespotch is, after all, the best model. To be incessantly frivolous, to try in every phrase to be diverting, to round unctuously and a little smartly every sentence, to conduct with so Mozartian a grace his glassy passages of sustained bravura from page to page—can one, by this method, achieve the best? It is true that occasionally he manages this sort of

[1] 'Collection of everything,' i.e. hodge-podge.

thing with delightful skill. 'Nuns at Luncheon' could hardly be better. It is perhaps as triumphant an example of a dexterous and heartless *playing* with a tragic theme as one could find. Not wholly satisfying— for the click of the spring at the end is too sharp, too prepared, too small, and serves only to reveal the story as an anecdote (like many of Mr. Huxley's stories) comparatively empty of beauty, of feeling, of intensity, and indeed actuated more by a desire to toy with the theme, holding it at arm's length, than by any deeper concern. This externalism has a peculiar and delightful effect in this instance: an effect as of an inverted sentimentality, a deliberate frolic in the presence of tragedy. But the method is not one that can be used *passim*; and, unfortunately, the habit of doing so, of trying always to remain cynically aloof, has been indulged by Mr. Huxley too long to be easily broken. In *Antic Hay* it is obvious that he wants to concern himself more deeply and frankly with his characters, and invites his readers to do so; but the Mr. Huxley who enjoys buffoonery and burlesque insists on introducing his satirical ingenuities, which are ungainly rather than diverting, and his saffron interludes, which are pawky rather than frank. It is not, in consequence, a satisfactory satire, since one believes in the characters too much; it is not a satisfactory novel, since one believes in them too little.

The same difficulties must be urged against *Those Barren Leaves*. It is Mr. Huxley's best work, and it marks, perhaps, the sharpest single advance that he has made. It is rich, it is witty, it is admirably if ornately written. But if Mr. Huxley the buffoon is less in evidence, Mr. Huxley the non-stop conversationalist, and Mr. Huxley the cynical onlooker, are still all too tediously here. It is difficult, therefore, to judge his capacity for 'seeing' a character in the round. Has he, indeed, as yet, created a single character in whom one can believe, who escapes the Huxleyan gesture and intonation, and obeys a *daimon* of his own? He comes closer to Miss Thriplow and Irene than he did to their many prototypical predecessors, with whom they share their bell-like bobbed hair, round eyes, and doll-like faces. Chelifer and Calamy and Cardan— these, too, have moments when they come alive, are perhaps a little more recognisably and dimensionally real than Gumbril, with his pneumatic breeches and false beard, or Mercaptan with his sofa. But Mr. Huxley still has his uncontrollable appetite for talk, still strives to be that 'miracle of nature, breathing libraries.' Scarcely has a character begun to take on the warmth of the actual, or the action to be enticing, when off he goes once more into endless discussion; the drawing-room style puts on its quotation marks; effective phrase is added to effective phrase, paragraph to paragraph, page to page, no matter who it is who happens to be speaking; the reader's will to believe is remorselessly defeated; and we are presented at last not so much with a story, or a series of character studies, as with another tremendous example of Mr. Huxley's highly cultured conversation. Chelifer, Cardan, and Calamy become interchangeable shadows, and, if all three are divinely articulate, it is not themselves they talk into existence, but their author. Chelifer's 'autobiography' is indistinguishable in tone from any other part of the story. Was it—one asks after closing the book—Calamy who was the poet, and Chelifer, who, wearying of his amorous successes, became a mystic? Was it in this novel, or in *Crome Yellow*, that the dashing young lord, with his lisp and high-powered car, flew from one house-party to another? Was it Calamy or Chelifer or Cardan who talked so well, and who so perpetually and wearily fell into love and out again?

But this is ungrateful. The book is, when one has weathered the first hundred pages, extremely entertaining. The Chelifer section is managed with a technical virtuosity that any novelist must envy; and many of the interpolated discussions—notably that of Cardan on art—contain admirable criticism. If only Mr. Huxley could abjure his habit of cynical intrusion, and wear for a little, without shame, his heart on his sleeve, one feels that he might achieve something very fine indeed. Could he not also, for a time, give up these emancipated house-parties and exquisite boudoirs? We encounter them, in his pages, far too often.

37. Carl and Mark Van Doren on Huxley

1925

Carl Van Doren (1885–1950) served as editor for The Literary Guild 1926–34 and received a Pulitzer Prize in 1939 for his biography of Benjamin Franklin.

Mark Van Doren (1894–1972) was literary editor of the *Nation* 1924–8 and wrote many critical essays, some collected in *The Happy Critic* (1961). He was President of the American Academy of Arts and Letters in 1959, when the Academy gave Huxley its Award of Merit for the Novel.

The following two excerpts are from the Van Dorens' *American and British Literature since 1890* (New York: Century, 1925), pp. 162, 210–11.

[The authors have been discussing the emergence of 'radical poetry' in early twentieth-century England. Several of Huxley's early poems appeared in *Wheels* from the 'second cycle' of 1917 to the last issue in 1921]

. . . It was not until 1916, however, that the new movement seriously began. In that year appeared an anthology of queer, wayward poetry called *Wheels*, which shocked a public accustomed to traditional poetic themes and melodies. The authors of *Wheels* were so delighted at such a reception that they issued four other volumes in quick succession. The spirit of this new literature is iconoclastic. The poets are satirists with a vengeance, bent upon mocking conventional minds at every turn. The most gifted of them is Aldous Huxley, a brilliant, perverse young man whose two volumes of poetry[1] have deservedly attracted great attention. He is the most fitting representative of a satiric school which is likely to leave a deep mark on English poetry. At least he is the most fascinating

[1] *Leda* and *Selected Poems* (1925)—selections from *The Burning Wheel* and *The Defeat of Youth*, which had not been published as such in America.

spokesman of a generation disillusioned by war and intellectual confusion everywhere. In 'Frascati's,' a characteristic poem, he shows his contempt for the well-fed middle class which, as will later be seen, has been a target throughout the twentieth century for attacks from important dramatists and novelists.

[The following excerpt is from pp. 210-11]

The tendencies of prose fiction in the present decade are carried by Aldous Huxley to much the same conclusion as that to which he carries its poetry. From irony like his it will be possible for his followers to escape only by turning to romance, by resolutely shutting their eyes to doubt and by deliberately feeding upon hope. In the meantime, his position is very striking. With the rest of his generation, he has come to suspect the validity of the ways of life which were generally accepted during the past century but which were broken up in the turmoil accompanying the recent war. He has seen the established virtues practised without reward and the established vices practised without penalty. He has seen prudence dejected and folly triumphant. Moreover, the unusual amount of learning which he possesses confirms him in his pessimism. History has assured him that the general direction of mankind is full of purposeless drifting; science has assured him that men, if more than puppets, are at best no more than animals. The mystery of life itself may possibly be discovered to reside in the atom. The mystery of character, of love, hate, ambition, devotion, may turn out to depend upon the chemical action of obscure glands. Human existence may therefore be best regarded as a dance, either a dance of life or a dance of death. Thus, indeed, the matter is regarded in Huxley's novels and short stories. He fills them with persons, mostly belonging to a leisured class, who profess the maddest ideas and follow the most unregulated careers. His masterpiece, *Antic Hay* (1923), exhibits a group of smart and intellectual Londoners all contending in their different ways with the discomforts of boredom. They are not, strictly speaking, a group, for they come and go with only occasional contacts, weaving a pattern which Huxley knows is meaningless. He does not seem to be distressed by their eccentric habits. He at least allows them to say and do whatever they will, concerned himself with nothing but making an ironic comedy out of the performance. Always perfectly self-possessed, he plays his sardonic wit over his characters, finding something absurd in every step they take. Yet back of this apparently irresponsible mood of his lies something more austere. He genuinely admires the undeluded intelligence. He has a secret longing for a universe which should be orderly and just, harmonious and beautiful. Not finding it, he suffers disappointment, which imparts to all he writes that note of bitterness which is as obvious as his mirth. His bitterness gives him, as an artist, one of his chief merits. However ironically he may represent his whirling world, he holds his materials well in hand and shapes them with cutting outlines.

Repellent to many readers as Lawrence and Huxley are, they at any rate are noteworthy as indicating an honesty and an energy in the new generation which must insure distinction to fiction in the future. Whatever the younger novelists decide is important or unimportant, they may be trusted to follow their decision to its bitterest end. They will be savage, perhaps; they will in spite of that, or possibly because of it, unearth unexpected facts of human nature, and they will present these facts with a sincerity and a genius which fiction at no time in the twentieth century has been without. They will only carry on a work begun by Moore, Conrad, Wells, Bennett, Galsworthy, and Maugham.

38. Edmund Gosse on *Along the Road*

Sunday Times (London), 4 October 1925, p. 8

Sir Edmund Gosse (1849–1928), prolific essayist and widely honored scholar, author of the novel *Father and Son* (1907) and many books on international literature. This essay was entitled 'Wander-Birds and Mr. Huxley' for Gosse's World of Books column, which was a regular feature of the *Sunday Times*. The sub-headings are here omitted.

Yoi Maraini, after an interview with Huxley, wrote of this essay: 'That his place in the world of letters is fully recognized can be judged by the fact that Sir Edmund Gosse—ever ready to acclaim those who have won their crowns—wrote a long article on this last book [*Along the Road*] in the *Sunday Times*' (*Bermondsey Book*, p. 80). See Introduction, p. 12.

This is the ninth book which Mr. Aldous Huxley has published, and he has become what my dear friend R. L. Stevenson used to call 'quite a little Man'. In the quotidian crop of promising young sprouts which every decade puts forth, there are always some few who are not withered by the frost of incapacity or mown down by the sickle of economical distraction. They are saplings who, while we are going about our daily chores, unobtrusively push up into the light and become trees. Mr. Aldous Huxley has already overtopped most of his fellows, and boasts a trunk with branches. I cannot hope to live to see him a finished ornament of the forest, but I believe that my descendants will so see him. My earliest impression of him was as a poet, with a little mythological epic of 'Leda,' which was agreeably objective and un-Georgian. The form of it was founded, I thought, on that of Keats's 'Lamia'; I believe I said so, without, I hope, giving offence, since all good early work is founded on some masterpiece. Apparently, the Muses did not seriously adopt Mr. Huxley, as he has developed into a prose-writer, pure and simple. I will say, without reserve, that he has already become one of the best English prose-writers of his generation.

His prose takes the shape of novels, among which the latest, *Those Barren Leaves*, is the best; of short stories, where he gives way to a certain wilful madness, which I like best in *Limbo*; and of essays, of which the specimens now before me are the first which I have met with. I am almost afraid to say how much I have enjoyed *Along the Road*, because I am not quite sure how far I am prejudiced by the circumstance that many of these impressions of travel reflect to a quite singular degree my own whims and recollections.

In his early works of fiction I have been conscious of a certain turbidity, a stirring up of the lees with the wine, a palpable design to show himself uncompromising, which the author seems to be now steadily outgrowing. He strains his imagination more than he used to do through the jelly-bag of experience, and this is a very good thing if it does not carry him too far. I am not one of those who have ever been seriously 'shocked' by Mr. Aldous Huxley, though I confess myself a little averse from the scatological. He has shown himself an apt student of the caprices of the flesh, and I am not ready to throw a stone at him on that account. But I am pleased to find him growing tamer even in this respect.

He must not grow too tame, since it is the privilege of his age to be outspoken. I should be sorry if his chrome yellow turned to decayed vegetable colour. I cannot avoid a smile when I remember that the irony of the generations makes him the grandson of that magnificent puritan of science whom we all admired so justly half a century ago. Professor Huxley was kind to me in my early youth, and I had (and still have) an unbounded respect for his genius. But in æsthetic matters he was a John Knox, if not a Savonarola. I shudder when I speculate what he would have thought if he had lived to read *Antic Hay*. I have a distressing memory of my being openly reproved by him at a dinner party for praising Rossetti's poetry. 'Nothing in it but devilish sensuality!' the great man roundly declared, reducing me to abashed silence and impotent indignation. When young critics inveigh against the narrowness of Victorian morality, they are apt to forget that it was the giants of scientific investigation who held the fort for Mrs. Grundy. By the side of Huxley and Faraday and Darwin even Tennyson seemed dissolute and Matthew Arnold a trifler. It was curious how the roundhead came out in the heroes of biological revolution.

There is nothing in *Along the Road* which would alarm the illustrious professor. Perhaps the fact that all these chapters (as I suppose) were contributed in the first instance to the periodical Press has checked the flow of the author's extravagance. When we write for the million we have to curb our tendency to paradox. The subject of these essays may be roughly defined as a confession of the illusions of travel, and of the limitations which its practice presents to us in advancing life. The curiosity of change of scene, for its own sake, has never, I gather, vehemently swayed the nerves of Mr. Aldous Huxley; he has never been a traveller of pure rapture, such as Pierre Loti[1] was, to whom the discomforts of the route were rather a stimulus than a discouragement. Mr. Huxley can never have breathed the poet's prayer:

> Let loss of luggage count as gain
> To them who travel by the train,

yet there evidently was once a time when he enjoyed travelling in a sense which now fairly fails him. He once walked; and then he came to depend upon the railway; now nothing serves but he must indulge his whims in a motor-car; and even in his attitude to the car we detect a heresy which must soon become fatal. He yields to the mania of more speed. His reflections on racing are as deplorable as they are amusing. He no longer cares what country he goes through, if he only can go through it fast enough. He hankers after the insolence of 40 h.p. The way in which he paints his jealousy of motorists more rapid than himself is extremely diverting, but it unconsciously reveals a sad decline, since the traveller who becomes a mere glutton for speed is a genuine traveller no longer.

The unity of these brilliant and amusing essays consists, then, in their disillusion. The book is a confession of the futility of travel. It is the clear and even poignant lament of a soul which once murmured by the running brooks a music sweeter than their own, but now cares for no sound less raucous than the voice of 'a huge red Alfa-Romeo road-racer'. It is true that the transformation is not complete. Mr. Huxley still thinks that he hates the road-racer, but his error is patent in the obsession which that dreadful object has for him. It fills his thoughts; the mountains and the lakes, the cathedrals and the castles, have no longer any power to arrest his attention. Mr. Huxley conceives no pleasure any more in travelling at less than fifty miles an hour. To do this he will, doubtless, presently contrive; he will be able to change his modest Citröen for such a shrieking scarlet monster as he longs for. And then he

---

[1] Pierre Loti (1850–1923), French writer whose travels provided an exotic décor for his novels and reminiscences. Huxley thought he was 'rather maudlin' (*Jesting Pilate*, p. 226).

will certainly travel no more, since what will be the use of motion any longer? The nemesis of h.p. 40 is an armchair by the fire.

The Germans call a tourist a Wander-Bird, and the name is quaintly appropriate to a quiet, aimless species of travel. Mr. Aldous Huxley, approaching the fatal turn of his happiness, looks back on the time when he was himself content to be a hovering wander-bird, and he sees it without illusion. He enjoyed his picture-galleries and his cascades immensely when they were new to him, but he detects elements of distress even in those recollections, and he yields to an almost conscientious scruple when he warns us of their inevitability.

Mr. Aldous Huxley, let me hasten to add, if disillusioned, is never cynical. Sterne declared that Smollett should have reserved his impressions of Italy for his physician. There is nothing morbid about Mr. Huxley's candour. Simply, he has tried Europe and found it wanting. The H.P. racing-car has destroyed his sensitiveness, and he is lost to the simple pleasures of the golden age. This volume of his essays is a *vademecum*[1] for the traveller who is ceasing to care for travel and cannot tell why his appetite is failing. Mr. Huxley tells him why, and shows him that a man who has once yielded to 'violent and purely physiological stimuli' must never even wish to taste again the glory and the joy of sauntering.

For a spirit so cloyed it is remarkable how freshly the memory of Mr. Huxley retains the impression of its earlier raptures, and how gaily it is able to transmit them to us. The earliest section of this book, containing the author's reflections on travel, is the most original and even amusing, yet it is likely that the others will be read with even greater satisfaction. So much has been written since the comparatively colourless days of Evelyn and Addison about the picturesqueness of Italy that the subject might seem to be exhausted, but Mr. Huxley has found several nooks in that rich country which have been hidden from other eyes. His attitude towards Italian resentment of foreign admiration is sympathetically droll; but while he is trying to persuade himself that he is a Marinetti, Mr. Huxley remains at heart more a Beckford than ever.[2]

In some of these studies he attains a fine completeness of impression. Dozens of travellers have tried to bring before us one of the most vivid survivals existing in Europe, the yearly ceremony of the Palio in Siena.

---

[1] 'Handbook.'

[2] Filippo Tommaso Marinetti (1896–1944), Italian writer, founder of the literary Futurist movement; William Beckford (1760–1844), English man of letters and patron of the arts, who scandalized society by his extravagant ostentation and defiance of convention.

It has never before been painted so successfully as by Mr. Huxley in an essay where he has allowed himself more space than usual. The Palio itself is the painted banner presented to the successful jockey at the end of the race. As an object of art it offended Mr. Huxley's taste, when everything else in this living restoration of a Pinturicchio fresco delighted him.

Into his critical judgments of the works of art presented to the notice of the Wander-Bird, most of which might as well be presented to the docility of a sheep, Mr. Huxley brings a keen independence and a mixture of rapture and irony. Instances of the latter are 'Conxolus', a study of an imaginary old master of the thirteenth century, on whom the reputation of a fashionable art-critic can be based; and 'The Pierian Spring', an examination, no less just than humorous, of the chaos of taste which prevails in the art world to-day when no single canon is recognised, but a thousand warring conventions are timorously welcomed:

[Quotes 'Gone is the blessed ignorance . . .' p. 195]

This is sound, yet it is difficult to see what can be done to prevent the breaking-up of the old standards of taste. The tendency rather is to add to the confusion of our æsthetic values, and to invent new watchwords for the vigilant snobbishness of our connoisseurs. The great advantage of the old masters was that they flourished when there was nothing to distinguish a good painter from a mediocre one except the excellence of his draughtmanship and his modelling. One definite type being alone accepted, individuality was not tempted to exhibit itself in anything but pure technical proficiency.

TWO OR THREE GRACES

May 1926

39. L. P. Hartley, review in
Saturday Review (London)

5 June 1926, cxli, pp. 686, 688

For a biographical note see No. 20.

However good Mr. Huxley's work may be one rarely reads it without a small pang of disappointment. To surpass themselves is for many novelists a comparatively easy task; but here is one who has contrived to set his own standard so high that, captivate and divert us as he may, he still seems to fall short of a proposed excellence. The shadow of a commanding talent and a distinguished mind is thrown across each page, but though Mr. Huxley has many altitudes that are visible enough we can never quite descry that single peak which puts so much, even Mr. Huxley's own work, into the shade. Perhaps it is to his disadvantage that he makes his meaning so clear: he is the victim of his own lucidity. He has such a gift for expression that for the imagination to look beyond the written word in search of private overtones seems an impertinence. And the imagination, always eager to contribute its little quota, however futile and irrelevant, resents being warned off in this way, and sulks because it may not co-operate. It complains that Mr. Huxley makes Aunt Sallies of his characters, setting them up simply to bowl them over with a few good shots, and that these figures of unreason are sometimes too near and too flimsy to justify their impressive bombardment by Mr. Huxley's heavy guns. Grace Peddley, for instance, in the first and most important story: is she made substantial enough to carry our interest through her various metamorphoses, her ungraceful,

137

almost disgraceful, antics as one man's wife and two men's mistress? Are we prepared to shed tears, as Mr. Huxley seems to require us to, over such a figure of fun? But the mind delights in the humours of Grace's progress, rejoices in the deft exposure of Peddley, Rodney and Kingham, never withholds its laughter when for the hundredth time Mr. Huxley demonstrates that futility is futile. It is even impatient of the softer note that has lately crept into Mr. Huxley's voice and makes a faint deprecating undertone to the brilliant derisive music with which he plays his characters out of his pages.

'Half-Holiday' is the best story of the collection. The poor young man whose romantic day-dreams have led him, on behalf of two beautiful young ladies, to interpose in a dog-fight and get bitten, cannot restore the creature because of his stammer:

[Quotes Peter's embarrassment, pp. 208–9]

After this delicious bit of comedy it was a pity to give the story a bitter and unhappy ending: it does not quite 'come off'. At his best Mr. Huxley 'comes off' as few living novelists do. And our enjoyment of his work depends upon its successfulness. If there is no 'pop' we know the wine is flat. Mr. Huxley's work has no intermediate quality; it is flat or it is effervescent. He is a literary acrobat, setting out to do a difficult feat perfectly; he makes no attempt to conceal his virtuosity; he calls upon one to hold one's breath. He may take a tumble, but his successes, of which there are many in *Two or Three Graces*, are as undeniable and as instantly recognizable as if they were the work of the hand, not of the pen.

40. Joseph Wood Krutch, review in *Nation* (New York)

2 June 1926, cxxii, p. 612

For a biographical note see No. 14. The title of Krutch's review is 'More Barren Leaves.'

Krutch's continuing insistence that Huxley's early work contains a strong moral undercurrent may be compared with a remark in the *Letters*: 'I never really feel that I am performing a wholly *moral* action, except when I am writing' (p. 191). See also *B*, I, p. 201.

Mr. Aldous Huxley, probably the most intelligent of *les fauves*,[1] exhibits alternately the two moods, the disdainful and the explosive, of his mind. In the first he is an aloof satirist regarding human follies with an air of great detachment and describing them in a style of limpid simplicity; in the second the mask drops from his face and reveals the pain which lies behind it. Tolerant contempt gives way to ferocious hatred, classic irony to raging disgust, and the author descends from his Olympian height to struggle desperately with the problems which he had mocked others for not solving.

This second mood, definitely foreshadowed in the satiric poems which formed the bulk of the volume called *Leda*, received its fullest expression in that hideous masterpiece *Antic Hay*. An obscene farce at the heart of which lay an utter despair, it seemed to reach the uttermost possible limits of hatred for a world in which nothing could be believed and nothing, not even debauchery, could be enjoyed. Beyond it lay nothing except the desperate conversion of a Huysmans, and perhaps for that reason Huxley has never since let himself go completely. In

---

[1] Literally 'the wild men' or 'beasts'; refers to a group of early twentieth-century artists who splashed brilliant, jarring colors onto their canvasses in rebellion against the sober browns and blacks of Victorian painters.

Those Barren Leaves as well as in the present volume there are occasional glimpses of the black abyss from which *Antic Hay* was born, but the mask is resumed and confession is checked. The author, turning his eye upon this character or that situation, regards it with an aloof ironical gaze and pretends to have found his own fixed point of peace—though he never reveals to us just where it is—in the midst of the flux which he describes.

The world with which he deals is essentially a world where there are no faiths but only an infinitude of poses. Biology, anthropology, psychoanalysis, and the rest have made it impossible for anybody to be sure of anything. There are people who pretend to believe in art, in science, or even in morality, but at bottom they know that they have only taken up attitudes and they are so used to pretending at faiths and passions that they do not themselves know when they come closest to sincerity. Painters talk glibly of forms, physiologists of glands, and philosophers of complexes, but none of them know where they are or have continued very much to care. At their best they manage, like the painter Rodney in the present volume, to obtain a success by some simple device; his consists of painting provocative green nudes in a distorted setting. At their worst they merely stand, like one of the minor characters, in the midst of a drunken party and bawl: 'We're absolutely modern, we are. Anybody can have my wife so far as I'm concerned. I don't care. She's free. And I'm free. That's what I call modern.' Between them there is not much to choose and they meet on a common ground. One and all they drink and couple, the only real difference being the extent to which they can dramatize their monotonous experiences.

Such is the milieu of the story 'Two or Three Graces,' which gives its title to the present volume and which constitutes more than two-thirds of its bulk. Its central character is a pleasant, simple, and rather stupid woman who is drawn into the chaos which she understands rather less than those who make it. Somewhat after the manner of Chekhov's 'Darling' she assumes in desperate earnest the tastes and the poses of her lovers. While she lives with the painter she talks of 'drinking life like champagne' and of 'the duty of obeying one's whims'; when she becomes the mistress of the neo-Nietzschean philosopher she tries her best to be the vampire 'possessed by a devil of concupiscence' which it pleases him to pretend that she is; but all the time she cannot help taking the poses more seriously than those do from whom they are imitated. While they pretend to suffer she really does, and we leave her desperate at the end of one of her affairs, yet inevitably destined to do an eternal *da capo*.[1]

It is a grotesquely tragic story, one which might, indeed, have been woven in as one of the many threads of *Antic Hay*, but it differs in that it is written with an air of ironical detachment which conceals the desperate disgust the former book set out clearly to reveal. In it Mr. Huxley no longer shrieks. He pretends almost to be writing again in the mood of mere satiric extravaganza which marked *Crome Yellow* and which caused him to be compared to Peacock. His clear self-possessed sentences are polite and calm, his analyses minute and unexcited. And yet for all the careful impersonality of manner it is the essential serious-ness of his mind, his real concern with the world and its ways, which gives to him his strength. He is at heart no aesthete and no mere Olympian satirist. As surely as the most solemn of moral philosophers he is in search of the good life, and it is the bitterness of his disappointment in not having found it that sets his work so far above that of our merely precious sophisticates. Essentially too serious of mind to be content with the cleverness which is so abundantly his, and possessed of a mind too powerfully critical to fall a victim to any sham philosophy, he has wandered unhappily through a life which has so far revealed to him nothing in which he could believe; and if he has described nothing but folly his descriptions have been significant for the very reason that he would so infinitely have preferred any wisdom that he had been able to find.

[1] 'Going back to the beginning and repeating.' A familiar musical notation used in Huxley's story.

41. Unsigned review in *NYTBR*

14 November 1926, pp. 4, 18

Before the following extract the reviewer has been discussing Huxley's reactions to India and America as expressions of the individual mind of 'a young English intellectual rebel.'

. . . Mr. Huxley, behind all his descriptions and analyses and pertinent comments, is asking a question, and that question is the famous one that Pilate put forth and to which he received no answer—'What is truth?' It is the basic truth of humanity for which Mr. Huxley seeks, and he has about as much chance of finding it as Pontius Pilate had.

Mr. Huxley's book is always informed with a wit and lightness of manner that carry agreeably enough the deeper tones implicit in the subject matter. He writes with great ease, and the informal diary-manner in which *Jesting Pilate* is composed is, if anything, an added charm to the book. The emanation of a defiant and individualistic personality rises from the pages, a personality that is essentially modern as we understand modernity today—inquisitive and restless with the shackles of custom and convention, a personality intellectualized and thoroughly sophisticated. His book, therefore, is as much an expression of the time as it is a fleeting glimpse of many strange places that girdle the earth. It is the type of travel book that should please the reader who is as much concerned with the spirit of the world as he is with the colorful material aspects of foreign lands.

42. Unsigned review in *Spectator*

30 October 1926, cxxxvii, p. 764

According to the paper's files, the reviewer was E. J. Strachey—neither John St Loe nor his son John, but probably Edward Strachey, b. 1882, quite likely John St Loe's nephew.

A new kind of travel book seems to be emerging. They are 'travel diaries' rather than descriptions of topography; they record the spiritual rather than the physical voyages of their authors. Keyserling's *Travel Diary of a Philosopher* was an early and remarkable example of this kind of book. Mr. Huxley has now produced another.

Mr. Huxley has, in the flesh, been round the world, but his mind has travelled even further than his body. He has found, it seems, a new and far firmer moral outlook upon the world than he has ever achieved before, and the result is, to put it bluntly, that he seems in a fair way to be becoming a great writer. Perhaps he has found a medium in this travel diary which is really more suited to him than fiction. Each new sight and sound that his circumnavigation brought to him has evoked the most amusing and often the most stimulating reflections. Take, for example, the very first entry in the book. A cargo is being unshipped in Port Said; Mr. Huxley watches quintal after quintal of potatoes being swung out of the hold and dropped into the lighter alongside—

[Quotes from p. 3]

The next part of the book is about India and Burma. Many of the things which Mr. Huxley says about the architecture and institutions of that country will strike English ears as unusual. They may even give offence; but Mr. Huxley must not always be taken too seriously. What seems to have happened is this: Mr. Huxley, confronted with the 'immemorial East,' suddenly discovered himself to be very definitely a Westerner. The spirituality of the East might seem very attractive amidst the rush and clangour of a Western Metropolis or even from the comparative distance of Port Said. But amidst the filth, the despair, the lackadaisical degradation of India, the thing had a different appearance.

[Quotes passage on Hindu 'spirituality,' p. 109]

This reaction has perhaps led Mr. Huxley to be unfair to India. He certainly says some apparently unjustifiable things about its architecture.

Cruising down the Hooghly on his way still further East, and away from India, he is led to these desperate reflexions:—

[Quotes reflection on suffering populace, pp. 159–60]

But perhaps the most entertaining and certainly the most fantastic part of the book is the section on America. What could be at once more brilliant or more illuminating than the beginning of the entry headed 'New York'?

[Quotes from pp. 280–1]

The most notable of Mr. Huxley's observations concern London. He has returned from all his voyages and wishes to sum up.

A great growth of scepticism is, he tells us, the most striking result of his journey:—

I set out on my travels knowing, or thinking that I knew, how men should live, how be governed, how educated, what they should believe. I knew which was the best form of social organization and to what end societies had been created. I had my views on every activity of human life. Now, on my return, I find myself without any of these pleasing certainties.

But more interesting still he feels that this scepticism itself has its limits. He sums this up in a sentence: 'The established spiritual values are fundamentally correct and should be maintained.'

[Quotes long passage on 'our sense of values,' pp. 290–1]

This is indeed a remarkable conclusion for the author of *Antic Hay*. Yet the circumspect reader of Mr. Huxley's early works could, we think, have foretold that something of the sort would ultimately occur.

43. T. S. Eliot on Huxley

1927

Thomas Stearns Eliot (1888–1965), poet, essayist, and critic, a renowned writer and powerful shaper of literary opinion in his time, recipient of a Nobel Prize for Literature in 1948.

The excerpt is from Eliot's essay on 'The Contemporary English Novelist,' *La Nouvelle revue française*, 1 May 1927, pp. 669–75. The translation is by Thomas M. Donnan, a member of the staff of the Foreign Language Department, State University of New York at Geneseo.

Huxley and Eliot had met at Garsington (*MV*, pp. 30–2) and kept up correspondence into the 1930s (*L. passim*). See Introduction, p. 15.

Mrs. Woolf's work is something Mr. Lawrence's could never be; the perfection of a type. Although it faithfully represents the contemporary novel, there is nothing to be found in it that completely resembles it. It is perhaps more *representative* than the work of Mr. Joyce. To take up another line, a novelist must possess not only great gifts but a great deal of independence as well. 'Moral interest' cannot be simply 'restored': Conrad's strong man, fallen, is already nothing more than a sentimental relic. This interest has to be rediscovered like something new. Mr. Aldous Huxley, who is perhaps one of those people who have to perpetrate thirty bad novels before producing a good one, has a certain natural—but little developed—aptitude for seriousness. Unfortunately, this aptitude is hampered by a talent for the rapid assimilation of all that isn't essential and by a gift for chic. Now, the gift for chic, combined with the desire for seriousness, produces a frightful monster: a chic religiosity. It is at this point that one should fear for Mr. Huxley. In his last long novel, *Those Barren Leaves*, the adolescent self-analysis, in its scathing caricature, seemed as though it had been written under the influence of some momentary mystical or ascetic impulse although it was only the lyrical outcry of a destitute heart. It wasn't yet definite enough to give form to the characters or to the atmosphere in which they lived. Mr. Huxley is at least dissatisfied with himself and the society which he photographed with such precision and desolation in his recent story, 'The Monocle'. But his nature is very strongly imbued with sentimentality, and he still runs the risk of falling into the rank of an amusing modern variant of René or Werther.[1]

[1] René I (1409–80), French prince who wrote a mystical dialogue, *The Mortification of Vain Pleasure*, which was resurrected in an edition by F. Lyna in 1926; Werther, hero of Goethe's *The Sorrows of Young Werther* (1774).

POINT COUNTER POINT

October 1928

44. Unsigned review in *TLS*

4 October 1928, p. 706

The reviewer's observations on Huxley eschewing 'the craft of fiction' (itself a reference to Percy Lubbock's study of fictive technique, *The Craft of Fiction*, 1925) may be compared with the analysis by Frank Baldanza (No. 137). See Introduction, p. 14.

At the end of *Those Barren Leaves* a man named Calamy went away to meditate upon reality. In Mr. Aldous Huxley's new novel, *Point Counter Point*, a man named Rampion propounds a notion of reality which Calamy was very unlikely to have found in solitary meditation, because it is a discovery that could only be made in active social life. For Rampion the 'central norm' was humanity. He was ready to explain what he meant by humanity, and therefore was not talking through his hat when he declared the world to be 'an asylum of perverts' from that norm, 'perverted towards goodness or badness, towards spirit or flesh,' perverted by the imagination, the intellect, its principles, its tradition and education, perverted in morals, in politics, in science, in business, in war, in love, trying always to be something other than human.

That is the theme; and the counter point is made of several different departures from the norm. The sort of departure that most allures and most offends Mr. Huxley's mind is excess of sexuality; and once more, with no sparing of physical detail, he reveals the various kinds of dislike with which he regards it. But though carnal lust is the showiest it is by no means the only divagation from the norm of humanity which exercises him. Into this long, loosely made, episodical book he has poured, out of a dozen different vessels of his thought, his anxieties about many a difference between human life as it is and human life as he thinks it should be, and his indignation with those who, in one way or another, are leading men astray from their humanity. The reader has no right to commit Mr. Huxley to Rampion's notion of what human life ought to be; but there is every sign that he shares Rampion's disgust, anger, and distress at human life as most people are made to lead it. More than any of Mr. Huxley's previous books this is 'a novel of ideas', as one of the characters, a novelist, would call it; and some of the difficulties which Philip Quarles saw in the novel of ideas seem to have beset Mr. Huxley. 'I never pretended to be a congenital novelist,' wrote Quarles; and the phrase suggests a warning from Mr. Huxley that he has not tried to make this new book a good example of the craft of fiction. It does not weld story and ideas into one: it cares little about progression, proportion, climax, and so forth. In spite of a few masterly scenes and descriptions, the persons always come second to the ideas. But that is not to say that the book is without form. The author's purpose was to set point counter point: to pose these various forms of rottenness against each other and against human soundness. He sometimes jolts us, sometimes for a moment bewilders us; and sometimes he strains our credulity because he has allowed the idea which the character stood for to dictate the plot (cocaine, not murder and suicide in search of the absolute, would have been the end of the Spandrell whom we meet at first). But the book does what it set out to do; and does it with all the strength and sensibility, the acuteness and the impatience, of Mr. Huxley's mind.

45. L. P. Hartley, review in
Saturday Review (London)

20 October 1928, cxlvi, pp. 514–15

For a biographical note see No. 20. See Introduction, p. 14.

Mr. Huxley's new novel contains all the ingredients of his former books, but hotter and stronger and in greater abundance. It is an imposing and a dangerous dish, not meant for queasy stomachs. One naturally thinks of the stomach in connexion with Mr. Huxley's work; he does so love to turn it. He feints at the heart, he attacks the head, but where he really hits one is in the wind.

It is difficult to review him. His work is never raw; it is in an extraordinary degree pre-digested. The able critic and reviewer who is sleepless (too sleepless) within Mr. Huxley himself leaves little scope for the comments of external colleagues. Moreover—a personal matter—to criticize him one cannot help identifying oneself in some measure with the literary men who throng the pages of *Point Counter Point*, men who have taken to journalism 'as a drug', men like Burlap, whose talk is specious but whose private lives . . . [sic] However, here goes.

Point Counter Point is a novel of some six hundred pages, a crowded canvas filled with all sorts and conditions of men and women, for the most part interested in art, science, politics, philosophy and love, generally intelligent, always articulate, and liable to be seen at Lady Edward Tantamount's evening parties in Pall Mall. Mr. Huxley arranges them in little groups, each with its own centre of interest, each with its relation, conversational, or amorous, to the rest; and these groups he manipulates (as far as prose can do it) contrapuntally, the various motives succeeding and interlocking with each other. It is said that art should approximate to the condition of music, and Philip (one of the most sympathetic figures in the book) explains how he means to apply the theory to novel-writing. But the 'condition of music' cannot be attained merely by imitating musical technique. Prose can convey a

149

sequence of single moods and mark the transition between them. It can only feebly present the interaction of ideas, it is too fluid a medium of expression. The motives that should enhance and illustrate each other converge like rivers and forfeit their identity. In Mr. Huxley's work the supply of ideas is enormous, the play of mood limited.

For a general criticism of the novel, and all Mr. Huxley's novels, one cannot do better than refer to Philip, that clever, gentle, diffident, sensitive creature, welcome whenever he appears, a piano passage in the general blare:

'I wish one day [says his wife] you'd write a simple straightforward story about a young man and a young woman who fall in love and get married and have difficulties, but get over them and finally settle down.'

'Or why not a detective novel?' He laughed. But if, he reflected, he didn't write that kind of story, perhaps it was because he couldn't. In art there are simplicities more difficult than the most serried complications. He could manage the complications as well as anyone. But when it came to the simplicities he lacked the talent—that talent which is of the heart, no less than of the head; of the feelings, the sympathies, the intuitions, no less than of the analytical understanding. The heart, the heart, he said to himself. 'Perceive ye not, neither understand? Have ye your heart yet hardened?' No heart, no understanding. . . . 'That simple story of yours,' he said aloud, 'it wouldn't do. . . . It would have to be solid and deep. Whereas I am wide; wide and liquid. It wouldn't be in my line.'

This passage, of course, overstates the case. *Point Counter Point* is both solid and deep; but its solidity and depth are intellectual, its foundation in life is more flimsy. The reasons for this are plain. Mr. Huxley is a puritan, perhaps a Manichee, and a moralist. He regards the physical and intellectual functions of mankind as hopelessly irreconcilable; men are, as the verse says, 'vainly begot and yet forbidden vanity, created sick, commanded to be sound'. The consciousness, tormented by this self-division, must take one side or the other, and he throws in his lot with the intellect. But so self-lacerating is his sensitiveness that it takes perverse delight in dwelling on all the more discreditable links between man and matter. In his jaundiced regard imperial Cæsar is always clay stopping a hole. Sick-room incidents, the phenomena of illness, revolt him so much that he harps on them for pages. One of his characters in youth gets hold of a pornographic novel describing the amorous adventures of a major. The book inflicts on him so deep a psychic wound that when, later, his mother marries *en secondes noces*[1] a military

---

[1] 'In a second wedding.'

man he never forgives her. Towards the end of the book the wretched Philip's house is the scene of a double tragedy, his little son dying of meningitis, his father-in-law dying of cancer. Mr. Huxley's world is a hospital, in which there are no screens and all the physical signs of illness are ruthlessly insisted upon.

These dismal convictions Mr. Huxley illustrates by a thousand manifestations of modern life. He seems to omit nothing; there is even mention of a Baby Austin. He overwhelms us with knowledge, wit, feats of caricature. Almost everything Mr. Quarles says is funny. There is an unremitting crescendo of pace, volume and excitement, until with murder and melodrama symbolizing the activities of the flesh, and Beethoven's air in the Lydian mode signifying the aspirations of the spirit, the book reaches a violent end. One gasps. Mr. Huxley, like Mr. Dreiser, has given life a very bad name. But was it worth while collecting all this curious evidence to establish a charge, the groundlessness of which is obvious to anyone? I think it was; for setting aside Mr. Huxley's conclusions, where else shall we find so brilliant and compendious a diagnosis of the modern world? Most novelists are content to describe it without reference to the progress of scientific discovery; Mr. Huxley takes all knowledge for his province and simplifies without vulgarizing it. A curious scientific fact awakes him to passion; he has a power akin to Donne's of investing it with poetry. His mind finds categories everywhere; no two objects so dissimilar that he cannot fit them into a relationship. Under the fire of his scrutiny the most prosaic, concrete object, a poker for instance, loses its material quality and is melted into a solution where pokers are as abstract as thoughts. It is not his technique, excellent as that is, but the unifying power of his vision that exalts his work into the condition of music.

46. R. A. Taylor, review in *Spectator*

13 October 1928, cxli, p. 498

Rachael Annand Taylor (1896–1960), poet and critic, was reviewing almost weekly for the *Spectator* at this time.

Mr. Aldous Huxley's new novel, like its predecessors, communicates an intellectual excitement and a nervous exasperation. It is an experiment in what his Philip (a novelist within a novel, like André Gide's Edouard) calls the 'musicalisation of fiction'. The two-part oppositions of voices, imploring, blaspheming, lamenting and resigning, weave a contrapuntal fabric that seems to cease in mid-air. Mr. Huxley begins by describing the heavenly pattern of Bach like any angel; his own music of humanity is of the Stravinsky kind. Certainly his effort towards capturing simultaneousness in time, though not entirely novel, is stimulating to the intelligence. In the first half of the book, at least, the two-part themes well up wavelike, one beneath the other, with a wonderful iridescence and fluidity of texture. 'Story, God bless you, Sir! I've none to tell you,' says Mr. Huxley with the Needy Knife Grinder. His London intellectuals and libertines, philosophic and otherwise, disenchanted, sardonic, too deliberately satyric, go on talking; and, for all his fling at Proust, remembering. Enraged idealists all of them, wreaking their disappointed hopes in excesses of materialism, and exploiting viscera instead of hearts with a rather undergraduate kind of blague. Story? Well, there's a murder towards the end, of an incredibly casual kind. If somebody had murdered the verbose Mark Rampion, perversely put forward as the wise and normal man among his perverse neurotic friends, it would seem more natural. All of the talkers being contemptuous of love, they are consequently rather obsessed by the problem of sex. Mr. Huxley takes too many of his types from the pathology textbooks: old Mr. Quarles, Spandrell, Carling, Lucy Tantamount, that young Messalina with the manners of an ill-conditioned schoolgirl, are 'cases' in need of the alienist rather than the novelist. Yet the book is crowded with provocative creatures, some of whom are mere birds of passage, like the enchanting Polly Logan. The exposure of Burlap, that merchant of the world of sentiment, is masterly as well as ferocious. Moods of sad and lovely regret flower like groups of jonquils in the corners of the bitter chapters. A learning both wide and ardent enriches the pages with remote fair images. The passage in Time which forms this novel, with all its chords of ironic pathos and desperate disdain, has a plangency that must echo long in the disturbed memory.

47. Review in *New Statesman*

20 October 1928, xxxii, p. 56

Signed 'C.C.' and identified in the paper's files as Cyril Connolly, b. 1903, critic, novelist, founder of the British *Horizon* (1939), regular reviewer for the *Sunday Times*, author of, for example, *Enemies of Promise* (1938) and *The Modern Movement* (1965).

Connolly was a persistent reviewer and acquaintance of Huxley's (a detailed account of their relationship appears in *B*, I and II, *passim*). See also Nos 90, 113 and 141.

This review is entitled 'The English Morand.' See Introduction, pp. 4–6, 14.

This, if not Mr. Huxley's best book, is certainly his most important. Though it occasionally happens that the mind of an author continues to develop with the years, there is in every writer a period when his emotions are not only most intense, but most in harmony with their surroundings. Mr. Huxley, admirably gifted for a modern Petronius, was also blessed with a Petronian universe to be young in. Paul Morand,[1] who resembles him in many ways, equally was able for a moment to

[1] Paul Morand, b. 1888, French writer, author of some of the best short novels in the language, a perceptive and witty observer of the modern world.

voice that post-war world, and almost to direct it; but while M. Morand has flung himself rather convincingly into the modish subjects of Hollywood, Harlem, and the Yellow Peril, travel seemed to have had on Mr. Huxley only the pernicious effect of broadening his mind. Robbed of the unity which his intellectual and picaresque bias gave him, he seemed to be more and more reasonably adapting himself to the reasonable man. Progress is a steady accommodation to the second rate, and Mr. Huxley was clearly progressing. This is why *Point Counter Point* is such a critical book. Were it a re-hash of the world of *Antic Hay* it would be a sequel; were it a sincere and worthy recantation of intellectual dandyism, a burning of the vanities, it would be a failure and only bear out the 'Too old at Forty' rule which seems to be spreading over literature as over sport. Luckily it is neither. There are worthy passages, as irrelevant as they are worthy, and there are worthy people; but they are treated intellectually and the result is a novel with a finer grasp of the emotional realities of ordinary people than the author has ever managed before. Yet all the old cleverness remains, and practically all the old intensity.

The beginning is the most difficult part, for there are several rather august digressions, and the characters, described so fully, turn out all to be minor ones. Also the method by which the affairs of a great many people are described simultaneously necessitates the introduction of the whole of the orchestra at once, a rather bewildering confusion. Essentially a satirist, the author succeeds best with the characters he has borrowed and the situations he has observed. The wide scope of the novel, however, and its elaborate construction tend to make him trespass on the domains of other writers, and one is being perpetually surprised by these resemblances. The clever, sensitive woman managing her home and dealing with a thoughtless husband and an adoring lover, the rather shy-making tea party wit, Mr. Sita Ram, in Bombay, suggest two obvious authors, while other passages even resemble Mr. Galsworthy and Mr. Maurice Baring. The novel is mainly the picture of a group of people; the author seems most interested in their intellects if they have intellects, and, failing that, in their attitudes to sex and, if they are capable of it, to intimacy. There is also a novelist writing a novel about the other characters, and we are given some interesting extracts from his diary. In one of these he schemes to write a novel about a novelist, and to illustrate the themes from analogies to be made in an aquarium with deep-sea fishes. The *Faux-Monnayeurs* of Gide is exactly this method, even down to the analogies with deep-sea fishes.

Either Mr. Huxley is steeped in the *Faux-Monnayeurs* and is reproducing its form in English, or he is as ignorant as his own novelist (who naively suggests two other inventions for his novel, the themes of Proust and *Ulysses*). Even the sensational murder at the end of the book is close to Gide's and exhibits the same interest in pathological extremes of human temperament which will make stupid people, quite erroneously, call the book unpleasant. But it is surely slavish even to send his salt-water moralist to the same aquarium as Gide sent his to, that of the Prince of Monaco.

Point Counter Point is a slice of life, with a tentative moral, perhaps, in the idea that nothing happens to anyone which it is not in their nature to bring on themselves. This truism is elaborated in a brilliant piece of conversation, till it appears a paradox, and we see the book as a study in the mathematics of justice, not divine justice, but the indifferent, ruthless action of cause and effect which is fascinating to the spectator, but of little consolation to those implicated. There are several nice people in this book, but the author is careful not to be too nice about them, and preserves his impartial cleverness both for the new types and solider emotions he has experienced and for the brilliant, unpresentable intellectuals who continue the tradition of *Antic Hay*. Unfortunately, Rampion, who talks a great deal and whom the author treats almost with reverence, is a crashing bore and no better than the Burlaps and Bidlakes whom he so pitilessly flays. There is a far greater depth of emotion in this book than in any other of Mr. Huxley's and a far wider range of it. His prose has improved and his gift for rendering conversation seems to have become more humanised; the talk, except in the rather wooden opening party, is that of human beings, and the reader can follow it as keenly as he could a broadcast tennis match. Spoken essays have given way to real conversation, the free play in talk of ideas and intelligences. The faults of the book lie chiefly in the beginning. Of the typical Huxley characters, Spandrell, his 'Evil-be-thou-my-good man', lies in a deeper epigrammatic hell than even the satanic Coleman, and his sophisticated young vamp is more flawlessly sensual, futile, cold and heartless. The style of Mr. Huxley is now impeccable, and there is more plot in this book than he has ever given us. Had he lifted less from Gide and incorporated fewer germs for articles and promiscuous reporting, the book would have been technically better. Nevertheless, though not so finished as *Crome Yellow* or so continuously of a piece as *Antic Hay*, *Point Counter Point* is a more constructive satire than either and a more promising one.

48. Joseph Wood Krutch, two reviews

1928

Perhaps Huxley's most persistent American reviewer in the 1920s, Krutch published two reviews of *Point Counter Point* in as many weeks.

For a biographical note see No. 14. See Introduction, p. 14.

(a) Following is an extract from Krutch's review in the *NYHTBR*, 14 October 1928, Section XII, pp. 1–2

Considered as a conventional novelist, Mr. Huxley's defects are obvious enough. His characters are never more than either mere caricatures or, at best, the embodiments of certain points of view. They are not fully alive as the characters of a pure novelist must be and though they have words and ideas they have no blood. His plots have, moreover, singularly little continuity and it is as true of *Point Counter Point* as it has been true of most of his books that there is not, properly speaking, any climax or any conclusion. The book might have been only half as long or it might, so far as any inner necessity is concerned, have gone on for another volume. But *Point Counter Point* is not in any conventional sense a novel even though its superficial form is more like that of a novel than some of Huxley's other books have been. It is, on the contrary, a collection of very brilliant satiric sketches which combine a most accomplished fantastic picture of contemporary manners with comments, at once searching and agile, upon the ideas out of which these manners grow. Unflagging in its spirits and unflagging in its intelligence, throughout more than four hundred pages it vindicates Mr. Huxley's right to be considered the most able of contemporary satirists and the most perfect representative of the mood which he describes. Far less esoteric than certain of those who have reacted against it, and far less superficial than others who have exploited its mere impudence, he has given the most lucid and most complete possible statement of that disillusion which is not the exclusive property of philosophers but which in some form or other manifests itself today in every class of society, from that of the shop girl who is lost in her own way on up to that of the latest product of the best education who is lost in his own way.

(b) Following is Krutch's review of *Point Counter Point* for the *Nation* (New York), 31 October 1928, cxxvii, p. 456

Those who have read Aldous Huxley's novels as they appeared will find nothing in *Point Counter Point* to surprise them except the increased richness and solidity of its satire. The very first of his short stories announced his theme and exemplified his method, but it is not likely that even their author suspected how these stories would expand into longer and longer novels or how every addition to his knowledge and wisdom would fit the pattern there laid out. He has gone on year after year saying the same thing and yet saying it with such unflagging vivacity and such increasing richness of illustration that to many (myself included) he has not only been perpetually interesting but has come to seem the most considerable of those writers who have taken the contemporary intellectual as their subject.

What attracted us first was the depth of his sophistication; among the many smart young men he seemed quite the smartest. No other impudent modernity, no other insolent flippancy in the treatment of respectable platitudes was so accomplished as his and no one else seemed so capable as he of vindicating, by the width of his knowledge and the force of his mind, his right to be scornful. But soon we came to see how far he rose above those of his contemporaries who were content to raise an easy laugh and to float with their characters down a stream of cocktails and kisses. He was impelled to understand the forces which had produced the phenomena he was describing and to grapple with the problems which, whether they are aware of it or not, lie unsolved in the minds of those living, as most sophisticated people do today, on the loose. Without destroying his lightness of touch, even without abandoning the farcical elements which always play a part in his novels, he has managed to make them serve as vehicles for a most comprehensive analysis of the contemporary soul. In them religion and science and sociology wear motley, but they join issue and the joke which knowledge has played upon human nature is fully revealed.

Point Counter Point runs to over four hundred closely printed pages peopled by a score of the most diverse characters. They range all the way from Lord Edward Tantamount, the grave survival from Victorian biology, to sick little Spandrell, the latest model of the eternal wastrel, and they gyrate, one and all, in that spiritual void to which modern thought has reduced them. Tantamount can go about grafting the tails of newts upon the shoulder-blades of the animals from which they have been cut in order to see what will happen; Spandrell can conduct his experiments also with the more esoteric vices; but neither they nor any one else in the book can discover any direction to take which promises them anything at the end of the road.

'What a relief!' said Lord Edward, as he opened the door of his laboratory. Voluptuously, he sniffed the faint smell of the absolute alcohol in which his specimens were pickled. 'These parties! One's thankful to get back to science.' Illidge shrugged his shoulders. 'Parties, music, science—alternative entertainments for the leisured. You pays your money and you takes your choice. The essential is to have the money to pay.' He laughed disagreeably.

But the cream of the jest is simply that there isn't any choice except a choice of escapes. Most choose cocktails and kisses and they are not much more futile than those who pretend graver preoccupations. Illidge seeking social righteousness and Spandrell seeking a thrill assassinate the leader of the British Fascisti; Burlap, editor of a mildly pious literary weekly, slips gently into his lady-assistant's bed; Lord Edward sticks to his newts. Of which is the kingdom of heaven?

Point Counter Point is a terrible book, endurable only because it is also hilarious, and it illustrates once more how remarkable is the balance which its author is able to maintain between mere wit on the one hand and mere indignation on the other.

There were moments in certain of his earlier books (*Crome Yellow* for example) which did not rise above smartness and which might conceivably have been written by any one of the innumerable clever young men who constantly thank heaven that they are so naughty; there were, on the other hand, moments in *Antic Hay*, the most impassioned of his novels, when loathing made him write with the turbid vehemence of a Huysmans; but he is most characteristically himself when he manages, as in *Point Counter Point* he does, to achieve some mood, some acceptance of the material with which he deals, wholly his own.

It is neither the lightness of the joker, the detachment of the pure artist, nor the self-righteousness of the Juvenalian satirist, for he is himself too much a part of the confusion which he describes to attain any of these; but it is something which does enable him to maintain a sort of balance in the midst of events where all balance has been lost. The motley world which he describes—a world in which all sorts of people, from the frank wastrel to the scholar, are united by a common inability to think their way through the confusion of their age—is a painful one and its creator is, at bottom, as lost as any of his creatures, but his very ability to describe and to analyze supplies him a refuge. He looks down from no mountain top and achieves no real serenity; he solves no problems and he sees, in a word, very little further than his characters do. Yet he manages to exist—and to live and to write—in a world where all of the others die some kind of death.

49. Robert Morss Lovett, review in *New Republic*

5 December 1928, lvii, pp. 75–6

Robert Morss Lovett (1870–1956), editor, critic, and teacher, served on the editorial board of the *New Republic* 1922–30 and wrote books on fiction.

The title of his review is 'Vanity Fair Up-to-Date.' See Introduction, p. 14. Lovett's opening paragraphs are omitted.

Point Counter Point is the modern *Vanity Fair*, and Mr. Huxley is the Thackeray *de nos jours*.[1] Both are fundamentally satirists, and play with their characters in a spirit of mockery. Thackeray usually checked the impulse this side of caricature while Mr. Huxley lets it run. Major Pendennis is more real than life itself, while Mr. Huxley's old men,

[1] 'Of our days.'

John Bidlake and Sidney Quarles, are considerably less so. Similarly, Thackeray's Becky Sharp, the *arriviste*,[1] is a finished portrait, while Mr. Huxley's Lady Edward Tantamount, who has arrived, is a poster lady. And in Burlap, Mr. Huxley has stood too near his model and set down something in malice. Both Thackeray and Mr. Huxley are masters of worldly wisdom. They know a great many things about a great many people, but Mr. Huxley is freer to communicate his knowledge. The peculiar attraction which a woman of doubtful reputation has for men, observed by Thackeray, is explained by his successor. 'A bad reputation in a woman allures like the signs of heat in a bitch. Ill fame announces accessibility.'

To neither author is Vanity Fair a moral place. Thackeray had, indeed, an honest code of Christian virtues, but he saw their inapplicability to the society wherein he lived. Indeed, the same charge that is made against Mr. Huxley was levelled at Thackeray, that he presented an ambiguous moral world. In both, virtues have always the defects of excess. Thackeray drew in Amelia Sedley an admirable little woman, whose love, first for her husband and afterwards for her son, defeats its object and becomes a bore. Mr. Huxley, in Marjorie Carling, pictures a woman who has sacrificed everything for her lover, and though she sees the fatal result, she cannot restrain herself from trading on her love and her dependence. Both show a kind of cynicism in marking down the virtues on the moral bargain counter. Thackeray applies the great Victorian test of a renunciation in Fanny Bolton, who nurses Pendennis in his illness, only to be trampled on by the virtuous ladies of his family; and gives him up not to die a nun but to find consolation in the arms of Samuel Huxter. Mr. Huxley saves Elinor Quarles from giving herself to a lover, only through the accident of the illness of her little son, but her virtue does not give life to the boy. And the same accident, by making Elinor miss her appointment, brings Everard Webley, the fascist leader, to his death—but the assassination is not a splendid revolutionary crime, but a mere murder for thrills.

Mr. Huxley, like Thackeray, is fond of having a novelist within his novel. From Philip Quarles' notes upon fiction we can understand his author's attitude toward his form.

[Quotes Quarles's theory of music in fiction, Chapter XXII, pp. 408–9]

There is a Thackerayan touch in the style of this (see Smith and

---

[1] 'Careerist, social climber, go-getter.'

Jones and their respective pastimes), and it is a fair description of Thackeray's structure. He would not, indeed, have thought of himself as 'modulating from theme to theme,' but this is in fact what he does, not as a musician but as a conversationalist. His *Vanity Fair* has been described as a long essay, animated by word pictures or occasional dramatic scenes. Both novelists present a vast inchoate world of events and opinions morally unorganized and socially corrupt. Thackeray, it is true, takes full advantage of his license to appear as showman, a liberty for which Mr. Huxley wistfully pleads but forgoes.

It might be said in its own day that Thackeray's *Vanity Fair* was the richest novel in substance and the most comprehensive that had appeared in English. The same thing might be said today of *Point Counter Point.* It is rich in the experience of many characters, completely understood if not always completely realized. It is rich (and here it passes beyond *Vanity Fair*) in the intellectual background furnished by science in two forms, the mechanics of life and knowledge of its biological and social processes, and by the arts, painting, music, poetry as well as the *ars amatoria*.[1] It is rich in speculative ideas and points of view. Mr. Huxley has given a synthesis of modern culture, and has made it, if not always its exponents, alive. The reader is constantly surprised by the scope of his knowledge and the depth of his understanding, by the keenness of his intuitions and the soundness of his logic. Throughout the wide range and variation of scale and color and mood, in his rendering of action and thought, elevated or vulgar, tragic or obscene, he maintains a largeness of comprehension and a fine equilibrium of feeling that justifies the term, human comedy.

But the English tradition demands a comedian to give relief to his puppets of human futility. This Thackeray understood when he made himself the showman of *Vanity Fair*. This Mr. Huxley understands when he makes Philip Quarles defend the personal appearance of the novelist, but is too self-conscious, in the presence of masterpieces of detachment, to play the part himself. Deprived of this, *Point Counter Point* seems hard, relentless. Yet we must remember that to Thackeray's contemporaries *Vanity Fair* seemed a cruel exposure of mankind, and what impressed them in its author was his cynicism, not his pity. Every age tends to see itself in the cold light of the evening of the world, after the golden morning and the silver afternoon. Perhaps to the next century Mr. Huxley's Georgian London will seem sweet and mellow and inviting.

[1] 'Art of loving.'

50. Amos N. Wilder, review in *Outlook and Independent*

21 November 1928, cl, pp. 1210–11

Amos Niven Wilder, b. 1895, poet, essayist, theologian, writes especially on the relation between the modern temper and the life of the spirit. Two of his most recent books are *The New Voice* (1969) and *Grace Confounding* (1972).

Wilder below has been reviewing several books, among them Virginia Woolf's *Orlando*. His review is entitled 'For Today or for Keeps.'

. . . We are accustomed to think of art in terms of order as we see it, and, if this is especially true of the plastic arts and of music, we must still think of novels and poetry as the products of the creative impulse disciplined by a sense of order into a commonly comprehensible form. And it often seems as though the best of the post-war novelists had discarded form as we know it so that the line between their work and the critical essay, the satire or the expanded character sketch is a faint one. This has been especially true of Virginia Woolf and of Aldous Huxley.

[Wilder's review of *Orlando* is omitted]

We dare not speculate upon the permanence of contemporary work. 'No good book,' says Carlyle, 'shows its best face first.' We believe that *Orlando* will not open all its beauties to the casual reader nor cease to disclose new excellences to him who reads it for the seventh time.

Carlyle also said that 'readers . . . should understand that cases may occur when a little patience and some attempt at thought would not be superfluous in reading.' If that is applicable to *Orlando*, which reads as sweetly as a stream flows in May, how much more is it true of *Point Counter Point*, which reads like a palindrome, the same backward as forward, indeed of all of Aldous Huxley's work, however much the superficial reader may damn it as merely smart or as esoteric. Both patience and thought are demanded in reading *Point Counter Point*, for it is very long and extremely complicated. There is in it incessant contrapuntal play of character against character and situation against situation. It must be indeed shocking to some of the presumably tender minded among the subscribers to the Literary Guild, which circulates it, and even the hardened reader will shrink from some of its brutality. Aldous Huxley's world is minute in its detail, and peopled with men and women who, having found out that nothing is worth doing, do not know what to do next; there is no game worth their playing even if there were a candle to light the board. So they expend their energies, scientist and soldier, big brother and sweet philosopher, stenographer and misunderstood wife and aristocratic tart, in thinking up new ways of doing the oldest thing in the world, only to discover at the crucial moment that there is no new way. Out of such colossal disillusion Huxley has made *Point Counter Point* the most scintillating, the most bitter and the most serious of his novels. It is a notable piece of work and one of which this decade may very well be proud, but, as compared with *Orlando*, its permanence seems doubtful.[1] Huxley's creative talent, his critical sense, constantly at war with it, and his noble background of massed information combine to make his work as provocative as it is entertaining. But the very brilliance of its timeliness must work to date it indelibly. Our children, if they read *Point Counter Point* at all, will probably read it for data on a lost generation.

[1] Huxley's reaction to *Orlando*: 'a tiresome book' which is so 'terribly literary and *fantaisiste* [fantastic] that nothing is left in it at all . . .' (*B*, I, p. 198).

51. Louis Kronenberger, review in *NYTBR*

14 October 1928, p. 5

Louis Kronenberger, b. 1904, critic and editor, is a professor of theater arts at Brandeis University. His books include *Kings and Desperate Men* (1941), *Company Manners, A Cultural Inquiry into American Life* (1954), and *The Republic of Letters* (1955).

The review is entitled 'Mr. Huxley's New Novel Is Savage Satire.' See Introduction, p. 14.

It seemed once, most of all perhaps in his first novel, *Crome Yellow*, that Aldous Huxley had in him, not only brilliant gifts of satire, wit, fantasy and style, but the makings of an important creative novelist. With the passing of time and the writing of other novels, however, he seems less likely to have them. He remains where he began: a satirist, a sophisticate, a worker in the 'novel of ideas.' His people are created statically, they almost never develop, they almost never influence one another, they almost never work together in the interests of a central theme or story. They speculate about life, rail against it, wound and weary one another. That is their function as people. And they call forth in the reader a moral protest against their kind, a moral abhorrence, or dismay, or indignation. That is their function as satire.

In *Point Counter Point* Mr. Huxley is more scathing and savage than ever before in his picture of contemporary intellectuals. In *Antic Hay* the underlying tone was futility, in *Those Barren Leaves* it was boredom. But the underlying tone of *Point Counter Point* is disgust. We go into a world of writers, editors, artists, scientists, musicians, wastrels, dilettantes, society women; and to put it tersely, one is worse than another. These people stoop to trickery, bait the helpless, wound the decent, trifle with young men sincerely in love, drive a woman to suicide, murder a man. Those who are not ridiculous or silly are for the most part vicious or cruel. Only three or four of these people can be deemed humanly worthy.

The aim of this book is not idle amusement for the sophisticated, but a grasping of the intellectual Zeitgeist[1] and a biting criticism of it. Even as a novel of ideas the book attempts to reveal the character of those who express the ideas. We have a hint of this intention in the notebook of one of Huxley's characters.

The great defect of the novel of ideas is that it's a made-up affair. Necessarily; for people who can reel off neatly formulated notions aren't quite real; they're slightly monstrous. Living with monsters becomes rather tiresome in the long run.

Is this an apologia, or just another 'idea'? At any rate, in *Point Counter Point* the people are slightly monstrous. But the fault lies in this particular book rather than in the limitations of the novel of ideas. Huxley himself proves this. In *Antic Hay* the people are not monsters, but valid satiric representations; satire does not run away with itself, but has pertinence and point. This book is ruined by overstatement.

That there is powerful writing to the book cannot be denied. Certain parts of it have great force. But it is force exerted without restraint or cumulative meaning, good only in terms of itself. There is a brilliant malice in some of the portraiture, an almost diabolic ability to reveal man in ridiculous and mean and embarrassing situations. But one misses the supremely judicious, controlled, comic, pathetic implications of *Antic Hay*; one misses what seemed so promising, and proved so beautiful in the earlier Huxley; things like the fantasy of the dwarf in *Crome Yellow* and the tale of the half-witted girl in *Those Barren Leaves*. Here one must be content with an astringent, brittle wit, a maturity of observation, a powerful outburst of disgust. These may well be extraordinary gifts, but they are not new ones. And as they have served their usefulness to better advantage before, one may be justifiably guarded in praising them. The needless length of this book, too, is at least possible evidence of its disorder. If *Point Counter Point* is the most powerful and vitriolic indictment of the intellectual world we have had in years, it is also the most exaggerated and unrelieved.

[1] 'Spirit of the times.'

52. Henry Seidel Canby, review in *Saturday Review of Literature*

2 February 1929, v, pp. 637–8

Henry Seidel Canby (1878–1961), editor, writer, professor, edited the *Saturday Review of Literature* 1924–36 and was later a Fellow of the Royal Society of Literature.

Huxley replied to Canby's suggestion that he should write treatises instead of novels:

In very belated reply to your letter and the enclosed article, I'd like to say that the novel form is preferable to the treatise because the fictionally embodied idea is different from, and much more alive than, the 'same' idea in the abstract. My book contains both abstract and (more or less effectively) embodied ideas. It would have been less effective if the embodied ones had been omitted (*L*, p. 312).

In his opening paragraphs, here omitted, Canby refers to Lee Wilson Dodd's mockery of the 'high-brow thinker' in *The Great Enlightenment*.

Canby's review is entitled 'The Adventures of Libido.' See Introduction, pp. 3, 14.

The Great Enlightenment flicks a cracking whip over the tough hide of the intellectualist as Critic and Wise Man, but another current book discusses the animal as such, the end-product of a psychological evolution, civilized man very sure that he is civilized and unhappy over the result, not man proud, but man weary. Man weary of living, sated with experience yet irritable with nervous desires, immensely intelligent yet puzzling over the utility of the simplest acts and suspicious of the slightest inhibitions—you find him in all the really modern plays and novels, most pointedly depicted in Aldous Huxley's *Point Counter Point*.

For here is a study, miscalled a novel, since it is as much of a social document as Mr. Huxley's grandfather's deductions from the fossil horse, which, with an admirable honesty, carries society as Mr. Huxley sees it to logical conclusions. The book is as witty as Mr. Dodd's poem and as full of fornication unblushingly carried out as the old sentimental novel of suggested situations left to the imagination. It is certain that many have read *Point Counter Point* only for its frank realism, since if they had read it for its ideas and the really appalling significance of its scenes, a cry would have gone up from Bloomsbury, London, to Bloomsbury, Indiana. For this novel is a shocker in the only sense which shocking really counts, an intellectual shocker intended to be literally true, illustrating a great despair, and a wholesale decadence of will, registering by the easy terms of narrative in which alone the populace will take their ideas, a moral lesson which is all the more affecting because Mr. Huxley is clearly uncertain whether preaching it is worth the effort.

He is, I think, a better preacher than novelist. He is so eager (like his mouthpiece and favorite character, Philip Quarles) to think all round the human race, that he quite loses, or never gains, that illusion of reality in characters created by the author in accord with some law of their own personality which makes them personalities as you and I are personalities, and total not partial in their contacts with life. Huxley is far too interested in ideas for such creativeness. He takes his characters raw out of experience, very much as a man at a club window might illustrate his argument by gestures at well-known figures in the crowd. One gets sound evidence this way but not life, for life in fiction is synthesis not analysis. In this book it seems that only lack of knowledge prevents the naming of an original for each of the *dramatis personae*— Lucy Tantamount, Burlap, Bidlake, Spandrell, Rampion. They are not new creations, but Huxley's interpretation of people he knows—a wide difference, for in that half-way stage between discovery and recovery of the personality John Smith, who might be on the way to become a Pendennis or a Richard Feverel, is abstracted for a moment into typical qualities with the photograph of the original upon them, talks with his own voice, but stands for the type into which the discerning novelist will put him. All Huxley's characters (like those of Wells, of Sinclair Lewis, of so many moderns) are like that. They are not convincing as people, like the men and women of far less intellectual students, Jane Austen for example, no matter how true may be their words. Yet they are indubitably good specimens—collected for the laboratory, powerful as evidence, if only because one feels so sure that they are documented.

They are part of London, 1926–1927. One feels sure that most of them are discoverable in London, 1929.

Yet if I call Huxley a mediocre novelist, I call him a reporter of genius and a philosophic thinker acute and unafraid, with a background of erudition and an intellect of great subtlety and poise. Huxley is a social critic of a high order and must be taken as such.

Rampion is the spear-head of his indictment, but it is the brooding spirit of Quarles, half-stoic, half pyrrhist ready to suspend judgment, that interprets the action. Here is a set of people, not living comfortably, as Thackeray said of his Vanity Fair, without God in the world, but violently and self-consciously seeking some substitute for God and some corrective of their slackened grip upon living. Lord Edward Tantamount, futile and helpless in active life, has discovered the abstractions of science and happily makes two newt's tails grow where one grew before with no concern for the human species except a puzzle as to the probable rate of their extinction. Lucy Tantamount, his predatory and oversexed daughter, has exhausted sensation and wearied of intellect. Like the Roman decadents she seeks for sexual experience divorced from any sentiment that might interfere with direct physical pleasure, and longs for the days of easy violence when debauchery ended in blood. Spandrell, the rotter, most terrible and most pathetic of Huxley's figures, who makes Dreiser's crude instinctive villains seem like childish Goths, has been mentally wounded in youth by his mother's sensual remarriage. He revenges himself on love by seductions, and in the last desperate attempt to feel the response of a moral self, tries cold-blooded murder, which leaves him where it found him, a worn-out pervert incapable of interest in living. Burlap—a hideous caricature—is the 'Christ pervert,' a self-deluded hypocrite whose weakness leads him to idealize his sensual vices, until, as Rampion says, he goes to bed with women as if he and they were angels—a jellied soul that slips away from life, when it is fouled, into a pretense of spirituality. These are the intellectual leaders of a civilized London, and they believe in nothing, except music, the common language, the only undissected happiness of all, the one experience of humanity not subject to analysis because it has no ideas but only form.

[Discusses Huxley's attack on scientists and businessmen]

Only Rampion, the man with a Jehovah complex . . . has any zest for real life in this book, gets something that he wants from it, and has a good wife who won't leave him (as every one else is about to do).

But Rampion has become such a surly Carlyle of a bear from contemplating the folly of intellectuals afraid of life and philistines making
dust of it, that he isn't much help. He is a Jonah, a Jeremiah, not a
Saviour. The penalties that all pay in this book, save Rampion, are
horrible.

Is *Point Counter Point* another defeatist book, discoursing of the
futility which sterilizes a generation that has given up its convictions
because they no longer square with known facts? Scarcely defeatist,
though Mr. Huxley may so have intended it, but certainly fatalist. For
his thesis seems to be enkernelled in Spandrell's remark that the sort of
things that happen to you are the sort of thing that you are. These
subtle, sensation-weary Londoners are conditioned by an environment
that has made desire a nervous itch of the brain which can never be
eased. They are quite clearly degenerates in the accurate sense of the
word, retrogressive as a human species for all their fineness, brittle and
neurotic. You cannot argue from them on the positive side because they
are no longer quite human. They are like Rampion's picture of the outline of history with little foetuses, all brain, tickling or disembowelling
each other in the misty future of time. 'The intellectual life,' I quote
from Quarles again, 'is child's play, which is why intellectuals tend to
become children and then imbeciles and finally, as the political and
industrial history of the last few centuries clearly demonstrates,
homicidal lunatics and wild beasts.' 'Clearly' here is a strong word,
but we can accept it for intelligent people who lose their grip upon the
vitalities of living; the subtler or the more energetic, the quicker they
rot. Lucy Tantamount, the tigress woman, is one of the logical end-
products of an intellectual civilization.

It is a fatalist book, but too narrow, too provincially restricted to the
rarefied region of weary intellectualism to be convincingly defeatist. It
is more stoic than pyrrhist. Mr. Huxley has not suspended judgment
until he should see what those who are not world weary would do when
they turn, if they ever do turn, from strenuously knocking things about
to the cultivation of life itself. There is a just comparison between
Spandrell afraid of sex, afraid of God, and sadistically wreaking himself
upon every sexual and godly manifestation, and the scientist taking
refuge in the simplicities of relativity or mutation from the hot complexities of his own life. Yet there is no question which is worth more
in any scale of human values that does not depend upon an ultimate and
unguessable result. The logical answer to Aldous Huxley's fatalistic
pessimism is that since all men are not conditioned alike, the things that

happen to them may sometimes very safely and happily be the things
that they are.

I am aware that Mr. Huxley is stirring deeper water, that he is asking
whether any philosophy or any course of action can save the mind from
perdition once it has become conscious of its own nature. Bidlake who
followed physical pleasure till it turned to pain is not an answer, nor
Marjorie sunk in a trance of Christian resignation, nor the disgusting
Burlap, playing baby with his latest paramour in the bath tub. And
Rampion is only a voice crying, or rather, bellowing, in the night.
Huxley would agree with Mr. Joseph Wood Krutch that a life constructed as a conscious work of art is sure to be a failure in a real world;
he would agree with all the young futilitarians that there is no objective
reason, not physical, why one should not do always what one wants, no
matter where it leads. He agrees too much and with too many. It is the
fault of an acutely logical mind. He accepts reason against instinct even
in the defence of instinct. Such a failing may account for Christ's
preference for babes, Buddha's distrust of experience, and the wisdom
of the Catholic Church in making intellectual pride a deadly sin.

Every great religion would have had its comment upon the characters
of this book, modern as they seem to be; but not a solution because
there is no solution, but only an explaining. If you atrophy against life
as apparently the best of the Pagans did in the late Roman period, you
can construct irrefutable arguments against the significance of living,
for argument is only a rationalization of what you are. The kind of
man determines the kind of argument quite as much as the kind of
thing that happens. And if one asks how to avoid this atrophy of living,
the answer may be (*ad hominem*) not to live in the counterpoint of
Huxley's London, no matter how much one loves Bach and good conversation. For there are an extraordinary number of things that the
people in Huxley's novel never try, even those with their moral fibre
intact like Quarles, among others the civilized humility of which the
poet sings:

> All mockers of false gods, who loved the True,
> As all who labour for perfection do:
> Yea, mocking, they revered the mystery,
> Its fine discriminations and far sweep,
> As Atom thrills to Atom, Deep to Deep.

Mr. Dodd's reference is to Voltaire and Rabelais and Butler who, if
what one desires is a measure of civilization, were certainly as civilized

as Spandrell, Quarles, or Lucy Tantamount, and seem to have carried their liquor better.

I have not discussed Mr. Huxley's novel as art or Mr. Dodd's poem as poetry because the one is actually a philosophic treatise and the other frankly a philosophic satire. . . . And I have already said of Mr. Huxley's novel, that it should be a social treatise, as witty as he has made it, even more thoughtful, and illustrated by 'cases,' frankly such, which he would be at liberty to anecdotize as much as he pleased, if only we were sure that they were absolutely authentic. It is the laziness of readers that brings work like his into fiction. Not that he is unskilful. On the contrary, he weaves his point and counterpoint with complete mastery. His story never falters, although it carries a burden of discussion that might make an elephant stagger. But that sort of thing oughtn't to have to be put into fiction and never would in any right thinking age. Lift the social or economic pressure which makes a fine mind like his tell us stories because only so can he get our attention, and *Point Counter Point* would have been the biting philosophic essay which it so clearly longs to be. Huxley wants to 'get the new way of looking at things, whose essence is multiplicity.' He wants to look with the biologist's, the bishop's, the chemist's, the historian's, the common-sense man's, the flirt's eye, all in a single book. He wants, in fine, to see *through* eyes, not inside of them, and is more interested in what he finds about living than in life itself. A scientist-philosopher, an essayist like his grandfather, with more wit and less concentration, with a broader background, and perhaps less industry, yet with the same kind of quest-ing, analytic imagination—that is what Aldous Huxley is. I wish he would go beyond his note-taking on the interesting aspects of his brilliant, but somewhat neurotic, acquaintances and proceed from provocative stories to the outspoken book he has in his power.

53. D. H. Lawrence on *Point Counter Point*

1928, 1929

David Herbert Lawrence (1885–1930), famous British novelist, poet, and essayist, was a close friend of Huxley's, especially from 1925 to 1930. Perhaps the most helpful account of Lawrence's influence on Huxley is Jerome Meckier's in *Aldous Huxley: Satire and Structure*, pp. 78–123. See also *B, I, passim*.

For related comments on *Point Counter Point* by Lawrence, see Introduction, pp. 13–14. The text below is from Huxley's edition of Lawrence's letters (New York: Viking, 1932), pp. 765–6, 791.

(a) Extract from a letter to Huxley, late October or early November 1928

I have read *Point Counter Point* with a heart sinking through my bootsoles and a rising admiration. I do think you've shown the truth, perhaps the last truth, about you and your generation, with really fine courage. It seems to me it would take ten times the courage to write *P. Counter P.* than it took to write *Lady C.*: and if the public knew *what* it was reading, it would throw a hundred stones at you, to one at me. I do think that art has to reveal the palpitating moment or the state of man as it is. And I think you do that, terribly. But what a moment! and what a state! if you can only palpitate to murder, suicide, and rape, in their various degrees—and you state plainly that it is so—*caro*,[1] however are we going to live through the days? Preparing still another murder, suicide, and rape? But it becomes of a phantasmal boredom and produces ultimately inertia, inertia, inertia and final atrophy of the feelings. Till, I suppose, comes a final super-war, and murder, suicide, rape sweeps away the vast bulk of mankind. It is as you say—intellectual appreciation does not amount to so much, it's what you thrill to. And

[1] 'Dear.'

if murder, suicide, rape is what you thrill to, and nothing else, then it's your destiny—you can't change it *mentally*. You live by what you thrill to, and there's the end of it. Still for all that it's a *perverse* courage which makes the man accept the slow suicide of inertia and sterility: the perverseness of a perverse child. . . . I can't stand murder, suicide, rape—especially rape: and especially being raped. Why do men only thrill to a woman who'll rape them and S——on their face? All I want to do to your Lucy is smack her across the mouth, your Rampion is the most boring character in the book—a gas-bag. Your attempt at intellectual sympathy!—It's all rather disgusting, and I feel like a badger that has its hole on Wimbledon Common and trying not to be caught. Well, *caro*, I feel like saying good-bye to you—but one will have to go on saying good-bye for years.

(b) Extract from a letter to Lady Ottoline Morrell, 5 February 1929

Aldous and Maria were here for ten days or so—neither of them very well, run down. Aldous with liver, and Maria going very thin and not eating enough. I think the *Counter Point* book sort of got between them —she found it hard to forgive the death of the child—which one can well understand. But, as I say, there's more than one self to everybody, and the Aldous that writes those novels is only one little Aldous amongst others—probably much nicer—that don't write novels—I mean it's only one of his little selves that writes the book and makes the child die, it's not *all* himself. No, I don't like his books: even if I admire a sort of desperate courage of repulsion and repudiation in them. But again, I feel only half a man writes the books—a sort of precocious adolescent. There is surely much more of a man in the actual Aldous.

54. Arnold Bennett on *Point Counter Point*

1929

An extract from Bennett's article, 'The Progress of the Novel,'
The Realist, April 1929, i, pp. 3–11.

For a biographical note see No. 29.

Bennett has been discussing novelists of the generation of Proust,
Joyce, and Virginia Woolf.

Of the still younger novelists, a few, such as Henry Williamson, author
of *The Pathway*, may emerge from the ruck of competence. *The Pathway*, while a very fine novel indeed, and covering a large expanse,
shows absolutely no symptom of an innovating mind. In attitude and
technique it looks backward instead of forward. One younger novelist,
however, has quite definitely emerged from the ruck: Aldous Huxley.
Among novelists under forty (he is thirty-five) Aldous Huxley rises
high above everybody else as a figure in the world of imaginative prose
literature. His novels are anticipated with eagerness; and it is impossible
for anybody critically interested in fiction to ignore them. He has
matured gradually and surely, which is a good sign. What he will
ultimately achieve no one can foretell. What he has so far achieved is
one sound and complete novel, *Point Counter Point*, issued last autumn.
He is immensely well-informed about the social structure; his intelligence is acute; he has generally, but not always, a scientific mode of
thought; he has taste and erudition; he has power and style; he is
courageous, perhaps more courageous than he feels himself to be. He
influences his contemporaries, and it may be said that, in the matter of
the progress of the novel as an artistic vehicle, he stands for his generation; his generation may fairly be judged by him.

We will therefore test *Point Counter Point* by settling its place in the
three groups of categories. The task is easy.

First: breadth of outlook—particularly sociological outlook. No
fresh progress is to be observed, but rather a retrogression from the

standard of Balzac, and certainly from the standard of Wells. (I do not mean here merely the Wells of the Utopias.) I do not see how the contrary can be argued with any hope of success. The novel deals with authors and their mates; three of the principal characters are authors; and yet I remember in *Point Counter Point* not a single passage in which are broadly treated the repercussions of literature upon life, or vice versa. Here, if ever in a novel, was an opportunity for imaginatively and dramatically portraying those relations. It was refused.

Second: destructiveness and constructiveness. The book is almost, if not quite, wholly destructive. It is a very formidable and uncompromising attack on the society which it depicts, and there are few or no implications which might pass for constructive criticism. The ground is littered with the shapeless rubble of demolished images. Never was ruin so ruthlessly accomplished.

Third: sympathy or antipathy towards individual characters. The attitude is almost uniformly hostile. In one case, that of Burlap, the treatment accorded amounts to virulent persecution. Of all the chief personages, one alone is sympathetically drawn. Indeed, the author gives the impression that he hates and despises his characters. He is without pity in the exposure of their weaknesses and their turpitudes, and his censure can only be justified on the assumption that their iniquity and absurdity are the fruits of individual naughtiness and original sin, and not in any degree to be attributed to ancestry, to environment, or to the mysterious but unescapable influences of a defective social structure.

Hence I do not see in the representative serious novel by a young man any appreciable sign of evolutionary development of the vehicle. I am judging it comparatively, not positively. As a positive achievement it ranks high; it has rightly aroused enthusiasm. The author is entitled to be proud of it. And one willingly admits that it contains a large dose of antiseptic straight talking—corrective of the pervading, timid sentimentalism of the British novel. Personally I exulted in its tonic brutality. But it is not a progressive book, save in the respect just noted. I should call it reactionary, in both a spiritual and a technical sense. And the milk of human kindness is not in it. Having read it—yes, and having sardonically enjoyed it—one comes to the conclusion that Jesus may have preached the Sermon on the Mount in vain.

DO WHAT YOU WILL

October 1929

---

55. Richard Aldington, review in *Sunday Referee*

15 December 1929, p. 6

Richard Aldington (1892–1962), poet, critic, and novelist, was married to 'H.D.' [Hilda Doolittle] 1913–37.

This review is reprinted in *Richard Aldington: Selected Critical Writings, 1928–1960*, ed. Alister Kershaw (Carbondale: Southern Illinois University Press, 1970), pp. 19–23.

I have to confess my ignorance, as one so often has to do. I have not followed Mr. Huxley's work closely; and this seems ridiculous since I find myself so much in sympathy with him and admire what I have read of his so much. In 1919 and 1920 I think I read everything he wrote; and I have always maintained that his poetry is estimated far below its real worth. But between 1920 and *Point Counter Point* I admit with shame that I read nothing of his—an omission I intend to repair. It was entirely my fault or misfortune. For reasons not unconnected with the War, I turned away from modern literature (except certain sections of it) and plunged into a gluttonous reading of other ages. So I come to *Do What You Will* with a particularly open mind. Perhaps that is why I like it so much.

In *Do What You Will* Mr. Huxley has said a great many things extremely worth saying, things I should have liked to say myself if I had his ability. I don't agree with all he says, and I think he might be attacked successfully along certain lines, but I prefer to write about what I like and admire in his book.

The most important thing I admire is Mr. Huxley's valiant, and I believe successful, attempt to say something positive, to set up a sanction for life. I am sick of death and death-worshipping in all its forms, from senile gentility to the cold butchery of intellectual suicide. Let me give an example. A greatly admired poem by the most admired poet of the day may be summarized in the following excerpted words:

[Alludes to T. S. Eliot's 'The Hollow Men' and expresses his dislike of 'this exhibitionism of a perpetual suicidal mania']

It is the War despair which involved so many of us and from which the healthy-minded have been struggling to escape, not yearning to wallow in. Mr. Huxley has struggled tremendously and bravely, and I think he has escaped. He has got back to a positive belief in life, a positive enjoyment of life. And he has not done it by yielding to the old nauseating humbugs, the false official optimisms which are like a bad but insipid smell. Perhaps Mr. Huxley's escape is only valid for himself and for a few who by education and temperament are predisposed to sympathy with him, but at least he has found *a* way to life—that's something.

A life-worshipper, so Mr. Huxley describes himself. One up to him! With all the various forms of death and death-worship now popular, real courage is needed to take up such a position and great skill to defend it successfully. But what is meant by 'life'? (The question must be asked with a would-be-superior sneer.) Well, I think Mr. Huxley has answered the question by the whole of his book, which should be read by everyone who is interested in our life here and now. But he has also answered it in a very quotable passage, which may stand as a definition of what he means by 'life':

[Quotes summary of Pericles, p. 81]

By one of those pleasing coincidences which sometimes happen in life, I received Mr. Huxley's book after a day spent in Pompeii. All the way back I had been thinking, not of Bulwer Lytton's absurd and mythical Roman sentry, but of the past life whose ghost has been imprisoned there for us by the volcano. Heaven knows, Pompeii was a common little provincial town, a kind of Southend. But it keeps a pleasant fragrance of pre-Christian European life. While I was still trying to find words to express the impression it gives my eyes chanced on the passage I have just quoted. That is it. There was still enough Hellenism in that small Campanian town for the inhabitants to wish to be men, and not gods or devils.

I am not setting up the Pompeians as ideal people, and I don't mean to play the easy game of attributing to the past the virtues or qualities neither it nor we possess. But I do think that we can live out our own lives fully as human beings, just as those Romanized Hellenes and Oscans and Samites of Pompeii seem to have done. I think that is the gist of what Mr. Huxley says so cogently (and often wittily) in these essays. His conviction that we must live here and now dictated his admirable analysis of monotheism, his exposition of the diversity of the human being, his ruthless exposure (how I welcomed it!) of the slobbered-over Francis of Assisi, his twenty-six rounds with Pascal—the best onslaught upon that formidable 'death-worshipper' I have read since Voltaire's. Further, Mr. Huxley's exposition of how the effort to live in a superhuman fashion inevitably results in sub-human compensations seems to me both convincing and valuable. It shows you exactly why the Unco Guid[1] are such ruthless persecutors and tormentors. His dislike for all unbalanced and cock-eyed living is very cordial. Even his analysis of Dostoievsky's characters (perhaps a little unfair) I greeted with a mild cheer—I am very sick of the Russian idiot-Christ.

At times I have meditated a modest apologue, based on the theory of the transmigration of souls, where a man spends each of his innumerable lives in maceration and misery, preparing himself to enjoy felicity in his next life and always finding it was quite different from what he had expected. One life at a time. The problem, as Mr. Huxley puts it, is for us worms to be the best of all possible worms. No self-maiming, either in the interests of Paradise or big business. The one objection I find to Mr. Huxley's philosophy of life is this. It is a most attractive, if difficult, programme, but it is infinitely easier for him and for me (who live on the margin of the commercial-industrial world as its spoiled amusers) than for those, the great majority, who have to live that life. Halcott Glover once said to me: 'No man who has managed to keep out of an office can be called a failure in life.' All well and good, but most men don't manage it. Most men *are* in offices or factories or industrial jobs of some sort. If they all took up their beds and followed Mr. Huxley he and I would be reduced to mendicants in a few months. 'Life' cannot be the monopoly of a few intelligent upper middle-class people and artists. To do Mr. Huxley justice, he makes a strong effort to deal with this in his essay called 'Revolutions'. But that is extremely pessimistic in its conclusions. 'It will be a Nihilist revolution. Destruc-

[1] Unco Guid—those who are professedly strict in matters of morals and religion.

tion for destruction's sake. Hate, universal hate, and an aimless and therefore complete and thorough smashing up of everything.'

Most depressing, and I don't believe it. Here Mr. Huxley is a little inhuman, as he is in his attack on the talkies and movies—attacking them from the basis of the world's worst film (Al Jolson's beastly Mammy sentimentalism) seen in Paris, where there has been a trade blockade for months of American films, where German and Russian films appear ruthlessly cut, where the native producers seem to me mostly imbeciles, who have never grasped the elements of film production. (If you are ever tempted to go to a Jean Epstein film, don't.) The movies are part of the life of our time, and I refuse to clip that little head from my hydra because Mr. Huxley objects to the merchants of film production. I might just as well object to his book because it is printed by a machine and not exquisitely calligraphed by hand. The camera can produce results as surprising and beautiful as those of paint and brushes. If Mr. Huxley disbelieves this, let him go and see what Mr. Man Ray can do. Besides, the mere rhythm of action and vitality in films like *Tempest over Asia* and *The Mad Czar* is enough to refute Mr. Huxley's criticisms—or prejudices.

56. Unsigned review in *TLS*

10 October 1929, p. 787

Those who can look back to the world of academic philosophy as it was before the War will recall the hubbub aroused when the Nirvana of Hegelian Monism was abruptly broken by the request of William James for a fresh examination of the claims of Pluralism. That the ground of the universe might possibly be not the Absolute One but a diversity of Forces seemed an impious insinuation. We can barely conjecture what the feelings of those philosophers would have been if they had been driven to cope not with James's mild doubt, but with Mr. Aldous Huxley's breezy denial of their monistic creed. In this collection of metaphysical and moral essays he not only admits but positively revels in Pluralism, in the ultimate diversity and inconsistency of

Reality. He tears the robe of Hegel to tatters and stitches the fragments into a motley of *le gai savoir*.[1]

Even those who reject most thoroughly Mr. Huxley's philosophic preferences and professions cannot fail to admire the mastery with which he expresses them. It is a minor point that the irrepressible jests well up to relieve the tensity of abstract reasoning, the definition of the lion as 'a desert-coloured animal with a mane and claws and an expression like Garibaldi's'; the remark, in a tirade against the barrenness of Hebrew monotheism, that 'we may be pardoned for wishing that the Jews had remained not forty but four thousand years in their repulsive wilderness'; the exhortation to the human species to 'be the best of all possible worms'. Mr. Huxley's more remarkable achievement here is the lucidity and firmness of exposition; there are pages in which the most baffling concepts of philosophy are placed before us with the un-wavering outlines of statuary, paragraphs in which Mr. Huxley triumphantly competes with such masters of philosophic style as James, Bergson and Santayana.

This clear style sets out as clear a substance. All the essays exhibit, in effect, different facets of the same principle, the principle that man, who should be as diverse, undulating and supple as the infinitely varied reality in which he plunges, is for ever enslaving himself to some artificially simple system in the hope of dignifying his existence by an artificial consistency.

[Comments on the content of the various essays and calls the study of Pascal 'perhaps the most powerful psychological exploration that Mr. Huxley has ever conducted']

It is small boot, doubtless, to accuse of inconsistency a thinker who glories in the badge. But there is certainly a divergence between the Mr. Huxley who demands 'the making and holding of a psychological harmony within the individual and an external social harmony between the individual and his fellows', and who praises the ordered diversity of the Hellenic ideal, and the Mr. Huxley who cries for 'systematic inconsistency', who asserts that 'there is no such thing as Historical Truth', and who claims that the wise man of his ideal will be 'at times a positivist and at times a mystic; derisively sceptical and full of faith'. What assurance can faith have that admits it will crumble before scepticism next week? What edge is left to scepticism that flirts with the ghost of faith? Yet at times we discern beneath the mask of 'jesting

[1] 'Merry knowledge.'

Pilate' a believer with remarkably energetic affirmations. Very transient, if they exist, must be the moods in which Mr. Huxley rejoices in his *bêtes noires*,[1] mechanical civilization, the vulgar pleasure-hunting of 'the Good-Timer' or the slobber of the Talkie Palace. 'In the depths of the human soul', he remarks in one place, 'lies something which we rationalize as a demand for justice.' What a shamefaced psycho-analytical circumlocution for the plain statement that man has the sense of justice! Can the sceptic, and particularly the moralizing sceptic like Mr. Huxley, afford to doubt the ultimate human values and truths that alone give a basis to his critical assertions? They remain ineradicable, 'do what you will'.

57. Desmond MacCarthy on Huxley's limitations

1930

Sir Desmond (Charles Otto) MacCarthy (1877–1952), close associate of the Bloomsbury Group, literary editor of *New Statesman* (1920–7), senior literary critic of the *Sunday Times* (1928–52), author of, for example, *Portraits* (1931) and *Shaw* (1951).

The text below is from *Life and Letters*, September 1930, v, 198–209. Reprinted in MacCarthy's *Criticism* (London: Putnam, 1932), pp. 235–46.

Mr. Aldous Huxley's last volume of stories, *Brief Candles*, has met with a somewhat tepid reception from reviewers who a few years ago would have praised enthusiastically, but their comments will only influence opinion in so far as these reflect an already existing discontent or satiety in his many admirers. There is no falling off, quite the reverse, in Mr. Huxley's penetration and execution; the merits of these stories must,

[1] 'Pet aversions.'

indeed, have been embarrassing to those who wished to convey their disappointment. Each story is a complete expression of its theme, and the words in which every detail is described are precise and, when occasion requires, charming. The style is his own fine blend of intellectual curiosity and æsthetic sensibility; at the same time it is faultlessly correct. It is not, it cannot be, the craftsman who has disappointed his critics. His reviewers must have started by asking themselves another question: Are these stories worth telling? That an inclination to underrate his aims should appear already asserting itself is due to a common phenomenon—satiety. All authors are musical-boxes which play a limited number of tunes, and sooner or later in the case of every author readers become aware that they are listening to variations on tunes heard before; and the crucial period in the history of every literary talent occurs when an author's merits are thus taken for granted while his limitations are discussed. Mr. Aldous Huxley is on the edge of it. Yet every real talent survives it, and not infrequently after the ordeal by satiety those books which were received with indifference are recognized as the flowering of that talent. Even the letters of the inexhaustibly resourceful Dickens betray now and then an uneasiness lest readers of some forthcoming number will exclaim: 'Hullo, the same old stuff'; *David Copperfield* was a tremendous effort on his part to draw from a fresh and deeper spring.

With Aldous Huxley this period was bound to occur early in his literary career because the attitude towards life he has hitherto compelled us to share, is one in which no one can remain contented for long together. It is detached, exacting—and inconclusive, and we find ourselves perpetually looking down on human nature; we never have the exhilaration of looking up. To share his detachment is for a while, flattering; for though we may often recognize our own failings and ignoble predicaments in his pages, these facts exist in our lives, we know, in contexts which are omitted from his books and relieve them of much of their meanness. It is primarily, therefore, other people who appear to us to be mercilessly exposed. This is agreeable until we realize that, after all, it is as necessary to respect and like at least a few other people as it is to respect ourselves. And this Mr. Aldous Huxley seldom, or never, allows us to do.

[Protests, nonetheless, that the few amiable traits in Huxley's characters are not stressed, even though the people 'are not so bad as they appear in his pages']

I can imagine the author interrupting me here by saying: 'Well, since my characters have apparently suggested that to you, I don't see ground for complaint.' To which I would reply: 'It is a matter of emphasis. You always leave to my imagination to supply what is amiable or exhilarating, while employing your skill in fixing my attention on what is not.' What is the explanation? This is a question which the analyst, confronted by Mr. Aldous Huxley's work, must attempt to answer.

Before attempting to do so it is necessary to define his position in the world of letters. For although his limitations are not inevitable consequences of his peculiar gifts, they are affiliated to the qualities which make his work important.

No one can deny its importance to his contemporaries; and the interest which it has roused confirms it. He has succeeded in recording modes of feeling and thinking characteristic of his own generation which have never been described before. He has made his contemporaries more aware of their own responses, moral, amoral, æsthetic and intellectual; their indifference, impatience, obtusity, disappointment, sensibility. He has diagnosed subtly and mercilessly the diseases of modern self-consciousness, and described the ignobly comic falsifications of emotion which result from them. But this is not for the critic the central fact about him. His distinguishing mark is that he stands out as the most deeply and widely cultured of modern novelists. I am not sure that even in the past one can point to any other writer of fiction who has made so obstinate an attempt to illumine his picture of life with criss-cross lights drawn from an equal familiarity with contemporary knowledge and theory. George Eliot only comes near him. It is one of the great merits of Mr. Wells that his imagination has absorbed his knowledge of science, but Mr. Wells is far from being a cultured man in other respects. The peculiarity of Mr. Huxley's work is that not only science in all its branches is laid at moments under contribution, but also the history of art, music, poetry, medicine, society and philosophy. What is disconcerting is the contrast between the extraordinary many-coloured richness of the light he pours upon his subjects, and the fact that they are taken from small and often stuffy corners of the big common world of experience. He is the most universal of novelists in his references and one of the most limited in focus. His constant theme is love and sex, and the result of his investigations is dissatisfaction, or more positively disgust. The two questions which he continually asks are what is the right attitude towards sex-attraction, and is it all-important, or unimportant, or of moderate importance? This preoccupation he shares with his age, which is thinking as hard and confusedly about sex as the one preceding it thought about religion. Hence the peculiar interest of his fiction to his contemporaries. No one in his senses could say that sex was a small corner of experience; it is, after all, the staple theme of fiction. But it is either the falsifications of emotion by self-consciousness or the dullness of mere promiscuity which he studies. The failure of the intellectually honest to fall in love romantically, or the failure of the frankly canine to get satisfaction without romance are aspects of sex he has made his own; and he has done them extraordinarily well—the lovers who try to drag their feelings up to emotional heights, and those who, equally fatally, endeavour to satisfy instinct without committing their emotions. He is a merciless analyst of emotional playacting in love; that tendency to pretend one feels like someone else or like some character in a book. He is the student of 'Bovaryism' in all its forms.[1] Those who are not interested in his drift either enjoy, or detest, his careful lubricity, for his skill in the rapid suggestion of such scenes is equal to that of Anatole France. To those scenes he owes not a little of his popularity, though they are not the substance of his work.

Point Counter Point is the most ambitious of his novels, but he does not achieve in it more than he had done in *Antic Hay*. That book also took us from scene to scene in which different characters were interpreting experience, chiefly amorous, according to their different sense of values. The effect was desolating, though often amusing. The title *Point Counter Point* suggested that he had hoped in this later book to make the music of humanity audible: 'It's all like music; harmonics, and counterpoint and modulations.' But we heard only distressing confusion. The author had not pulled the world together in his own head any better than in *Antic Hay*. That feat so necessary to the artist, who, if his work is to have balance must pretend, at any rate, that he has done so, is one of enormous difficulty to him. To begin with he cannot pretend, and no novelist is more sensitive to the inconsequent queerness of life, and the inconsistency of what is happening simultaneously in every moment of experience. His scientific awareness makes it harder still for him to unify his impression of life, except as a patternless confusion in which any sense of proportion is as good as another, and all moral judgments equally valid. Intellectually, therefore, he is entirely sceptical,

[1] Bovaryism—an exaggerated, glamorized concept of oneself—from Flaubert's *Madame Bovary*.

184

but temperamentally he seems to be one who is driven into making passionate, not to say acrimonious, distinctions. It is this perpetual discord between the indulgent scepticism of his intellect and the severity of his uncorroborated reactions, that is responsible for that acrid discontent which emanates from his fiction, shot though it is with gleams of beauty.

[Quotes extensively from Quarles's reflections on what kinds of books to write, Chapter XIV, pp. 268–71]

Clearly there is little that the critic can tell Mr. Aldous Huxley about his work that he does not already know himself; but this passage contains much that his critics should remember. They must accept him as a writer not 'deep' but 'wide'. They must accept the fact that, since his supreme merit lies in width of reference, in putting facts in juxtaposition which his omnivorous reading and perpetual reflection have assembled, his novels and stories must perforce be disquisitions illustrated by characters. The deep pleasure in reading Mr. Huxley lies in following the movement of his mind. He is aware also of the irritation produced in some readers by his inevitably discursive methods. There is an amusing self-critical bit of dialogue on this point between 'Philip' and his wife. They are driving in a motor and they have just run over a dog.

[Quotes Quarles's intellectual digression on the dog's death, Chapter VI, pp. 110–11]

Not unnatural, but still Elinor's 'desire to scream' was not a good criticism. Mr. Aldous Huxley's loyalty is committed to 'a cool indifferent flux of intellectual curiosity'. It is his point; it makes him unique among English writers of fiction. He is an Anatole France, only far more learned, who has not attained to the suavity of indifference. He is therefore more interesting, but less successful as an artist.

58. André Maurois on Huxley as a great Englishman

1930

André Maurois (1885–1967), highly honored critic, biographer and historian, was one of the leading men of letters in twentieth-century France. His many books include *Aspects of Biography* (1929), *A History of England* (1937), and *Victor Hugo and His World* (1966).

Maurois's essay appeared as the Preface to the first French edition of *Point Counter Point*, trans. Jules Castier (Paris: Plon, 1930). The text below is from *Living Age*, September 1930, cccxxxix, pp. 52–5. See Introduction, pp. 1, 15.

'Intelligent to the point of being almost human.' In these words Aldous Huxley describes one of his heroes, the novelist, Philip Quarles. This character bears a singular resemblance to its creator and Huxley several years ago might well have been defined as Philip Quarles, but his talent from book to book has followed an ascendant progress from pure intelligence to a pure humanity which does not exclude intelligence but which cannot be satisfied by intelligence alone. Huxley's first novels had a familiar ring to French ears. In *Crome Yellow* the learned, sensual characters, dominated from far above by their author, exchanged against an English countryside remarks worthy of a Jérôme Coignard or a Bergeret, but a Bergeret who was more a doctor than a philosopher and who would have studied science rather than have taught literature. Through its fantasy, skill, and grace this was an astonishing beginning in which charm rather than force predominated.

His next novels, *Antic Hay* and *Those Barren Leaves*, and two books of short stories, several of which are excellent (*Two or Three Graces*, *The Gioconda Smile*), revealed both an enrichment and a deepening. With *Point Counter Point* it seems that Aldous Huxley has joined the company of the greatest novelists. Such, in any event, is the opinion of those who believe that André Gide's *Faux-Monnayeurs* is one of the great French novels, and I am one of them. *Point Counter Point*, unlike the classic novels of Balzac and Stendhal, is not a continued history of a central event or the life of one or more characters. It is not a 'novel-river,' but rather a novel of additions. One scene is laid in an intellectual milieu of writers, painters, scholars, and men of the world. All the elements thus isolated are described and through them appear the beliefs, sentimental reactions, and absurdities of a certain group of the British intelligentsia of about the year 1926. It is not a thesis novel, for such an intellectual counterpoint only looks upon doctrines as themes and the author develops them, weaves them together, but does not judge them. It is rather a novel of ideas. 'The chief defect of the novel of ideas,' says Philip Quarles, 'is that you must write about people who have ideas to express—which excludes all but about .01 per cent of the human race.' Perhaps, but the hundredth of one per cent that remains is very interesting and its human importance is greater than its numerical importance.

[Maurois observes the contrapuntal themes of the novel and declares that Huxley, through Rampion, is advancing the philosophy of psychic balance explained at greater length in *Do What You Will*]

What is the value of this novel, considered as a work of art? To the English reader it brought something very new. Huxley is the first writer, or perhaps the second, because E. M. Forster in *A Passage to India* may have been the first, who reëchoed in English literature the notes struck by Proust and Gide. And to the French reader he is no less rich. He reveals to us an England that we do not know—cynical, anarchistic, brilliant. It is only a little group and even since 1926 it has changed. But the æsthetes of the 1880s were no more numerous and their influence was great. Lucy Tantamount and Illidge are elements that one must take into account if one wishes to understand contemporary English society.

But perhaps the greatest originality of Huxley's lies in the fact that he is the only living novelist with a solid scientific culture, so assimilated that it has transformed his whole conception of the world. I say the only living novelist because Proust possessed that culture and the medical metaphors he used are some of the most beautiful elements in his work. Gide is a naturalist but I do not believe a physician. Huxley has a very exact vision of the image the universe presents to a great scholar of our time and he distills from this vision a poetry of his own.

187

There is in *Point Counter Point* the outlines of a new *De rerum natura*.[1] In certain passages, scientific learning submerges the novel, just as archæological erudition did with Anatole France. This is the greatest danger that Huxley as a novelist faces. But I believe he knows it, for, more and more in his work, simple humanity is regaining the ground once occupied by the dazzling paradox. 'It's the substitution of simple intellectual schemata for the complexities of reality,' says Philip Quarles. 'It's incomparably easier to have profound ideas about metaphysics and sociology than to know personally and intuitively a lot about one's fellows and to have satisfactory relations with one's friends and lovers, one's wife and children.' In *Point Counter Point* Huxley shows himself master of this faculty. His gifts as a satirist are brilliant. Mrs. Betterton, Mr. Sita Ram, and above all the admirable Burlap are creations possessing all the force of Dickens. But the opening scenes between Walter and Marjorie, so tragic and true, are worthy of the great Russians, which is a new kind of eulogy to pronounce on a great Englishman.

[1] *On the Nature of Things* by Lucretius, whom Huxley admired.

59. André Gide on *Point Counter Point*

1931

André Paul Guillaume Gide (1869–1951), famed French novelist and dramatist, recipient of a Nobel Prize for Literature (1947). Gide's *The Counterfeiters* (1926) was mentioned often as a possible model for *Point Counter Point*.

The excerpts are from *The Journals of André Gide*, trans. Justin O'Brien, Volume III (New York: Knopf, 1949), pp. 154–5. See Introduction, p. 13.

18 March [1931]

For the third time (I believe it may even be the fourth) I gather up my strength to launch into Huxley's *Point Counter Point*, for I have been told that one must get beyond the beginning. But what can I think of a book of which I read attentively the first seventy pages without being able to find a single line somewhat firmly drawn, a single personal thought, emotion, or sensation, the slightest enticement for the heart or mind to invite me to go on?

Went as far as page 115 with great effort. Illegible. Yet I have plenty of pluck for reading. I cannot even understand how there were people able to go on.

20 March [1931]

I definitely drop Huxley's book, in which I cannot get interested. Mme Théo very ingeniously compared it to Mauclair's *Couronne de clarté*. There is probably more intelligence in Huxley, but just as much rubbish.

MUSIC AT NIGHT

September 1931

60. Unsigned review in *Spectator*

19 September 1931, cxlvii, 361–2

Identified in the *Spectator's* files as by L. A. G. Strong. For a biographical note see No. 65.

The essay is entitled 'A Most Handsome Compliment.'

'I have,' says Mr. Huxley, near the beginning of 'Those Personal Touches', 'in the course of a strenuous journalistic career, written articles on an extraordinary variety of subjects, from music to house decorating, from politics to painting, from plays to horticulture and metaphysics.' It is characteristic of him that this sentence reads as an admission rather than as a quite legitimate boast. Yes, thinks the reader: and if anyone is going to write about all these things, who will do it better? For Mr. Huxley shows himself, in this volume, an excellent journalist. It is not, one immediately realizes, that a brilliant mind has been switched this way and that, like a searchlight upon a number of casually selected topics. It is that the topics, however selected, have excited Mr. Huxley's insatiable curiosity, and provoked that passionate instinct for synthesis which makes him the most normal, and the most humane among the writers of his generation. That does not mean that he possesses one of those tiresome minds which is never happy unless it is saying that something is 'like' something else:

In the remote future, when a science infinitely better informed than ours shall have bridged the now enormous gulf between immediately apprehended qualities, in terms of which we *live*, and the merely measurable, ponderable quantities in terms of which we do our scientific thinking . . . the juxtaposition will then be a juxtaposition of compatibles, not of incompatibles.

That is Mr. Huxley's faith. In the *non sequiturs* of the universe he finds a continual reproach to the thinking man: but, for the present, *non sequitur* is the too frequent answer to human investigation. The paragraph concludes:

But all this is for the future. So far as we are concerned, the bringing together of remote discoveries and near feelings is productive of literary efforts which we recognize as ironical.

Irony is the moralist's answer to a *non sequitur*. It follows that much of Mr. Huxley's writing is ironical. 'Ethics in Andalusia' and 'To the Puritan all Things are Impure' show him at his happiest in this vein. He is no irresponsible Jix-baiter: no one could see and express with more deadly seriousness the incompatibles dividing the late D. H. Lawrence and Mrs. Grundy, the system of thought which distinguishes morally between the Graeco-Roman and the Anglo-Saxon vocabulary for the expression of certain facts. *Music at Night*, however, is by no means preoccupied with these matters:

We are grateful to the artist, especially the musician, for saying clearly what we have always felt, but never been able to express. Listening to expressive music, we have, not of course the artist's original experience (which is quite beyond us, for grapes do not grow on thistles), but the best experience in its kind of which our nature is capable—a better and completer experience than in fact we ever had before listening to the music.

In like manner, if we may paraphrase, we are grateful to the journalist for a gift of expression so natural as to seem inevitable. The apparent simplicity and readableness of Mr. Huxley's style may well blind us to its art. He wastes neither words nor energy. He never mistimes a blow, nor hits harder than the ninepin needs. Only in the first pages of the title-piece do we realize with a start that he is deliberately 'writing': only in the essay on 'Liberty' does he seem, after an excellent opening, to fall below his own standard. (The point about travel, for instance, is ill-considered: for the value of a thing to the individual is not to be measured in terms of rarity or even of difference.) The book's final charm lies in Mr. Huxley's courtesy to his readers. He supposes them to be as humane and intelligent as he is himself. Closing *Music at Night*, one is aware of having received a most handsome compliment.

61. Louis Kronenberger, review in *NYTBR*

12 July 1931, pp. 2, 20

For a biographical note see No. 51.

The title of the essay is 'Versatility, Charm and Wit in Mr. Huxley's Essays.'

One might have supposed that it would be better, or been prepared that it should be worse, but one would hardly have guessed that Mr. Huxley's *Music at Night* is simply a good book of essays. There is nothing particularly profound or brilliant about it, and nothing careless or ill-balanced or underweight. He has published a book that is in the proper tradition of literary essay-writing: it has point, it has force and variety, it is written well and it reads well. The proof that these essays are good, and yet neither extraordinary nor unique, is that they so often remind us of other good essayists. It is not that they echo people, but that they resemble them: certain paragraphs might have been written in turn by Rebecca West, Walter Lippman, Max Beerbohm, G. K. Chesterton, H. L. Mencken and Bertrand Russell.

Yet, protean and versatile as this might seem to make Mr. Huxley, he is of course, in the long run, very much himself. But being himself consists to some extent in being versatile, in having an interest in many things and ideas on all of them; in having something of Beerbohm's literary playfulness, Chesterton's love of paradox, Mencken's witty forthrightness, Rebecca West's modernity, Walter Lippman's ability to reduce contemporary thought to simple, popular terms. Judged not by relative present-day standards, but by absolute ones, Mr. Huxley is important for width, not depth. He is a critic who sees modern life in its multiplicity and in the interdependence of its forces; who, whatever the conclusions he may reach about things or the temperament through which he may sift them, is interested in the causes and investigation of the facts; and the breadth of his range is fortunately not greater than the breadth of his equipment. Being really well educated and really civilized, Aldous Huxley, though not unjournalistic in his mission, nor even at times in his manner of going about it, stands yards above the ordinary competent journalist. For to communicate is not his initial, but his secondary object; his primary purpose is to learn for himself.

If the present book of essays is in most respects like other good books of essays, it still differs from them in one particular. It has a timely and contemporary quality. . . . His range is considerable; it covers politics, science, sex, morality, psychology, not to mention people and the arts. In most cases he displays double merit; he has something to say and his own manner of saying it. Thus he is far superior to the usual journalist not only because he is more of a scholar but also because he is more of a personality. So far as that goes he has, unlike most journalists, a definite point of view, and so is more of a critic also.

This point of view is, in a phrase, a sane skepticism. It is really far saner and more 'disciplined' than most people who first heard of him as a kind of enfant terrible and now remember him for his bitterly satiric novels, will suppose. True enough, Mr. Huxley today seems mellower than he was a few years ago. But actually, one can see now his skepticism was always pretty sane, his judgment always pretty sound, even in his 'violent' novels; for though Mr. Huxley has never seemed, and will probably never seem, detached concerning what he saw around him, the fact remains that it was what he saw, and not himself, which was awry—which was fatuous and shoddy and discontented and off-centre. A sane enough skepticism motivated *Antic Hay*, and if it failed to motivate *Point Counter Point*, it has returned to motivate *Music at Night*. We can perceive it the more readily here, chiefly because it plays upon ideas and not upon people; but perhaps also because Mr. Huxley, though not an autobiographical novelist, is a 'personal' critic.

One suspects, indeed, that Mr. Huxley has himself steadily gained in balance through his treatment of unbalanced people. None of his opinions are those of an extremist, and very few of them are any longer those of a 'smart' writer. If he is occasionally paradoxical, it is in order to make people perceive obvious but neglected truths, or discard obvious but persisting falsities. There is very little really original observation in this book, very little unprecedented opinion, almost no new theory about any important aspect of contemporary life. But Mr. Huxley's restatements must still be of immense help to an intelligent popular audience that is not familiar with 'sources.' Papers like 'Of Grace,' 'The New Romanticism,' 'Obstacle Race,' 'To the Puritan All Things are Impure' and 'Tragedy and the Whole Truth' should, each in its own way, be read because they are—the word exactly sums up their value—sensible essays, and if they say nothing to surprise us, they re-phrase familiar thought freshly and with personality. As for a half-dozen playful intellectual exercises like 'Wanted, A New Pleasure' or 'Selected Snobberies,' surely these things (for all their magazine connotations) aren't to be judged by intellectual standards: they are the concoctions of our old friend the 'familiar essayist,' and read much better than our old friend usually does.

As criticism and interpretation there is nothing about this book that glitters. Mr. Huxley's real criticism of modern life is in his novels, and the criticism, if not the novels themselves, is often first-rate—a social, intellectual and moral indictment which, for all its exaggerations and telescopings, is unanswerably just. In *Music at Night* Mr. Huxley has done something easier and commoner; but also different. In work of this kind Mr. Huxley has a kind of divine facility which, because it enables him to be interesting and intelligent without half-trying to be either, takes toll by never letting him be anything more. But while this book is certainly not first-rate criticism, perhaps it is not to be regarded as criticism at all. It is primarily the work of an essayist. In it we are introduced not simply to Huxley's ideas, but to his temperament, his personality, his point of view; and by no means least of all, to his literary gifts. And this side of him has something to give us as well as the *Antic Hay* side has. Surely, to give but one example, it is interesting to find this thorough-paced determinist moved by a strong sense of moral responsibility and born with an almost ascetic temperament.

For the narrow way commands an incomparably wider and, so far as I am concerned, an incomparably fairer prospect than the primrose path; fulfilled, domestic duties are a source of happiness, and intellectual labour is rewarded by the most intense delights. It is not the hope of heaven that prevents me from leading what is technically known as a life of pleasure; it is simply my temperament.

To find, in the same book, such a man railing against Puritanism in all its forms with both a fine logic and a powerful indignation, and elsewhere throughout the same book denouncing extremities of viewpoint and conduct which too-tolerant men have condoned as 'steps toward progress' is to feel that Huxley's own sanity, no less than his unbalanced characters, may prove significant in modern life.

62. Ernest Hemingway on Huxley

1932

Ernest Hemingway (1899–1961), famous American novelist, recipient of the Nobel Prize for Literature for 1954, is perhaps best-known for *The Sun Also Rises* (1926) and *The Old Man and the Sea* (1952).

The extract is from *Death in the Afternoon* (New York: Scribner's, 1932), pp. 190–2. Hemingway quotes Huxley's reference to *A Farewell to Arms* at the opening of 'Foreheads Villainous Low' (*Music at Night*, p. 201), where Huxley chides him for passing quickly over an allusion to Mantegna because he wishes 'to feign stupidity.' See Introduction, p. 15.

What about that, you say? Mr. Huxley scores there, all right, all right. What have you to say to that? Let me answer truly. On reading that in Mr. Huxley's book I obtained a copy of the volume he refers to and looked through it and could not find the quotation he mentions. It may be there, but I did not have the patience nor the interest to find it, since the book was finished and nothing to be done. It sounds very much like the sort of thing one tries to remove in going over the manuscript. I believe it is more than a question of the simulation or avoidance of the appearance of culture. When writing a novel a writer should create living people; people not characters. A *character* is a caricature. If a writer can make people live there may be no great characters in his book, but it is possible that his book will remain as a whole; as an entity; as a novel. If the people the writer is making talk of old masters; of music; of modern painting; of letters; or of science then they should talk of those subjects in the novel. If they do not talk of those subjects and the writer makes them talk of them he is a faker, and if he talks about them himself to show how much he knows then he is showing off. No matter how good a phrase or a simile he may have if he puts it in where it is not absolutely necessary and irreplaceable he is spoiling his work for egotism. Prose is architecture, not interior decoration, and the Baroque is over. For a writer to put his own intellectual musings, which he might sell for a low price as essays, into the mouths of artificially constructed characters which are more remunerative when issued as people in a novel is good economics, perhaps, but does not make literature. People in a novel, not skillfully constructed *characters*, must be projected from the writer's assimilated experience, from his knowledge, from his head, from his heart and from all there is of him. If he ever has luck as well as seriousness and gets them out entire they will have more than one dimension and they will last a long time. . . . A writer who appreciates the seriousness of writing so little that he is anxious to make people see he is formally educated, cultured or well-bred is merely a popinjay. And this too remember; a serious writer is not to be confounded with a solemn writer. A serious writer may be a hawk or a buzzard or even a popinjay, but a solemn writer is always a bloody owl.

BRAVE NEW WORLD

February 1932

---

63. Rebecca West, review in *Daily Telegraph*

5 February 1932, p. 7

Dame Rebecca West, b. 1892, novelist, critic, political writer, contributes to leading English and American newspapers and has written, for example, *The Strange Necessity* (1928), *Black Lamb and Grey Falcon* (1942), and *The New Meaning of Treason* (1964).

The review is entitled 'Aldous Huxley on Man's Appalling Future.' Titles of sub-headings are omitted here. See Introduction, p. 16.

Those who are easily shocked had better leave Mr. Aldous Huxley's new fantasy, *Brave New World*, on one side; noting, as they pass, that since this is a free country they are not compelled to read it.

Those who are not easily shocked can settle down to enjoy what is not only the most accomplished novel Mr. Huxley has yet written, but also the most serious religious work written for some years. His tendency in his other novels has been to select subject matter which might fairly be described as a fuss about nothing. Even the characters in *Point Counter Point* were carefully docketed as interesting individuals—they were, in relation to the depicted imbroglio, as lacking in allure as sexually-maladjusted cockroaches. But the argument in *Brave New World* is of major importance. One could sanely ask for nothing more than it gives.

One would say that the book was about a Utopia if it were not that a line of dreamers have given that originally noncommittal term a sense of imagined perfection; for the book describes the world as Mr.

197

Huxley sees it may become if certain modern tendencies grow dominant and its character is rather of a deduced abomination.

If one has a complaint to make against him it is that he does not explain to the reader in a preface or footnotes how much solid justification he has for his horrid visions. It would add to the reader's interest if he knew that when Mr. Huxley depicts the human race as abandoning its viviparous habits and propagating by means of germ cells surgically removed from the body and fertilised in laboratories (so that the embryo develops in a bottle and is decanted instead of born) he is writing of a possibility that biologists are seeing not more remotely than, let us say, Leonardo da Vinci saw the aeroplane. And it would add to the reader's sympathetic horror if he realised that the society which Mr. Huxley represents as being founded on this basis is actually the kind of society that various living people, notably in America and Russia, and in connection with the Bolshevist and Behaviourist movements, have expressed a desire to establish; and that this is true even of the least pleasing details.

There is, for instance, one incident which immensely enhances the impressiveness of the book if one knows its counter-part in reality.

In this new world there are various grades of human beings to do various work, ranging from Alphas, who hold all the positions of power and do all the intellectual work, to the Epsilons, who do all the drudgery and are too stupid to read or write. These are all bred for the purpose from selected germ-cells, exposed to various treatments during their bottled stages, and then educated by various devices depending on the theory of the 'conditioned reflex', which holds that any animal or human being can be taught to dislike an object, even if inherently pleasing, if it is always presented to them in association with an object that is inherently unpleasing to them. Mr. Huxley gives an example of one of these devices.

[Summarizes the conditioning of the babies, Chapter II, pp. 14–16]

This device serves two purposes. Since the Deltas have to perform fairly intricate work they cannot be bred below a certain fairly high level of intelligence, above that which would make it possible for them to read or write; but since the community cannot afford to have them waste their time on what must necessarily be a fourth-rate mental life, it seeks to make books hateful to them. And it has to discourage any native love of flowers, because they are not machine-made; and the appetite of citizens must be directed away from the natural to machine-made goods, so that the nightmare of over-production may be laid for ever.

Now the interesting thing about this experiment is that it is in technique exactly the same as those constantly conducted by Dr. John B. Watson,[1] the founder of Behaviourism, a philosophy which has probably made more adherents in the last twenty years than Christian Science did in the last twenty years of the nineteenth century, and finds them in a more influential grade.

I hope some time to try out the experiment of having a table top electrically wired in such a way that if a child reaches for a glass or a delicate vase, it will be punished, whereas if it reaches for its toys or other things it is allowed to play with, it can get them without being electrically shocked.

He believes in 'building in the negative reactions demanded by society'; and the society he belongs to is one that would certainly, if it could, have demanded such reactions as Mr. Huxley's new world demanded from the Deltas. Was it not that society in which, just before the Wall Street crash, a conference of automobile manufacturers expressed an intention of 'stimulating the two-car sense'?

There is, indeed, nothing at all impossible in Mr. Huxley's vision of a world where the infants are conditioned by such experiments, and by the dormitory loud speakers that whisper moral education into their sleeping ears (his pages on hypnopædia, or sleep-teaching, are among the most amusing in the book) into a lack of all characteristics save those which tend to uphold the stability of the State. Much of it is actual in America.

There is this salesmanship, which enjoins them to make a division between that which is valued and that which is preserved; they are taught to acquire an infinity of gimcrack objects, display them, throw them away. They are taught to dissipate their force on silly crowd pleasures. The talkies have become the feelies—they feel the kisses and the tears—but have not changed their fatuous essence. The chemists have found that drug they have been looking for, which intoxicates without deleterious effect on the nervous system. Leisure hours, therefore, become a blandly drunken petting-party; for promiscuity is a social duty, since it discourages far more than puritanism the growth of that disintegrating factor, love.

The religious instinct has been transferred by skilful conditioning to

[1] John Broadus Watson (1878–1958), U.S. psychologist, codified and forcefully publicized the theoretical program of behaviourism.

a deity known as Our Ford, whose beautiful and inspired sayings such as 'History is bunk' are reverently handed down. Age has disappeared, youth is artificially prolonged till 60, when there comes death, which is not feared. We are privileged to visit now a co-educational establishment under the headship of Miss Keate, a freemartin (for details refer to the first chapter of this book), and see five 'busloads of her pupils singing or in silent embracement', rolling home from Slough Crematorium for a stage in the death conditioning which begins at eighteen months.

Every tot spends two mornings a week in a hospital for the dying. All the best toys are kept there, and they get chocolate creams on death days. They learn to take dying as a matter of course. Emotional and intellectual life is entirely flattened out, so that the State which supplies the material needs of the citizens shall run with a triumphant smoothness, as it is intended in Bolshevist Russia. If the individual is drowned, at least he is drowned in a bath of communal happiness.

Into this world comes a Savage: a white child who has been born, through certain odd circumstances, in an American Indian reservation which has been kept untouched for psychological research reasons. His mind is governed by the harsh conceptions of Indian religion. He believes in the vileness of man that can be made acceptable to the gods only by fasting and scourging, and again scourging; so that blood must be drawn from the back if the gods are to let rain fall on the pueblo and the corn grow; and the delights of love must be fenced away by restriction upon restriction, and cancelled afterwards by shuddering loathing of them and contempt for the object who afforded them.

Towards those who begot or conceived one (so obscenely, compared with the decent technique of bottling and decanting) one is fixed in a torturing relationship of loving concern which it is almost impossible to destroy.

Far from blood and hatred and anguished passion being eliminated from life, they are ritually preserved; and nothing is done to veil the threat that, at the end of all this agony, there is nothing but a door painfully opening into emptiness. To this harsh existence there are no palliatives save the joy to be found in hunting and dancing, in the craftsmanship of the potter and the weaver: unserviceable æsthetic joys. It happens that the Savage has found in the Indian reservation an old volume containing the works of Shakespeare, an author forbidden in the new world on account of the reprehensibly private nature of the emotions he chiefly describes. They supply him with an almost complete language to express these blood-stained primitive beliefs; since the poet, also, for all that the literature teachers have done to disguise it (as one may read in an entertaining essay by Mr. Lytton Strachey), held beliefs not very different.

The Savage is, therefore, aware of his own world. It is not merely strangeness that makes him detest the new world and use the more denunciatory passages from Shakespeare to express what he thinks about its arrangement.

He finds contentment everywhere, but no nobility. Relief from the fear of death is no gain. As he sees his mother die in the Hospital for the Dying ('something between a first-class hotel and a feely palace, if you take my meaning,' says the nurse) doped with the new drug, canned music, and perfumes, while Epsilon dwarf twins munch chocolate eclairs round her bed as part of their death-conditioning treatment, he realises that to know the terror of death is better than to be drugged out of that knowledge. As he says when he talks to Mustapha Mond, one of the ten World Controllers (a cynic who reads Shakespeare, too, behind locked doors), things are too easy. One pays no price and one gets nothing valuable. He quotes Othello, 'If after every tempest come such calms, may the winds blow till they have wakened death.'

It is only at the end of the book that one sees precisely what literary task Mr. Aldous Huxley has set himself. He has rewritten in terms of our age the chapter called 'The Grand Inquisitor' in *The Brothers Karamazov*. In these days Dostoevsky is out of fashion, partly because he writes with heat and passion of the sort that Mr. T. S. Eliot's sham classicism has taught us to despise, and partly because the simple and elephant-sized neuroses of Tolstoy are easier for the inattentive eye to follow than the subtle spiritual ferments of Dostoevsky. But 'The Grand Inquisitor' is a symbolic statement that every generation ought to read afresh. In it Christ revisits earth, works a miracle in the streets of Seville, and is immediately, by order of the Cardinal, thrown into the prisons of the Inquisition.

The Cardinal visits the captive in the middle of the night and tells him that he has recognised him as the Christ, but means to burn him at the stake, because he insists on the freedom of man, and man cannot be happy unless he is a slave. 'For now' (he is speaking of the Inquisition, of course) 'for the first time it has become possible to think of the happiness of men. Man was created a rebel; and how can rebels be happy?'

The words are almost the same as Mr. Huxley's World Controller's. But instead of the Inquisition, instead of the orthodoxy that in the nineteenth century crushed spiritual endeavour, Mr. Huxley is attacking the new spirit which tries to induce man to divert in continual insignificant movements relating to the material framework of life all his force, and to abandon the practice of speculating about his existence and his destiny. Equally a denunciation of Capitalism and Communism so far as they discourage man from thinking freely, it is a declaration that art is a progressive revelation of the universe to man, and that those who interfere with it leave men to die miserably in the night of ignorance.

The book is many other things as well. One could cover many columns with discussion of its implications. It is, indeed, almost certainly one of the half-dozen most important books that have been published since the war.

64. Joseph Needham, review in *Scrutiny*

May 1932, i, pp. 76–9

Joseph Needham, b. 1900, internationally acclaimed professor, biochemist, and sinologist, has been Master of Gonville and Caius College at Cambridge since 1966. His numerous publications include the three-volume *Chemical Embryology* (1931) and *Within the Four Seas* (1970).

Needham begins his review, entitled 'Biology and Mr. Huxley,' by quoting the Berdiaev passage which serves as an epigraph to *Brave New World*. See Introduction, p. 16.

Mr. Huxley's book is indeed a brilliant commentary on this dismally true remark. It is as if a number of passages from Mr. Bertrand Russell's recent book *The Scientific Outlook* had burst into flower, and had rearranged themselves in patches of shining colour like man-eating orchids in a tropical forest. Paul planted, Apollos watered, but who gave the increase in this case, we may well ask, for a more diabolical picture of society (as some would say) can never have been painted.

Mr. Huxley's theme, embellished though it is by every artifice of that ingenuity of which he is master, is primarily dual, one of its aspects being the power of autocratic dictatorship, and the other, the possibilities of this power when given the resources of a really advanced biological engineering. The book opens with a long description of a human embryo factory, where the eggs emitted by carefully tended ovaries are brought up in the way they should go by mass-production methods on an endless conveyor belt moving very slowly until at last the infants are 'decanted' one by one into a highly civilised world. The methods of education by continual suggestion and all the possibilities of conditional reflexes are brilliantly described, and we are shown a world where art and religion no longer exist, but in which an *absolutely* stable form of society has been achieved, firstly, by sorting out the eggs into groups of known inherited characteristics and then setting each group, when adult, to do the work for which it is fitted, and secondly by allowing 'unlimited copulation' (sterile, of course) and unlimited sexual gratification of every kind. Here Mr. Huxley, whether consciously or not, has incorporated the views of many psychologists, e.g. Dr. Money Kyrle. In an extremely interesting paper* Dr. Kyrle has suggested that social discontent, which has always been the driving force in social change, is a manifestation of the Oedipus complexes of the members of society, and cannot be removed by economic means. With decrease of sexual taboos, these psychologists suggest, there would be a decrease of frustration and hence of that aggression which finds its outlet in religion, socialism, or more violent forms of demand for social change. This doctrine is indeed an extremely plausible one, and provides an answer to the question of what the 'born' reformer is to do when the ideal communist state, for instance, has been brought into being. Supposing that we have what we regard as an ideal state, how shall we ensure its continuance? Only, says Dr. Kyrle, by removing the sexual taboos which make the 'born' reformer. Accordingly, Mr. Huxley shows us the state of affairs when the attack on post- and pre-marital, and pre-pubertal taboos has long succeeded. The erotic play of children is encouraged, universal sexual relations are the rule, and indeed any sign of the beginning of a more deep and lasting affection is rebuked and stamped out, as being anti-social.

But Mr. Huxley, of course, sees so clearly what the psychologists do

* R. M. Kyrle, *A Psychologist's Utopia* (Psyche, 1931).

not see, that such a world must give up not only war, but also spiritual conflicts of any kind, not only superstition, but also religion, not only literary criticism but also great creative art of whatever kind, not only economic chaos, but also all the beauty of the old traditional things, not only the hard and ugly parts of ethics, but the tender and beautiful parts too. And it may well be that only biologists and philosophers will really appreciate the full force of Mr. Huxley's remarkable book. For of course in the world at large, those persons, and there will be many, who do not approve of his 'utopia', will say, we can't believe all this, the biology is all wrong, it couldn't happen. Unfortunately, what gives the biologist a sardonic smile as he reads it, is the fact that *the biology is perfectly right*, and Mr. Huxley has included nothing in his book but what might be regarded as legitimate extrapolations from knowledge and power that we already have. Successful experiments are even now being made in the cultivation of embryos of small mammals in vitro, and one of the most horrible of Mr. Huxley's predictions, the production of numerous low-grade workers of precisely identical genetic constitution from one egg, is perfectly possible. Armadillos, parasitic insects, and even sea-urchins, if treated in the right way, do it now, and it is only a matter of time before it will be done with mammalian eggs. Many of us admit that as we walk along the street we dislike nine faces out of ten, but suppose that one of the nine were repeated sixty times. Of course, the inhabitants of Mr. Huxley's utopia were used to it.

And it is just the same in the philosophical realm. We see already among us the tendencies which only require reasonable extrapolation to lead to Brave New World. Publicism, represented in its academic form by Mr. Wittgenstein and Prof. Schlick, and in its more popular form by Prof. Hogben and Mr. Sewell, urges that the concept of reality must be replaced by the concept of communicability. Now it is only in science that perfect communicability is attainable, and in other words, all that we can profitably say is, in the last resort, scientific propositions clarified by mathematical logic. To the realm of the Unspeakable, therefore, belong Ethics, Religion, Art, Artistic Criticism, and many other things. This point of view has a certain attraction and possesses, or can be made to possess, considerable plausibility, but in the end it has the effect of driving out Reason from the private incommunicable worlds of non-scientific experience. We are left with science as the only substratum for Reason, but what is worse, Philosophy or Metaphysics too is relegated to the realm of the Unspeakable, so that Science, which began as a special form of Philosophy, and which only retains its intellectually beneficial character if it retains its status as a special form of Philosophy, becomes nothing more nor less than the Mythology accompanying a Technique. And what will happen to the world in consequence is seen with perfect clearness both by Mr. Aldous Huxley and by Mr. Bertrand Russell. 'The scientific society in its pure form' says Mr. Russell, 'is incompatible with the pursuit of truth, with love, with art, with spontaneous delight, with every ideal that men have hitherto cherished, save only possibly ascetic renunciation. It is not knowledge that is the source of these dangers. Knowledge is good and ignorance is evil; to this principle the lover of the world can admit no exception. Nor is it power in and for itself that is the source of danger. What is dangerous is power wielded for the sake of power, not power wielded for the sake of genuine good.'

Such considerations, of course, do not solve the problem, they only convince us that a problem exists. But Mr. Huxley's orchid-garden is itself an exemplification of the contention that knowledge is always good, for had it not been for his imaginative power, we should not have seen so clearly what lies at the far end of certain inviting paths. To his convincing searchlight, humanity (it is not too much to say) will always owe great debt, and it must be our part to get his book read by any of our friends who suppose that science alone can be the saviour of the world.

65. L. A. G. Strong, review in *Spectator*

13 February 1932, cxlviii, p. 224

Leonard Alfred George Strong (1896–1958), novelist, poet, critic, was director of Methuen's publishing house 1938–58. His critical studies include *Common Sense about Poetry* (1932), *Synge* (1941), and *The Sacred River* [on Joyce] (1949).

Mr. Huxley has been born too late. Seventy years ago, the great powers of his mind would have been anchored to some mighty certitude, or to some equally mighty scientific denial of a certitude. To-day he searches heaven and earth for a Commandment, but searches in vain: and the lack of it reduces him, metaphorically speaking, to a man standing beside a midden, shuddering and holding his nose. For some years now Mr. Huxley has stood and shuddered. The obvious solution, to run away from the midden, is not possible for him. The mere knowledge of its existence must poison the whole landscape; and when it is apparent that, for him, the midden is the human body and its processes, his difficulty seems insuperable. *Brave New World* is the converse of Mr. Huxley's old theorem. Disgusted with the world of to-day, he imagines a scientifically perfected world in the dim future, and finds it equally unpleasant. In this new world children are of course born in laboratories, decanted, graded, and 'conditioned' so as to be suited for a particular status and vocation in the body politic and to be satisfied with it. Morality and convention, though stronger than ever, have changed their tune, and under the new motto 'Everyone belongs to everyone else', the height of immorality is to desire one man or one woman exclusively. 'Hypnopaedic' education—suggestion during sleep—standardizes all emotional reactions. To follow Mr. Huxley's erudite imagination through all the details of 'feelie' palaces, laboratories, helicopter excursions, etc., is a stimulating experience. There is no living writer, with the possible exception of Mr. Wells, who could have brought to the task such knowledge, such skill in the use of words, and such a savage sense of the ludicrous. The story which animates this essay concerns one or two characters with whom, despite all scientific precaution, something had gone wrong. They were individuals, and they met their inevitable fate—banishment to a remote island where the few misfits who demanded the right not to be happy could enjoy it together. This novel will shock some people, and shake a good many more. It is an astonishing feat of sheer intellect: but disgust, its driving force, if it is to be the mainspring of great art, needs to be coupled with exceptional *human* imagination, as in Swift: and of human imagination Mr. Huxley has little. Scientific imagination he has and to spare. The first chapters of this book are an amazement, but it does not finally satisfy the high demands it rouses in us, and this, I suspect, is the reason.

66. Charlotte Haldane, review in *Nature*

23 April 1932, cxxix, pp. 597–8

Charlotte Franken Haldane, b. 1894, novelist, translator, journalist, author of a study of Proust (1951) and *The Last Great Empress of China* (1968), among others. She was at this time married to the well-known scientist, J. B. S. Haldane, who may be the original of Shearwater in *Antic Hay* (see Clark, p. 223). J. B. S.'s sister, Naomi Mitchison, says her father 'is in a sense the original of Lord Edward in *Point Counter Point*' (*MV*, p. 53).

The review is entitled 'Dr. Huxley and Mr. Arnold.'

It is difficult to resist the conclusion that the writing of 'Utopias' is far more entertaining than reading them. This is probably due to the fact that the planning of a novel of the future gives an author an enhanced sense of power unobtainable from a novel of the present. The present is too full of the past not to limit that pleasant sensation; which is probably why so powerful a creator as Mr. Wells turned more than once to the future for his material.

It was inevitable that Mr. Aldous Huxley should sooner or later write a novel of the future. *Brave New World* is his second-best book, for he will never surpass *Antic Hay*. It proposes to describe a scientifically organised world, in which, however, one cannot imagine any scientist of to-day being able to live and work successfully. It is throughout a parody of the scientific point of view—shifting it ever so slightly but sufficiently towards the ridiculous—coupled with an exposition of Mr. Huxley's objections to what he conceives the scientific point of view to be. The reasons for these are two, of which the second will be described later.

In the first place, biology is itself too surprising to be really amusing material for fiction. If one wrote to-day a plain description of the work of Dr. Butenandt[1] on the male sex hormone, it would probably seem funnier than Mr. Huxley's detailed opening chapter on the 'Central London Hatchery and Conditioning Centre', where humanity is 'raised' on model factory lines. But never mind. What happens to these Alphas, Betas, Gammas, Deltas, and Epsilons, who are, of course, people, produced and conditioned and reared all nicely class-conscious and contented?

Mr. Huxley's genius here reveals itself: he knows their jokes, and they *are* funny; he also knows their sorrows and a cunning method for dealing with them, the ingestion of a pleasant dream-producing narcotic called 'soma'. He knows their pleasures, of which the foremost is promiscuous intercourse without fertilisation. Here he makes a slight mistake, for no young lady six hundred years hence would wear so primitive a garment as a Malthusian belt stuffed with contraceptives when a periodic injection of suitable hormones would afford her ample protection. But on mass entertainment, such as the 'feelies'—heirs to 'Talkies'—he is quite sound.

In his search for dramatic relief Mr. Huxley follows Voltaire. Borrowing from him the idea of 'L'Ingénu', a nice, simple savage, he provides one, a poor boy born mistakenly of a European father and mother, the latter a Beta-minus and all named Linda, who had got lost on an exploratory excursion to the New Mexican reservation where Indians were allowed to remain on sufferance. While Linda here relapses into a horrible state of pre-scientific squalor, her son John discovers the works of W. Shakespeare. Henceforth his speech is that of the bard.

Now, however, a terrible thing happens which brings us back to the

[1] Adolf Friedrich Johann Butenandt, b. 1903, German biochemist, was awarded a Nobel Prize for Chemistry (1939) for his work on sex hormones.

second reason for saying that Mr. Huxley is unable to do justice to the scientific point of view.

The savage is brought back to his kind in Europe and goes beserk in their brave new world. That is nothing. The terrible thing is this: Mr. Arnold appears once more and goes berserk on Dr. Huxley. (Everyone knows that Mr. Huxley is the grandson of T. H. Huxley. He is also the great-nephew, I believe, of Matthew Arnold, and therefore the great-grandson of 'Arnold of Rugby'.)

Dr. Jekyll and Mr. Hyde are nothing to Dr. Huxley and Mr. Arnold. Mr. Arnold is always doing it. He did it in *Point Counter Point*; he does it in *Brave New World*. Dr. Huxley, who knows and cares about biology and music, science and art, is once again ousted by this double of his, morbid, masochistic, medieval-Christian. Mr. Arnold takes charge of the last chapter of *Brave New World*. . . . [sic] The result is distressing. Nevertheless, this is a very great book.

67. Bertrand Russell, review in *New Leader*

11 March 1932, p. 9

Bertrand Arthur William Russell (1872–1970) was the foremost British philosopher of the twentieth century. He was awarded a Nobel Prize for Literature in 1950. Russell was among the Garsington group during and after the First World War, and may have been partly behind the figure of Scogan in *Crome Yellow*. Russell in fact objected to Huxley putting forward seriously, through Scogan, ideas which Russell says he discussed jokingly at Garsington (Clark, p. 224).

Philip Thody suggests that Russell's *The Scientific Outlook* was a source for *Brave New World*: 'Indeed, so much of *Brave New World* resembles *The Scientific Outlook* that one wonders at times if Huxley put any original ideas into his book' (*Aldous Huxley*, pp. 50–1).

The title of the typescript of the review was 'A Manipulator's Paradise,' changed in the printed version to 'We Don't Want to be Happy.' Indicative sub-headings are here omitted. See Introduction, p. 16.

In the happy days of Queen Victoria men used to write Utopias to suggest the likelihood of even greater happiness in the future. In the unhappy days in which it is our lot to live, Utopias are written in order to make us still more unhappy. Mr. Aldous Huxley, in his *Brave New World*, has shown his usual masterly skill in producing this result upon the reader, for he has undertaken to make us sad by the contemplation of a world without sadness.

In the world that he portrays everybody has a job, and everybody likes his job; there is hardly any sickness, and people preserve their vigour almost to the day of their death; there is no fear of poverty, there are no unhappy marriages, and there are no wars. When the working day is over, everybody enjoys the benefits of an intoxicant which has no bad after-effects upon the system.

In spite of these merits, the world which Mr. Huxley portrays is such as to arouse disgust in every normal reader, and obviously in Mr. Huxley himself. I have been asking myself why, and trying hard to think that his well-regulated world would really be an improvement upon the one in which we live. At moments I can make myself think this, but I can never make myself feel it. The feeling of revulsion against a well-ordered world has various sources: one of these is that we do not value happiness as much as we sometimes think we do. We like adventure, self-determination, and power more than we like happiness. Most of us would be unwilling to live in an opium dream even if it could go on and on without any reaction.

Another unpleasant aspect of Mr. Huxley's world is the method adopted for producing contentment. Human beings are no longer born in the old-fashioned way, but are artificially incubated and ultimately 'decanted'. During incubation they are treated in various ways which determine their mental, physical, and social status throughout their future life. Moral instruction is given to children by means of machines under their pillows, which whisper to them while they sleep the same moral platitude over and over again for years. This has an hypnotic effect, which makes them incapable of moral revolt. They are 'conditioned' against a dislike of death by being taken into hospitals and given sweets while the patients die. Those who are going to be workers underground are taught to dislike the beauties of the open air by having flowers shown to them when they are babies and getting an electric shock whenever they touch them.

The system is almost perfectly successful; almost everybody is happy almost all the time. But we are shocked—more, I think, than we ought to be—by the idea of moulding people scientifically instead of allowing them to grow. We have a notion that we can choose what we will be, and that we should not wish to be robbed of this choice by scientific manipulators drugging us before we are born, giving us electric shocks in infancy, and whispering platitudes to us throughout our childhood.

But this feeling is, of course, irrational. In the course of nature the embryo grows through natural causes. The infant learns haphazard lessons of pleasure and pain which determine his taste. The child listens to moral propaganda, which may fail through being unscientific, but which, none the less, is intended to mould the character just as much as Mr. Huxley's whispering machines. It seems, therefore, that we do not object to moulding a human being, provided it is done badly; we only object when it is done well. What we cling to so desperately is the illusion of freedom, an illusion which is tacitly negated by all moral instruction and all propaganda. To us human life would be intolerable without this illusion. In Mr. Huxley's *Brave New World* men live quite comfortably without it.

What is the reformer to do in this dilemma? Pride and self-direction and all the other kinds of anarchic glory that have made our great saints no less than our great sinners are becoming incompatible with the continued existence of a civilised society. In the Middle Ages all Christendom hated the Turk. The Turks and Christians, in spite of their utmost endeavours, failed to do each other more than a very moderate amount of harm. In our day the same degree of hatred would bring both sides to complete destruction. We must learn not to hate. A few saints and mystics can love without hating, but for the bulk of mankind the only way not to hate is not to have any strong feelings at all.

If you follow out this thought you will be led straight to Huxley's world as the only civilised world that can be stable. At this stage most people will say: 'Then let us have done with civilisation.' But that is an abstract thought, not realising in the concrete what such a choice would mean. Are you prepared that ninety-five per cent. of the population should perish by poison gases and bacteriological bombs, and that the other five per cent. should revert to savagery and live upon the raw fruits of the earth? For this is what will inevitably happen, probably within the next fifty years, unless there is a strong world government. And a strong world government, if brought about by force, will be tyrannical, caring nothing for liberty and aiming primarily at perpetuating its own power. I am afraid, therefore, that, while Mr. Huxley's prophecy is meant to be fantastic, it is all too likely to come true.

Is there, then, no hope? Yes, of course there is. Disband the world's armies and navies, forbid the construction of aeroplanes even for commercial purposes, and abolish all tariffs. If this is done, it may be possible to preserve a civilisation worth having. Meanwhile we have the Disarmament Conference and the bombardment of Shanghai.

68. Gerald Bullett, review in
Fortnightly Review

March 1932, cxxxvii, pp. 402–3

Gerald (William) Bullett (1893–1958) wrote numerous works of fiction, criticism, essays and reviews, such as *Modern English Fiction* (1926) and *The Quick and the Dead* (1933).

Mr. Aldous Huxley's new novel is definitely a disappointment—the least of the many good things he has given us. As prophecy it is merely fantastic; as satire it overshoots the mark (if indeed there *is* a mark); as a story it lacks interest. It is, in fact, an elaborate and somewhat tedious joke. And what else? There are signs, alas, that Mr. Huxley would have us take his satire seriously, would have us applaud him as he pelts with ridicule, damns with ironical praise, one scientific Aunt Sally after another. The book's intention seems to be suggested in the passage from Nicholas Berdiaeff quoted on the fore-page:

[Cites Berdiaeff]

. . . But nothing is more grotesquely improbable than that the world will ever be so efficiently ordered, and human beings so accurately conditioned and controlled, that all our present spiritual values will be meaningless to us. This is the state of affairs in Mr. Huxley's *Brave New World*.

[Recounts some of the startling features of Fordian London]

Into this world the author brings a young man called John, who has been born and brought up in one of those Savage Reservations which exist in places held to be not worth the trouble of civilizing. From the point of view of satire—for satire is nothing if not didactic—this does not help us much. Between John and the typical Alpha or Beta there is precious little to choose: they represent opposite extremes of folly. John is a psychological mess: he has an uneasy conscience, he is a raging

213

prude, he has a powerful appetite for self-mortification. It is impossible that Mr. Huxley should intellectually approve of John, of whom the best that can be said is that he loved his mother with maniacal extravagance and had assimilated into his own speech many of the utterances of Shakespeare. Yet if we were to unravel all the implications of this allegory I fancy we should find reason for supposing that Mr. Huxley is at one with John in respect of certain important opinions or sentiments: that physical pain is good for the soul, that discomfort is a holier state than comfort, that pleasure is a necessary evil. The other novels of Mr. Huxley suggest that ordinary human nature (of which there happens to be no example in *Brave New World*) is something for which he has small admiration and much contempt. Angry puritan as he is, he can never forgive himself and his fellows for being, among other things, animals. I am inclined to prophesy that within ten years, unless meanwhile he becomes reconciled to our sad condition, he will be received, with loud applause from the faithful, into the bosom of the Church of Rome.

69. Henry Hazlitt, review in *Nation* (New York)

17 February 1932, cxxxiv, pp. 204, 206

Henry Hazlitt, b. 1894, an American economist, was literary editor of the *Nation* 1930–3 and served on the *New York Times* editorial staff 1934–46. His books include *The Anatomy of Criticism* (1933) and *Man vs. The Welfare State* (1970).

Hazlitt's review, entitled 'What's Wrong with Utopia?,' opens by citing the Berdiaev epigraph to the novel, here omitted.

Mr. Huxley has portrayed here a Utopia that obviously he would wish to avoid. It is set ostensibly in the far future, the year of Our Ford, 632. One has not read very far, however, before one perceives that this is not really Mr. Huxley's idea of what the future will be like, but a projection of some contemporary ideals. So far as progress in invention is concerned, there is very little in this Utopia, outside of the biological sphere at least, that does not seem realizable within the next twenty years—though people do go to the 'feelies.' Economically, the ideals that prevail are those usually associated with Henry Ford—mass production and particularly mass consumption. Everyone spends freely, and games and other pleasures that do not require the use of elaborate and expensive apparatus are frowned upon. The social organization is communistic—there is a World State managed by ten World Controllers, who head an almost Catholic hierarchy; everyone is assigned his job, is educated to identify his interests with those of everyone else, and is suspected if he is ever found alone. The official religion is Fordianity; people under stress of emotion say 'Ford forbid!' or 'Ford's in his flivver; all's well with the world,' and make the sign of the T. *My Life and Work* has replaced the Bible, and all old books are forbidden to circulate because they suggest the past and history is bunk. Moreover, reading wastes time that should be given to consumption.

The sexual *mores* stem from the ideals associated with the names of Freud and Bertrand Russell.

[Describes the 'complete promiscuity' and the 'rigid caste system' of Huxley's future]

. . . The purpose of the caste system is social stability. There could obviously be no social stability if everyone were an Alpha. The lower castes are prevented from being dissatisfied by having brains geared down to the work they have to do. In addition to these hereditary and prenatal precautions, conditioning along the lines discovered by Freud, Pavlov, and Watson begins at birth. The secret of happiness and virtue, as one director points out, is liking what you've *got* to do; therefore all conditioning aims at making people like their unescapable social destiny. Children are conditioned to hate flowers by giving them regularly an electric shock when they touch them. In their sleep certain maxims, like 'Everybody belongs to everybody else,' are repeated to them over and over again, so that the adult mind accepts them as axioms. Finally, these people are also protected from whatever physical and emotional pain there may be left in the world by regular doses of *soma*, a drug somewhat similar in its qualities to morphine, with none of the latter's bad after-effects.

What is wrong with this Utopia? Mr. Huxley attempts to tell us by the device of introducing a 'savage,' brought up under other ideals on an Indian reservation, and having read that author unknown to the Model T. Utopia, Shakespeare. In the admittedly violent and often irrational reactions of the 'savage' we have the indictment of this civilization. Not only is there no place in it for love, for romance, for fidelity, for parental affection; there is no suffering in it, and hence absolutely no need of nobility and heroism. In such a society the tragedies of Shakespeare become not merely irrelevant, but literally meaningless. This Model T. civilization is distinguished by supreme stability, comfort, and happiness, but these things can be purchased only at a price, and the price is a high one. Not merely art and religion are brought to a standstill, but science itself, lest it make discoveries that would be socially disturbing. Even one of the ten World Controllers is led to suspect the truth, though of course forbidding the publication, of a theory holding that the purpose of life is not the maintenance of well-being, but 'some intensification and refining of consciousness, some enlargement of knowledge.'

Brave New World is successful as a novel and as a satire; but one need not accept all its apparent implications. A little suffering, a little irrationality, a little division and chaos, are perhaps necessary ingredients of an ideal state, but there has probably never been a time when the world has not had an oversupply of them. Only when we have reduced them enormously will Mr. Huxley's central problem become a real problem. Meanwhile reformers can continue to strain every muscle in the quiet assurance of their own futility. They may, for example, form their Leagues of Nations, draw up their Kellogg Pacts and Nine-Power Treaties, and hold their disarmament conferences, in the calm confidence that a Japan will still brutally attack a China.

70. Margaret Cheney Dawson, review in *NYHTBR*

7 February 1932, p. 5

Margaret Cheney Dawson, author of a novel entitled *City Harvest* (1934).

The review is entitled 'Huxley Turns Propagandist.' See Introduction, p. 16.

Mr. Huxley has the jitters. Looking back over his career one can see that he has always had them, in varying degrees, that the flesh and the intellect have exasperated him in almost equal proportions, that love and lust and art and science and religion and philosophy have been so much pepper to his nostrils. Time was when these and other phases of the human experiment appeared to him ridiculous and he exposed them, brutally to be sure, but with charming malice and suave literary grace. As the years went and novels came, the dry wine of his wit began to sour and his satire to toughen into something closely resembling didacticism. To the astonishment of those who had counted as much on his thoroughgoing erudition as his brilliance for stimulation, the second phase of his development failed to produce any outstandingly powerful or original results. The fine edge of his bitterness was worn down to querulous argument. And now, with what can only be called a straight case of jitters, he abandons his genius for mere ingenuity and rushes headlong into the great pamphleteering movement.

Brave New World is intended to be the Utopia to end Utopias, the burlesque of grandiose modern schemes for futurity. It is described by the publishers as 'witty and wickedly satirical,' but unless the substitution of Ford for God ('Ford's in his Flivver, all's well with the world') and the introduction of such scintillating nursery rhymes as 'Streptocock-Gee to Banbury T, to see a fine bathroom and W.C.' can be relied on to stop the show, it must stand on its merits as a lugubrious and heavy-handed piece of propaganda.

[Describes the methods of achieving stability in the new world]

The description of the fertilizing room, the decanting room, the predestinating room, etc., have a horrible fascination. Every detail is conceived and depicted with the utmost ingenuity, and if Mr. Huxley had confined himself to such vivid grotesqueries, he might have given us a first rate case of the horrors. It is when he runs into plot development that the illusion fails. By way of supplying adverse comment on the system, he brings on the scene a 'savage,' i.e., the child of a 'civilized' woman who had been abandoned with her viviparous shame in a New Mexican Indian reservation. This boy, John, had grown up in a very confused state, his mother extolling the wonders of civilization on the one hand, while his Indian playmates and an old copy of Shakespeare taught him an utterly different set of values on the other. He learned to prize heroism, to honor self-discipline, to believe in chastity. In the new world to which an enterprising Alpha Plus transported him, these virtues were useless, in fact, incomprehensible. But John could not relinquish his belief in them nor resist trying to convert the placid herds to his own credo of divine discontent. Trouble ensued, and at last John the Savage was arrested and brought face to face with his Fordship Mustapha Mond, Resident World Controller for Western Europe. There follows a dialogue that contains the meat of the matter, during which John pleads for the 'right to be unhappy' and protests against 'getting rid of everything unpleasant instead of learning to put up with it.' Both arguments the Controller meets with commendable placidity, while showing John out the door. The unhappy savage retires to seclusion and eventually to suicide. And then at the very end, after all the sound and fury, Mr. Huxley relents for a moment and gives us a few plangent phrases in which lie the only echo of his former work, the only whisper of better things to come.

71. Granville Hicks, review in *New Republic*

10 February 1932, lxix, p. 354

Granville Hicks, b. 1901, was an assistant professor of English at Rensselaer Polytechnic Institute, 1929–35, and a contributing editor for *Saturday Review* 1958–69. Among his books are *The Great Tradition—An Interpretation of American Literature since the Civil War* (1933) and *Literary Horizons* (1970). See Introduction, p. 16.

With war in Asia, bankruptcy in Europe and starvation everywhere, what do you suppose Aldous Huxley is now worrying about? If you happen to have read an article he published about a year ago in *The Virginia Quarterly Review*,[1] you will be able to guess. He is worrying about the unpleasantness of life in the utopia that, as he sees it, is just a century or two ahead.

Brave New World is, as one would expect, a somewhat amusing book; a bright man can do a great deal with two or three simple ideas. Mr. Huxley assumes that, six hundred years from now, mass-production methods have been perfected, Freudian psychology has triumphed, and certain biological experiments, notably in the field of ectogenesis, have born fruit.

[Summarizes the society and the story]

. . . It is difficult to suppose that Mr. Huxley is really much concerned about God and romance and the beauty of motherhood, but he

[1] 'Boundaries of Utopia,' *Virginia Quarterly Review*, January 1931, vii, pp. 47–54.

sees that there is something to be said for them, and the whole argument does show that after all human nature is human nature. Anyway, two of the rebels are sent to Ireland, and the savage commits suicide.

This is a pretty horrid picture Mr. Huxley paints, and he can be sure that any of us, after reading his book, will think twice before taking steps that might bring about such a calamity. Perhaps we had better not do anything about social injustice or international anarchy. A quotation in the front of *Brave New World* points out that utopias are almost inevitable and that a day will come when intellectuals will dream of ways of avoiding utopias and returning to a society less 'perfect' but freer. The better way, the book shows, is here and now to nip the utopias in the bud. After all, Mr. Huxley must have his chance to suffer and be brave.

Apparently we have been doing Mr. Huxley an injustice in thinking of him as a bored, cynical and generally rebellious young man. He is, on the contrary, quite well satisfied with life as it is. And why, when you stop to think of it, shouldn't he be? He has money, social position, talent, friends, prestige, and he is effectively insulated from the misery of the masses. Of course he demands the right to suffer bravely. Of course he wants something to worry about—even if he has to go a long, long way to find it.

72. Hermann Hesse, review in *Die Neue Rundschau* (Berlin)

May 1933, Supplement, p. 2

Hermann Hesse (1877–1962), famous German novelist and poet, recipient of a Nobel Prize for Literature (1946), wrote for example *Siddhartha* (1922) and *Steppenwolf* (1927). See Introduction, p. 16.

The translation is by Professor G. Wallis Field, Chairman of the Department of German at Victoria College, the University of Toronto.

Huxley's utopian novel has all the pleasant characteristics of his earlier books, the good ideas, the nice humour, the ironic cleverness. Its effectiveness is only diminished by the utopian element itself, through the unreality of its human beings and situations. With perspicuity and irony a completely mechanized world is depicted, in which the human beings themselves have long since ceased to be human but are only 'standardized' machines. Only two of them are not wholly machines, one superior and one inferior; they still have remnants of humanity, of soul, of personality, of dream and passion. In addition there is a savage, a complete human being who, with logical consistency, quickly succumbs in the standardized civilized world: the last human being. There survive the two half-human beings and one of them may well be the symbol of Huxley's own tragic fate: the figure of the clever, gifted, successful, brilliant man of letters who, to be sure, has been too far engulfed by civilization in order to be a poet, as his ambition desired, but who knows well enough about the magic and miracle of poetry, perhaps has plumbed the depths of what it means to be a poet more thoroughly than any real poet ever could, for he sees with perfect clarity that poetry rises from other roots than technology, that like religion and genuine learning it thrives on sacrifices and passions, which are impossible on the asphalt of a standardized superficial world with its cheap department-store happiness.

221

This book does not reach the level of tragedy. We remain on the level of a slightly melancholy irony, but one loves Huxley for the sake of this figure, one loves his deep love for Shakespeare and his gently ironic gesture of resignation.

73. Two opinions of Huxley's significance

1933

Review article, based on Huxley's *Texts and Pretexts*, by C. P. Snow (for a biographical note see No. 136), entitled 'The Case of Aldous Huxley,' *Cambridge Review*, 17 February 1933, liv, pp. 249–50, and a letter by Elizabeth Downs in reply to Snow, 24 February 1933, liv, p. 272. See Introduction, pp. 1, 17.

(a) C. P. Snow, 'The Case of Aldous Huxley'

All the bright things have already been said about Huxley—all the bright things and some not quite so bright. Angry men with strong views have used words which make a nasty hissing sound, like 'salacity' or 'lubricity'; when they have done this, they feel that the situation and Huxley are dealt with. On the other hand, equally angry men with equally strong views call him 'the last of the Puritans'. Sometimes he is compared with his grandfather and his brother, in a way apparently intended to disparage all three. In Marseilles he is regarded as the leader of the Neo-Classical movement in English letters; Mr. John Strachey, however, sees him as the last writer of a dying civilisation (along with Proust and Lawrence, between whom Mr. Strachey detects a resemblance which no one has ever seen before or will again).

Gerhardi finds Huxley impossible to accept as an artist; and Mr. Middleton Murry regretfully feels that he is over-rated as an authority on human nature.

I would not like to add to the confusion or the brightness. Brightness has been enough nuisance to Huxley as it is; through his books, one gets rather wistful references to it—'brilliant as a smile of false teeth' comes in *Antic Hay* when, for a moment, he writes about the almost morbid shyness which seems to lie behind that brightness and that heavily-carried erudition. Brightness has got in his way, just as it got in Shaw's way. For both of them it gained readers, and obscured their importance. For if you can call a man 'amusing', there is no real need to call him anything else, and if you can call him 'amusing and intelligent', then he might as well write revues.

Whoever we are, we tend to take views seriously only when they have been pounded into us so long and so heavily that we are bored— and unwillingly impressed. In the same way, we only esteem creative writing fully when we go through the words, the pages, the chapters, without a glimmer of relief; it is only then that we are persuaded of the truth of the artists' emotions; we read steadfastly through the Father Zossima part of *The Brothers Karamazov* and the arid genealogies of the second part of *The Guermantes Way*—and by their sheer unrelieved dulness, they add, they actually and indisputably add, to the effect of the creation. Dulness adds to a work of art as much as brightness takes away. Perhaps some day, if ever critical appreciation gets quicker and more impatient, that is if we get more agile mentally, we shall change all this. At present, however, it is true, even though we regret it.

Usually it doesn't matter; but with Huxley it does, for it prevents even those best disposed towards him, including Huxley himself, from realising that he is saying some very important things. Lawrence got his gospel home, by a reiteration which was guilty of many crimes but not of brightness. He hammered at us until we were bored—but yet impressed. Huxley himself has had his revelations: but he has put them in with a joke in order to excuse them: and though we appreciated them intellectually as we read, they didn't sink any deeper. The heart is a humourless organ completely insensitive to brightness. It prefers to be battered at by the unintelligent.

It is a pity. We have, however, to admit that Huxley produces less effect on us than writers who are inferior to him in every possible way. He has the best intellect of any considerable writer that I can remember reading; his mind is certainly the most completely equipped (even the pinnacle of erudition once announced that 'Huxley is the only man of letters with a sound elementary education': which means, if you know the language, that Huxley is capable of talking with authority on seventh century architecture, the meaning of the positive solution of the wave equation, and the earlier works of Lope de Vega.)

He has the mental qualities which other writers have not at all; and because he has, it is too easy to imagine that he has nothing else. While in fact he has a great deal more. He has the response to the sensuous world which has been bred in every major novelist since Proust wrote about his bedroom at Combray. He does not give us the sensuous moment with Gerhardi's casual breath-taking rightness, or Forster's delicate ease, or Virginia Woolf's enthusiasm. But those three, who are masters of the sensuous moment, stop short while Huxley is conveying emotions and ideas about human beings—which perhaps should be the greater part of a novelist's art. When he does this, he shows an intuition, an emotional sensitivity, which very few of the great novelists have surpassed—Dostoievski certainly, Tolstoi certainly, perhaps Turgeniev, perhaps Lawrence (in a left-handed sort of way).

One reads *Antic Hay* or *Those Barren Leaves* or *Point Counter Point* and feels all this. And yet all the time there is a feeling of uneasiness, the disturbing question—is he an artist like the others after all? Isn't he a very clever man, with, as it were, an imitative-colour of the artist? Isn't he a wonderfully constructed synthetic model of the real thing?

Many of us have had these doubts, I think. As I have said, the fault seems to me to be more with us than with Huxley. I don't believe in the divine right of the reader, not even when the reader is myself. There are, probably, one or two technical reasons which are responsible for something of the effect of his words; but far more it is that he is intellectually too mobile for us, too 'bright' in the right sense as well as the wrong. There is a packed beautifully quick-moving mind behind the bad jokes; we admire, are a little disturbed for a time—and reserve our homage for someone nearer our own intellectual pace.

So, through our own incapacity, we are missing the vital thing he has already expressed, the attitude which is the essence of so many men of his age and younger, both in their hopelessness and their hope. More than any writer in English, he represents the 'consciousness of motive' which a few but increasing number of people are beginning to show. By 'consciousness of motive' I mean some grasp of the reasons behind the actions that one does and other people do, some idea of the causes behind the words we speak. I am not suggesting that the greater portion of our civilization is suddenly acquiring an intense psychological insight; of course, almost everyone still believes that the reasons they give to themselves for their own actions are the true ones; the words they speak seem still to mean nothing but their face-value. That is the present stage of things, and it will be so while men are anything like their present selves. To be interested in the regions beyond consciousness, to possess the technique for exploring other people as ourself, needs a sort of intelligence and intuition which will always be rare. 'Consciousness' will never be as popular as Anglo-Catholicism. It is not a good basis for a group movement. But there are a growing number of people who are aware of it as a factor in the modern world: and Huxley has used his wit and wisdom to describe how they think and what they think.

They are mostly of Huxley's age or younger; in so far as meaningless generalisations like 'generations' mean anything, the division between the intellectual 'old' and 'young' is better marked by 'consciousness' than by any other line. They are usually products of a liberal tradition: the Fabian of 1900 or the Wellsian humanist of a little later has been replaced by someone sympathetic to both—yet uncomfortably knowing *why* he is sympathetic. You will find Huxley in all his later works trying to disentangle his own progressive prejudices; he performs feats of fair-mindedness in explaining how St John of the Cross's interpretation of experience may be as valid as Proust's (though he himself, for reasons which he is prepared to indicate, has a predisposition in favour of Proust).

What they will do with this consciousness is difficult to say. Perhaps it will be swept away by communism (which like any religious movement would kill the complete consciousness in individuals). Perhaps it will express itself in a psychology like Jung's and a few works of art, which would promptly be misunderstood as we misunderstand Huxley. Almost certainly, it will not make for much difference in action. Knowing why one acts doesn't make one act differently; it may occasionally prevent one acting at all. There may not be much to look forward to. There is, however, just this: that consciousness should make life more complicated, richer, and that anything built with it as a basis, from the friendship of two people to the society of many, has some chance of being free from the grosser stupidities and meannesses. That is all; it may be a good deal.

Meanwhile, as Huxley says in *Texts and Pretexts*, it remains 'to pipe up for reason and realism and a certain decency'. If you want to see him doing it and to follow his mind through some of its illuminating states, to see 'consciousness' at work, you should read this pleasant anthology. It is a selection that very few men could have made; the commentaries are Huxley at his best—and then just to remind us that he has his weaker side, he includes a poem (presumably obscene, from the context) in the original Spanish.

It is a spare time collection, thrown off in the interval between novels. It is interesting enough for its own sake, but above all it should be read for the insight it gives into his own creations. Huxley is on the way to becoming an English institution; it would be a pity if he became one before his interpretation of consciousness has gone home, for otherwise it never will. This anthology ought to be read: and then some of the essays such as *Do What You Will* and *Jesting Pilate;* and then *Antic Hay, Those Barren Leaves,* and *Point Counter Point*; after that he ought to seem the most significant English novelist of his day. And if he doesn't, the reader should at least have learned enough about himself to know why he can't like Huxley.

(b) Letter in reply from Elizabeth Downs

Sir,—Dr Snow has presented a challenging view of Aldous Huxley as 'the most significant English novelist of his day' and as one who can bear comparison with all but the very greatest of the past. He regards him as combining brilliance and comprehensiveness of intellect with an intuition and sensitiveness in communicating emotion which the average, and even the intelligent, reader misses through an incapacity to keep pace with Huxley's quickness of mind. The result of this incapacity is that he fails to appreciate 'the vital thing' in Huxley—the quality which Dr Snow calls 'consciousness of motive' and which seems from his description of it to be the union of an honest mind with a knowledge of up-to-date psychology.

It is rash to dissent from Dr Snow, and so automatically to brand oneself as a slow-witted dullard, but I do still find myself among those whom he describes as suffering from 'a feeling of uneasiness' when he brackets Huxley with Dostoievski and Tolstoi. Dr Snow brings forward no illustrations of the richness and variety of Huxley's emotional intuitions, and I do not quite know where we are to find them. His conclusion about life *seems* to be summed up at the end of *Antic Hay*:

'To-morrow,' said Gumbril.
'To-morrow,' said Mrs Viveash, 'will be as awful as to-day.'

He can, as Dr Snow points out, report and analyse and describe the position of the mystic, with the most penetrating critical brilliance; he can make Calamy *say* that life is 'beautiful, terrible and mysterious, pregnant with what enormous secret, symbolic of what formidable reality?' But who has ever *felt* it to be so in the pages of Huxley? Its symbol to him, indeed, seems to be that of the gigantic bubble of hypocrisy and humbug which he explodes with his masterly and effective satire. Has his 'consciousness of motive' made him aware of many motives which are not either actively base or passively stupid, or has his intuitive sensitiveness given him any more positive emotion (in his books) than an almost brutal dislike and contempt of the very limited range of characters he presents? His art is the art of exposure, not of creation.

And that is why, in spite of his quite first-rate qualities of mind and personality, and the richness of his intellectual range; in spite of his bracing and sane rationalism and his amazing precision of critical insight and analysis, all of which make his books some of the most stimulating and thought-provoking of the age, one continues to question whether he is more than a minor novelist, with a very meagre emotional scope. It is because, when one puts his work beside that of the really creative writers of even his own day, let alone the past, one feels, for example, that he has none of the depth and variety of patient human understanding of the author of *The Old Wives' Tale*; none of the fine heady enthusiasm and rich creative zest of the author of *Tono Bungay*; none of the exquisitely subtle intuitive grace of the author of *The Waves*; none of the completely original technique of seizing and presenting human experience of the authors of *A la recherche du temps perdu* or *Ulysses*; none of the intensity of sustained vision of the author of *Nostromo* or of the single-minded passion of the author of *St. Mawr*.

74. G. K. Chesterton on Huxley

1933

Gilbert Keith Chesterton (1874–1936), renowned essayist, critic and novelist, author of such books as *The Victorian Age in Literature* (1913) and *The Everlasting Man* (1925). Maisie Ward's observation in the *DNB* summarizes Chesterton's position: 'Never did Chesterton give in to the "rather weakminded reaction", the mood of pacificism [sic] and appeasement that followed the war of 1914–1918.' See Introduction, p. 15.

The text is from Chesterton's essay 'The End of the Moderns,' *London Mercury*, January 1933, xxvii, pp. 228–33. The essay was reprinted in *The Common Man* (London: Sheed & Ward, 1950), pp. 196–205.

In the opening lines of the essay, here omitted, Chesterton contends that the age of revolt in art and thought is over.

. . . As for the present, no period could be entirely dull when Mr. Aldous Huxley was writing in it; but it is significant to notice what he writes. In one of his latest books, *Brave New World*, he shows that however grimly he may enjoy the present, he already definitely hates the future. And I only differ from him in not believing that there is any such future to hate.

I take these two names[1] as typical of what has been called in the last decade modernity or revolt; but the thesis I would seriously suggest covers something larger and perhaps simpler. The revolutionary elements in our epoch do not mark the beginning, but the end, of an epoch of revolution. I should hesitate to describe a number of distinguished and often honest literary gentlemen as Dregs; or I would have given that short and convenient title to this article. I prefer to put the same meaning, or even the same metaphor, into the words of a

[1] Huxley and D. H. Lawrence.

revolutionary poet (whose present unpopularity is enough to show how insecure is the future of revolutionary poetry) and while I drink to the memory of Lawrence or the health of Huxley, murmur the words:

> All thine the last wine that I pour is
> The last in the chalice I drain.

That will suggest the same idea in less offensive language. In short, it is doubtless true, in the words of Mr. Jefferson Brick (that pioneer of revolt), that the Libation of Freedom must sometimes be quaffed in Blood; but whether it be in blood or wine, that cup is very nearly dry.

[Attacks what he calls 'the literature of blasphemy' and says that it leads to suicide]

. . . And when we turn to the more subtle and suggestive writers, such as those I have named, we shall find that this is exactly their own condition. They are not opening the gates either of heaven or hell; they are in a blind-alley, at the end of which there is no door. They are always philosophising and they have no philosophy. They have not reached that reality, that reason of things, or even that fully realised unreason of things, for which they are obviously and indeed avowedly seeking. But, what is here more to the point, they do not (like the old revolutionists) even know the direction in which they are to seek it. They have failed to discover, not only any purpose in the world, but even any purpose in the will. They are witty, brilliant and fashionable bankrupts. They have come to an end; and they have not come to an End. The earlier rebels were happy in being pioneers of the actual forward movements of their time; as Walt Whitman, axe in hand, walked before the actual march of industrial democracy. But Mr. Aldous Huxley can hardly be roused by the word Democracy.

[Criticizes Lawrence for stressing things earthy]

. . . [Huxley cuts] down his own standard to something so thin that it can hardly stand. In one of his recent novels, a character sums up much of the general teaching of the author, by saying that Man must not hope to be either an animal or an angel. He adds, significantly, that it is a tight-rope sort of business.[1] Now walking on a tight-rope is both difficult and dangerous; and the author makes the good life really more difficult than it is for an ascetic. He has not only to avoid being an animal, but he must guard against any unlucky accident that might turn

---

[1] Rampion in *Point Counter Point*, 560.

him into an angel. That is, he is forbidden to have the enthusiasms and spiritual ambitions that have sustained the saints, and yet he has got to become in cold blood something much more exceptional than a saint. Nobody asks such a realist as Mr. Huxley to idealise the real. But such a realist must surely know that human nature cannot show, at every instant, the valour and vigilance of a spiritual tight-rope walker, cannot suffer more for this ideal than all the heroes, and yet be forbidden even to idealise its own ideal. The plan of life is simply obviously unworkable; where the plans of the wildest mystics and martyrs have proved workable.

I say that I do not abhor these men as the first figures of an advancing anarchist army. On the contrary, I admire these men as the last figures of a defeated anarchist army. I take these two original and forcible writers as types of many others; but the point is that they are not, like the anarchists of history, at the head of an army marching in a determined direction. That is exactly what they are not. Lawrence rushed out against almost everything; Huxley, being more sensitive, recoils from almost everything. But, however valuable be the vivid description of the one or the sharp criticism of the other, they are not valuable as guides; and certainly not as guides to a revolution. They had not the simplification given either by religion or irreligion. There was something grand about D. H. Lawrence groping blindly in the dark; but he really was in the dark, not only about the Will of God, but about the will of D. H. Lawrence. He was ready to go anywhere; but he did not really know where to go next. Aldous Huxley is ideally witty; but he is at his wit's end.

. . . People will call Mr. Aldous Huxley a pessimist; in the sense of one who makes the worst of it. To me he is that far more gloomy character; the man who makes the best of it. He gives the best advice he can; in conditions of converging impossibility. I do not write here in a hostile spirit about any of these recent realistic or revolutionary writers; on the contrary, I sincerely sympathise with them, because, unlike the earlier revolutionists, they know they are in an intellectual hole. Doubtless, there are thousands of gay and buoyant innovators, who are not intelligent enough to know it. But the same plan of defeat is spread over the whole situation. It can be seen, for instance, in the thousands of thoughtless 'sexual' novels, the writers of which are evidently unconscious that they have got into a logical contradiction about the whole position of sex. They inherit the notion that sex is a serious crux and crisis; for indeed this is necessary to the very nature of a novel. In this they are living on the last legacy of Romanticism; which, in its turn, was living on the last legacy of religion. But their new and simple philosophy teaches them that sex is only the sort of necessity that is also a triviality; that sex is no more crucial than smoking. So that the modern novelist, torn between two ideas, has to attempt to write a story about a man who smokes twenty cigarettes and tries to think that each of them is a crisis. In all these things there is an intellectual tangle; the sort of thing that eventually tightens and throttles. Of this sort of philosopher it is exactly and literally true to say that, if you give him rope enough, he will hang himself. It is consoling to reflect that suicide holds a sublime place in his philosophy.

75. Huxley's literary criticism

1933

Extracts from an article by Hans W. Häuserman, 'Aldous Huxley as Literary Critic,' *PMLA*, September 1933, xlviii, pp. 908–18.

Hans Walter Häuserman, b. 1902, critic, editor, translator, is a professor at the University of Geneva, Switzerland. He is the author of articles on Defoe, Yeats, and T. S. Eliot, and has written *The Genevese Background* (1952) and *Modern American Literature* (1965).

Häuserman's is the first significant essay on Huxley's criticism and one of the few intelligent discussions of Huxley's own concept of literature to appear during his lifetime. See Introduction, p. 17.

Häuserman's footnotes, purely documentary, are omitted, as is his opening paragraph, which discusses the broadening of traditional molds of literature by Shaw, Galsworthy, and Wells.

Among the members of this group Huxley stands out as the most erudite, cultured, and 'scientific' writer. The orthodox history of literature declares that the scientific spirit of the nineteenth century dominated the philosophical outlook of the representative Victorians. In reality, however, none of them endeavors to realize, in terms of literature, the genuine scientist's ideals. It is another thing to seek truth for truth's sake than to seek it for some ulterior end, be it beauty, vitality, or some ethical good. George Eliot makes an exception, she alone has power of detachment and intellectual universality. She does not write, as Browning and Meredith, primarily from a preoccupation with ethical questions, but chiefly intent on bringing order and clearness into her conception of the world. Apart from her there is hardly another novelist, either contemporary or in the past, who can be compared to Huxley. For him too, literature is only a possible approach to an end to which science as yet fails to provide an access.

Consequently, as a literary critic, the first quality he looks for is scientific integrity or whatever its literary equivalent may be. Any writer is condemned who betrays not the same passionate intellectual honesty that guides Huxley's own hand when he depicts the various types of modern people. Some critics reproach him with materialism; the rigorous self-discipline demanded by his analytical method is, how-ever, a redeeming factor which is too often overlooked. In the domain of literature he champions the same empirical idealism that his grand-father, Thomas Henry, claimed for his biological studies. 'Legitimate materialism,' the great anatomist once wrote, 'that is, the extension of the conceptions and of the methods of physical science to the highest as well as to the lowest phenomena of vitality, is neither more nor less than a sort of shorthand idealism.' Similarly, Aldous Huxley demands that a writer should take all the forms of life under observation, and forbids him to erect artificial barriers against less exalted, but for all that not less real, aspects of existence.

[Traces Huxley's views on a variety of writers, and notes, especially, his affinities with Balzac]

It is interesting to watch Huxley pursuing the analogy between Balzac and himself even further. Studying the author of the *Comédie humaine*[1] as a sociological phenomenon, he exposes him as a writer in whom the times have attained consciousness of themselves. The spectacular period of the French Revolution and the Napoleonic Wars has found in him an adequate and comprehensive expression. On this ground Huxley ventures the generalization that profound, dramatic changes in the political and economic conditions of society call forth the historiographer of Balzac's proportions. Huxley probably made this averment on the instance of writers like Compton Mackenzie, Arnold Bennett, Galsworthy, who, in the midst of our troubled times, were and still are engaged in writing novels of the same monumental kind. Their work is, if not in bulk, in conception at least, equal to Balzac's. Although Huxley is not very explicit about the subject, it is clear enough that he considers himself as one of them. If his work does not form an organic whole like the *Forsyte Saga*, but takes rather the shape of a series of loosely connected studies of human types, the individual bent of his mind (which is more analytical than synthetic) must be held responsible.

He not only feels himself called upon to perform the same task, he

[1] 'The Human Comedy.'

is even conscious of the superiority of his own work over Balzac's. The French novelist's character-drawing lacks artistic restraint, it is too melodramatic, it reminds one too strongly of a film-scenario to be consistent with literary dignity. The limits to which even vitality and an exuberant imagination have to conform themselves are the limits imposed by a judicious intelligence. Like Victor Hugo, Verhaeren, and G. K. Chesterton, those crusaders mounted on rocking-horses, Balzac has for all his surpassing genius a touch of childishness.

The reader of Huxley's novels may well be surprised to see how this author, as a literary critic, champions unrestrictedly the Elizabethan ideal of literature. One perhaps rather expected him to place his sympathies with those less vigorous but so much more enlightened poets of the Augustan era. It is for their ethical rather than their intellectual or even aesthetic qualities that Huxley prefers the Renaissance to the Classic writers. Mere learning is not essential in the making of a poet. On the other hand, there is nothing more damnable than the wilful shutting out, the deliberate, narrow-minded exclusion of certain domains of vitality from the scope of literature. The Elizabethans understood that the sublime and the grotesque, the high and the low, tragedy and farce, are inseparable. Unhampered by conventions, they gave its due to both spheres and assigned to each its proper expression and fitting place in the picture. What Huxley praises in the Elizabethans is not their poetic force, their flights of imagination, although he is conscious of them too, but their unprejudiced view of the world. The criticism is highly characteristic of Huxley himself: what he strives at, and what he wants every writer to make his ideal too, is a complete and unforeshortened conception of life. Thus the most erudite author of our days stands up as the champion of an age which Voltaire called barbarian, and he champions it for its very barbarity.

Huxley, however, does not include Spenser in his general praise of the English Renaissance. In the face of the unanimous opinion of critics and poets he confesses his inability to admire the author of the *Fairy Queen*, in whom he sees only a virtuoso, a highly gifted versifier with the knack 'of extracting perfectly rhymed stanzas by the hundred, out of an empty mind.' He counts for nothing the aesthetic pleasure derived from the pageant-like flow of Spenser's poetry and, by this judgment, places himself resolutely by the side of moralists like Shaw and Tolstoy. Literature, according to Huxley, must above all contribute to a better understanding of the bewildering spectacle of life. Spenser, on the contrary, causes the reader to lapse into a kind of intellectual torpor—the one unpardonable sin in Huxley's eyes. For him mental alertness and universal curiosity are the indispensable qualities of a writer.

He professes, on the other hand, the greatest admiration for 'that strange old Dean of St. Paul's three hundred years ago'—John Donne. He honors him as one of those rare poetical master-minds, like Lucretius, Dante, and Goethe, who were capable of including in the range of their poetry the mind as well as the life of their times. And again, as in Balzac's case, he finds a close resemblance of the present period with that of Donne. In both epochs we see a reaction against the rich but formalized poetical tradition of the preceding century. The new generation demands a wider scope of subject-matter for poetry and a nearer approach to reality and nature.

[Sums up Huxley's reactions to Gide, Proust, Wordsworth, Shelley, and others, and sees a similarity between Percy Lubbock's *The Craft of Fiction* and Huxley's 'traveller's-eye view' remarks in *Along the Road*]

The essential function of literature, therefore, is, according to Huxley, to give a picture of life in its totality, excluding neither its spiritual nor its material aspects. He dislikes being classified, and he vigorously objects to the denomination of a neo-classical writer with which a French critic designated him. In his refutation, Huxley ventures a definition of classicism which is entirely based on this conception of the function of literature. Classicism means to him an arbitrarily limiting the scope of art to the expression of rationalized emotions only, a disregarding the particular and immediate quality of experience in favor of its general, simplified aspect. Thus, the French tragedy of the seventeenth century excommunicates the body, and with its a priori psychology of passion and reason reduces man to an algebraical equation. Huxley, therefore, denounces the classical discipline as essentially a shirking of artistic difficulties which lie in rendering the quality of immediate experience. Whereas the classical ideal is perfectly realizable, the naturalistic writer, whose task it is to express the finally inexpressible, can only approximately attain his end.

It is obvious that Huxley does not grasp the full import of classicism. His favorite plea for totality of artistic outlook, his insistence on freedom from conventions in literature, are chiefly responsible for the insufficiency of this definition. It is, in fact, the definition given by the primer for literary history which considers the observance of rules and restrictions as the essential quality of classicism.

A deeper conception of the matter goes beyond his ideas as developed in 'Vulgarity in Literature'. Huxley's judgment is clearly biassed by his militant opposition against Victorian literary conventions. And, what is more, the fundamental elements that go to the formation of classicism are themselves to be found at the root of his own work. Man is the subject not only of his poetry and fiction but also of his theoretical thinking: his most important collection of essays bears the significant title *Proper Studies*, with reference to Pope's precept that 'The proper study of Mankind is Man.' Huxley's literary creed is an essentially classical one and he defines it with all desirable clearness in this statement: 'Art is not the discovery of Reality—whatever Reality may be, and no human being can possibly know. It is the organization of chaotic appearance into an orderly and human universe.'

76. Wyndham Lewis on the opening of *Point Counter Point*

1934

Percy Wyndham Lewis (1882–1957), British novelist, artist, and critic who held pronounced views on modernism and politics, wrote *The Childermass* (1928) and *The Apes of God* (1930).

The extract is from 'The Taxi-cab Driver Test for Fiction,' *Men Without Art* (London: Cassell, 1934; reprinted New York: Russell, 1964), pp. 295–304. See Introduction, p. 1.

Lewis has been arguing against contemporary fiction as a formal art.

I would go so far upon that purist road myself as to say that *no* book that could possibly be made to fit into the schemes of things suggested by the word 'fiction,' could possibly be a work of the least importance. No book that would not pass my taxi-cab-driver test, that is, would be anything but highly suspect as art—though it might be an awfully good aphrodisiac, or a first-rate 'thriller.'

But I will at once proceed to a demonstration of how my fiction-test would work.

The *taxi-cab-driver test* can be applied, in the absence of a taxi-cab driver—though not so effectively—by merely opening any book of 'fiction', at the first page, and seeing what you find. I will now give a hasty demonstration of that method, selecting, for the purpose, two of the only 'fiction' books I have within easy reach. Here displayed intact upon the next page, is *first-page* No. 1.

[Cites as 'Specimen A' the first page of *Point Counter Point*]

That is the first page of the most important work of 'fiction' of a very famous author, published in 1928, and regarded as one of the landmarks in English literature of the last decade. There is no occasion to name the author, as it is only my purpose here to show you my taxi-cab-driver test in operation, and to indicate what results may be expected. This single tell-tale page appears to me to be terribly decisive: for no book opening upon this tone of vulgar complicity with the dreariest of suburban library-readers could, from my point of view, change its skin, in the course of its six hundred long pages, and become anything but a dull and vulgar book.

'"*You won't be late?*" *There was anxiety in Marjorie Carling's voice.*' That is surely so much the very accent of the newspaper serial (even down to the cosy sound of the name of the heroine) that the sort of person who would be at home in such an atmosphere is not a person likely to clamour for the 'highest standards in literature'. The 'only two years; and now already he had ceased to love her!'—the sentimental repetitive in the 'she knew that her importunity would only annoy him, only make him love her the less'—the 'she loved him too much, she was too agonizingly jealous'—all this is the very voice of 'Fiction', as practised by the most characteristic of lady-novelists. Whatever else may be true of such a production, it is safe to say that out of such material a serious work of art decidedly cannot be manufactured.

[Cites as 'Specimen B' the first page of James's *The Ivory Tower*]

I think that I will change my mind, and (for the sake of effect and because that may promote a more immediate understanding) reveal the name of the book whose first page I reproduced, as my specimen A. It is *Point Counter Point*! If you do not believe me, you may turn to that work, and you will find that I have indeed placed before you the first page of that famous piece of super-fiction.

77. Huxley's humanism

1935

An excerpt from Winfield H. Rogers, 'Aldous Huxley's Humanism,' *Sewanee Review*, July–September 1935, xliii, pp. 262–72. I have regrettably been unable to obtain biographical information on the author of this important essay.

Huxley a few years earlier described his aim in writing to J. W. N. Sullivan: 'I believe that mankind is working towards some definitive and comprehensive outlook on the world, and I regard my work as contributing something towards that' (pp. 15–16). Rogers's essay is a penetrating summary of Huxley's position in the early 1930s. See Introduction, p. 17.

Mr. Aldous Huxley does not interpret life, on his own admittance, in those exciting and emotional terms which persuade the generality of men. His followers are confronted, moreover, with the astonishing fact that even some of the intellectual and sophisticated minority fail completely to understand or to like his work. Very few of Mr. Huxley's readers, apparently, take the trouble to discover the true implication and importance of his satire. As with all satire worthy the name, the reader must discover in this instance the point of view or philosophy that in the first place dictated the satiric criticism, which is, with novelists who are not also essayists, an inductive process of no little difficulty. Fortunately, to construct the positive philosophy from the negative material of satire, though entirely possible because his philosophy is implicit in each of his works, is not necessary with Mr. Huxley. In numerous essays and in isolated passages in his novels, he has clearly set forth his attitude. A true understanding of Mr. Huxley's philosophy indicates, contrary to the common American conception, that his novels are genuinely significant works; the unit of his thought, his intellectual acumen, his humanity, above all, his morality (for he describes immorality only to condemn it) become crystal clear. Mr. Huxley then stands out as one of the important social thinkers, as well as critics and creative writers, of our time.

The inability of many American readers to arrive at an understanding of Mr. Huxley's attitude, as well as of his importance, may be illustrated from several points of view. One intelligent reader of *Point Counter Point* pronounces it sewage; another, a scholar of distinguished ability, states, in effect, that readers put up with the immoralities of the book because of the author's intellectualism; a writer in one of the foremost learned journals emphasizes the scientific element in Huxley, without making clear exactly what he means by this term. And other readers frankly are baffled. The American reader of Mr. Huxley, piqued at the foreign conception that Mr. Sinclair Lewis portrays accurately the American scene, might well consider that he is falling into a similar error. The exaggerated pictures drawn by either writer must be taken for what they are, satiric pictures of segments of their respective societies. The great difference between these two satirists, on the other hand, is that Mr. Huxley has a far more definite, an infinitely more valuable philosophy behind his criticism. His philosophy, though often formulated in intellectual terms, is shot through with emotional conviction. It is the produce of a fine brain and a sane emotional attitude. This philosophy is inherent in all of Mr. Huxley's work, in every satiric portrait, in every comedy and tragedy of his novels. So completely does it dominate his work, that whatever he touches must in some way be brought into contact with it. It is this philosophy which dictated the essential pattern of *Point Counter Point* and which keeps it from being a mere literary freak.

Mr. Huxley's attack on Wordsworth indicates at once the essential basis and sufficiency of his philosophy. Wordsworth, he believes, committed the unpardonable sin of making an intellectual generalization from the emotional particular. Not that the emotion itself was invalid, but the resulting rationalization has no validity, for it is 'suspiciously anthropocentric.' He recognizes and insists upon the small value of truth in the emotional experience, though condemning the poet for attempting to erect a life philosophy upon it. That most intellectual philosophies are ultimately based on emotional attitudes, he believes is natural and right and inevitable by virtue of their human origin; indeed, the emotion is given force and permanence through embodiment in an idea. Nevertheless, this basis assuredly must not be an emotional particular.

The emotional basis of his own philosophy Mr. Huxley expresses in various places—Coleman's statement in *Antic Hay*, for example. Late at night when he and his companions are walking through the streets,

Coleman asks them to think of the '. . . seven million distinct and separate individuals, each with distinct and separate lives and all completely indifferent to our existence . . .' who are about them. He asks them to think of the 'Hundreds of thousands' experiencing similar activities and emotions; and yet '. . . they are all alive, all unique and separate and sensitive, like you and me.' Mr. Huxley is definitely fascinated and influenced by the thought. This incongruous quality of life—its oneness and simultaneous diversity—is the basic emotional conception of his philosophy. It gives him his zest for life and his pessimism; it determines his philosophic position, which he defines as *pessimistic humanism*.

The salient difference between the humanism of Mr. Huxley and that of the humanists of the school of the late Professor Irving Babbitt[1] is found in Mr. Huxley's modernity, at the center of which is his reconciliation of the psychological and humanistic points of view. He can best be described as a 'psychological humanist.' Inherent in the term is the pessimism which he himself uses to describe his attitude. The terms of many so-called humanists seem vague and outmoded when compared to those of this psychological humanism. The fine humanistic tradition of the Greeks and the life worship of the Elizabethans are reinterpreted for the benefit of the twentieth century man in terms which he can understand.

The only facts, Mr. Huxley thinks, in which we can believe are psychological. In one sense these facts are only rationalizations, but in any case the only possible ones in the new state of mind of humanity. Everything else, apart from these psychological facts, I presume with the exception of the physical sciences, is either man's projection, in some way, of himself, or pure conjecture. Thus, with this irrational absolute, man's attention should be concentrated on his psychological well-being in the present. Our mode of living and our social institutions must be brought into harmony with the individual's psychological necessity. I do not think I am misinterpreting in saying that Mr. Huxley believes that our time has given itself alternately to two tendencies, that of theorizing and that of living for the moment in an unreasonable enjoyment of what he calls 'direct perceptions and spontaneous feelings.' In the mean between reflection and spontaneity we find that humanistic ideal.

The essential difference between this type of humanism and the

[1] Irving Babbitt (1865–1933), U.S. critic and teacher, leader of that twentieth-century movement in literary criticism known as the 'new humanism.'

purely psychological point of view may not, at this point, be clear. With Mr. Huxley, emphasis upon material psychology does not, as with many modern thinkers, lead him to anything approaching a materialistic, naturalistic, or behavioristic outlook. To him the human spirit is distinct from the body; for, in comparison, the capacity of the spirit is limitless and subject to profound modification; the spirit is the result of all experience. This conception is a very adequate reconciliation of the findings of modern psychology to the individual sense of oneness. The capacity of the spirit gives a oneness to the obvious diversity within the individual man. Mr. Huxley's conception of sin illustrates the psychological basis, the profound modernity and the true nature of his philosophy. A sin is not a sin because it has been somewhere prohibited, but because it is hygienically unsound, either to the mind or body. On the other hand, the virtues might be described as those things which are hygienically sound because they make it possible for a man to develop his potentialities, unhindered by disease and agitation. Capacity for development, for modification on the part of the human entity, is the cornerstone of his humanistic philosophy. The reader of Mr. Huxley's work who emphasizes his scientific attitude, or his demand for scientific integrity in literature, should absorb his idea that scientific explanations are not the whole truth.

[Discusses Huxley's belief in the individual's need to develop his being in all its diversity]

. . . As the individual is actually many persons, he should sincerely try to be all of them. Man's almost infinite potentiality he should recognize and do his best to realize. His potentialities allow him to live in the universals of human experience rather than in the individual and one. The validity of the experience of oneness and simplicity, however, or even the occasional consciousness of oneness with the whole universe, though only true of one psychological experience, is not destroyed.

To this end of developing the harmonious adult man, of attaining perfection in all the diverse aspects of the human entity, our entire attention should be concentrated on this world. In realizing his potential humanity and primary duty to himself, it is necessary for man to keep himself at a pitch of efficiency which will allow him to give life to all his elements and latent capacities. The conscious mind, the instincts, and the body must be allowed life, so that man may become a perfect animal and a perfect human. The best life consists of: 'Multiplicity of eyes and multiplicity of aspects seen.' The right of all the diverse components of human nature to real life is important to Mr. Huxley. When he says that each man, by virtue of his heredity and his acquired habits, is domiciled in several universes, he carries his sense of diversity to the extreme. Yet when he states that the whole of a single man's universe is composed of a series of 'non sequiturs,' all connected by the individual, we begin to realize the emotional reality behind his idea.

[Finds that, for Huxley, the gentleman is the person most capable of achieving an ideal balance in living]

A real bird's eye glance at Mr. Huxley's novels at this point reveals their true import and the significance of the satiric characterization. He believes that a great many modern writers, because of their reaction to the 'excesses of popular art', and because they have confined themselves to 'only a tiny fraction of existence' have neglected the important things in life. The inclusiveness, for example, of *Point Counter Point* is an attempt to indicate the diversity of human nature and human life, and an implied plea, as well, that we do not let a single aspect of our beings dominate our lives. Each character who is satirically condemned in this novel, as well as in his satiric works, in some way violates the humanistic code of the life-worshipper. Each in some way fails to be the harmonious adult man.

[Cites examples of this failure in some characters in *Point Counter Point*]

Of Mr. Huxley's positive statements on this contemporary tendency I have already spoken. Strikingly, Mr. Huxley's deep conviction and sincerity cause him to turn whatever he touches into a humanistic document. He looks upon his novels, I believe, as he does upon poetry; they exist primarily as instruments '. . . for the modification of existence patterns.'

[Considers some of Huxley's attacks on modern substitutes for religion—Socialism, Nationalism, Progress—and observes that Huxley consistently tests these idols against his pessimistic humanism]

The philosophy of Mr. Huxley must be synthesized into the organic whole from which it came. As we see it in its isolated manifestations, a sharp eye, considerable curiosity and constructive power are required to discern its true importance. The humanism of Mr. Huxley, here set forth, differs from that of the noisier humanists contemporary with him in that it is rationally acceptable, clear in terminology, and more powerful in creative force. He makes us vitally aware of the enormous possibilities of life and living, of the opportunities in knowledge and art. The fact that we are on earth is quite enough. We must adventure, and gain knowledge, and advance—not necessarily for any particular reason—towards an unattainable goal. As a novelist, moreover, Mr. Huxley becomes extremely important when it is realized that he is among the remarkably small number of distinguished English and American novelists who have raised their work upon a coherent philosophy. With the realization that his novels have behind them a philosophy which is an acceptable working hypothesis for modern man, they become definitely significant. There are many who will agree with Mr. Huxley that the greatest need of our times is to make this humanistic philosophy generally assimilable.

EYELESS IN GAZA

June 1936

78. John Sparrow, review in *Spectator*

19 June 1936, clvi, p. 1138

John Hanbury Angus Sparrow, b. 1906, educator, barrister, and essayist, is Warden of All Souls College at Oxford and author of *Sense and Poetry* (1934) and *Controversial Essays* (1966). See Introduction, p. 20.

Sparrow's review is entitled 'Mr. Huxley among the Philistines.'

Two things are remarkable in Mr. Huxley's new book: the method and the moral. The method is what first strikes the reader with surprise; the time-scheme is confused in a bewildering fashion: for ten pages we are in 1933, then for half a dozen in 1902, thence we jump to 1926, after twenty pages we find ourselves in 1912, and a little later we are back where we started. 'The cinema,' say Mr. Huxley's publishers, 'has accustomed people to the use of similar methods.' The cinema, it is true, telescopes, it omits, it speeds time up and slows it down, and gives a bird's-eye view, as it were, of simultaneous happenings—but it does not turn topsy-turvy the series of events in time, as does Mr. Huxley in this book. The only machine that does that is the human mind, in its efforts to remember and in its sub-conscious re-creation of the past. Mr. Huxley has not used a psychological method of presentment, he writes as an impersonal narrator, recording from outside the happening of events. The result is a book which is at a first reading considerably more puzzling than *The Waves*, and irritating as *The Waves* is not, because the feature which causes the difficulty has no obvious artistic justification. So skilfully, however, has Mr. Huxley used his method that, as one reads on, one instinctively recognises and co-ordinates these different *strata*, and on a second reading everything falls more or less naturally into its place. In this respect, the book is a *tour de force*: the thing is done so well that really it is almost as satisfactory as if it had not been done at all.

The method, none the less, has its advantages. Indeed, something of the sort is necessitated by the absence of a continuous plot and by the nature of the task which Mr. Huxley has set himself. For his aim is not to tell a story; it is to preach a sermon. And his collection of snapshots of the pre-War and the post-War world is presented to us simply in order to make that sermon more effective. We do not feel that interest which attaches to events which play their part in the development or the interplay of character. Mr. Huxley simply takes a piece of the life lived by his chief figures at their private school in 1902, cuts it into slices, and scatters it through the book, interlarded with slices from their lives in 1912–14, in 1926, in 1933. Each of these slices indicates the squalor of the treadmill to which the hero, Anthony Beavis, and his contemporaries are condemned. Mr. Huxley is an adept at this kind of picture, and we do not wonder at the impulse which finally drives Anthony away from the London world made familiar to us in *Point Counter Point* and *Antic Hay*, to Mexico. It is in Mexico that he meets Dr. Miller; and Dr. Miller is in some ways the most important figure in the book. It is Dr. Miller who introduces the moral; and the moral is the other remarkable thing about *Eyeless in Gaza*.

Not that it is remarkable that a novel of Mr. Huxley's should contain a moral; it would be a much stranger thing if it did not. For Mr. Huxley is at heart a Puritan, and in almost every book that he has written it has become more evident that his fundamental purpose as an artist is satiric. But his satire hitherto has been conveyed mainly by means of the reflections of some detached, some balanced, intellectual, who does not commit himself doctrinally any further than is involved by putting a record on the gramophone and declaring, amid the hopeless and aimless debauchery of his contemporaries, his faith in the Seventh Symphony.

Now Mr. Huxley has discovered that the serene temples of the intellect, from which he used to look down smiling, not without pity, upon the blind and desperate struggles of humanity, are open themselves to a most insidious assault. For there has broken out, as is well known, among the intellectuals of today, as there did among their mid-nineteenth-century predecessors, a serious epidemic of religious doubt.

History is beginning to repeat itself, with the difference that our intellectuals are discovering that they have found, not lost, their faith. In *Eyeless in Gaza* Mr. Huxley for the first time frankly abandons a detached and intellectual standpoint: Dr. Miller preaches the Way and the Life; Anthony Beavis is his evangelist.

[Describes some of Miller's views]

So Anthony becomes an Active Pacifist, and we leave him at the end of the book (at the end, according to the time-series; according to the page-series, throughout it) going up and down the country addressing Dr. Miller's meetings, preaching against Fascism and Communism, against hatred and butcher's meat; in favour of love, and compassion, and a proper diet, and, above all, unity: 'Unity beyond the turmoil of separations and divisions. Goodness beyond the possibility of evil.' In these passages from Mr. Huxley's book there is no trace of irony; no touch of the 'distaste, the intellectual scorn' which his hero reprehends, and it appears that the writer himself is speaking.

It is in the moral, therefore, that the explanation of the method is to be sought. The topsy-turvy jumble of pictures reflects the shapelessness, the aimlessness of a life which Dr. Miller has not sanctified with purpose, while the pictures themselves are made horrible in order to show the true nature of the hell from which Dr. Miller offers us deliverance.

Indeed, the horror of Mr. Huxley's descriptive passages deserves to be recorded as the third remarkable feature of the book. There is a serious danger that *Eyeless in Gaza* may fail in its evangelistic aim because those of its readers who have not the very strongest stomachs will put it aside in disgust before they realise the seriousness of its purpose. 'Writing is dirty work', as a distinguished contemporary writer has assured us; and Mr. Huxley himself in this book reminds us of the adage that a dirty mind is a perpetual feast. There are those who after reading a very little of this book may be inclined to exclaim that Mr. Huxley knows his job, and that enough is to them as good as that particular kind of feast; for the glimpses which Mr. Huxley affords, with that suggestiveness of imagery and significance of detail of which he is a master, into the private school, the public lavatory, the concentration camp, and into many a bedroom, are an advance (if that is the right word) on anything that he has done before. But they are all in a good cause, for they serve to point the more vividly to Dr. Miller's moral.

At the moment, then, it seems that Dr. Miller (true to his doctrine of unity and the avoidance of all hatred) has persuaded Mr. Huxley that the best way to vanquish the Philistines is to join them, and he and Mr. Huxley are safe together in a region where they cannot be touched by the intellectual scorn of Mr. Huxley's own earlier books. One is left regretting that Dr. Miller and Mr. Cardan can never meet—and wondering where Dr. Miller will next lead the author of his being.

79. David Garnett, review in *New Statesman and Nation*

20 June 1936, xi [n.s.] p. 970

David Garnett, b. 1892, prolific novelist, editor, and essayist, wrote for example *Lady into Fox* (1923), *War in the Air* (1941), and *Ulterior Motives* (1966). See Introduction, p. 20.

Battered, seasick, and bored, the passengers suddenly wake up; through the portholes the outline of a green hill passes by, a bell clangs and the ship's rhythm is altered. Land! Land at last. Life will be interesting and amusing once more. The sight of a new large novel, *Eyeless in Gaza*, by Aldous Huxley was for me, a passenger with a weak stomach, like the sight of land. Here was a world in which one would know one's way about, in which the characters would feel and think and talk like educated people with open minds. Sure to be delightful company, though perhaps rather like *Gryll Grange*. Peacock. Yes, Mr. Huxley has often been compared with Peacock and quite rightly. Gumbril might have been a guest at *Nightmare Abbey* and Myra Viveash might have been caught in Mr. Aquarius's net. Happy to be ashore, with a good appetite, it was a shock at first to find the streets of the town blocked with notices: No Thoroughfare, and one's happy stroll constantly interrupted. The dust-cover gives warning: 'instead of a chronological sequence, a counter-point of four narratives at different epochs of the hero's life.' . . . At first the No Thoroughfare notices annoy and the reader regrets having to pop about after the counterpoint, but practice reconciles; it is not as difficult as one might expect to keep the sequences clear in one's head, and one is thankful for anything, anything that will take one away from 1934. That indeed, and no nonsense about counter-point, seems to me the reason and justification of the method. Had the chapters been arranged in chronological sequence, nobody could have ever finished the book, just as no one can read the last chapters of *War and Peace*. Mr. Huxley's happy device enables his hero's philosophical reflections to be broken up and scattered through the book. Even so, there are moments when one rebels.

Anthony shut his book, feeling he couldn't read even one line more.

He was reading his own manuscript and Mr. Huxley has given us three whole pages; we could understand the reason of Anthony's feeling with less.

In July 1914 (ch. 48) Anthony betrayed his best friend in a particu-larly stupid way and Brian committed suicide. Partly owing to that, and partly owing to reading too much, Anthony has lost the capacity of having intimate personal relations; he has love affairs, but he funks love and for the sake of his work becomes 'a man in a burrow'. When Helen leaves him, he realises that he has never been really there during their relationship and feels that he has no personality of his own.

In fact, of course, Hamlet didn't have a personality—knew altogether too much to have one.

He imagines that he is like Hamlet and that his enormous accumula-tion of knowledge and over-education is the reason. His real trouble seems to be that he is a victim of words; that he can never stop pinning out facts and ideas like an entomologist arranging a collection of dead butterflies. The trouble is that there are a terrible lot of cabbage whites and meadow browns among them. Anthony and his friend Mark Staithes are intellectuals, *pur sang*,[1] but they are always saying profoundly untrue things such as:

Life is so ordinary that literature has to deal with the exceptional.

The limit is reached when, after re-reading *Anna Karenina*, Mark Staithes complains of what it lacks:

[1] 'Pure blood,' hence 'thoroughbreds.'

No mention of the part played by mere sensation in producing happiness. Hot bath for example, taste of bacon, feel of fur, smell of freezias, or of the sudden accession from unknown muscular sources of more than ordinary health.

Since this is exactly what Tolstoy does do, and which is the foundation of Levin's happiness, and Stephan's delightful good nature, one can only conclude that Mark had never read *Anna Karenina*, much less re-read it. Anna laughing aloud at the feeling of delight that came over her when she laid the cool smooth surface of her paper knife on her cheek is one of innumerable instances which he could not have missed. Yet Mr. Huxley cannot have intended us to draw the conclusion that his characters were bombinating in a vacuum. He has simply forgotten the book and used its name at random, just as, at random, he makes his heroes read Edward Thomas's poetry years before it was published, or written, and discuss the Brewers' movement for True Temperance before the war when it was a post-war answer to Prohibitionist propaganda. One is tempted to give a list of such howlers if only because Mr. Huxley, like Anthony, is obsessed by irrelevant facts, and crams his pages with them. Even when these ideas are really interesting they are out of place and spoil the book. Unlike Hamlet, Anthony has not got an original mind and the inventory of its acquired contents should have been avoided.

Every word of this criticism is justified—yet it is beside the point: since *Eyeless in Gaza* is nevertheless Mr. Huxley's finest novel. Though the spate of ideas has now more resemblance to H. G. Wells than to the discussions in Peacock, the characters are alive and not mere pegs. There is a new depth of understanding. Mary Amberley, with her crooning way of speaking, has features in common with Mrs. Aldwinkle, but if we compare chapter 34 with anything in *Those Barren Leaves*, we see the tremendous development of Mr. Huxley's sympathy. Mary Amberley is not only perfectly observed, but perfectly understood, a really living woman, and her tragedy, though incidental, is the most moving thing in a book which is full of moving things. Mr. Huxley has gained in depth, but he has lost none of his lightness and his gift of making us laugh. There is nothing even in *Antic Hay* so amusing as chapter 5 when Helen, *pour épater sa soeur*,[1] bets that she will steal something from every shop she goes into.

[Quotes Helen's search for something to steal at the butcher's shop, pp. 48-9]

[1] 'In order to shock her sister.'

Oh, how delightful it is to meet girls like Helen, how alive she is and how grateful one is to Mr. Huxley. All the road may be up in the little port and the loud speaker in the café may insist on delivering a talk on sociology, but one is on land again. On land and in a world of civilised people. As observation Mr. Huxley has written nothing better than his description of the Rev. Mr. Thursley waving his empty inkpot about in fury before saying grace. And Joan, his daughter, is extraordinarily good. *Eyeless in Gaza* is a delight, but on the whole the plan of popping about in time is a mistake. If the chronological method had been followed, I should have stopped reading at page 500 and have missed almost all the boring parts of the book; Anthony ends up with a new wisdom, part of which is to concentrate like a Yogi on the act of putting on his shoes because the means is of more value than the end. What a bore.

80. Q. D. Leavis, review in *Scrutiny*

September 1936, v, pp. 178–83

Queenie Dorothy Leavis, b. 1906, wife of F. R. Leavis, co-founder of *Scrutiny*, editor and essayist, wrote *Fiction and the Reading Public* (1932) and is co-author, with her husband, of *Lectures in America* (1969) and *Dickens the Novelist* (1970).

Mr. Peter Quennell recently wrote (in a book reviewed in the last number of *Scrutiny*): 'Huxley, supremely intelligent, appears to suffer from the very complexity of his apparatus.' This, as one might expect, is an echo of the stock Bloomsbury account of Huxley. His 'intelligence' is popularly considered to be so great that it inhibits his other powers as novelist, particularly his ability to 'feel'; this account is supposed to explain what it is that even Mr. Quennell feels to be wrong with Mr. Huxley's novels. But supreme intelligence in other literary artists—

Shakespeare, Blake, for instance—is not a handicap or disability: on the contrary, it is the condition of their outstanding achievement. It is obvious that 'intelligence' here needs examining. There must be different kinds of intelligence and Mr. Huxley's an inferior and inherently defective kind.

The generally accepted explanation of Huxley's fatally supreme intelligence originates, it is of interest to note, with Mr. Huxley himself. What he had hinted earlier and made explicit in *Point Counter Point* (in the character of Philip the novelist-protagonist) is repeated in his new novel, though Anthony, the new hero, is only writing an amateur literary *Elements of Sociology*; nevertheless we read again of 'the temperamental divorce between the passions and the intellect', etc., and we are repeatedly given to understand that though the feeling powers are admittedly weak the intellect is first-class. There is an instructive instance in Chapter VI of *Point Counter Point* of the way Mr. Huxley's intellect functions and the value the reader is instructed to place upon it. There is only space to quote the conclusion:

[Quotes from pp. 110–11]

Philip's wife wanted to scream because her husband's mental processes struck her as being inhuman, but some readers may with more justice object that the product is not brilliant, nor wonderfully interesting, and that Mr. Huxley's *procédé*[1] is not even amusing for very long. In a novelist it is a form of laziness: a Henry James, a Stendhal or a Flaubert dissolves his general ideas into his particular material—their novels are saturated solutions, whereas Mr. Huxley's are a preposterous mixture like the White Knight's pudding. This extract also betrays our novelist's over-estimate of his own bright ideas—for of course Philip's intellect, like Mr. Huxley's, works by stringing together in a rapid conversational way dubious generalizations from other people's printed conclusions. *Il prend son bien ou il le trouve*,[2] and he doesn't risk looking the *trouvaille*[3] in the mouth. On inspection his learning is found to be painlessly acquired like his information from such obvious sources as encyclopædias, the scientific best-sellers, the current popular sociological, psychological, anthropological, etc. works, the more expensive and less well-known equivalents of Benn's sixpenny series (if, on reading *Eyeless in Gaza*, you notice that he has been using *Patterns of Culture* as a

---

[1] 'Process, method.'
[2] 'He takes his advantage where he finds it.'
[3] 'Lucky find,' 'brain-wave,' hence 'gift horse.'

source-book, you will equally reflect that it is just the sort of book he finds useful and congenial); nor does he discriminate between one borrowed theory and another, all grist. He remarks himself (*Eyeless in Gaza*, p. 171) that this is a form of laziness and self-indulgence, and continues, characteristically, to include in this charge all 'Higher Lifers': scholars, philosophers, and men of science—all are rather contemptible escapists. He asserts that all intellectual efforts are identical in kind with his own undisciplined and slipshod filching of other people's labour. Of course it is impossible to tell how far this too may be merely an irresponsible bright idea. But 'sincerity' at this level can mean nothing; it doesn't signify.

Mr. Huxley's intelligence looks like being merely a matter of a great deal of reading and a great deal of note-taking (significant that all the novelists in his books take copious notes of ideas and extracts to be worked up into their texts) combined of course with a natural flair for picking up superficially impressive ideas. This goes along with his flair for embodying the Zeitgeist, and it is cheering to see how the naughty nasty short-story writer of the 'twenties has become the earnest essayist of the 'thirties. The serious element in *Eyeless in Gaza* is represented by a crusade for an academic kind of pacifism based on the Shelleyan or *Prometheus Unbound* perfectionism (see pp. 170–1). However, we are not here concerned with this but with the novel to whose tail it is very clumsily and perfunctorily tied. As a piece of fiction it reveals the death-throes of a novelist. Mr. Huxley is so bored with it that the characterization and bits of experience are for the most part merely repetitions of those used in previous novels of Mr. Huxley and other people; they don't even come out of a new note-book. This sterility of invention is the nemesis of the novelist who has chosen to resort to books instead of to life for his raw material. It is the logical result of the boredom with and contempt for humanity so evident in *Beyond the Mexique Bay*, and of course to a less degree in his previous novels and stories. The novelist who is bored is also, inevitably, boring.

Mr. Huxley's defects of intelligence are seen to be the source of his defects as novelist (thus contradicting the orthodox account of his make-up). There is no relation between his bright ideas (his 'intelligence') and his sensibility, so his technique accordingly remains a matter of bright ideas too. His 'technique' in the textbook sense was always a matter of lifting dodges from Gide and Proust and applying them from outside; in the present novel the by no means new device of the time-shift is used quite arbitrarily and in practice merely to the reader's confusion. As for technique in the important sense, the incompetence here is pronounced. For instance, if the social drama part of the new fiction and of *Point Counter Point* serves any end, it must be to expose the futility of the lives of the pleasure-chasing members of the opulent classes; any novelist who takes so many words to achieve so simple an effect ought to read the novels of Mr. Evelyn Waugh and blush for himself. At showing the middlebrow fear in a handful of dust Mr. Waugh outclasses Mr. Huxley every time. And Mr. Huxley's radical defect as a novelist, his lack of interest in the novelist's raw material, is responsible for his insensitiveness to speech and emotional idiom; his characters are identifiable if at all by gross verbal mannerisms, and Mr. Wyndham Lewis, in a pamphlet *Have With You to Great Queen Street*, reproducing the first page of *Point Counter Point*, remarked with justice that it might nearly all come from a penny novelette.[1]

The one hopeful sign in *Eyeless in Gaza* is that Mr. Huxley represents his hero Anthony as turning, if only on theoretical grounds, from the *Antic Hay* attitude to his fellows—the attitude of would-be scientific contempt ('My original conception was of a vast *Bouvard et Pécuchet*, constructed of historical facts. A picture of futility, apparently objective, scientific, but composed, I realize, in order to justify my own way of life. If men had always behaved either like half-wits or baboons, if they couldn't behave otherwise, then I was justified in sitting comfortably in the stalls with my opera-glasses. Whereas if there were something to be done, if the behaviour could be modified . . .')—to a use of 'his raw material of life, thought, knowledge' as a means, apparently, in the service of humanity. The writer who has taken up for so many years the stalls-and-opera-glasses position can hardly be outstandingly intelligent, nor equipped with the understanding and courage that are the accompaniments of real intelligence in an artist. The inability to follow up any line of thought, to resolve his bright ideas beyond the elementary stage of indiscriminate acquisition, has produced Mr. Huxley's notable distaste for committing himself to any position. His characters, it is generally recognized, mostly represent positions Mr. Huxley has liked to see himself in, was afraid of seeing himself in, or was trying himself out in. It is interesting to see how he protects himself against the possible charge of taking seriously any serious position he is advancing by loading the mouthpiece with some ridiculous characteristic (*e.g.* Brian Foxe's stammer). Mr. Quennell's distinction between thinking and feeling doesn't look very sensible.

[1] See Lewis in *Men Without Art*, No. 76.

Brave New World and some of the less pretentious essays are so much better than the ponderous novels because Mr. Huxley has had there, by the nature of the undertaking, to commit himself to a line and take serious thought in advance about where he was coming out. As literary critics it is our business to assess merely Mr. Huxley's possibilities as a man of letters. And it seems evident that Mr. Huxley's talents are not those of a novelist but of a populariser of ideas: this, if we had the reasonably serious large reading-public we have a right to expect after nearly seventy years of compulsory education, would be a function needing several hundred middlemen of Mr. Huxley's calibre, nor would the crop be difficult to raise. But in fact the market for such writers disappeared with the old heavy reviews. There remains the public Mr. Huxley has secured; with that his success depends on keeping up with the intellectual fashions and getting his wares early to market, for it is a public that is always looking for tips.

81. Newton Arvin, review in *New Republic*

19 August 1936, lxxxviii, p. 51

Newton Arvin (1900–63) was a professor of English literature 1922–60, winner of a National Book award in 1951, and author of books on Hawthorne (1929), Whitman (1938), and Melville (1950). See Introduction, p. 20.

It is a matter of course that Aldous Huxley should abound as much as ever in paradoxes, and the intentional, the systematic ironies of *Eyeless in Gaza* will have, to his old readers, a ring of almost amiable familiarity. The things men think they share with the demi-gods are set off here, as mockingly as they were in *Crome Yellow* and *Mortal Coils*, by the things they actually share with the higher primates. What is new in the novel, however, is an apparently unintended contradiction in its very substance and scheme. In addition to its deliberate antitheses of detail, *Eyeless in Gaza* is itself one long oxymoron. The explicit aim of the novel—for, as always, Huxley is frankly both story-teller and pamphleteer—is to inculcate a transcendental gospel of love, unity and peace; to preach, as a means of salvation from the prevailing violence and disorder, a way of life based on self-discipline, non-resistance and expansive good will. With this aim the actual content of the book is sensationally out of harmony.

Aside from the intrinsic merits of Huxley's new doctrines, it is wholly conceivable that he might have given them at least a literary plausibility; might have realized them momentarily for the imagination by embodying them, tangibly and illusively, in dramatic terms. A book about men and women feeling, speaking and acting more or less in the light of these high admonitions would have silenced the skeptical reader until the last page was well behind him. *Eyeless in Gaza* is not such a book. On the contrary, it is a book mainly about that Huxleyan world with which we are already well acquainted—a world not of potential order, dignity and purposeful struggle, but of pointless confusion, of physical and moral disgust and of derisive futilities.

That is just the world, Huxley of course intends us to understand, from which we are only to be freed by 'learning to use the self properly,' by 'communicating with and contemplating goodness' and by transcending the limitations on the love of which we are all capable. No doubt; but is it too much to ask that a novelist who comes to his readers with so strenuous and so ideal a message should seem to have made it so completely his own that it has colored the whole aspect of human life for him? Certainly it is what other novelists, to say nothing of poets, have done; Aldous Huxley has still to reinforce his message with his fable. The possibility of doing the things he pleads with us to do seems hardly real enough to be interesting so long as we are in the company of the nymphomaniac, Mary Amberley, with her morphine and her malice, or of the impotent narcissist Hugh Ledwidge; of Mary Amberley's neurotic daughter Helen, or of the pedantic philological bore John Beavis; of Mark Staithes, with his angry misanthropy, or of the tormented suicide Brian Foxe, exploited emotionally by his mother and then betrayed by the woman he loves and by his best friend, Anthony Beavis.

These are the people who fill the foreground of the book, who give it its pervasive tone, and it is hard to see that they take us a step beyond the Mercaptans, the Mrs. Viveashes, the Burlaps and the Spandrells of

Antic Hay and *Point Counter Point*. It is true that, just as there was a Rampion in the latter novel, there is a Dr. Miller, the expounder of proper self-use and of anthropological pacifism, in the present book; but alongside of Mary Amberley and Mark Staithes, Dr. Miller is a mere sketch—and he remains only the promise of a character at the end. Huxley's protagonist, Anthony Beavis, the cynical sociologist, has been won over to Dr. Miller's program during the last few months of the long period covered by the novel; and at the very end, having conquered his fears and his apathy, he is about to go out and address a meeting at which he has been threatened with violence by a Group of Patriotic Englishmen.

Here is a really new motive in Huxley's fiction; a new willingness to imagine and to represent a deliberate purpose, a conscious choice, and action in the light of it that may not be—that in fact will not be, whatever happens—sardonically futile. The novel that Huxley might write around such a motive, dominant and definitive throughout, it is impossible not to speculate on; but with *Eyeless in Gaza* he is far from having written it. The Anthony Beavis of the last sections is an almost disembodied potentiality; the Anthony Beavis of the book as a whole—the Anthony who, even after his 'change,' catches himself 'taking intense pleasure in commenting on the imbecility of my audience and human beings at large'—this is the actual and the dramatically credible man. Whatever Huxley may later write, there is still an immense vacuum between his premises and his conclusions.

The seriousness of thought and feeling behind this novel cannot, however, be mistaken; and one is bound to wonder whether the vacuum will ever be filled in; whether, with his new interest in the active defense of culture and peace, Huxley will sometime write a novel of contemporary life that will carry complete conviction. *Eyeless in Gaza*, to tell the truth, does not make one very hopeful. The habits of thought that have enabled Huxley to write wittily and destructively about little groups of bored and idle sophisticates are not habits that adapt themselves very suitably to the rendering of European society in its present period of acute and omnipresent crisis.

With all his learning, with all his fine cultivation, Huxley is almost wholly without the sense of history, almost wholly without the sense of social dynamics; and to judge from the novel before us, his recent about-face is a change of front on one plane only. If he formerly viewed men with a largely undiscriminating scorn, he now views them with an equally undiscriminating love, or recommends the attempt to do so;

and in both cases it has been the attitude of a romantic individualist, now Byronic, now Dostoevskian. He may speak of order and unity as transcendental goals, but he has astonishingly little understanding of the actual tightness with which human destinies are intertwisted or of the necessity of postponing individual to collective reconstruction. 'States and Nations,' writes Anthony Beavis in his diary, 'don't exist as such. There are only people. Sets of people living in certain areas, having certain allegiances. Nations won't change their national policies unless and until people change their private policies.' With such perilous half-truths ringing in one's ears, one is tempted to reflect that Milton's Samson, sightless among the slaves of the Philistines, was at any rate not self-blinded.

82. George Stevens, review in *Saturday Review of Literature*

11 July 1936, xiv, pp. 3–4, 12

George Stevens, b. 1904, journalist and publisher, was managing editor of the *Saturday Review of Literature* 1933–8 and an officer of J. B. Lippincott Co. 1940–70.

The review was entitled 'Aldous Huxley's Man of Good Will.'

Aldous Huxley is undoubtedly the most interesting writer of non-fiction among English novelists today. At forty-two, the author of twenty-four published books, he has written only six novels. Besides these there are five books of short stories, leaving thirteen—more than half the total—of essays, poetry, and travel. And in all his longer novels there are frequent disquisitions on general ideas which interrupt, even when they illuminate, the narrative. These passages are often memorable, whether the author is writing about music or science or Pareto or psychoanalysis—or, as in his new novel, about freedom.

This explains why his narrative abilities have sometimes been under-estimated. Those of us who believe that *Point Counter Point* is among, say, the half dozen most distinguished novels of the twenties, have often had to counter the criticism that Huxley's characters are merely the mouthpieces of a succession of arguments; that his drama dissolves into dialectics and his sympathies into satire. He has been given much the same kind of critical treatment—with notable exceptions—that Shaw was receiving thirty years ago. Writers who get the reputation of being long on ideas but short on emotions arouse the uneasy suspicion that they cannot be quite as good as they look. But *Point Counter Point* stands up, after eight years, as the kind of enrichment of experience that first rate fiction can provide; if it was widely read at the time for enter-tainment, for its richly satiric portraits and scandalous episodes, it is remembered now for its dramatization, through its leading characters, of a large phase of modern intellectual life. It marked Aldous Huxley's transition from a promising novelist to a mature novelist. *Crome Yellow* and *Antic Hay* had represented an attitude; *Point Counter Point* repre-sented a point of view. Mr. Huxley had progressed from sarcasm to satire, from disillusionment to skepticism.

Skepticism is implicit in *Point Counter Point*; if it is a story of intelli-gent men trying to live intelligently, it is permeated with a distrust of absolutes; the characters in the novel who deluded themselves with absolutes ended by being either tragic or ridiculous. In *Eyeless in Gaza*, the point of view is no longer skeptical, nor is the meaning implicit. Mr. Huxley says precisely what he means in so many words, and thus raises once more the question of how much non-fiction a novel can hold. This is not merely a matter of splitting hairs. No one questions Mr. Huxley's privilege, as a novelist of ideas, to write as he pleases: to introduce elaborate technical devices, to let his characters—so long as they are characters—say what he thinks about things in general. Like *Point Counter Point, Eyeless in Gaza* can be read on two levels, for enter-tainment or experience, or for both at once. It is comparable to *Point Counter Point* in humor, insight, and originality; it contains superb narrative passages, many of which can be read as independent short stories; it is the product of a first rate intelligence; it is always readable and often exciting, both in its ideas and in its general dramatic event-fulness. In short, it is interesting for every incidental quality. It has everything that Mr. Huxley's admirers will expect. But it also has some qualities which they will not expect.

The theme of *Eyeless in Gaza* is freedom. Does freedom mean merely financial independence and spiritual detachment? Anthony Beavis, the characteristic Huxleyan intellectual who is the chief character of this novel, reaches the age of forty in the conviction that he is a free man because he has money, a professional interest in sociology, and an independence of mind which lifts him above popular fallacies and sentimentalities. He carefully avoids responsibilities; he even carefully prevents himself from falling in love with his mistress. But he finally discovers that all this is merely sham freedom: that genuine freedom consists not in detachment, but in identifying himself with other human beings. Human freedom is the result of human solidarity.

Now the idea of human solidarity is in the air. It is a translation into terms of individuals of the idea of internationalism. It is the same idea precisely as that signified by the phrase, 'Men of Good Will,' which is the title of Jules Romains's monumental novel. It means that the differences which separate human beings are far smaller, and far less important, than what human beings have in common. And that this must be recognized, and become part of our consciousness, before any of the problems of the modern world can be dealt with.

Since Mr. Huxley expresses this idea in the form of fiction, it would be irrelevant to criticize his novel according to whether or not one believed the idea to be valid. The question is whether or not the novel successfully dramatizes the idea. Certainly it is not a propagandist novel; human solidarity is not a partisan issue, it is universally acceptable. We are not concerned (fortunately) with how it is to be brought about, but with its place in Mr. Huxley's story. If the events of the novel and the lives of the characters excite our imaginations with the idea of freedom, the novel is a success. It is not, however, if the thesis does not emerge from the events, but seems merely tacked on as a postscript.

[Presents a synopsis of the story]

This synopsis is necessary to any criticism of *Eyeless in Gaza*, but it does not, of course, begin to convey the richness of the story. There are many excellent characters, some of them brought to life with sympathy, some of them satirically observed under glass, all of them precisely delineated. Brian Foxe, the idealist, never becomes the neurotic another novelist might have made of him; his relationships with Anthony, with his mother, with his fiancée, come out in a succession of moving and compassionate passages. Helen Amberley first appears in an early chapter which, as an amusing episode of a spoiled brat, could stand by itself and win any of the short story prizes of the year; she develops into a brittle and superficial young woman with more experience than her intelligence can cope with; and she finally catches up with her experience in another superb short story, this time a tragic one, in which she sees her German lover kidnapped by the Nazis. The magnificent episode of Mark Staithes has already been mentioned. Except for the chief character and his development—which is the central part of the book—*Eyeless in Gaza* would be a consistent, vigorous, and veracious observation of modern individuals at the mercy of catastrophe.

But Anthony Beavis is something else. He is not at the mercy of catastrophe; it is he who creates or observes the melodrama of others. And it is he who tries to discover the solution for the individual victim of the contemporary world. Anthony is presented as a sensitive and civilized person, with some of the weakness that is supposed to be the defect of those qualities. But there is a considerable difference between the character Aldous Huxley evidently intended to create, and the character of Anthony Beavis as the reader sees him. It would have taken more than weakness, it would have taken most extraordinary obtuseness and lack of imagination, for him to carry through the Brian Foxe episode. The whole difficulty is that Beavis's intellectual life is the subject of the novel, and Beavis is not very intelligent. His character is that of a man who has been favored by circumstance, who has never had to battle for his education or his point of view, who accepts intellectual fashions—the best ones, to be sure—but never is obliged to think out anything for himself. His final conversion to the idea of human solidarity is reminiscent only of a Princeton senior's conversion to Buchmanism.[1] The technique is the same: Anthony has, in the language of the Buchmanites, 'faced up to' his previous shortcomings.

So the final chapter, which develops the idea of freedom, comes out not as a spiritual experience of Anthony Beavis's, but as a metaphysical essay of Aldous Huxley's. And that is why—with the best will in the world, as an enthusiastic admirer of the author—one reads this essay with more detachment and bewilderment than conviction. It is deeply sincere and beautifully written:

[Quotes Chapter LIV, pp. 614–15]

But the reader stays on the outside looking in. The essay follows, intellectually, from the story; but it is not organic to the story, because

[1] The principles of the international movement for Moral Re-Armament, or of the Oxford Group, named after its founder, the U.S. religious leader Frank N. D. Buchman (1879–1961).

the reader has not sufficiently shared the preceding emotions of the leading character. Since a musical analogy is appropriate to this 'contrapuntal' novelist, it may be said that Aldous Huxley has translated Schiller's 'Ode to Joy' into modern metaphysics but without the transfiguration which Beethoven gave to it in the last movement of the Ninth Symphony.

In any event, it is a surprise to see Aldous Huxley embracing the millions. Admirers of *Point Counter Point* may well continue to prefer him as a skeptic. His skepticism was a valuable quality; it cast a clear light over the 'color of his times' (in Rebecca West's phrase): he made it emerge as a positive literary force, he made it carry a conviction that is lacking in *Eyeless in Gaza*. What lies behind this development Mr. Huxley alone could say; the relevant fact here is that he has found fiction an inadequate medium to express his new point of view.

Since the war, there has been a procession of British novelists who seem, for one reason or another, to have found the novel an insufficient medium for what they had to say. H. G. Wells was the first of the major novelists to abandon the novel. When Bennett and Galsworthy died, the literary scene which had so long been dominated by imaginative writers no longer cohered under any domination. The next generation had produced significant novelists in Aldous Huxley, Virginia Woolf, James Joyce, D. H. Lawrence, E. M. Forster. But Lawrence died in his forties and Forster wrote his last novel in 1924. Joyce began his *Work in Progress*, and Mrs. Woolf wrote *Orlando, Flush*, and *The Waves*. *Work in Progress* is an abandonment of the novel in the direction of case history; and *The Waves* was an abandonment of the novel in the direction of poetry. Which left Aldous Huxley, who took a satirical holiday with *Brave New World*, and now, four years later, in his most serious attempt to unravel an intellectual problem, finds narrative insufficient for his purposes.

It seems that an intellectual novelist like Huxley, and like Wells before him, although possessed of enormous imaginative powers, cannot subordinate those to his immediate interest in the problems of contemporary life. Whether it is because the danger of a breakdown in civilization makes the ordinary materials of fiction—stories, characters, and individual relationships—seem trivial, or whether it is because contemporary life is too complex for any treatment other than the purely analytical, the result is that the intellectual novelist comes finally to some form of non-fiction between journalism and philosophy. If Aldous Huxley had maintained a detached point of view towards Anthony

Beavis, *Eyeless in Gaza* would have been a novel comparable in every respect to *Point Counter Point*. In fact, nine tenths of it is comparable: this new novel is magnificently readable, acutely intelligent, and, in its succession of narrative episodes, humorous, compassionate, and dramatic. But the point of the book is in the ten per cent that is not comparable to *Point Counter Point*—and this ten per cent is non-fiction.

83. William Troy, review in *Nation* (New York)

11 July 1936, cxliii, pp. 49–50

William Troy (1903–61), educator and critic, wrote essays for such magazines as *Perspectives USA*, *New Republic*, and *Partisan Review*.

The review is entitled 'Huxley Agonistes.'

Somewhere in this novel the hero quotes the closing lines of the most magnificent of Gerard Hopkins's sonnets-written-in-blood; and the thought occurs that with this book Aldous Huxley proves that his whole career has been moving toward a rediscovery of the truth, re-stated in the same sonnet, that 'selfyeast of spirit a dull dough sours.' At least it will seem true if we take the liberty of identifying an author with his hero, which is here somewhat more justifiable than usual in view of the fact that the hero is a prosperous sociologist, renowned for his ironic detachment and given to a kind of finicking distaste for any form of experience that is too unpleasantly concrete. Anthony Beavis is the Huxley hero, the one and only Huxley hero, aged forty-three, and finally confronted with the ancient problem of salvation for himself and the world. He is a projection, that is to say, of everything that his creator has thought, felt, and read in the seven years since his last novel (one may ignore the unhappy interruption of the fantasy that appeared in 1932). And to say that he represents a distinct enlargement in every sense over his earlier self is one way of indicating the considerable advance that this book marks in Huxley's development as a novelist. Whatever else remains to be said about it, *Eyeless in Gaza* is the deepest, the most serious, and the most complete novel of his career.

After the erudite snickerings and Rabelaisian guffaws, after the admirable collection of protozoic analogies, after the tired fornications in Mayfair boudoirs, the Huxley hero has become a stern but ardent moralist. Just before this transformation, it is true, he has begun to have doubts about the existence even of his own personality; he has apparently been reading Proust; and there are several pages of denatured metaphysics for the readers of the lending libraries. But all such doubts are dissolved in the warm light of his recognition that he can no longer live irresponsibly, that he has 'duties toward himself and others and the nature of things.' For twenty years he had thought all this nonsense— 'nonsense, in spite of occasional uncomfortable intimations that there might be a point, and that the point was precisely in what he had chosen to regard as the pointlessness, the practical joke.' His shock is the result partly of the lesson of experience, partly of his meditations on society and its institutions, and partly of his friendship with a certain Dr. Miller. Or it may be said that the doctrines of this spiritual reformer provide an interpretation, as well as a direction, for a life that would otherwise be without significance. Life and its interpretation are therefore presented simultaneously, so to speak, out of what may be called the drowning man's point of view in fiction.

This method, reminiscent both of the Jamesian 'process of vision' and the movie flash-back, involves a discarding of the normal time order of narrative for the more or less fortuitous order of the memory. For Huxley, translating the lesson of experience, such a method has the advantage of dispensing no more of the lesson than the reader's preference for experience enables him to take, like a physician administering an otherwise too saccharine fluid drop by drop over a period of time. Moreover, it has the advantage of distributing more equally the disquisitions that are the fruit of the hero's recent readings in biology, chemistry, sociology, and anthropology. But it may be questioned whether this wilful playing with the normal time sense is not really evidence of a last infirmity in a writer headed toward nobility. The substance of the experience, as a matter of fact, is reducible to a single

situation. It is that complication in his youth which caused Anthony
Beavis to betray the feelings of his best friend's fiancée in order to win
an idle bet from his mistress. As a revelation of the 'piddling, twopenny-
halfpenny personality' of the modern man it is a situation admirably
suited to Huxley's general theme. The remorse suffered by the hero is
an adequate psychological explanation for his over-eager surrender to
the persuasive Dr. Miller, uttering from a mule-back in Mexico the
immemorial formula of the Buddhist redemption, 'love and compassion.'

To summarize the stages of speculative reasoning by which Anthony
arrives at the same formula would be to give more order to his thought
than Huxley himself has troubled to give it. We know that he is
opposed to both fascism and communism because each sacrifices the
means to the end. Revolution always fails of its aims because it operates
from the wrong motives and puts the wrong people in power. It
merely creates new institutions to enslave the individual and set him
against his fellow-men. Politically, therefore, Anthony—or Huxley—
is an anarchist, unless the pacifism that we leave him practicing as well
as preaching at the end can be considered a system. But 'Millerism' is
perhaps more strictly a spiritual and psychological discipline, like Yoga
or Christian Science. There is much talk of 'the proper use of the self,'
and also a serious defence of vegetarianism. Anthony's final meditations,
to tell the real truth, read like the lucubrations of a Bloomsbury intellectual sunk irrevocably into the downy folds of the Buddhist heaven.
Not the high strength of the Miltonic Samson struggling with real good
and real evil, within and without, but Annie Besant and the 'peace
beyond peace.' It is perhaps the last irony of this novel that it will be
most appreciated by the Stigginses and the Burlaps, by those accustomed
to commit the greatest enormities in the name of love, by the sort of
people that Huxley has grown famous in satirizing.

The report that Huxley has turned sentimentalist will probably be
little credible to many people. Sentimentalism implies lack of intelligence, and surely Huxley is among the most intelligent of living writers.
Yet the contradiction may be somewhat diminished if it is admitted
that the professional *homo sapiens*, 'the chimpanzee on the upper side of
humanity,' is more likely to be thrown off his base than the so-called
average man. Between his brittle intelligence and his sense of experience, between his intellect and his sensibility, there has always been in
Huxley a breach which has prevented him from being a great imaginative writer. Confronted in mid-career with the reality of certain values

to which he had hitherto paid little attention, his intelligence gives the reins to his sensibility with an abandonment that will shock some very much less 'intelligent' individuals. For while a sense of the reality of human life does not make for any less love, it does render impossible a bubbling romantic belief in the kind of disembodied human goodness and justice in which Huxley finally puts his faith. It makes impossible any program for men or societies that is not based on some objective system of organization and control. But there is a sense in which Huxley, without undergoing a profound reorientation of mind and temperament, could have arrived at no other solution to his problem. From thinking too little of humanity the romantic ironist has ended by thinking too much: the wheel has come full circle back to Rousseau.

84. J. Donald Adams, review in *NYTBR*

19 July 1936, pp. 1, 20

James Donald Adams, b. 1891, edited the *New York Times Book Review* section 1925–43 and has written *The Shape of Books to Come* (1944), *Literary Frontiers* (1951), and *Speaking of Books and Life* (1965). See Introduction, p. 20.

It is a pity that Aldous Huxley is not a better—perhaps one should say a completer novelist—for he has written a novel which is at least the equal, if not the superior, in intellectual and spiritual content, of any in our time. For all its structural faults *Eyeless in Gaza* is an important and portentous book—one that no thinking man or woman of the twentieth century can read without stimulation and deep respect. In this novel Huxley has faced his age more fully than any other novelist writing in English: he has shut his eyes to none of its terrifying aspects, he has evaded none of its problems, and he has given us, in result, the picture of an individual man groping for a way of life that will bring meaning and purpose to his existence which is quite without parallel in our contemporary literature.

This novel rings down the curtain—and not through the medium of escape—on a literary age of disillusion and despair. By that I do not mean to say that it lifts a curtain on the millennium. But Aldous Huxley, quite evidently speaking for himself, has posited a way of life from which he derives courage to face the future. It is not a solution which will satisfy everyone who reads this book; it may not even satisfy many, but all will recognize the sincerity which informs it and respect the reasoning by which it is approached. I had hoped that such a book as this might have come first from an American writer, and certainly there is more in the contemporary American novel to justify the expectation than there has recently been in England. But it has remained for Huxley to sound, for the first time clearly, and in accents that are familiar and valid for our generation, that note of definite affirmation which has been absent from creative writing for so many years.

[Comments on Margaret Mitchell's *Gone with the Wind*]

. . . This is a more tolerant—no, a more compassionate Huxley than the young man who wrote *Point Counter Point*, or even that more recent self who wrote *Brave New World*. It is a man who has thought much and deeply, who has his feet set in the path to wisdom; and his eyes, if they can watch 'the awful unconsciousness of that unconquerable, crawling desire' revealed in a film picturing the fertilization of a rabbit's ovum, can also see beyond to the unity of all life and to the realization of goodness and peace through its recognition.

Aldous Huxley is not, as was long ago observed, a natural novelist, not a writer predestined by temperament and gifts to express himself in the form of fictional narrative. But an essayist, which Huxley is by nature and talents, cannot make himself adequately heard in our time, and he, like many others, has found it expedient to work in a form which would make possible a wider audience. As a novel, *Eyeless in Gaza* is more awkward technically—perhaps perversely so—than anything which Huxley has done. But in a man of his gifts, some of them, like his sure psychological sense and his remarkably acute powers of observation, of the utmost value to a novelist, this difficulty with the form of the novel, with the art of telling a story, may largely be overlooked.

In this book he has created characters, one of whom we identify closely with himself, in whom it is impossible not to become interested as people. They are real and their problems are real; they are also, in large measure, the problems of all of us who look out with misgivings and dismay upon a disordered world in which we find it increasingly hard to create for ourselves a satisfactory base upon which to build our lives. One by one he interests us in these people exceedingly, and then he proceeds to tell their stories in a peculiarly maddening fashion. . . . It is difficult to conceive precisely what Huxley expected to gain from this method, and the best evidence of the interest he creates in his ideas and the figures through whom he works them out, lies in the fact that one reads on in admiration, annoyed, but scarcely impeded, by the method.

[Summarizes the book]

Aldous Huxley bears inerasably upon him the scabrous imprint of the world in which he, like Anthony, grew to maturity. It lay like the hand of death on *Point Counter Point*, and brought him to the contemplation of that horrible future which he pictured for mankind in *Brave New World*. In this book he has done his manful best to slough it off, and he emerges a moralist, a believer in the efficacy of the spiritual life, in the necessity that one demands of oneself the achievement of the impossible. Peace for the individual, peace for the world itself, only through the individual exercise of love and compassion. That, in essence, is what Aldous Huxley has to say in this novel. And he has said it persuasively and well.

85. Gabriel Marcel, review in *L'Europe nouvelle*

21 August 1937, xx, pp. 815–16

Gabriel Marcel, b. 1889, notable French philosopher and author, is a key twentieth-century inquirer into the challenge of existence for man. Marcel contributed dramatic and literary criticism to numerous periodicals and wrote several important philosophical books, among them *Being and Having* (1935) and *The Mystery of Being* (1951). See Introduction, p. 15.

The extract is translated by Thomas M. Donnan, member of the Foreign Language Department of New York State University at Geneseo. The opening sentence refers to Guy de Pourtalès's *Pêche Miraculeuse*, which Marcel has been reviewing.

Aldous Huxley, whose book also undoubtedly includes a major auto-biographical element, wasn't able to stick to this kind of procedure, and I think that I understand just what preoccupations caused him to adopt the procedure—albeit annoying in itself—which can be observed in his book. With a little astonishment the reader will acknowledge that the first chapter is dated: '30 August 1933,' the second: '4 April 1934,' the third: '30 August 1933,' the fourth: '6 November 1902,' the fifth: '8 December 1926,' the sixth: '6 November 1902,' the seventh: 8 April 1934,' etc. We are confronted with a composition in zig-zags entailing displacement in time, as contrasted with the continuous development of normal narrative. The reader is thus constrained to the relatively arduous task of putting things back in order. It is as though someone had given him a deck of shuffled cards and he had to redispose them in some systematic way. The author himself admits today that one could easily wonder—and not without some irritation—why the novelist didn't carry out this necessary arrangement. The answer is twofold; I am not saying that it is wholly convincing, but it certainly deserves some consideration. Mr. Huxley started out from a psychological observation (an incontestable one, in my opinion): he has remarked that I, for instance, can on a certain date, say 20 October 1936, feel myself nearer, in a way which is at once precise and unexplainable, to what I was twenty-five years earlier, nearer to much more recent events, but events which we cannot call 'brought nearer' except by putting ourselves on the level of an objective, impersonal passage of time. Upon bending over to kiss the shoulder of his mistress, Helen, Anthony Beavis perceives a faint but none the less penetrating odor, both salty and smoky, which carries him off to a chalk quarry of the Chilterns, where, in the company of Brian Foxe twenty years earlier, he had spent an inexplicably pleasant hour striking two pieces of flint together and sniffing voluptuously at the spot where the spark had left its characteristic mustiness of marine combustion. Thus the palpable ground of Helen's presence opens up and he finds himself precipitated into another time and another place.

[Quotes Beavis's reflections on time, Chapter III, p. 23]

But who knows if it isn't necessary to go even further, that is, if the reason for a happening to be registered by the consciousness doesn't reside *in the future*, in the fact that it has yet to be evoked much later under certain circumstances. One sees here that Mr. Huxley has been profoundly impressed by certain contemporaneous studies on time, and in particular by the curious research of Dunn (*An Experiment in Time*). But we should naturally go into the esthetic sphere in order to understand Mr. Huxley's basic intent. No doubt he thought he would (keeping in mind the subjective order in the succession of the evocations, or moreover, in another manner of speaking, of our inner space—that is, the way of arranging successive present-times for consciousness itself), or shall I say, he *hoped* he would make us participate much more directly in the intimate life of his hero this way than by restricting himself to reciting its course. By this he has applied himself to what I would venture to call spatial psychology as opposed to the plane psychology of the usual novelists. It is doubtful, really, that he succeeded at it. Besides the fact that the reasons—emotional or life-ordering—for putting such and such a scene after such and such aren't clear, and that consequently the linking seems arbitrary here, Mr. Huxley works counter to a kind of exigency of the mind that the Germans would rightly call transcendental and requires just that strict ordering that he claims to overthrow. But I doubt whether a work that sets itself up as a challenge to the fundamental postulations of consciousness can, in fact, triumph over them.

With this reservation, the richness of Mr. Huxley's book cannot be too much admired; one can find in it the same gift for implacable and almost sadistic analysis that burst forth in *Point Counter Point*. But there is another thing which shows a profound development in the writer. Anthony Beavis, who has been successively the lover of Mary Amberley and of her daughter Helen, who, to win a bet, has driven his friend Brian Foxe to despair and death by turning his fiancée from him, in brief, who has behaved in life like one devoid not only of moral sense but even of a heart, is won over in the end by a sort of religion more Ghandist than Christian and which is, however, somewhat related to the conceptions professed by the 'Oxford groups.'[1]

[Quotes from Beavis's meditation, Chapter LIV, pp. 618–19]

It is this canticle to peace that brings to an end an otherwise most cruel, most willfully dissonant book. But in this the book is a milestone. It brings a definitive close—not only for its author, but also for those who admired and imitated him—to a whole period in which the mind thought it had found, even as it was disintegrating, the full potential of its powers. What will tomorrow bring? I don't think Mr. Huxley is the one who can tell us. The uchrony of the *best of all possible worlds* already belongs to . . . [sic] the past.

[1] See note to No. 82, p. 261.

86. C. Day-Lewis on Huxley's pacifism

1936

Cecil Day-Lewis (1904–72), English Poet Laureate from 1968 to 1972, editor, professor, and director of Chatto & Windus publishers, was a leading figure among that group of 1930s writers urging a reawakening of social consciousness. Stephen Spender also replied to Huxley's pacifist position in an open letter to the *Left Review* (see Introduction, pp. 19–20).

Following are excerpts from Day-Lewis's *We're NOT going to do NOTHING: A reply to Aldous Huxley's 'What are you going to do about it?'* This thirty-one-page pamphlet was issued in a limited edition of fifty copies by the *Left Review*. Huxley replied to Day-Lewis, *L*, pp. 411–12.

Mr. Aldous Huxley's recent pamphlet, *What are you going to do about it?* has had a considerable success. Published at a time when the ordinary Englishman feels tempted to sell his birthright for a reliable gas-mask, and even the English intellectual can no longer ignore the bayonets that are being brandished beneath his nose, this pamphlet puts forward a specious plea for what seems to me in fact a policy of final inactivity. Mr. Huxley is a writer of great brilliance and achievement: in consequence, when he enters the sphere of practical politics, we are bound to listen to him with respect. We have listened, and we feel that his pamphlet does more credit to his heart than to his head. His *Case for Constructive Peace* constructs nothing more solid than a great, big, beautiful idealist bubble—lovely to look at, no doubt; charming to live in, perhaps: but with little reference to the real facts and inadequate protection against a four-engined bomber.

We are at one with Mr. Huxley in detestation of war and determination to prevent it. We agree with him that pacifism is more than a Utopian dream. We disagree as to the methods which can make this dream into a reality. The core of Mr. Huxley's argument is that violence is morally wrong under every conceivable circumstance, for the reason that 'means condition ends', and therefore any end achieved by violence will itself be morally unsatisfactory—will be infected by the means, and thus will breed more violence in due season. I believe this argument to be both fallacious and self-contradictory. If it is proved so, then Mr. Huxley's policy of non-violent resistance to war must fall to the ground also.

[Day-Lewis argues in the body of his pamphlet that Huxley's position is unrealistic]

The doctrine of non-violence is an idealistic doctrine which, as far as I can see, may help the war-mongers, but, in existing conditions, cannot possibly advance the cause of peace. I call it a doctrine of despair, because non-resistance is the last resort of both brave men and cowards when they are up against overwhelming odds, and when it is only an attitude that can distinguish the one from the other. 'Since all our efforts can only end in frustration,' the despairing pacifist seems to say: 'let us refrain from effort.' It is a gesture which, however finely performed, is not very different from the gesture of Ivan Karamazof 'returning the ticket,' or Pilate washing his hands. Needless to say, Mr. Huxley does not see it like this. He makes much of the 'realism' of his proposed methods of 'active' pacifism. But that the words 'realism' and 'active' are misapplied has not been, I think, difficult to show. 'Hell is paved,' says Mr. Huxley, 'not only with good intentions, but also with the most exquisite sensibilities, the noblest expressions of fine feeling, the profoundest insights into ethical truths.' Aldous Huxley's own sensibilities are so exquisite that, together with his great talent in writing, they have made him one of the prophets of our time—the Prophet of Disgust. He feels so keenly the discrepancy between the fact and the ideal that he seems like some miserable figure, standing with face averted from the ruin and filth that surround him; though every now and then, half in fascination, half in disgust, he directs an exceedingly sharp glance at what so much appalls him. Now it looks as though he is turning his back on us for ever. Looking away from us, he has a 'profound insight into ethical truth', and we are still stewing in the same juice. Might we venture to beg him to turn right about and risk looking contemporary humanity in the face? There would be much there to hate and much to be disgusted at, but there would also be something which, without any 'expressions of fine feeling', could be loved and supported.

[Urges that the idealists have withdrawn into an inner world of simple truths which is not consonant with the complex actualities of life in the material world]

The real argument behind Mr. Huxley's case is clear and familiar. It is the argument that it is no use doing anything 'from without'. Reformation must come 'from within'. It is another form of the doctrine of despair, and there have been periods of history when it has been appropriate. When reform from without is clearly impossible, there is nothing left but reform from within. 'Spiritual exercises' are appropriate for a man in prison, to whom other activity is denied: but we are not in prison yet. Nowadays we usually find this argument in the armoury of individualists who, shrinking from contact with their fellows or disgusted with what seems to them the hopelessness of 'politics', take refuge in the thought that they themselves can keep un-contaminated, that they and their friends can at least save their spiritual skins. Once more let us ask Mr. Huxley to look at the real world. Are there not some circumstances in which, if not the Kingdom of Heaven, at any rate decent living, friendly feeling, love and hope thrive better than in other circumstances? Are there not indeed whole countries and whole economic systems where the conditions for a good life are better than elsewhere? For 'saints or trained pacifists' it may be easy to live well under any conditions. But for the mass of mankind an improve-ment in material conditions—more money, more leisure, more freedom, more peace—would be, to say the least, a great help towards living the good life which Mr. Huxley recommends. Let us talk sense and say that, although a saint (or trained pacifist) may be oblivious to material conditions, everyone else on earth requires a change from without before his strength and humanity can flower in him from within.

[Defends 'the Labour Movement' as the key instrument for preserving peace and democracy]

. . . We must compel our National Government to make up its mind whether it stands for democracy or Fascism: if for the former, let it declare its uncompromising support of democratic rights at home and of democratic governments abroad: if for the latter, we must take all steps in our power to overthrow it.

That is the one alternative for pacifists. The only other is the doctrine of despair advocated by Mr. Huxley and his friends. Let me say it again. There is still hope. We are not yet at the stage of absolute impotence where there is nothing to be done but while away the time with Mr. Huxley's 'spiritual exercises'. Public opinion is still a force of incalculable potency, and it is our business to organise it and lead it into action. We must remember that there is something more important for us to save than our own individual souls. And we must act *at once* if we are to save it.

87. Elizabeth Bowen on Huxley

1936

Elizabeth (Dorothea Cole) Bowen, b. 1899, British novelist and essayist, wrote, for example, *The Death of the Heart* (1938) and *Eva Trout* (1969).

The essay appeared as a review of *The Olive Tree* in *Spectator*, 11 December 1936, clvii, p. 1046, and was reprinted in Bowen's *Collected Impressions* (London: Longman, 1950), pp. 146–8.

Mr. Huxley has been the alarming young man for a long time, a sort of perpetual clever nephew who can be relied on to flutter the lunch-party. Whatever will he say next? How does he think of these things? He has been deplored once or twice, but feeling is in his favour: he is steadily read. He is at once the truly clever person and the stupid person's idea of the clever person; he is expected to be relentless, to administer intellectual shocks. This attitude to Mr. Huxley, to which his early work may have given credit, has been maintained, and strengthened, for about twenty years. Actually, he is now at an age which in any other profession would be considered sober: he is well into middle age—or maturity. This is a statement which may be considered slighting in a country that dreads maturity for its artists, in which there is a deep and horrific gap between the bright young fellow and the good old bustard, in which the dream-child and the prodigy dominate literature. Shocks apart, the growing pressure, behind Mr. Huxley's work, of adult seriousness may give his public unforeseen offence: he threatens to break a pact by which the clever person is not permitted to be in earnest right through. Whereas, if you are moral, to be clever is superfluous, even unbecoming. Happily for this country—while she makes this distinction—she has few grown-up writers, fewer grown-up æsthetes; Mr. Huxley is both. As a novelist, it is true, he still gives his readers pleasure by adolescent harshness, a dashing cynicism, the depiction of excruciating scenes and what are called 'unnecessary' incidents—like the dog on the roof in *Eyeless in Gaza*, or the moron's death in *Those Barren Leaves*. (Strictly, those two incidents are necessary; they are the moral pivots of the two books.) As a novelist, he still has a touch of the prodigy: in a great glare of intellectual hilarity his characters dangle rather too jerkily; they are morality characters with horrified puppet-faces. His novels, however, have it over his best collections of essays in one important particular: they are continuous. And Mr. Huxley's continuity—the transitions he makes, the positions he abandons, the connexions he underlines—is very important.

The Olive Tree is another collection of essays, written, with two exceptions, within the last few years. The piece (placed last) which gives the book its pretty and concrete name is pure reflection, a running-on of the mind. The quickness and limpidity of its flow remind one that Aldous Huxley was labelled a writers' writer—which meant, presumably, that he writes better than lay people are expected to understand. Few readers now are as dumb as the critics thought: we know technique when we see it. The vitality, aptness, structure and inherent beauty of Mr. Huxley's style is plain to, more or less, anyone. He is occupied, now, with something beyond this—though real style, it is true, cannot be involuntary. His analysis of T. H. Huxley's prose is instructive.

The preface to the D. H. Lawrence letters reappears, and is given context and fresh point by some of the other essays. The juxtaposition of subjects, in this collection, is telling; they lend one another interest and gain collective importance. One would gladly have the links that form in one's own mind tested by Mr. Huxley, and associations, however idle, explored. If he would write one long, embracing essay— those different sofas, for instance: Crebillon's and the sofa in the Spaxton billiard-room-chapel on which Brother Prince, the Beloved, redeemed the flesh. ('Justifications' is brilliant.) Exactly what divided

D. H. Lawrence from Laurence Oliphant of the *Sympneumata*?[1] What would Crebillon have made of *Lady Chatterley*? Again, there was Lawrence's 'Art for my sake' and there was poor B. R. Haydon's piteous arrogance: should one, in fact, like Lawrence, stand by one's genius if, like Haydon, one really has not got any? We should like this gone into.

Learning and frivolity polish all these essays, but there is something more. 'Writers and Readers' and 'Words and Behaviour' are as overtly serious as parts of *Eyeless in Gaza*. The foundations of the ivory tower are shaken; there are no longer untouchable palaces for the mind. Intellect cannot withdraw; it must go into the battle. Mr. Huxley is out to combat, with mathematical coldness, with chemical deadliness, the forces of unreason he sees destroying us. Actually, he can never write—can anyone?—without emotion: his statements are often given colour by horror. He sees us as hypnotized by abstractions, morbidly passive, herdable, driven on to our fate. Morality, a morality of the mind, is all we have against ruin.

[Quotes from 'Words and Behaviour,' p. 100]

In fact, he is preaching a new asceticism: if he presses this point further he will not be popular. Meanwhile, he has done, in this collection as ever, a great deal to amuse us: dug up the Perfectionist Bundlers, reclaimed Haydon and quoted his anecdotes, shown the way to Crebillon, painted an oasis, and given some notes on snobbery, examinations, fetichism and time. *The Olive Tree* goes to its place in that lengthening row on his shelf—perhaps he was born versatile: did he make himself diligent?

[1] Laurence Oliphant (1829–88), British author, traveler, and mystic, wrote the *Sympneumata: Evolutionary Forces now Active in Man* (1884) with his wife, after forming a small community in Haifa: the book is a plea for purification of the sexual life.

88. Alexander Henderson on Huxley

1936

Alexander John Henderson, b. 1910, critic, novelist, translator, and public servant, has been Chief Editor of the United Nation's Food and Agricultural Organization since 1953. He has written, among others, *The Dangerous World* (1949) and *The Tunnelled Fire* (1956), and has contributed to *Poetry Quarterly*, *Listener*, *Asiatic Review*, and others.

Extracts from *Aldous Huxley* (New York: Russell, 1964), pp. 1–2, 5–6, 141–4. Originally published in 1936, Henderson's was the first full-length study of Huxley.

Because we all know how to read, we imagine that we know what we read. Enormous fallacy!—'Vulgarity in Literature.'

Aldous Huxley has been writing for nineteen years. During that time he has produced twenty-five works of the most varied kinds, in each of which is immediately perceptible a mind and a sensibility of a distinction uncommon at the present time. There is no living author better worth re-reading. No one who can better inspire one with the courage of Europe in the face of the American big-shots, Hemingway, Dos Passos, and Faulkner. Few writers have more important things to say than Huxley, and none has a finer style, a politer malice, a deeper culture or a more secure artistry.

Huxley's serious reputation has, I believe, suffered from the fashionable and slightly scandalous success which attended certain of his novels. Among the smart, up-to-date sections of London Society and intelligentsia *Antic Hay* was, when it appeared in 1923, the one book it was unforgivable not to have read. At the same time the bigger public was shocked. It was reported by a popular London newspaper that *Antic Hay* had been burned by the Public Librarian in Alexandria because it

278

'smelled too strongly of the goat.' The 'burning' was, as I happen to know, a piece of journalistic licence. But that imaginary bonfire in Alexandria has cast its indignant glow upon a score of volumes.

Five, ten, fifteen years afterwards, Borough Councillors light upon one of Huxley's novels, and suddenly fearful that their children may grow up better men than they are, proclaim that though themselves above corruption, nevertheless they consider that such books should not be written. They may have a bad moral effect on the young (*i.e.* prevent them from being like father). And accordingly the book is banned from the public library. There is nothing like a Borough Councillor for stopping fun.

That, in 1935, is still the public reaction to Huxley. It should be sufficient indication that he is one of the most serious of living writers.

For the reviewers too there is a stock attitude. With magnificent, if perverted tenacity they go on year after year observing the Huxley of their own creation, and complaining that they do not like it. Their Huxley, then, is a pale-gray cardboard figure labelled: 'Intellectual—slightly unpleasant.' The first half of the tag appears to be inspired by the vanity of the critic, the second by his tender solicitude for the public. Time after time the reviewers complain that Huxley is too intellectual, too puritan, too abstract, or alternatively (in sudden panicky reaction), too voluptuous, concrete and obscene. And among reviewers of every class Huxley inspires plaintive wailings that he is too intelligent, and anyhow, unlike other writers.

. . . In dealing with Huxley's works the usual formula has been to apply the 'unpleasant' or 'lovable' classification, and on the whole his characters have been found unpleasant. From this conclusion, it is but a step to such peculiar mis-readings as:

'Is it surprising in the circumstances that Mr. Huxley is left with a puritanical disgust of life and a bleak cerebral pessimism?' (R. D. Charques: *Literature and Social Revolution*); or, 'His findings are always the same. Go where you like, "do what you will," you will never escape from the smell of ordure and decay' (John Strachey: *The Coming Struggle for Power*).

The only possible explanation for such remarks must be that the authors simply have not read Huxley with the care they would give, for instance, to D. H. Lawrence. Probably no important contemporary writer has been read with such superficiality, even by his most intelligent readers, as Huxley.

This is no doubt partly his own fault. His style invites to a swift, delicious glide. His irony charms continually. The firm easy movement of his prose lulls the mind into a quiet glow of admiration. With the reader thus drugged, Huxley can say anything and get away with it. Indeed it is his misfortune that he gets away with it too easily. Like Shaw he suffers from the consequences of providing too much jam with his pills. His readers will swallow pills indefinitely for the sake of the red delicious jam, and there is so much of it, that they never notice the hard white pill in the centre, which indeed, drowned in raspberry, leaves them unpurged and asking for more.

Because he is so easy to read, Huxley has never been read carefully enough, and because of that his books have never been subjected to a thorough, serious criticism.

[The rest of the excerpt is from the conclusion to Henderson's survey of the novels through *Brave New World*]

Huxley's novels have not come easily to him. In the twenty years of his writing career he has produced only five, as against nine volumes in the essay form. In each of those five the story is of secondary importance. They would be evidence, without his own admission in Philip Quarles's notebook, that he was not a congenital novelist. The absence of a story no one will regret, since he is able to get on without one. The only justification of the story, really, is that it may maintain the *writer's* interest, may encourage him to go on to the end when he would otherwise give up. What is important to note is that the novel form brings Huxley's natural qualities to a higher development. The precise psychological delineation, the close observation of man alone and in society, the irony, the wide ranging view—everything that distinguishes the essays is intensified by the glow of the creative imagination which the novel arouses in him.

The reason that he has done few novels, and has written those slowly, is because to compose fiction he requires the stimulus of ideas, of hitherto unexplored psychological peculiarities, of new technical tricks. Once stimulated by the possibilities of exploring this or that peculiarity of the psyche (he is working now on a novel dealing with the individual's experience of the past in the present), this or that technical literary device, his imagination begins to create characters, situations, names, and gradually a novel takes shape. The important point to note is that the novel does not occur to him in the form of a story. It is the dramatization of that talking to himself which proceeds at a lower level of excitement in the essays. It is a working model of his inner debate. In his characters he can see what his ideas look like dressed in human form.

But once his imagination is stirred into action, he creates with a firmness of construction, a sureness of form, which, despite his protest,* is of a kind only describable as classical. Artists speak of a draughtsman having a sure sense of the direction of a line. In the same way, we feel confident, in reading Huxley's novels, that he knows exactly which way he is going. We may not know ourselves, but we are sure he knows. There is never any danger of a mistake. The line never deviates into meaningless, uncertain darts and flurries. Besides Huxley I can think of only three writers who have the same assured sense of direction— Fielding, T. S. Eliot and Molière. . . .

Formally, art is only juggling. Huxley, like Molière, can circle blocks of words round his head with the arrogant grace of a master juggler. When you think everything will crash, he adds a glass of champagne, smiles, and continues, with Olympian unconcern. It is dazzling. It is intoxicating. It is perfection. And it is classical, not romantic.

The curious thing is, as every writer knows, that what may seem to the reader the perfection of controlled and conscious art, has not seemed at all like that to the author. So much of a novel suggests itself in the very process of writing. Scenes, characters and places not originally contemplated seem to spring from some dark, unexplored store-house of the mind. I do not doubt that many of the apparently most carefully planned set-pieces in Huxley's or any other novelist's works have been impromptus, have suddenly burst into the midst of quite other intentions. But this does not invalidate terms like balance, control, direction. Such classical qualities are as intuitive as the romantic ones. They show themselves in the ability to turn the impromptus of the subconscious to good account. Design which, in literature as in the plastic arts, must be learned at the beginning, becomes with much practice, intuitive.

Huxley, congenitally an essayist, has done his most lasting work in fiction. He has declined to stop at what came easily to him. Stimulated by the 'forme au travail rebelle'[1] of the novel he has produced five books which from their poise, irony and compact strength we feel to be works of bright and enduring beauty.

* 'For I have never had the smallest ambition to be a Classic of any kind, whether Neo, Palaeo, Proto or Eo.' 'Vulgarity in Literature' [*Music at Night*, p. 293—ed.].
[1] 'Form [which] rebels against the work.'

89. W. B. Yeats on Huxley

1936

William Butler Yeats (1865–1939), a foremost Irish poet, playwright and essayist, received a Nobel Prize for Literature in 1923.

The extracts are from *The Letters of W. B. Yeats*, ed. Alan Wade (New York: Macmillan, 1955), pp. 849–52.

(a) To Dorothy Wellesley, 6 April 1936

In my introduction to the translation of the *Upanishads* Purohit Swami and I are working at, I think I shall take up once more the theme of the sudden return of philosophy into English literature round about 1925. I will speak again of you and Turner, adding Huxley's *Barren Leaves*, which has the pessimism of modern philosophy. I read it a couple of weeks ago—it has historical significance but is not I think a lasting work. Its style belongs to the previous movement—it has precision but no rhythms—there is not a single sentence anybody will ever murmur to himself.

Can you recommend me some novels of the first intensity written in the last few years? I want to study the prose as I have studied the verse of contemporary writers—now that I have much time on my hands is a good moment. I want especially the names of any books that are philosophies, as *Barren Leaves* is. . . . Behind Huxley's satire is a satire which has for theme the whole of life. . . .

(b) To Olivia Shakespear, 10 April 1936

I am reading Aldous Huxley and Miss Sackville-West. I admire Huxley immensely and Miss Sackville-West a little and dislike both. Huxley seems unaware how badly his people are behaving. I sympathise however with his sadistic hatred of life. I want the reply and have half found it.

ENDS AND MEANS

November 1937

---

90. Cyril Connolly, review in *Sunday Times*

12 December 1937, p. 10

For a biographical note see No. 47. Connolly had done what
Evelyn Waugh called a 'silencing' parody of *Eyeless in Gaza*. See
Introduction, pp. 4–6.

This is Mr. Huxley's most important book. I also think it is his best.
Nobody could produce thirty books in twenty years of literary life,
without doing themselves considerable damage, and by the time he had
finished *Eyeless in Gaza* Mr. Huxley had done much harm to literature
as well. He had vulgarised and atrophied much of our current prose
vocabulary, tortured the novel and flattened the short essay, making
science and culture equally suspect to his uneasy admirers. Another
work of fiction would have driven them frantic. Instead he abandons
the novel to those with a more serious appreciation of their art, and
joins the philosophers.

Here his unique gifts are of the greatest value, for he has one of the
most lucid, penetrating, and best-informed minds of our time, and one
of the few which are also capable of assimilating the most advanced
ethics, physics, politics, and psychologies of today, and putting them
into a form comprehensible to the general reader. When he writes
about things I don't understand in this book I trust him, and there are
very few writers, only perhaps Gide, Valéry, and Bertrand Russell, of
whom one can say that.

Ends and Means is a synthesis of contemporary opinions on war,
education, society, religion, and ethics. Mr. Huxley examines various

attitudes to them and their future, and then describes his own. His own attitudes will be found to have a deep consistency, and to be based on arguments which grow cumulatively sounder and more impressive.

[Summarizes the gist of the book]

None of these ideas are new; they are found in primitive Christianity, in Buddhism, and in the Greek philosophies. What is new is Mr. Huxley's analysis of how they can be applied today. The Anarchists in Spain have tried them, and many small isolated communities have put them to work. What distinguishes *Ends and Means* is the penetrating grasp of why and how we fail to achieve them, why the lion will never lie down with the lamb. Huxley's great point is that the Means are never justified by the End. That violence in any cause, right or wrong, begets more violence. He is the complete pacifist. . . .

It is difficult in a book with which one is so much in agreement to find much to criticise. Mr. Huxley has one unfair advantage. He is a mystic, he has had mystical experiences; and when he talks of non-attachment to things of this world he is able to think of the mystical world as a compensation. For most of us it is not.

He has also one unfair disadvantage, a body which has given him only intermittent satisfaction, so that he cannot understand how happily the mind may reside in its shell, where health and moderate appetites permit. A man whose body will carry him equably for seventy years and even help him to realise many delicate sensations has every right to be attached to it. For many of us sudden illuminations of touch and smell and hearing are the only mysticism within our grasp.

I suppose the best minds of the war generation are now pacifist just as the best minds of the post-war generation are now militant. I can imagine one of them saying, 'It's all very well to say that human beings can only be improved from the inside—but it will take centuries— meanwhile we have to prevent them from being destroyed, and only direct action will do that. You preach yoga, blessedness, and non-attachment, we prevent war and remove slums—which of us is really doing most good?' To which Mr. Huxley will reply, 'For every slum you remove another slum grows up, and I don't believe you can pre-vent war, for your warlike instincts will find an outlet. Eventually someone will be shot.' I have given him the last word. Read his chapter on 'Beliefs' and see if he has not deserved it.

91. Honor Croome, review in *Spectator*

12 November 1937, cix, p. 852

Honor Renée Minturn Croome (1908–60), economist, reviewer, and short story writer, had recently written *An Economic History of Britain* (1936).

Croome's review is entitled 'Mr. Huxley's Testament.'

Eyeless in Gaza roused in many readers a sense of bewilderment and exasperation. Obscurity had succeeded clarity, the *bel canto*[1] had turned to thick-voiced exhortation . . . [sic] it was like seeing on some oddly reversed film a butterfly become a pupa; a disconcerting experience. What on earth had happened?

In *Ends and Means* the answer is given, an answer perhaps best indicated comparatively, by the following quotation from the penultimate chapter:

[Quotes the passage on Huxley's earlier response to value and meaning, pp. 269–70]

That is the early Huxley, the mocking virtuoso of *Antic Hay*, the irresponsible fantasiast of *Crome Yellow*, even the self-torturing analyst of *Point Counterpoint*. Vanity, vanity, all is vanity; and yet there is the *Heilige Dankesgesang*.[2] One constantly notices this juxtaposition of futilitarianism and a passionate pity, of disgusted *accidie*[3] and a rapturous recognition of that which for a moment enables futility to be forgotten. In the later essays the balance changes. There are psychological states in which futilitarianism is truth; there are others in which unity and meaning are truth; and one state is as valid as another.

In 'Pascal', in 'The One and the Many', in 'Wordsworth in the

---

[1] A smooth, cantabile style of singing.
[2] 'Holy song of thanksgiving,' in Beethoven's A minor quartet, referred to significantly in *Point Counter Point*.
[3] 'Acedia, sloth.'

Tropics', there emerge the general outlines of a sceptic's creed. Value lies where at the moment one may choose to find it; in unity and in diversity, in asceticism and in voluptuous appreciation, in a mutually controlled and balanced excess of every human attribute. Now, in *Eyeless in Gaza* and in the present volume, the development takes two further steps. The assumption of the equal validity and value of all psychological states is discarded and the interest broadens from the individual to society. Truth is no longer relative and personal, a matter of taste to be settled between a man's own soul, intellect and senses; it is absolute, universal, and essential to the salvation of mankind from physical and spiritual catastrophe. The One may have many names and attributes varying in time and in space, but there is a One; human ideals may vary, but there emerges an overriding ideal—essential freedom or non-attachment:

The ideal man is the non-attached man. Non-attached to his bodily sensations and lusts. Non-attached to his craving for power and possessions. Non-attached to the objects of these various desires. Non-attached to his anger and hatred; non-attached to his exclusive loves . . .

In the way of that ideal stand the seven deadly sins; and of these the deadliest is anger. For anger leads to violence, destructive not only to the individual but, in the form of modern war, to all humanity. It vitiates even the best of ends when it is used as a means towards them. Here is, once again, the thesis of the *Encyclopaedia of Pacifism*, partly summarised, partly amplified. It is this theme, indeed, to which the most energy and thought appear to have gone; and rightly, for it is the most urgent. But it does not stand alone; it is only one of several means to an end. It forms part of a whole 'practical cookery book of reform' with recipes for most aspects of social betterment. This section of the book is scrappy but stimulating.

[Summarizes the book]

. . . Such are his conclusions; and above all there stands the conclusion that these things are of the utmost practical importance. The tree is known by its fruits. The fruits of materialism, of anthropomorphic religion, of the separation of ideals and of means, are under our eyes today and their bitter and unwholesome taste in our mouths. All that we are is the result of what we have thought. That in the final analysis is the theme of the whole book. We must grasp our ideals consciously and intelligently and pursue them only by means which are themselves compatible with the ideal. Mental sloth is as deadly a sin as any other. Again and again we are brought back to this necessity; the tree is known by its fruits.

It is easy to pick individual holes in the argument here and there. The 'recipes' are sketchy to a degree. Economic and administrative difficulties are brushed aside with optimistic unconcern. On the gospel of non-violence itself one may feel that the last word has not been said. The power of non-violence depends, in the last resort, on the underlying decency of the aggressor. But are there not aggressors impervious to its influence? Could non-violence have done any good to the helots of ancient Sparta, to the Albigenses, to the Jews in modern Germany? Should the Good Samaritan allow the traveller to be beaten up before coming to his succour? Is there no good worth defending?

But the respect aroused by *Ends and Means* is independent of complete agreement with its practical conclusions. Its very shortcomings somehow increase that respect. It does not, as a matter of literary technique, rank anywhere near the novels and essays. Gone are the airy literary allusiveness, the delectable and flattering pyrotechnics of culture, gone the alluring ethical eclecticism, gone, except for a few rare flashes, the incisive and caustic wit. There remains a naked, almost stumbling sincerity. The futilitarian, the critic, the satirist, the connoisseur, has become a prophet in deadly earnest calling the world—calling each individual—to repentance before it is too late; to repentance bodily, intellectual and spiritual, and to action when repentance is complete. It is a curiously impressive personal testament, a whole lot more convincing than its constituent parts; a book to be read, re-read and thought about. The practical advice may be faulty but the essential method is surely sound. It is this combination of intense intellectual effort, intense preoccupation with ultimate truth, and intense emotional and artistic sincerity, which is the world's first need today.

92. Malcolm Cowley, review in *New Republic*

19 January 1938, xciii, pp. 315–16

Malcolm Cowley, b. 1898, prolific writer, editor, and translator, was associate editor of *New Republic* 1929–44 and has been literary advisor to the Viking Press since 1948. Among his books are *Exile's Return* (1934) and *The Literary Situation* (1954).

Cowley's review is entitled 'Mr. Huxley's New Jerusalem.'

It seems to me that most reviewers, whether they praised or disparaged it, have totally missed the point of Aldous Huxley's *Ends and Means*. And it seems to me too that the author helped to lead them astray by describing his new book as 'an inquiry into the nature of ideals and into the methods employed for their realization.' Judged on that basis it seems well intentioned, even noble, but at the same time badly argued, badly constructed, unscientific, often illogical and generally crammed with platitudes and misinformation. In spite of these faults it has a semi-hypnotic quality—not so much a persuasiveness as a compellingness—that is hard to explain at a first reading.

Going through the book a second time, I found the key to it on page 143, just at the end of an eloquent chapter that discusses the causes and the nature of war. The cure for it, Huxley decides, will have to be psychological:

[Quotes passage on the obstacles to peace, p. 125]

These are big words but their meaning, in the context, is simple: *If you want to stop war, start another religion.* Here is the 'good end' and here the 'appropriate means' proposed by this book. Essentially it is the testament of a new synthetic church, with Aldous Leonard Huxley (b. in 1894, educated at Eton and Balliol, Oxford) as its bookish Gotama Buddha and its non-polygamous Mohammed.

That seems a curious role to be played by a writer who used to be known as a chronicler of disenchanted and disappointing adulteries; as

the inventor of Gumbril's Patent Small Clothes. But the prophetic note
was already there, even in his poems and his early novels, if anybody
had tried to look for it. Remember the masque that interrupts the story
of *Antic Hay*? The hero of the masque is a very human Monster, wealthy
but neglected, who insists on saving the world through love—

[Quotes *Antic Hay*, Chapter XVI, pp. 181–2]

Like his own Monster, Huxley is establishing reforms in the social sewer
and then climbing out of it through the manhole. He is straining upwards, upwards, without being too sure of his balance. And he is
exhorting others to follow his pathway toward the stars.

When his book is judged not as an inquiry but as a scripture, it
suddenly assumes an intelligible form. The first nine chapters, up to and
including the discussion of war, serve as a picture of the present world
and the futility of our efforts to reform it. The last six chapters—more
than half the book—are a program and prayerbook for that new church
by means of which the world can be saved. Huxley believes that his
church will be established and spread by little bands of devoted
individuals gathered into religious communities. All these communities
will accept the same creed and will take the monastic vows of poverty,
obedience and something not quite chastity but pretty close to it. They
will spend part of their time in religious meditation modeled after Zen
Buddhism, and part of it in business enterprises conducted on scientific
lines, with plenty of capital. They will create an industrial democracy,
fight war by non-violent methods and, in general, build a new
Jerusalem in England's green and pleasant land.

That is Huxley's plan for saving the world: vastly more agreeable
than most plans, but most certainly the vision of a prophet rather than
the blueprint of a social engineer. Once this fact is realized, the faults of
the book are explained, and some of them are even transformed into
virtues. Thus, the bald, repetitive style ('It is time now to consider'—
'Let us now briefly consider'—'I will proceed at once to the consideration of my next topic') is one that has proved effective in religious
exhortation. The descent into platitude ('Birth control has reduced the
size of the average family'—'New methods of transportation have profoundly modified life in the village and small town') is a means of
assuring his audience that Huxley is, after all, a sensible fellow, even if
inspired. The authorities he quotes (some of them honest and able
but others easily identified as quacks, shamans, charlatans and faith-
healers) are those who share Huxley's religious impulse. His lumping

together of fascism and communism and his fierce attacks on both are explained by their being, in his own word, 'idolatries'—that is, rival religions.

There is simply no use arguing about what he says. Either through common sense or else by inspiration, Huxley is sometimes magnificently right where others are wrong, but he can also be stupendously wrong where others are right. In neither case do his conclusions rest on logic, evidence or history. He goes to the length of condemning all history, since, 'At the present moment of time, the "historical" is almost unmitigatedly evil.' There are pages in which he seems to be saying that, like the great mystics of all ages, he has been granted a direct insight into the nature of ultimate reality and thus is privileged to remodel not only the future but also the past. Humble people like myself who have never come face to face with Ultimate Truth are scarcely equipped to contradict him.

Yet there were times when I wanted to stand up in Mr. Huxley's church and shout, 'Go read a book!' For example, when he said that the iron dictatorship of the Jacobins destroyed the French Republic by leading to foreign war and reaction at home—when he blamed Danton and Robespierre for every misfortune of the twentieth century, including conscription, Hitler and quite probably the sack of Nanking—then I felt like referring him to any honest and scholarly history of the French Revolution, whether radical, conservative or middle-of-the-road. The foreign wars began on April 20, 1792. The reaction at home had begun much earlier but, in the spring of 1793, it led to the revolt of the Chouans and the treachery of Dumouriez. It was then and only then that the Convention passed a law creating the Committee of Public Safety. The iron dictatorship of the Jacobins was not the cause but the result of 'foreign war and reaction at home.'

Again, I felt like standing up in my uneasy pew to say that Huxley never discusses the general problem of ends and means (should we let a steer be killed in order to eat roast beef?) but only the special problem of whether fundamental reforms are possible without violence. Huxley says they are, and I hope that he is right. But he befogs and bedevils the whole issue by confusing non-violent resistance (as advocated by Richard Gregg)[1] with non-violent non-resistance (as advocated by the Hindu mystics). He argues that insane asylums, prisons and colonial possessions have been vastly improved since keepers, wardens and *pukka*

---

[1] Huxley wrote an introduction for Gregg's *Training for Peace* (Philadelphia: Lippincott, 1937).

sahibs have been using less violence toward their charges. From this he deduces that the same non-violent methods can be used by France and Great Britain toward the fascist nations. But these nations are not imprisoned lunatics or convicted petty thieves or conquered Black-fellows. In effect, Huxley is saying that because dogs respond to petting, we should also approach tigers with a cheerible voice and empty hands.

There were other passages that almost brought me to my feet—especially the one in which Huxley misinterprets Baudelaire in such a fashion as to transform the terrible poet into a YMCA secretary lecturing on sex. But after all, I reflected, the wiser course was to sit the sermon through. There is no use pointing out his errors in mundane logic when Huxley is moving far above them, in the sphere of the ultimate entities.

93. Thomas Wolfe on Huxley's ideal

1937

Thomas Clayton Wolfe (1900–38), well-known American novelist, was the author of *Look Homeward, Angel* (1929) and *The Web and the Rock* (1939).

The excerpt is from a letter to Mary Louise Aswell, 31 December 1937, in *The Letters of Thomas Wolfe*, ed. Elizabeth Nowell (New York: Scribner's, 1956), pp. 698–9.

I've been reading Huxley's book [*Ends and Means*] which you gave me for Christmas. He's a brilliant writer, isn't he? His mind is so clear and penetrating, and he sees so many things, and yet I got the impression he was puzzled and confused, too. To be partisan about anything almost implies hatred. Apparently Huxley's ideal is a kind of non-partisan man —or rather, a man who is partisan only in his belief in life. And yet, I wonder if in this world of ours to-day we can be non-partisan. Of one thing I am sure: the artist can't live in his ivory tower any more, if he is, he is cutting himself off from all the sources of life. Tremendous pressure is brought to bear from all sides upon people like myself: we are told that we must be partisan even in the work we do. Here I think the partisans are wrong; and yet a man does feel to-day a tremendous pressure from within—a kind of pressure of the conscience. There are so many things that are damnable, and which must be fought—we all ask ourselves the question: can we be free and be effective at the same time? I think nearly all of us have a pretty strong and clear feeling in our hearts about the larger humanity we would like to achieve. But when we see such wrong and cruelty and injustice all around us we ask ourselves if we have any right to refrain from taking sides and joining parties, because taking sides and joining parties are likely to limit and distort us so. I wish it were also possible for me to feel like Candide that the best thing in the end is to tend one's garden. A tremendous lot can be said for that, a tremendous lot of good, but somehow garden tending doesn't seem to be the answer either, the way things are to-day.

94. René Lalou's view from France

1938

Lalou's 'The Ends and Means of Aldous Huxley,' *Études Anglaises*, October 1938, pp. 353–71, has been translated and edited for the Critical Heritage by Clémentine Robert in collaboration with Nina Lavroukine (Sorbonne, Universities of Paris III and IV). Their introduction here follows.

René Lalou (1889–1960) can be considered one of the most prominent figures on the French literary scene of his time. As early as the 1920s he established his reputation as a critic and a historian of modern French and English literature. The two companion studies *Histoire de la littérature française contemporaine, 1870 à nos jours* (1922) and *Panorama de la littérature anglaise contemporaine* (1927) exemplify the comprehensive manner which was to be characteristic of his critical outlook. These 'panoramas' were followed later in his career by other surveys on the present state of the French novel, *Le Roman française depuis 1900* (1941), and drama, *Le Théâtre en France depuis 1900* (1951). Still more wide-ranging, *Les Étapes de la poésie française* (1942) and *La Littérature anglaise des origines à nos jours* (1944) are further instances of the synoptic approach.

Lalou was one of the last representatives of the now lost generation of humanists: his extensive culture made it possible for him to escape provincialism in literature. But he was by inclination a man of his time open to the latest trends of the literary production in France and in England. Like so many of his contemporaries Lalou was a man of many excellences. Literary history brought him international fame, but he also made his mark as an essayist, a weekly contributor to *Les Nouvelles Littéraires*, and a distinguished editor and translator of Shakespeare.

Thanks are due to the editors of *Études Anglaises* for permission to bring out a translation of the article in the present volume.

Our translation follows pp. 358–70 of the original; omissions are indicated by [. . .]. Footnotes have been provided, except in those few instances marked [R.L.]. In its attempt to reproduce the distinctive features of the original, which is truly representative of an epoch and a certain style of criticism, this translation has kept as close as possible to the text, even as far as retaining some of the French mannerisms. Special thanks go to Mr Nicholas Lorriman, University of Paris-Sorbonne, for his careful reading of our manuscript. [See Introduction, p. 15.]

No fame can escape the price of a certain amount of misunderstanding. Though not altogether wrong, our view of Huxley in this country was to call for more than one correction. [. . .] Shall we say that his didacticism showed more clearly through the veil of fiction. For there is hardly a work by Huxley, be it ever so whimsical and casual in appearance, but has a moral to it. The amazing thing is that this writer should have acquired the reputation of a dilettante. [. . .] When the translation of one of his travel books [*Jesting Pilate*] appeared in 1932 under the title *Tour of the World by a Skeptic*, I protested against this double inaccuracy. As far as geography is concerned, to see India, Malaya, Japan and the United States, is to accomplish, at best, half a world tour. As for *Jesting Pilate*, it is common knowledge that Huxley borrowed his title from Bacon's first essay: 'What is Truth? said jesting Pilate; and would not stay for an answer.' Why not? because the Roman Proconsul knows for certain that the doctors of Israel will give him of truth a thousand definitions intricate to a degree; hence this man of action will not tarry. Rather than waste his time listening to idle disputations, away he goes to perform the duties of his office. Is this a mark of scepticism?

In orchestrating what I would call the theme of Pilate's fugue, did Huxley rank among the sceptics? The conclusion of his enquiry leaves no room for doubt: 'The traveller,' he writes, 'will distinguish between harmless perversions and those which tend actually to deny or stultify the fundamental values. Towards the first he will be tolerant. There can be no compromise with the second.' [. . .] Edmond Jaloux was more perceptive when he called him a 'fanatic of truth'.[1] But this truth, to be sure, did not seem to imply any metaphysics: it remained wholly human and thereby relative. An open-minded individualist, the author

[1] Preface to *Two or Three Graces*, trans. Jules Castier (Paris: Stock, 1931), p. xii.

of *Jesting Pilate* sympathizes with all the beliefs that bespeak human diversity; he wages a pitiless war against all the superstitions that belie human unity.

Such was already the meaning of Mark Rampion's message. But at this point a more serious ambiguity needs to be resolved. We have seen that Lawrence had served as a model for the portrait of Mark Rampion. Huxley was Lawrence's friend, the editor of his *Letters*, the champion of his memory; it has even been hinted that the depiction of Denis Burlap was an anticipated vengeance. Thus to associate Lawrence and Huxley in terms of affection and gratitude is amply justified; to endow them with a common creed would be to confuse and distort notions which Huxley has very subtly distinguished. At the very most we can only go as far as conjecturing that Lawrence's thought was one of Aldous Huxley's great temptations. Could he be otherwise than captivated by the generosity of this lyrical naturism? And yet, as is evidenced in *Beyond the Mexique Bay*, he vigorously reacted to it. For he has gauged the weakness of the Lawrencian gospel, on the level of art and of life as well. Rereading *The Plumed Serpent* in Mexico, he rediscovers some admirable passages; but the work as a whole strikes him as an 'artistic failure' in which he sees 'the evidence of some inner uncertainty of conviction'. Putting aside all manner of oratorical or poetic effect, it is clear that Lawrence has cheated: he and his protagonists claim they reject civilization, when in fact they have secured its most valuable achievements. Huxley, on the other hand, invites to a more honest assessment: 'When man became an intellectual and spiritual being, he paid for his new privileges.' At what cost? By giving up 'a treasure of intuitions, of emotional spontaneity, of sensuality still innocent of all self-consciousness.' But could we not recover such by-gone treasure by renouncing our latest acquisitions? Vain imaginings, Huxley will retort, 'we must be content to pay, and indefinitely to go on paying, the irreducible price of the goods we have chosen.' For all those who advocate the return to blind instincts come up against this obstacle: the 'goods chosen' by man have been for centuries those of conscious intelligence.

To be sure, Huxley does not regret the choice. In *Jesting Pilate*, after labelling Edmund Spenser a 'virtuoso' in 'the art of saying nothing', Huxley professes himself, on the contrary, 'perhaps . . . unduly prejudiced in favour of sense'. And in *Brief Candles*, he puts the following formula into Fanning's mouth: 'What *is* a novelist, unless he's a person who understands?' I dare not say that this definition applies to

Dickens or to Dostoevsky, but it is admirably suited to Huxley. So much so that one seldom refrains from blaming him for it. Most critics would approve of Edmond Jaloux's epigram in his preface to *Two or Three Graces*: 'Huxley . . . so implacably intelligent, I mean intellectual' (p. vii). And yet I do not think that Huxley would agree to the shifting from the one adjective to the other. In *Point Counter Point* already, he was upbraiding the 'impregnable' intellectual; Elinor Quarles was riddling her husband with piercing arrows: 'You're like a monkey on the superhuman side of humanity. . . . *you're* trying to feel down with your intellect.' Huxley has never deceived himself into thinking such a divorce from average humanity to be other than a permanent snare in the path of intellectual pride.

I even tend to think that he would be surprised if he were accused of having fallen a prey to it. He is not to be identified with Philip Quarles any more than with Mark Rampion on the assumption that he has sometimes given them leave to speak in his name. Fortunately enough, we possess other reports wherein he commits himself entirely—essays and travel books in which he addresses the reader without any proxy. Does he then fall into the trap by becoming abstract or dogmatic? What is striking about his attitude is that it never stiffens, that his curiosity is as brisk as his humour, and that he conducts his enquiries with unquestionable honesty. I was but now praising the integrity with which he stripped Lawrence's arguments of their captious enticements: does it necessarily follow that this desire to return to nature is all nonsense? The possibility of a union between primitive and civilized virtues still subsists in a form which Huxley presents in qualified terms: 'Partially to industrialize and civilize primitives may be impossible. But to introduce a salutary element of primitivism into our civilized and industrialized way of life—this, I believe, can be done.' At the close of *Beyond the Mexique Bay*, after examining the perils entailed by the progress of industrial civilization, he will formulate, with equal modesty, the conclusion which he considers of vital importance: 'The problem is to evolve a society that shall retain all or most of the material and intellectual advantages resulting from specialization, while allowing its members to lead to the full the life of generalized human beings.' Aping the ways of the primitive will not do: the point is to acquire his ability to be 'whole—a complete man'. The Savage of *Brave New World* is a worthy opposer of standardized society, inasmuch as he shaped his own human vision of the universe when in his solitude he conjured up the world of Shakespeare's imagery.

[Portion here omitted]

The great quarrel that opposes Huxley to his contemporaries can be summed up as follows in a sentence from *Brief Candles*: they allow themselves to be lured, under the pretence that 'being alternately a hero and a sinner is much more sensational than being an integrated man'. This apologist of 'the complete man' could not possibly, in troubled times, think of withdrawing into an ivory tower. In June 1935, Aldous Huxley was attending the first World Congress of Writers for the Defence of Culture: the paper he read on this occasion unfolded a penetrating psychological analysis without any trace of oratorical display. It confirmed the judgments he had passed in *Beyond the Mexique Bay*. The enemy he had come across everywhere on his journey was nationalism which he defined as 'the justificatory philosophy of unnecessary and artificial hatred'. If he proclaimed the insufficiency of the Marxist theory as taking only, so it seemed to him, economic factors into account, Huxley, however, levelled most of his attacks at the barbarian ideologies of the fascist regimes: 'The Nazi movement', he wrote, 'is a rebellion against Western civilization. In order to consolidate this rebellion, its leaders are doing their best to transform modern German society into the likeness of a primitive tribe.' It is to be remembered that in tracking the teachings conducive to this mentality, Huxley was convicting two French thinkers: 'Gobineau was responsible for that doctrine of race superiority used by the Nazis as an aphrodisiac to arouse hatred for Gobineau's own countrymen. And it was Bergson who led the intellectuals' disastrous attack on the intellect, and so prepared the way for the systematized paranoia of Hitler.' Through these lines we apprehend Huxley, the 'fanatic of truth'. The objection that conclusions reached by intoxicated disciples are no fault of the teacher carries no weight with Huxley: any breach of intelligence contains a seed of hatred that, sooner or later, shall give poisonous fruits.

These reflections from *Beyond the Mexique Bay* are, to my mind, the best introduction to the central drama of *Eyeless in Gaza*. The symbolism of the title is perfectly rigorous, for so John Milton's Samson voices his bitterness:

> Promise was that I
> Should Israel from Philistian yoke deliver;
> Ask for this great deliverer now, and find him
> Eyeless in Gaza at the mill with slaves,
> Himself in bonds under Philistian yoke.

And so are we, Europeans, bound to the same old mill of hatred and of war. Will Anthony Beavis be able to escape the bondage? Will he be able to make a tentative effort to set his fellow bondsmen free, or, at least, to show them the way towards this liberation? Such is the problem that dominates the whole of Huxley's novel. When the book came out in this country, in the summer of 1937, the publisher announced that it had been the most controversial work of the preceding season in London. Nevertheless a doubt persisted: was the polemics aroused by the revolutionary technique which Huxley had used, or by the denouement of the tragedy with the allegiance of the protagonist to the doctrine of non-violence? I am personally convinced that the two elements are inseparable, and only for clarity's sake will I briefly distinguish them.

There is no denying that the reader of *Eyeless in Gaza* may be disconcerted, at the outset, by the headings of the first seven episodes: 'August 30th 1933, April 4th 1934, August 30th 1933, November 6th 1902, December 8th 1926, November 6th 1902, April 8th 1934.' But it will not take him long to realize that had Huxley followed the chronological sequence, the novel would have fallen into five periods —November 1902–January 1904; May–July 1914; December 1926–April 1928; August 1933–February 1934; April 1934–February 1935— with five connecting chapters for 1912 and 1931. Why then is the fabric presented as a jig-saw puzzle? The first answer to this is that Huxley is striving after a dramatic effect: the parallel elaboration of these five actions permits close involvement of their denouement and the build-up of a powerful crescendo. And in the process, Huxley brings out the clash between time as measured mathematically, and duration as lived psychologically. At this point, the French reader has every reason to believe that Aldous Huxley comes close to Marcel Proust. But this is not so: Huxley departs from him, and Anthony Beavis treats Proust like his 'personal enemy'. The reason for this is that the chronicler of *A la recherche du temps perdu*, 'for ever squatting in the tepid bath of his remembered past', was doggedly working at reestablishing some continuity within his sentimental life. Anthony Beavis will not be burdened with such chains, and parodying two well-known lines by Wordsworth, he proclaims: 'I would wish my days to be separated each from each by unnatural impiety.'

To set the problem of time in these terms is but a preliminary step leading up to the major question of personality. Proust was not without knowing that the two are closely related: 'For with the troubles of memory are closely linked the heart's intermissions. It is, no doubt, the existence of our body, which we may compare to a jar containing our spiritual nature, that leads us to suppose that all our inward wealth, our past joys, all our sorrows, are perpetually in our possession.'[1] But every one of Marcel's efforts was meant to recapture what is most precious in the personality so as to preserve it, through the magic of art, within 'time regained.' Anthony Beavis's ambition is just the reverse. There is nothing more simplistic to him than the design of Ben Jonson who flattered himself he could arrest human beings, 'every man in his humour.' Anthony's model is Hamlet who, 'of course . . . didn't have a personality—knew altogether too much to have one.' The Prince of Denmark refused to be compared to 'a penny whistle with only half a dozen stops.' He is one of such men as feel they are 'potentially at least . . . a whole symphony orchestra', and claim for their masters Michel de Montaigne and William Shakespeare.

Were Anthony's soliloquies to be enjoyed merely for their dazzling variations on the theme of 'psychological atomism'? My personal opinion is that they amount to much more than a clever 'burlesque', and this I tried to show in one of the literary sections of *Europe*.* In a remarkable article of *La Revue de Paris* [No. 23, 1 December 1937, pp. 685–700], Marcel Thiébaut proved equally responsive to the earnestness with which Anthony developed his propositions and their corollaries. On the other hand, Edmond Jaloux, in one of his contributions to *Les Nouvelles Littéraires* [28 August 1937, p. 4], carefully avoided bringing Huxley's proselytism under discussion: he simply found it embarrassing that Anthony should be at once a biologist and an apostle of pacifism. Edmond Jaloux was probably of the same mind as André Rousseaux. Reviewing the two latest works of Virginia Woolf and Aldous Huxley [in their French translations], the critic of *Le Figaro* came to the following conclusion: 'Between *The Waves* and *Eyeless in Gaza* lies the boundless realm of psychological investigation. But to introduce social concerns into it would be dangerously ineffectual. The social dreams in which Mrs. Virginia Woolf's characters are bogged, while Mr. Huxley's flounder about, derive in fact from a unanimism in every respect akin to that of M. Jules Romains, and no less hazardous' [28 August 1937, p. 6]. The desire to restrict the matter is here much too openly expressed to bear the semblance of an artifice. However, it is hard to believe that to follow the author's wish and to develop the

[1] *Remembrance of Things Past*, Vol. 7, *Cities of the Plain*, trans. C. K. Scott Moncrieff (London: Chatto & Windus, 1929), I, p. 219.   * 'October 1937, xlv, pp. 266–72' [R.L.].

argument would be dangerous and ineffectual. That Anthony's example should be dangerous, or that it should be ineffectual, either hypothesis is tenable in theory; and yet, the two are most likely to be mutually exclusive.

Since our main preoccupation is an understanding of Huxley's intentions, we can say that André Rousseaux was not far wrong in using the term 'unanimism'. The word 'unity' would round off the picture. We have seen Huxley obsessed with the ideal of the 'complete man'. Imagine he should read those pages from *Degas, Danse, Dessin* where Valéry confesses wistfully that 'the complete man is dying out.' Huxley would certainly retort that the 'complete man' will not disappear, provided he can combine the virtues of the primitive with the qualities of the civilized man. With Anthony the process is achieved by degrees. Mention has already been made of the first two stages—the liberation from a cumbersome past and the indefinite expansion of the 'personality'. The third step consists in recapturing 'the unity of all life'. Once again, Huxley parts company with Lawrence. The author of *Aaron's Rod* was urging every individual to withdraw into the 'central aloneness' of his being. The word *oneness*, by which Lawrence meant this irreducible *unicity*, takes on again with Huxley the idea of *unity*,★ necessarily implying that of communion. Precisely because he is a biologist, Anthony first acquires the certainty of this unity in his own field: 'Physical unity, first of all. Unity even in diversity, even in separation. Separate patterns, but everywhere alike.' He does not deny the equal reality of division and goes so far as to admit that 'the point was in the paradox, in the fact that unity was the beginning and unity the end, and that in the meantime the condition of life and all existence was separation, which was equivalent to evil'. Mark Rampion professed that the ultimate fulfilment was to be a man, that is to say, in Lawrence's own words 'a fragment of the shell of life'.[1] Anthony Beavis now proclaims that the 'paradox' can be overcome, that non-violence can triumph, and all men can unite who descend to 'dark peace in the depths'.

[Portion here omitted]

The question arises as to whether it was not somewhat rash to have taken Anthony Beavis for Huxley's spokesman in 1936, thus adopting towards him a less qualified attitude than towards Mark Rampion or

★ 'Used in this sense in *Ends and Means* in opposition to *separateness*' [R.L.].
[1] *Aaron's Rod* (London: Secker, 1922), p. 277.

Philip Quarles. The matter is now settled with the publication of *Ends and Means* which bears the following sub-title: 'An Enquiry into the Nature of Ideals and into the Methods Employed for Their Realization.' Here again, from the very beginning we find a reaffirmation of the notion of unity. All the guides of humanity are agreed, according to Huxley, in assigning this goal to men—a 'Golden Age' where 'there will be liberty, peace, justice and brotherly love'. The transformation of our present-day society into this ideal state can only be the doing of individuals free from all self-interest, 'non-attached beings'. How is such a change to be brought about from within and from without? The aim of *Ends and Means* is to supply an answer to this twofold question. For this purpose Huxley provides us with a 'cookery book of practical recipes'. They concern public life, international life, and the private life of citizens. Huxley deals with social reforms, with the famous 'plans', with inequality, with centralization and decentralization. He treats extensively of the subjects of war and non-violence. He offers solutions to the problems of education, of the relationships between sexes, of individual contributions to collective progress. The three crowning chapters of his work are devoted to religious practices, beliefs and ethics: they represent as such a moving formulation of his personal philosophy.

[. . .] Aldous Huxley's evident generosity is given full scope in these final chapters which he holds to be the most important. At the risk of offending some of his French admirers, I observe that 'the accomplished intellectual' seems to him 'a far from satisfactory person' who 'is not concerned with humanity as human, as potentially more than human'. 'The rational idealist', such is Huxley's pseudonym throughout this panorama. He retraces his spiritual evolution in a few pages. There was a time, indeed, when he maintained that the universe was devoid of meaning. Like so many of his contemporaries, this belief helped him to free himself 'from a certain political and economic system' as well as 'from a certain system of morality'. With time, however, the men of his generation consented to reintroduce some meaning into the world. 'But only in patches', and with the 'disastrous results' which Huxley points out in 1937: 'We have thought of ourselves as members of supremely meaningful and valuable communities—deified nations, divine classes and what not—existing within a meaningless universe. And because we have thought like this, rearmament is in full swing, economic nationalism becomes ever more intense, the battle of rival propaganda grows ever fiercer, and general war becomes increasingly probable.' Provided this self-examination is not confined to one individual, some sort of recovery remains possible. Huxley has nothing of a Jeremiah: as a 'rational idealist' he proposes a revision of our methods in keeping with the ends that we have set ourselves. For it would be pointless to go on 'producing improved means' to be applied to 'unimproved ends'.

To have measured the limits of 'the accomplished intellectual' is fruitful to a writer like Huxley. It is excellent for him to have distinguished from amongst fools those who have a few glimmers of wisdom or intelligence: some, the 'wise fools', behave rather decently in their own limited spheres; the others, the 'intelligent fools', are incapable of 'apply[ing] their intelligence to the subject of themselves'. Their aberrations do not prevent Huxley from still ranking intelligence among the major virtues: 'Without intelligence,' he observes, 'charity and the minor virtues can achieve little.' He expresses the hope that with our becoming indifferent to riches and personal success, we should lose none of our intellectual nimbleness or interest in science. In the same way he remarks that if we are expected to 'transcend personality, we must first take the trouble to become persons'. But on the other hand, this clear-sighted analyst admits the validity of mystical experience, although his preferences go to the mysticism of health, to the author of *The Cloud of Unknowing*, rather than to Blaise Pascal. He calls the mystics to witness that there exists 'a spiritual unity underlying the diversity of separate consciousnesses'. And the confidence that this unity runs deeper than any division does not only dominate his thinking, it also conditions his attitude in daily living, since 'non-violence is the practical consequence that follows from belief in the fundamental unity of all being'.

Who would have thought in 1930 that the author of *Point Counter Point*—this Englishman endowed with an almost superhuman intelligence which drew a reaction of fascination not unmixed with fear—would soon dedicate himself to a mystical faith closer to Buddhism than to Christianity? Who would have dared to think that, without denying the cultural heritage of the civilized man, he would speak one day with the fervour and, at times, the humility so touching to the reader of *Ends and Means*? For the purposes of retracing this evolution, it is probably not without its advantages to have followed it from a French standpoint. As Jean Racine said in his second preface to *Bajazet*, 'the distance in place makes up in some sort for the too great nearness in time'.[1]

[1] *Complete Plays*, trans. Samuel Solomon (New York: Random House, 1967), II, p. 5.

Now, the Channel may lie as a great obstacle to writers, since on either side some are said never to have crossed it. Indeed, such was not the case of Aldous Huxley, welcomed in this country with enthusiasm, first treated like one of us, and whose every book by better disclosing his fundamental originality, will have compelled us to qualify our judgments. Perhaps the hope is not altogether unfounded that the role of France, as far as Huxley is concerned, will be seen as that of a precocious posterity. At least, there is nothing to prevent us from saying in his own words that 'even the fragmentary outline of a synthesis is better than no synthesis at all'. May this last sentence from Huxley's *Ends and Means* serve as a suitable if modest conclusion to this tribute.

95. David Daiches on Huxley

1939

David Daiches, b. 1912, a prolific critic, is a professor of English at the University of Sussex. He was an assistant professor at the University of Chicago 1939–43 and later taught at Cornell and Cambridge. The catholicity of Daiches's work includes *Critical Approaches to Literature* (1956) and *A Critical History of English Literature* (1960), as well as individual books on Virginia Woolf (1942), Robert Louis Stevenson (1947), Robert Burns (1950), Willa Cather (1951), John Milton (1957), and Sir Walter Scott (1971).

Following is most of Daiches's Chapter XI, 'Aldous Huxley,' in *The Novel and the Modern World* (University of Chicago Press, 1939), pp. 188–210, a chapter omitted by Daiches in the 1960 edition of this book because, as he explains in his Preface, Huxley and Katherine Mansfield 'do not really fit into the general scheme of the book and are not in any case "novelists" in the strict sense' (p. viii). See Introduction, p. 25.

Daiches's essay on Huxley as a 'frustrated romantic' may be regarded as a climax to critical objections to Huxley's work thus far. Too, the essay initiates a phase of critical response, to dominate for over a quarter of a century, which finds the value of Huxley's fiction to be limited almost exclusively to its reflection of the frenetic mood of the 1920s. Daiches's account thereby occupies a key position in the shaping of the Huxley critical heritage.

The breakdown of traditional standards of value under the influence of scientific and psychological thought—more fundamentally, perhaps, as the result of the decay of an economic and social system—was taken by some authors as an opportunity for looking for a more personal, less traditional or conventional, sense of significance, which was manifested in their method of selecting events in fiction. And thus it led to new developments both in attitude and in technique which characterize the literature of the transition, if we may use this term to denote the literature produced by those aware of the disintegration of the older values without attempting to co-operate in the establishment of new. Other writers, however, seeing the effect of this breakdown in terms of the behaviour of a limited section of one class, generally the upper middle class, were less interested in seeking out new artistic attitudes and much more interested in registering disapproval of this behaviour, either explicitly or implicitly, through satiric observation. Two types of writers in particular were likely to take this approach: these are the frustrated romantic and the frustrated traditionalist. The former is the kind of person who would like to believe in love and progress and spirituality and the worth-whileness of life, but finds that reality, as he sees and understands it, will not let him. And why will not reality let him? Simply because, possessing the attitude that we call romantic, he sees reality in terms of individuals and their experiences, and if these individuals act in such a way as to deny all those things that he would like to believe in, then he feels bitter with reality as a whole. There is no appeal from the individual experience, which is not regarded as a particular event conditioned by its environment (and therefore likely not to be repeated if that environment is changed) but simply as representing things in general and therefore sufficient cause for despair if unsatisfactory. Swift, for example, who is shown by the *Journal to Stella* to have possessed an essentially sentimental nature, was not allowed by the facts that he saw around him to believe in the things that his sentimental nature wanted to believe in. Hence the bitterness of his satires: life— i.e., the conduct of the individuals with whom he came in contact— did not come up to his preconceived standard, and so he was furious with it. And because his preconceived standard was sentimental, because it was based on an unreal view of how the individual comes to be what he is, he was more furious with life than the objective facts warranted; he reached a point where he gloated over what was most horrible, torturing himself like a man with a toothache tugging at the aching tooth.

There is some parallel, though perhaps not a close one, between Swift and Aldous Huxley. Huxley was disgusted by the behaviour of his class. Instead of justifying the optimistic belief in science and progress (and we may note how essentially romantic this belief in science and progress as such is) that, for example, his own grandfather, the great T. H. Huxley, had held, the behaviour of the upper middle classes at the time when Aldous began to sit up and take notice was such as to indicate the essential hollowness in the modern view, or lack of view, resulting from the disintegration of traditional values. You had killed, or your grandfather had killed, the bad bogieman—namely, Victorian superstition and convention; and what was the brave new world that modern science and freedom was then able to build? Dust and ashes. Not only was the splendour gone from moonlight and roses (and Huxley was very much aware of this, too) but it was also gone from that other great stand-by of Victorian enlightenment—science and progress. The greater your desire to believe in what was gone, the greater your resentment at finding that it was not there. Hence you write satiric pictures of modern life, not out of a feeling of superiority or amused contempt or cynical indifference—not like Wells in some of his novels or like Shaw in his plays or yet like Norman Douglas in *South Wind*— but out of a feeling of horror, out of frustration, nostalgia, intense disappointment. And the more romantic you are, the fiercer will be your satiric picture of contemporary society, because the more disappointed and frustrated you will have been rendered by the modern scene. In the end you will either go crazy, as Swift did, or comfort yourself with a personal mysticism—a romantic view which will not require to be tested by the facts—as Huxley has done.

There is also the second type of writer who will be likely to turn to satiric observation: this is the classicist or traditionalist, who will be most upset by the lack of order and purpose in contemporary life. He, too, will be disappointed and nostalgic, but disappointed rather with the futility and lack of coherence in modern civilization than with its lack of personal values and ideals. And so, like the first type, he also will paint a dreary picture of modern life. He will give us *The Love Song of J. Alfred Prufrock* and the *Portrait of a Lady*, which emphasize futility and purposelessness; he will give us *The Waste Land* and *The Hollow Men*, where modern life is shown to be empty and dry and meaningless. It is interesting to compare T. S. Eliot's wasteland with the wasteland that Huxley paints in his early novels. They have much in common, though Eliot's is the wasteland of the thwarted classicist and Huxley's that of the thwarted romantic. Eliot emphasizes lack of pattern and purpose while Huxley stresses lack of worth-whileness for the individuals involved. And ultimately (again, if he does not go crazy first) your thwarted classicist will find refuge in some fairly rigid and institutionalized scheme of things to compensate him for his wounded sense of order. He joins the Roman Catholic church or, like Eliot, the Anglican church, which is almost the same thing. Huxley becomes a mystical pacifist with inclinations toward a personal interpretation of Buddhism, whereas Eliot lands up by becoming an orthodox member of a highly ritualistic and hierarchic religion. They represent two complementary types. Both, it may be added, avoid the issue, which is not personal compensation but the alteration of the environment which has produced the necessity for that compensation—the evolution and stabilization of a standard in which society can believe and with reference to which its activities can be given purpose and meaning and value.

Huxley's development from frustrated romantic to satisfied mystic is not difficult to follow; his novels trace the journey for us adequately. The early novels, from *Crome Yellow* in 1921 to *Point Counter Point* in 1928, tend to be at bottom re-writings of the same essential theme. We might begin by looking at *Antic Hay*, his second novel, published in 1923, and try to see what attitude on Huxley's part this book reveals.

[The following few pages present a reading of the major characters of *Antic Hay* as examples of 'the drying-up of traditional sources of value']

Those Barren Leaves (1925) is less a novel than a series of essays presenting various types of futility, cynicism, and disillusion. The author himself seems to appear indirectly, split up into the two characters of Chelifer, the cynical author, and Calamy, the reformed sensualist and seeker after truth. It is interesting to find Huxley's two selves talking thus:

'It is a pity,' put in Chelifer, in his dry, clear, accurate voice, 'it's a pity that the human mind didn't do its job of invention a little better while it was about it. We might, for example, have made our symbolic abstraction of reality in such a way that it would be unnecessary for a creative and possibly immortal soul to be troubled with haemorrhoids.'

Calamy laughed. 'Incorrigible sentimentalist!'

'Sentimentalist?' echoed Chelifer, on a note of surprise.

'A sentimentalist inside out,' said Calamy, nodding affirmatively. 'Such wild romanticism as yours—I imagined it had been quite extinct since the deposition of Louis-Phillippe.'

Huxley himself is not 'a sentimentalist inside out' in quite this sense. It is frustration rather than reversal that we notice in his case; and besides, it is not quite sentimentality that is frustrated but a quality we have preferred to define, if vaguely, as romanticism.

The characters which had been simple types in *Antic Hay* are slightly more individualized in the later novel, but they serve the same purpose. Here again the characters indicate dried-up sources of value. Love, art, literary creation, social reform, epicureanism, cynicism—all are exposed, each in a different character. The characters have a tendency to cancel out each other's claims, as it were, each seeing through the others. Mrs. Aldwinkle is seen through by almost everybody except her young niece, while the cynicism of Mr. Cardan remains the final verdict until Chelifer arrives to see through him, and finally Calamy sees through Cardan. Calamy is thus more nearly the author than any other single character, but Chelifer's importance as a commentator, and the amount of his autobiography that is included, gives him also some claim to speak for his author.

It is interesting to note how *Those Barren Leaves* concludes. Calamy, who has renounced the life of the senses, retires to the mountains to contemplate reality alone. Chelifer and Cardan seek him out and become cynical about his omphaloskepsis. But Calamy is not impressed by their arguments:

[Quotes Calamy on the 'axes of moral reference,' Part V, Chapter IV, pp. 377–8]

The arguments of his opponents inspire only a momentary doubt in Calamy's mind. The book closes with his reassurance: 'Perhaps he had been a fool, thought Calamy. But looking at that shining peak, he was somehow reassured.'

Calamy alone is not debunked; and Calamy has defended omphaloskepsis and has set himself the ideal of free personal contemplation and recollection. We see here the first real indication of the solution that Huxley was to find—the end of his search for a source of value; an end which is arrived at only by isolating the individual from the environment which had caused him so much despair, and seeking certain mystical absolutes alone. He is to find a solution by changing the problem.

Before we proceed to consider Huxley's later novels, it may be well to meet an argument that might be brought against the diagnosis of the bases of Huxley's thought which this discussion seeks to make. Huxley is not only a novelist; he has also written a great number of essays where he states his own position clearly and objectively. And in those essays he displays few direct and conscious symptoms of frustrated romanticism seeking a personal compensation. In fact, in his essay on 'Varieties of Intelligence' he gives us his own view of himself:

[Quotes *Proper Studies*, on 'the flux of reality,' p. 49]

This passage is from an essay published in the collection *Proper Studies* in 1927—two years after *Those Barren Leaves* and one year before *Point Counter Point*. Is it possible to reconcile Huxley's view of himself as expressed here with the view implicit in these novels? The question is irrelevant, at least to our present purpose. Throughout his career as a novelist Huxley has also been making conscious critical observations on men and affairs and ideas. Most critics, whether they approved or disapproved of Huxley's conclusions, would concede that these observations show a high degree of intelligence and even acuteness. Now, the objects to which a man applies his conscious intelligence and the conclusions which he draws are just as likely to obscure as to illuminate the real basis of his attitude. When a man writes critical or philosophical essays on problems of contemporary importance, he is on his guard; conscious cerebration is always in some degree inhibited. The truth about our underlying attitudes—if not the truth about our practical activities—can often be more readily told from our dreams and from other unconscious byproducts of activities which do not have for their admitted purpose the enunciation of a philosophy. This is a psychological commonplace. It does not mean, of course, that we have a right to dismiss all a man's conscious philosophy in a discussion of his thought; but it does mean that in the case of a novelist who is also an essayist we have a right to separate those indications of attitude which emerge, very often unconsciously, from the novels and consider them as a whole. It might even be urged that a novelist *qua*[1] novelist has a separate *persona* that it is profitable to inquire into even though it does not represent the whole man. Actually, in Huxley's case we are not driven to this extreme, because as a rule his essays, if not always consciously or obviously, corroborate the view which is implicit in the novels. This is especially true of his more recent writing, where essays and novels consciously make the same points. But if we build up in our minds a rather pathetic image of the thwarted romanticist and then turn to the essays and see a vigorous and confident intellect at work, the disparity is likely to be striking. The truth is that the basis of a man's attitude is much farther below the surface than we might imagine, and, further, we simplify unduly if we allow such an adjective as pathetic to float across our minds in this connection. Few would be so bold as to pity Swift, even though his inverted sentimentalism be granted.

[1] 'As.'

Except for a few passages, however, like the one quoted, the general tone of Huxley's thought in his essays corresponds very neatly with the views implicit in his novels. We find, for example, the same progress from destructive to constructive criticism that we find in his fiction, the latter becoming more emphatic with time, and also (though this is not so easy to see) tending to revolve around different questions. And the romantic element in the essays is even more obvious:

[Quotes passage on listening to Beethoven in *Music at Night*, pp. 51–2]

To label this passage romantic is not to condemn it; for romantic may connote a valuable type of human experience which only the peculiarly insensitive would wish away. But romanticism is an effect and not a cause, a result of value and not a source of value. Huxley is a frustrated romantic in the sense that his attitude is based on a search for sources of value among phenomena which, even at the best of times, would only represent the effects of value which existed elsewhere. There is no need to become upset with the phenomena themselves; they are neutral; they simply reflect value. Your criticism ought to be directed to causes, not effects. Huxley notes sadly that had Wordsworth visited the tropics he would not have been so confident about the good moral influence of Nature. This is to make a very acute point: but why become upset about it? Of course, Wordsworth was only deriving from nature what he or others had caused to be put there; but all values of that kind are created in that way. 'The Wordsworthian philosophy,' says Huxley, 'has two principal defects. The first . . . is that it is only possible where Nature has been nearly or quite enslaved to man. The second is that it is only possible for those who are prepared to falsify their immediate intuitions of Nature.' The first is no defect; there is nothing immoral or undesirable in reaping a value sown by your ancestors. Civilization would not get very far without that kind of activity. The second objection becomes an objection only because of the way it is stated. Why 'falsify'? Tamed nature does produce these emotions on people who have been conditioned in a certain way. Because untamed nature might not have that effect, or tamed nature might have a different effect on other people, it does not follow that we have here to deal with falsification. Huxley increases his sadness over Wordsworth in the tropics by relating the question to Wordsworth's later drying-up and the appalling smugness of his middle and old age. But that is quite another matter. Not that the Wordsworthian philosophy is immune to attack, but to attack it in this way proves nothing. It is one among many examples, drawn from his essays, of the type of approach and of attitude in virtue of which we are calling Huxley a frustrated romantic.

In his latest period Huxley's essays have echoed quite consciously and deliberately the message contained in the novels. But that comes only when journey's end is reached—when a source of value is believed to have been found, and Huxley turns to prophecy.

Point Counter Point followed *Those Barren Leaves* in 1928; again we are presented with a series of dismissals of traditional and other sources of value, and this time with a slightly clearer indication of where the solution is to come from. The book is, in many ways, a rewriting on a more elaborate scale of *Antic Hay*, with the novelist himself brought in, in the person of Philip Quarles, to register his dissatisfaction. As the solution approaches nearer, the author becomes more distinct. There was no trace of him in *Antic Hay*; there was some slight suggestion of his identification with two of the characters in *Those Barren Leaves*; he is quite clearly, at least in part, Philip in the following novel, and in *Eyeless in Gaza* he is completely identified with Anthony.

The first chapter of *Point Counter Point* presents us with Walter and Marjorie, a couple living together, but unmarried. Walter has discovered very rapidly that 'those months in the cottage hadn't been at all like *Epipsychidion* or *La Maison du Berger*'. Love outside wedlock, in fact, is no more ideal than the more conventional Victorian kind. The moonlight and roses aspect fades rapidly away in either case. Modern freedom is no better source of value, where love is concerned, than Victorian confinement. With this point are associated analyses of love in terms, for example, of chemistry, or with Swiftian lingering on bad smells. There is something very fierce about the rejection of love here. The Tantamounts introduce us to society—high society with Lady Tantamount, low society with Illidge. The inadequacy of both to give value to personality is illustrated completely and quickly. Lord Edward Tantamount, the aristocratic scientist, is a redrawing of Shearwater in *Antic Hay*. Scientific detachment is achieved at a wholly excessive cost in personal reality, and therefore provides no source of value. Even Philip himself, author by profession, finds that zeal in his profession provides no criterion of personal value. The portrait of Burlap is poisoned with the bitterness of personal satire and is not therefore a representative of a dried-up source of value in the sense in which the other characters are. But in so far as he does have a message, it is that unction and hypocrisy, while destroying the inner personality, yet make for external success, like the case of the painter Rodney Clegg in Huxley's short story, 'Two or Three Graces'. The death of young Phil adds a more sinister thought: in addition to the general barrenness we are struggling against, there is always fortuitous evil to reckon with, torture coming gratuitously, out of the blue. We are reminded of Gumbril junior's speculations in chapel on ulcers and God. John Bidlake, the aging artist, is the most mature picture Huxley gives us of apparent success ultimately manifesting itself in real failure: he is a rather better Rodney Clegg forty years on, and his personal inadequacy is now apparent even to himself. Webley, the would-be fascist leader, introduces a new theme: he is the man of action; perhaps action is the solution. But the man of action turns out to be a shoddy exhibitionist who comes to a melodramatic end. Spandrell, like his predecessor Coleman, is the representative of diabolism; the man who makes black his white out of disillusion or unhappiness, or out of a desire to prove good by evil. But diabolism provides no criterion either; it simply defeats itself. Even regarded as an attempt to prove good by evil, it gets nowhere.

There are other characters and situations in the novel which indicate other attitudes, each of which fails to provide a criterion of value. And who are the sympathetic characters? Mark Rampion and his wife. Rampion is allowed to deliver a complete exposé of his philosophy toward the end of the book. With his belief in love and emotion and the body, he is something of a mixture of D. H. Lawrence and the hero of a romantic film. Rampion believes in human nature if it is left to itself: 'You'd do more for peace,' he tells a representative selection of the other characters, 'by telling men to obey the spontaneous dictates of their fighting instincts than by founding any number of Leagues of Nations.' And again:

[Quotes Rampion's praise of instinct, Chapter XXXIV, pp. 561–2]

The way to a personal mysticism is being gradually paved. Depreciation of the intellect, the application of a criterion taken from an undefined natural man to civilization in general—we are beginning to see vaguely the nature of Huxley's final solution. Gumbril senior indicated that the hope, if any, was in some way in the past, not in the barrenness of the present. Calamy indicated that the hope was to be derived from personal contemplation. Rampion, the good and slightly prophetic man, believer in human nature if 'left to itself,' is a slight and very muddled sketch for the Saviour, Mr. Miller, of *Eyeless in Gaza*, who is a mixture of Jesus and the Noble Savage. Rampion dismisses Jesus, but he makes a good beginning with the Noble Savage.

Brave New World, published in 1932, amplifies in extended parable form a point he had made frequently before. The Victorian belief in science as guaranteeing progress, in science as an end and not as a means, must have been particularly bitter for T. H. Huxley's grandson to shake off: the drying-up of this source of value is therefore insisted on again and again. In his essay on 'Revolutions,' written a few years before, he had commented:

[Quotes passage on the mechanization of leisure, *Do What You Will*, p. 225]

Brave New World is a commentary on this text. That the scientific delusion should have been the subject of a whole novel, while none of the other dried-up sources of value gets the honor of a book to itself, illustrates the tendency we have noted in Huxley to tug hardest at the tooth that aches the most. We might note also the romantic undertones in all these novels; the musical references in *Antic Hay* and, particularly, in *Point Counter Point*, with their roses-wine-moonlight suggestions. The brave new world is horrible chiefly because it leaves no room for that side of life, with all that it implies.

So far Huxley had spent his time as a novelist looking down empty wells. With *Eyeless in Gaza*, published in 1936, he gives up this barren occupation and proceeds to dig his own well. The book is what earlier critics liked to call a spiritual autobiography: it is the record of his progress through the *Point Counter Point* life to a mystical-pacifist view, bringing final rest in the bosom of nonresistance. Nonresistance is not, however, a negative attitude called forth by certain specific circumstances; it is elevated into a philosophy of life. Having found the old positive values dried up, and being therefore scared of pursuing his investigation into those values any farther, he gives up the search and inverts a negative value into a positive, and reaction to a circumstance into a world-view. Sidney replied to the charge that poets lie by arguing that as a poet affirms nothing he cannot be said to lie in any respect. So Huxley replies to the crumbling of positive values which he sees in modern society by erecting a value which is dependent on nothing positive and therefore cannot crumble. That the solution is verbal rather than actual is inevitable in such a circumstance. Huxley has reached the point where he is content with a personal emotional solution so that, for all his intellectual acuteness, he is not aware that in constructing this new philosophy he is guilty of mistaking the subjective for the objective, of applying to an external situation what is true only of a personal emotion, and that there is both a false analogy and a bad psychology involved in the process. Mr. Miller may daunt a critic by allowing the critic to slap him—the critic may be made to feel a fool, and Mr. Miller may feel a glow of righteousness—but Hitler doesn't feel in the least ashamed when Chamberlain allows him to take Austria and then offers him Czechoslovakia. History, unfortunately, does not conform to Mr. Huxley's emotions. Though the view put forward at the conclusion of *Eyeless in Gaza* has been supported by Huxley in his nonfictional writing, we cannot help feeling that the special pleading and rather tricky argumentation that this involves is an indication that Huxley, in finding a solution to his problem, has unconsciously changed the nature of his problem and has not answered the question implicitly in his earlier criticisms of society. Huxley as a frustrated romantic creating his own compensation is now revealed. What his future course may be, it is no purpose of the present study to guess at.

From Gumbril senior to Calamy, from Calamy to Rampion, from Rampion to Miller and Anthony after his conversion—the evolution of the Huxley hero is one of the most instructive phenomena in recent literature.

Critics have shown a great deal of confusion in discussing the technical aspect of Huxley's novels. The fact is that Huxley is no novelist; he has never mastered—is not really interested in—even the elements of form and structure in fiction. We may note how frequently he makes his heroes write long diaries or autobiographical documents or makes them utter long philosophical monologues. His novels are either a series of character sketches or simple fables or tracts. The suggestion of mature technique in *Point Counter Point* and *Eyeless in Gaza* is quite misleading. It is as though Huxley deems it necessary to keep up with contemporary innovators in the technique of fiction by doing some jumping about in time and space, splitting up the action and taking it out of its chronological order, all of which devices are wholly unnecessary, having no functional purpose in building up the story at all. The musical analogy in *Point Counter Point* is quite false and the tampering with chronology there quite purposeless. As for the technique of *Eyeless in Gaza*, it would be comic if it were not so irritating. The novel would have been much more effective as straight autobiography or as the straightforward history of the development of his hero. Other innovators in technique may have had some compelling reason, in terms of plot and structure, for the innovations they introduced, but Huxley seems to be doing it only because he feels that it is expected of him.

His real genius is as an essayist. He has a gift for brilliant discussion, for sketching an atmosphere or a character, for making a point. His essays are always quite brilliant affairs technically. He is not really aware of the problems that face the writer of fiction of his day, but he does know how to handle—in isolation—exposition, argument, and description.

AFTER MANY A SUMMER

October 1939

96. Unsigned review in *TLS*

14 October 1939, p. 591

The review is entitled 'Mr. Huxley's Dark Vision.'

From an ivory and chromium-plated tower in California Mr. Huxley has seen everything that man has made, and, behold, it is not very good. So bad is it, indeed, so foolish or so vile are the things to which human beings have put their hand, that Mr. Huxley seems to wait for a different species of life to inherit the earth. Like the Lilith of Mr. Shaw's ultimate fancy,[1] he has spared men almost too long. Certainly he has written nothing bleaker or more chilling than *After Many a Summer*, a title borrowed with characteristic irony from Tennyson.[2] Not that this parable is without grace or stimulus: it is far from being dull. All the Huxleyan virtues are here in shining array—the Latin clarity and force of statement, the catholic learning, the encyclopaedic familiarity with the arts, the scientific curiosity, the wit and destructive satire—together with a more urgent economy of argument than he has practised in the past. But there is also the perfected bloom of Huxleyan pessimism, a graveyard aroma of the flesh, an enveloping glory of corruption and decay that induces a shudder and that is all the more oppressive for being translated by Mr. Huxley into a bliss of mystical experience in-communicable even in the symbols of eroticism.

[Recounts the situation and describes the major characters of this 'cunningly constructed parable']

[1] *Back to Methuselah.*
[2] 'Tithonus.'

. . . With a careless gesture of indulging narrowly conventional tastes Mr. Huxley also throws in poor Pete, Dr. Obispo's research assistant, who is fated to be simple and even kind. Pete, knowing no better, painfully adores Miss Maunciple and, again knowing no better, suffers the vanity and vexation of spirit, as Mr. Huxley sees it, of the idealist in a democratic cause.

From these elements Mr. Huxley has compounded a story as deso-latingly dark within as it is brilliantly polished without. His elegant mockery, his cruel aptness of phrase, the revelations and the ingenious surprises he springs on the reader are those of a master craftsman; Mr. Huxley is at the top of his form in this respect. In the cynicism of his view of the personal relationships he excels himself; the brutality of his human disgust here is unrelieved. What happens in the end is that Baby is initiated into the darker mysteries of the flesh by the recondite Obispo, whereupon Uncle Jo sees red and poor Pete, the only innocent among them all, pays with his life. For this transvaluation of accepted values of fiction Mr. Huxley offers a terse and stinging sort of apologia. To an adult mind, he says, the contemporary stream of merely descrip-tive novels is a burden and a weariness. 'All the innumerable, inter-minable anecdotes and romances and character studies, but no general theory of anecdotes, no explanatory hypothesis of romance or charac-ter.' No co-ordinating philosophy superior to common sense, only misplaced seriousness. It is a philosophy rising above the philistinism of common sense that he exhibits in this novel.

How does he do it? Of one of his characters it is said that 'the fright-fulness of the world had reached a point at which it had become for him merely boring.' If this were all, if St. Augustine's great statement of the problem of evil, for instance, had ceased to interest Mr. Huxley, then it might be sufficient to say of this latest novel of his that it is brilliant and bloodless. But it is not all. There is Mr. William Propter, who was bored by war and famine and the spectacle of misery. There are the baboons and the rejuvenated last Earl of Gonister, the hero of the Hauberk Papers. Mr. Propter has no organic connexion with the story, but his skilfully punctuated monologue in the middle is apparently its essential motive and justification, possibly the motive and justification of every-thing Mr. Huxley has written. For Mr. Propter has come into the haven of God, into direct intuition of non-human reality. His mysticism, or the expression of it, takes highly ratiocinative forms: there are difficul-ties, as he points out, of vocabulary. But God is not mocked. From the puritanism of the earlier novels, the misanthropical cerebration of *Point*

Counter Point, the disgust of *Brave New World*, the still deeper despair of *Eyeless in Gaza*, Mr. Huxley has passed to the absolute of mortal vision, which is 'liberation from personality, liberation from time and craving, liberation into union with God'.

Well, there it is. Perhaps it is to be expected that Mr. Propter should carry his mystical vision into what he calls strictly human concerns; perhaps the complacency, the sense of unfailing rightmindedness he exudes is natural enough in the circumstances. But what have Dr. Obispo's arts and the sexual behaviour of baboons to do with the apprehension of eternity? What is the foetal ape, who was once Earl of Gonister and outmoded the Marquis de Sade, doing in this mystical galley? Mr. Huxley's impulse of faith or religious experience seems to inhabit a human wilderness. The warring of flesh and spirit is both rational and daemonic in Donne, say, or in Swift. Here they embrace in strange darkness.

97. Anthony West, review in *New Statesman and Nation*

14 October 1939, xviii [n.s.], p. 524

Anthony Panther West, b. 1914, critic, novelist, essayist, author of *On a Dark Night* (1949), a biography of D. H. Lawrence (1950), *Principles and Persuasions* (essays originally in the *New Yorker*) (1957), and others.

Good as *Brave New World* was it gave one the impression that Mr. Aldous Huxley was imprisoned in a library and that he saw mankind through thicknesses of paper as a fish in an ill-kept vivary might see it through the slimy glass. And after reading *Eyeless in Gaza* the impression was strengthened; it could only be someone isolated from life who could imagine that amazing incident in which a terrier dropped from an aeroplane burst like a ripe tomato over a couple naked after copulation on a roof top—the incident was not made more credible by being related as if it might have happened to anyone. But disconcerting as the narrative was it did not inspire the doubt which attached to a synthetic yogo-buddhic-christian religion which cast a shadow across the book. The synthetic religion came into the light of day in *Ends and Means*. The new faith required certain things from the believer, the abandonment of all desires likely to lead to striving and rivalry, a complete control of the bodily functions, a concentration leading to St. Teresa's 'seventh mansion' in which one can be conscious of the mystical light while buying puppy-biscuit. It is perhaps not relevant to the ultimate virtue of the faith, but it is obvious that under existing conditions disaster comes to those who purge themselves of desire without first securing a guaranteed income of a fairly substantial sort, and the thought cannot have escaped readers of *Ends and Means* that the recipe it gave for acquiring complete control of the body was familiar from childhood—it was an elaboration of the two principles of the old-fashioned Nanny, Don't Fidget, Keep Regular. Be that as it may, the Evangelist of Mr. Gerald Heard's Neo-Brahminism has now published another novel in which the principles of the faith are displayed functioning in the everyday world, and the result is as depressing as that cloudy expository work led one to expect. It enables one to formulate an opinion of Mr. Huxley that it will probably be unnecessary to revise.

[Gives a brief description of the story]

Those who have followed Mr. Huxley's publications will recognise at once what they are in for. The kept woman is passed from hand to hand and used by people she does not like, there is a great deal of amorous activity which ignores the fact that the act can be enjoyable on a very simple level as resolutely as the fact that women frequently lie with men they enjoy. With the adolescent treatment of sexual activity as something thrillingly wrong goes the other adolescent excitement about intestines. The eighteenth-century Earl's remedy against old age was a diet of uncooked carp's guts, and there are some fine passages about the difficulty he experienced in keeping them down when he started the diet. The Earl is found at the age of two hundred and one in the cellars of a house in England, a gibbering ape with less than an ape's nicety about its faeces. The book is inspired with a hatred of the bag of guts tied to a sensitive brain, it is a cry of agony at the brain's slavery to the bag while it lusts and hungers, and at its partnership in its ultimate decay.

One sees here the penalty which is attached to all surrogates for religion and philosophy: they rationalize hell away and provide no other mechanism for relieving the individual of his burden of guilt, and by rejecting the conception of a personal immortality they leave men a prey to the crowding fears which account for most ill behaviour. They afford neither the defence offered by a philosophy nor the anaesthetic offered by a superstitious religion. *After Many a Summer* is the record of another spiritual failure; it is Mr. Huxley's petition in moral bankruptcy, and in presenting it he speaks for all those who are too sophisticated to accept the crudities of the established religions and are at the same time too credulous to accept a sceptical philosophy.

98. Thomas J. Merton, review in *Catholic World*

November 1940, clii, pp. 206–9

Thomas J. Merton (1915–68), author and clergyman, was instructor in English at Columbia's university extension in 1939. In 1941 he entered the Abbey of Gethsemani to become an ordained priest (1949). He wrote several volumes of religious studies and meditations in his quarter of a century as a Trappist monk. See Introduction, p. 22.

The review is entitled 'Huxley's Pantheon.'

A few years ago Aldous Huxley wrote *Eyeless in Gaza*, a novel which disappointed his followers for two reasons. First it was not a very good novel, and second it indicated his disillusionment in the comfortable and materialistic skepticism with which he had been, until then, apparently satisfied. His new opinions, instead, appeared to be those of a theosophic crank, but it was not altogether true that these opinions were as new or as startling in Huxley as they seemed. They had their roots in earlier work, like *Those Barren Leaves* in which Huxley exhibits the sneaking curiosity which intellectuals often feel toward mystics, who say they contemplate the truth face to face.

In all justice to Huxley he was always more than a mere intellectual. He is also an intelligent man. He even now sees more clearly than most of his contemporaries, the end for which man was created, but he shows himself both perplexed and confused in his discussion of the means of attaining that end. He is still a capable writer. He still makes criticisms of literature that are as full of erudition as they are of perspicacity. His personal charm is equal to his wit and his good intentions: but unfortunately as a philosopher he is *not* distinguished.

His *Ends and Means* seemed a little better than *Eyeless in Gaza* because he avoided, in it, some of the limitations that are imposed upon metaphysical concepts by the language of imagination and the accents of cultured dialogue. But the contradictions which were so perplexing in *Ends and Means* have become even more obvious in *After Many a Summer Dies the Swan*, his latest novel.

There is a good enough reason why his opinions frequently sound theosophic: it is that they often really are so. He has gone from one mystic to another, Christian and Oriental, and he has reached his own kind of pantheistic idealism, at last, not without having stopped by at the doors of Spinoza, Kant and Bergson. He now believes that the world is completely illusory. Matter does not exist, and it is evil. Of course it is evil by privation of reality, truth and goodness which are only to be found in the single substance that exists, God. This substance is also life itself; but although all living things participate in it, they are separated from it by matter, and imprisoned in the realm of death or karma. Existence on earth, then, is not good, and we are meant to escape from it by purification, detachment from matter, and union with the selfless One. Material attachments only bind us down to evil: they cannot help us to reach God in any manner. Huxley follows Buddhism this far, but abandons it on the question of metempsychosis, adding a further complicated twist of his own that makes it impossible in his system. He says that good is only impossible on the 'human level,' and exists not only above it, in eternity, but also below it on the level of animals!

The reason for this is probably a reminiscence of the old *Point Counter Point* days, in which animal instincts were good for their own sake: he thinks they still are, but they must be evil in men because they are self-conscious.

Matter, in any case, can be symbolized as death. That is a familiar enough convention in mystical literature, and that explains all the death symbols upon which Huxley's latest novel is built.

In the very first pages of the book we come upon a rather oppressive description of a cemetery called, not without reason, a pantheon, on the outskirts of Los Angeles. It is one of the great commercial enterprises of one of the characters, Stoyte, and it is a flamboyant place adorned with every possible kind of vulgarity and pagan display. Its more ambitious features include a Fountain of Rainbow Music, a Vestibule of Ashes, a tiny Taj Mahal, an Old World Mortuary, some catacombs and a perpetual Wurlitzer. But the most offensive thing about the place is that some of the graves are decorated with erotic statuary: for it is Stoyte's pride that he has 'put sex appeal into death.'

This heavy-handed joke would appear to be too extreme, if only it were not all too possibly, if not actually, true. But the importance of it is that it is a device Huxley uses to satirize materialism. For the materialist has to look for all goodness, all beauty and truth (if any) in materially desirable things. But since beauty, goodness and so on are not in material things alone, this is as absurd and as bad as trying to 'put sex appeal into death.' Nevertheless, the pagan hopes to get for himself as many material things and pleasures as possible before he dies: and if it ceases to be a case of every man for himself, at least one has a chance of getting his fair share if he unites to fight for it with other members of his 'oppressed class.' An extremely happy consummation, for him, would be to live on earth forever, enjoying everlasting youth and health: that is a characteristically pagan paradise. Therefore, the central theme of *After Many a Summer* is not death in general, but physical immortality.

The title of the book is taken from Tennyson's poem about a man to whom the gods gave everlasting life, in return for some favor. But unfortunately they did not give Tithonus everlasting youth, and he just got older and older and older, until he finally begged to be allowed to die, like all other creatures.

Huxley has created a Tithonus of his own; one who did the gods no favor, but whom at least the reader should thank for being the material cause of the only readable parts of the novel, the 'Hauberk Papers.' He is an English nobleman who found that he could be immortal on a diet of fishes' intestines, and lived for two hundred years in a hidden cave in Surrey. Unlike Tennyson's Tithonus, Huxley's does not lose his youthful vigor. Instead he suffers a different degradation. That degradation is only revealed in the surprise ending of the book, so perhaps it would not be just to reveal it. But in any case, it is very effective, and constitutes the most forceful indictment of materialism that ever came from Huxley's pen, even though somewhat the same idea was used, more crudely, in a Laurel and Hardy comedy in 1933.

The central theme is not at all a bad one, but it should have been treated in all its simplicity. Instead of that, it is buried in a lot of extraneous material. The interminable philosophizings of one Mr. Propter, the dullest character in the whole history of the English novel, are allowed to impede the movement of the story and to spoil the effect of the whole plan.

In the course of these soliloquies Huxley at the same time condemns most of the religious systems in the world and struggles with the contradictions of his own. His principal contention, in this, is a perfectly good one: it is that too many men have created God in their own image, and after they have done so, have called upon the God they have created to justify their own violent depredations upon their neighbors. The lowest form of anthropomorphic god is the dictator, who is not only a god in the form of a man but is a man, and who sets himself up as the embodiment of all the desires and strivings of his followers. Above this come polytheism and primitive monotheism and so on up the scale: and all the way up, even where God is the purest spirit, He does not cease to retain, in Huxley's eyes, some taint of anthropomorphism.

So he goes as far as he can, and reaches the same extreme as the Buddhists, to whom God is pure nothingness. But He is not nothingness in the metaphorical sense that no concept of ours can represent Him (which is the Christian view), He is really absolute nothingness. But at this point Huxley seems to realize that to say that God is nothingness is simply atheism, and so he falls back hurriedly upon the Christian notion of God as pure actuality, or 'pure working' as he says in the words of the German mystic John Tauler.

Nevertheless Huxley cannot assent to the Divinity of Christ (although he doesn't say how he feels toward the many incarnations of God worshiped in the East) and he thinks that Christianity, although it has 'the merit of being simple and dramatic,' is categorically 'wrong.'

He thinks that men like St. John of the Cross, by a lucky accident, transcended these 'errors' and managed to get a glimpse of pure and actual truth, but he condemns in the Spanish mystics a 'strain of negative sensuality' which only re-affirmed their self-will more strongly when they believed they were annihilating it.

But for Huxley any expression of will at all is 'self-will.' He believes all our acts are evil, and thus it would be absurd to designate special acts as sources of sin. He is convinced that 'the level of man is the level of evil' and he wants to lift the mind by main force out of that level, so that it may attain union with God through, not love, but knowledge.

In *Ends and Means*, Love was an important virtue, but now Huxley only mentions the word to say how much it embarrasses him. His mysticism operates exclusively in the order of speculation. Love, by which the will is directed to its proper end, the Good, has no place in that order. So naturally, since that is the only order Huxley accepts, Love must go.

Even the best intentioned activity only leads to evil consequences, and there is no longer any reason for Huxley to want to do anything for others. Gone, therefore, are the little groups of eight or ten proselytizers, familiar to readers of *Eyeless in Gaza*, schooled in self-control by the methods of F. M. Alexander, traveling about making speeches and opposing violence with non-resistance. In his new book, Huxley admits he doesn't want to save anyone, except perhaps three or four well-disposed individuals.

Yet in spite of all these opinions which are put into his mouth Mr. Propter is a very active person. He is as busy as he is talkative. He spends much time in a workshop, and he cares not only for his orange trees, but for the bodies and souls of itinerant fruitpickers. He dreams of a small agrarian community in some fertile valley, a sort of beaverboard Shangri-la, in which a few chatty contemplatives might wait out the war in seclusion and safety.

All Mr. Propter's attempts to help others seem false because of their inconsistency. Neither Propter nor Huxley really believes he can do anything for anybody else, and if they have any vocation at all, it is to the hermitage. There they will have no more worries about self-contradiction because they will no longer have to argue. There Huxley would be able to sit and think in peace, in between visits from cultured and amusing friends, and it would be very good for him. He should do that. He should stop writing about Mr. Propter, and, retiring to a suitable retreat, work in the medium in which he is really good: the Essay.

99. Harry Lorin Binsse, review in *Commonweal*

1 March 1940, xxxi, p. 418

Harry Lorin Binsse (1905–72), translator of works by Kant (1940), Bernanos (1945), Maurois (1956), and others, was managing editor of *Commonweal* 1938–47.

This is a disgusting book. But it's Huxley's best so far. First of all it isn't a novel. Secondly it is beyond the pale as far as sex is concerned. One of the principal characters draws curtains in front of the Virgin when she experiences a certain bestial joy in the sexual act—and that alone is a Catholic touch. We agree that there is a level beneath which the most earthy of us will draw the curtain. There is a point in sin where we have to stop, and without any merit for stopping. Unfortunately this stopping point is not recognized by Mr. Huxley. And there is another little matter—the matter of writing novels which really are novels.

Most of us assume that a novel is supposed to deal with human beings. Mr. Huxley insists that each character in his novel shall be a *porte-parole*.[1] Of course that is one way of handling the matter. But it isn't the way of the novel. There isn't in this latest dispensation a single human being, a real mixed-up human being. Everyone is crystal clear; here is the sensualist, here is the voice of the author, here is the damned-fool American millionaire. And it may be very unsophisticated to say it, but that's no way to write a novel.

Then we Americans should have another quarrel with Mr. Huxley. We may speak an outlandish language (I remember the awful quarter hour I spent with the daughter of a Cambridge don who found that I spoke 'such extraordinarily good English'), but it is our own. We resent people who don't really talk that way trying to write that way—which Mr. Huxley does all the way through. Imitation may be the sincerest form of flattery, but only when the imitation is clearly an imitation. Mr. Huxley is too good at it to be amusing.

[1] 'Spokesman, mouthpiece.'

But how about the book's philosophy? For it has one. There we can't be altogether ungrateful. For the philosophy is backhandedly Christian, via emasculated Buddhism. For so much may we be thankful. But the book is not only not *pour les jeunes filles*;[1] there are professors of moral theology to whom I should hesitate to recommend it.

100. George Catlin, review in *Saturday Review of Literature*

27 January 1940, xxi, p. 5

Sir George Edward Gordon Catlin, b. 1896, philosopher and educator, co-edited *The Realist* 1929–30 with Huxley, H. G. Wells, Arnold Bennett, and others. He has written such books as *Principles of Politics* (1930) and *The Atlantic Community* (1959).

The review is entitled 'Time and Aldous Huxley.' See Introduction, p. 1.

The Aldous Huxley of *Crome Yellow* expressed, as perhaps no other writer has done, the spirit of the 1920s, a spirit negative, disillusioned, and relaxed. He did not follow the 1920s into the mood of the Marxist 1930s, when youth identified idealism with revolution and economic toughness. He remained apart, like Job, meditating on humanity as Dr. Zuckermann meditates on Apes' Hill. The earlier spirit persisted beyond its season, became septic and gangrened with time. Mr. Huxley, best loved disciple of D. H. Lawrence, became a moralist, a new Juvenal and a new Swift, but there was an evil relish in his satire. He served us with a delicacy like a medlar, to be eaten when rotten. He satirized sexuality with an Arnoesque[2] exaggeration.

[1] 'For the young ladies.'
[2] Peter Arno, b. 1904, U.S. cartoonist and author.

After Many a Summer is the story of a wide-eyed English pilgrim, Mr. Pordage, quiet scholar of letters, who finds himself precipitated into the midst of the human fauna of California, ranging from the industrial baron in his castle, who owns a commercial crematorium, to the poor Joads at his gate. Amid vivisectors, murderers, and devotees of longevity, varied by sensuous ladies and adolescent idealists—such as Pete, who fought in Spain—Pordage, the scholar for scholarship's sake, finds Propter, the quietist philosopher. The kernel of the book lies in the contrast of these characters.

Superficially *After Many a Summer* is a study in the same colors as before, incredibly erudite, precious with 'Chippendale words,'[1] full of references to Molinos, St. Peter Claver, the Marquis de Sade, and Josiah Royce, admixed with descriptions, bright as new paint, of castles in California and Yosemitic seductions. The effect is oddly vulgar. Even the positive pacifism would appear to be lacking which characterized Huxley in his third period, when he and Mr. Gerald Heard—Heard of *The Social Substance of Religion*—were as David and Jonathan.

All that does show itself is Mr. Huxley as crown prince in the dynasty of H. G. Wells, heir to the socio-scientific novel. 'If you read old Schneeglock's work and the stuff they'd been publishing at Upsala, you'd know some of the sterols were definitely poisonous—much more so than chloresterol.' All that is purest Wells.

This, I submit, is the obvious judgment on the present book. It is, I believe, a superficial judgment. 'Literature,' says the philosophic Mr. Propter in *After Many a Summer*, 'is chiefly alcohol and cantharides.' Plato said that earlier, and profoundly I believe Plato and Huxley to be right. It may even be that the vulgar is best exposed vulgarly. But whether Huxley does himself justice by trying to sell philosophy to the nit-wits by seasoning it with aphrodisiacs, I leave him to judge. I doubt it. I don't think this garnishing will make Mr. Huxley's disquisition on the essential nature of Time any more palatable to those who believe that the test of significant truth is its lucidity to the glance of a mental twelve-year-old in a hurry. It is of course sad that this should be so; but it is so. 'A significance new not in respect to the entities connoted by the words, but rather in the mode of their comprehension, which, from being intellectual in character, had become intuitive and direct, so that the nature of man in his potentiality and of God in actuality was realized by an analogue of sensuous experience' . . . If this is what Mr.

---

[1] Thomas Chippendale (1718–79) was a celebrated English cabinetmaker in the florid rococo style.

Huxley means, it is well that he should say it. But he will only with difficulty escape being read by enraged critics their customary homily on ABC lucidity. It is not easy to explain to a mankind that demands its intellectual food peptonized why Pascal was right in distinguishing the human plane of living from the eternal, or just why Tithonus should pray about human day-after-day immortality, 'Release me, and restore me to the ground.' But I do not see that an injection of the style of the Marquis de Sade helps matters, in the context of what Mr. Huxley wishes to do. Those who want the food will take it without this dish . . . [sic] although for those who do not want the bolus, the method of getting them to take it is perhaps as good as the old one of Diogenes Laertius with his *Lives and Loves of the Philosophers*.

What does Huxley seek to do? It is to recall to our minds that there is a technique of the spiritual life which Eckhart and Loyola, in their different ways, sought to practise. The excellent life is by definition aristocratic. So good a democrat as Mahatma Gandhi has found it such. When the Protestant Revolt liquidated the monasteries, which were professional 'workshops of souls,' it was a catastrophe to civilization. Mr. Huxley would have us hark back by some Catholic-Quaker route. But indeed his philosophy is far older and more elaborated than that of Catholic mysticism. It is that of the Hindu Sankara and again of Buddha. And Mr. Huxley is its *guru* and apostle. One can no more belong to this church thanks to half an hour spent reading in an arm chair about the Fifth Earl of Gonnister, aged two hundred odd and clad only in the Ribbon of the Garter, leaping on his troll, than Gandhi could become Mahatma by reading smart literature.

Mr. Huxley re-expounds the old Buddhist doctrine of the Wheel of Life. His preoccupation is not really with castles in California or even with the circumambient Joads. This is not a novel of action. Its characterizations are after the style of Sears, Roebuck. It is that strange mutt of literature, a novel of ideas. And the idea here is that Time is essentially evil. Satire worthy of Donne or Swift is poured on the merely human, biological quest for long life. The true good is the quest for eternity, realizable now.

It is, however, Mr. Huxley's own affair how he chooses to express his ideas. What matters is that he has ideas of the first importance to express. He knows literature in the sense of *Belles Lettres* as a connoisseur, and very properly has a contempt for its pretensions. He is the best of our political philosophers. He is the only man today rewriting St. Augustine in letters of hell-fire. He does not fall into the lethal modern heresy that there is no pure or abstract truth, nor does he hold that, because we should all do good, it is the intellectual's task to 'serve at tables' or to rewrite history to forward a Cause, whether it be that Goebbels is always right or that Trotsky never existed. That was poor Pete's error in this book. Huxley, speaking by the voice of Propter, grasps that there is a structure of the nature of things, spiritual as also physical, superbly independent of our lusts and wishes, as unconcerned as Spinoza's God about how we feel about It. But in the comprehension of It lies our peace. There also lies the secret of that serene disinterestedness which is the sole pure well, *una sola sancta*,[1] whence flow, not murders and dictatures and wrath, but equity and social justice. Here is to be heard, by those who are willing, a still voice that searches the conscience.

101. Edgar Johnson, review in *Kenyon Review*

Summer 1940, ii, pp. 351–3

Edgar Johnson, b. 1901, has been a professor of English at the City College of New York (1927–72) and chairman of the English Department (1949–64). His books include *One Mighty Torrent; the Drama of Biography* (1937), as well as studies of Dickens (1953) and Scott (1970).

The review is entitled 'Amor Dei in Hollywood.'

Mr. Huxley's new novel is a sort of multi-decker literary sandwich with slices of burlesque, jazz, melodrama, and horror alternating with slabs of philosophical wry. The latter somewhat astringent cross-sections of the sandwich are devoted to Mr. Huxley's version of love, a rather thin and theoretical emotion explained in a series of monologues by the

1 'A lone holiness.'

Huxleyan raisonneur,[1] William Propter. Intellectually, Propter's connection with the story is quite clear: he is the commentator on its passions, and as such its most important character. Organically, however, his connection is tenuous indeed; he stands utterly alone, and all the others, almost as if he did not exist, fall into their own typical frustrations and damnations.

Nevertheless, the relation between the lives of these others and the harangues of William Propter is the key to Mr. Huxley's theme. Chief of them is Jo Stoyte, enormously wealthy, rapacious, terrified of death, and defying it with a senescent concupiscence for his Hollywood cutie, Virginia Maunciple, who dwells with him in a fantastic Gothic castle with Vermeers in the elevators, a swimming pool crowning the donjon keep, and a combination soda-fountain-and-bar in the boudoir. In his slobbering semi-incestuous passion, half parental, half obscene, for his 'Baby,' Stoyte is both grotesque and revolting, crazy with jealousy lest she may be two-timing him and with fear that he is a sinner in the hands of an angry God. Meanwhile, endowed by Stoyte's mortuary dread, the ferocious and metallic Dr. Obispo seeks the secrets of life and rejuvenation in the intestines of apes, rats, and carp, and cynically cuckolds his employer. His assistant, young Pete Boone, has idealistically fought Fascism in Spain, and worships Virginia's pneumatic charms so blindly that he cannot see her unambiguous relations. Overshadowing them all is the Earl of Gonister, known to us mainly through his journals found in the historic 'Hauberk Papers,' an emancipated 18th Century milord who had also sought the prolongation of life by delving in intestinal slime.

The Earl is first-rate, a vivid evocation of the rationalism, the brutality, and the assured classical tone of his age, even better than the dwarf Sir Hercules in Huxley's early *Crome Yellow*. But the others are crude and, indeed, only carelessly slapped-down caricatures of types he has drawn more skillfully before: Stoyte less subtle and penetrating in characterization than Chawdron, in *Brief Candles*; Virginia Maunciple mingling the vulgarity of Sidney Quarles's cockney mistress Gladys with the sexual humiliation of Rosie Shearwater at the hands of Coleman; Obispo a superficial and brassy variation on Coleman and Spandrell; Pete Boone a feebler echo of Gumbril, Denis, Walter Bidlake, all the sheeplike 'mild-and-melancholy Ones' of earlier novels. Huxley has, in truth, as Malcolm Cowley remarked in *The New Republic*, used 'commercial citric acid instead of lemon juice' and 'saccharine for sugar.'

[1] 'Reasoner, arguer.'

And the reason is that Huxley is interested in the people only as ingredients in the philosophic pill he has been preparing for his own consumption. In *Eyeless in Gaza* he had been 'converted' to love and shown his hero Anthony Beavis rather bitterly searching for channels in which to benefit humanity with that emotion; in *Ends and Means* his analysis had found a startling paucity of ways in which humanity could be helped; now he has brought himself to the cheering conclusion that it cannot be. That is to say, it cannot be helped on the 'human' level of ideals and desires. Stoyte's terrified longing for youth, and Maunciple's periodical ticklings of sensuality and repentances, the raucous disillusion of Obispo, Pete Boone's touching faith in mechanical solutions for the world's evils, all these are merely forms of the same fundamental delusion: that any good may be achieved in time and that ideals, which are only images of desire, represent any real goods. Even love for one's fellow-men is only a snare, an enticement into personal feelings, destructive of the only real aim, 'liberation from personality . . . liberation into union with God.' Only in the timeless and impersonal contemplation of God *sub specie aeternitatis* is there true good, true love only in the *amor intellectualis Dei*.[1]

The conclusion thus arrived at is obviously drawn from a fantastic mélange of influences: the Sankhya system of freeing the soul from its fetters by union with eternally existing essence, the Christian mystics, the renunciation of desire and the pantheism of Spinoza, Schopenhauer's analysis of the will as the origin of all suffering and evil, a dash of the New Humanism, D. H. Lawrence's diatribes against industrialism and idealism, even a little aroma of Ralph Borsodi.[2] The origin, however, is less significant than the destination and motive. Huxley does not love, and does not want to love humanity. Dostoevsky's Versilov advised his son to hold his nose in order to love his neighbor; Huxley has found in the love of God a substitute for all but a lipservice love for human beings. In the horrible anthropoid body of the Earl of Gonister, aged but still living in its underground dungeon, he has devised a fable to destroy belief in human ends, just as in the impersonal love of an impersonal God he has invented a fable to enable hate to masquerade as love. That is the subtle self-deception at the heart of *After Many a Summer Dies the Swan*. Huxley sees humanity tearing toward

---

[1] 'under the eye of eternity,' 'intellectual love of God.'

[2] Huxley refers approvingly to Borsodi in *Science, Liberty and Peace* (pp. 124, 143). In the 1930s Borsodi had established a 'School of Living' in the eastern United States to develop methods of small-scale production and decentralization.

perdition, and all his extraordinary mental maneuvers are the muddled rationalization of the desire to stand aside. But he does not like to admit to himself the cynicism and selfishness of that desire. Therefore love, but love to no tangible object and no ends. Out of such muddle no lucid work of art can grow. That is the cause, in *After Many a Summer*, of his flatness and his failure.

102. George Orwell on Huxley's anti-Utopias

1940, 1946, 1949

George Orwell (Eric Blair) (1903–50), well-known British novelist whose *Nineteen Eighty-Four* (1948) is inevitably compared with *Brave New World*. See Huxley's discussion of the two books in *Brave New World Revisited*, pp. 12–15, and his letter to Orwell, L, pp. 604–5.

Excerpts from *The Collected Essays, Journalism and Letters of George Orwell*, ed. Sonia Orwell and Ian Angus (New York: Harcourt, 1968): (a) Vol. II, pp. 30–1; (b) Vol. IV, pp. 73–5; (c) Vol. IV, p. 479.

(a) Extract from *Tribune* article (12 July 1940) in response to a recent reprinting of Jack London's *The Iron Heel*

Everyone who has ever read *The Sleeper Wakes* remembers it. It is a vision of a glittering, sinister world in which society has hardened into a caste-system and the workers are permanently enslaved. It is also a world without purpose, in which the upper castes for whom the workers toil are completely soft, cynical and faithless. There is no consciousness of any object in life, nothing corresponding to the fervour of the revolutionary or the religious martyr.

In Aldous Huxley's *Brave New World*, a sort of post-war parody of the Wellsian Utopia, these tendencies are immensely exaggerated. Here the hedonistic principle is pushed to its utmost, the whole world has turned into a Riviera hotel. But though *Brave New World* was a brilliant caricature of the present (the present of 1930), it probably casts no light on the future. No society of that kind would last more than a couple of generations, because a ruling class which thought principally in terms of a 'good time' would soon lose its vitality. A ruling class has got to have a strict morality, a quasi-religious belief in itself, a mystique. . . .

(b) Extract from *Tribune* article (4 January 1946) on the Russian Eugene Zamyatin's anti-Utopian novel, *We*

The first thing anyone would notice about *We* is the fact—never pointed out, I believe—that Aldous Huxley's *Brave New World* must be partly derived from it. Both books deal with the rebellion of the primitive human spirit against a rationalised, mechanised, painless world, and both stories are supposed to take place about six hundred years hence. The atmosphere of the two books is similar, and it is roughly speaking the same kind of society that is being described, though Huxley's book shows less political awareness and is more influenced by recent biological and psychological theories.

[Summarizes similarities between *We* and *Brave New World*]

So far the resemblance with *Brave New World* is striking, But though Zamyatin's book is less well put together—it has a rather weak and episodic plot which is too complex to summarise—it has a political point which the other lacks. In Huxley's book the problem of 'human nature' is in a sense solved, because it assumes that by pre-natal treatment, drugs and hypnotic suggestion the human organism can be specialised in any way that is desired. A first-rate scientific worker is as easily produced as an Epsilon semi-moron, and in either case the vestiges of primitive instincts, such as maternal feeling or the desire for liberty, are easily dealt with. At the same time no clear reason is given why society should be stratified in the elaborate way that is described. The aim is not economic exploitation, but the desire to bully and dominate does not seem to be a motive either. There is no power hunger, no sadism, no hardness of any kind. Those at the top have no strong motive for staying at the top, and though everyone is happy in a vacuous way, life has become so pointless that it is difficult to believe that such a society could endure.

Zamyatin's book is on the whole more relevant to our own situation. In spite of education and the vigilance of the Guardians, many of the ancient human instincts are still there. . . .

. . . It is this intuitive grasp of the irrational side of totalitarianism—human sacrifice, cruelty as an end in itself, the worship of a Leader who is credited with divine attributes—that makes Zamyatin's book superior to Huxley's.

(c) Extract from letter to Sir Richard Rees, Bt (3 March 1949). Huxley's book referred to is *Ape and Essence*

You were right about Huxley's book—it is awful. And do you notice that the more holy he gets, the more his books stink with sex. He cannot get off the subject of flagellating women. Possibly, if he had the courage to come out & say so, that is the solution to the problem of war. If we took it out in a little private sadism, which after all doesn't do much harm, perhaps we wouldn't want to drop bombs etc.

GREY EMINENCE

October 1941

---

103. C. V. Wedgwood, review in *Spectator*

5 December 1941, clxvii, p. 538

Dame (Cicely) Veronica Wedgwood, b. 1910, highly honored historian and educator, has written for example, *The Thirty Years' War* (1938) and *Seventeenth Century Literature* (1950).

The review is entitled 'The Mystic and the World.'

What exactly is this new book of Mr. Huxley's? Described as a biography on the dust cover and as a 'study in religion and politics' on the title page, its first chapter reads like a fragment of a novel. It is the spring of 1625 and Father Joseph is walking to Rome: here immediately is the Huxley touch, the biting, exact description of a man's brain at work, as though the author were walking about inside his creature's head, curiously, and with just a touch of malice, observing the mechanism. In the second chapter, a reconstruction of Father Joseph's youth, the novelist gives place to the historian, who in turn yields to the philosopher. So that the life of Father Joseph becomes the pivot of Mr. Huxley's further reflections on mysticism.

[Gives a brief summary of Father Joseph's career]

. . . How could a mystic thus serve the ends of worldly power, and a man devoted to the contemplation of Christ's agony so disregard the agonies of his fellow-men? This is the problem on which we see Mr. Huxley's brain at work. He does not solve it, and perhaps deliberately not, for he rejects the only two lines of research which provide a passable explanation—the historical and the psychological. Seen in his

335

place in history Father Joseph belonged to a gross and callous period whose standards of human suffering were not ours. Seen as a psychological case, Father Joseph was an example of the sadist-masochist to whom the infliction and the suffering of pain were essential. But Mr. Huxley is not studying Father Joseph, the psychological case, against a period background. He is studying Father Joseph, the mystic, against the background of eternity. It is a different and a far more important problem.

Since *Eyeless in Gaza* Mr. Huxley has, in a voice ever more authoritative, called for the recognition of the mystic's function in a world stifled by materialism. This is the authentic voice of Mr. Huxley; there was a whisper of it in those earlier urbane witty novels, until in Anthony Beavis he created an eloquent mouthpiece, and at length in *Ends and Means* spoke out in his own person. The voice may not at first sound so bold in *Grey Eminence*; pure history and pure biography must have their share of space, and neither the novelist nor the artist in Mr. Huxley could forgo the occasional comedy, the more frequent drama of the Friar's life. There must be the baroque tableaux—the horseman with the damascened pistols on the road to Rome, or Richelieu hastening from his private theatre among the flaring torches. These interruptions are inherent in the biographical form, but they are interruptions, for we read this book not to learn about Father Joseph's mind but about Aldous Huxley's. His voice, when it emerges, is more assured, more logical, than before, and yet more apt to our times. Not only has he progressed still further in the exposition of his doctrines, but he has realised the importance of historic proofs. Deference to the mystics, he argues, has repeatedly saved average men from their grosser follies; one mystic alone, Saint Benedict, by precept and influence, leavened the whole lump of the Dark Ages. Possibly he claims too exclusive a virtue for the mystic; surely the single-minded humanitarian serves as high a purpose. Who would be bold enough to decide between St. Benedict and Madame Curie? Or is single-mindedness itself akin to mysticism? But whatever the objections of historians or the arguments of philosophers, *Grey Eminence* is incontrovertibly the work of a thinker, whose undeviating integrity is one of the few spiritual torches left burning in the black-out.

104. Crane Brinton, review in *Saturday Review of Literature*

18 October 1941, xxiv, p. 17

(Clarence) Crane Brinton (1898–1969), famous professor of history at Harvard from 1923, was the author of many significant books, such as *The Shaping of the Modern Mind* (1953) and *The Fate of Man* (1961). See Introduction, p. 24.

The rather tame promise of the jacket, that this is 'a biography of Father Joseph, the right-hand man and collaborator of Cardinal Richelieu,' is indeed amply fulfilled. But just as no novel of Aldous Huxley's was ever simply a novel (there are indeed taxonomists of literature for whom no novel of his was ever properly a novel) so this, his first biography, is at the very least much more than a biography.

It is in part an account, in broad, but never text-bookish lines, of the power politics of the early seventeenth century which prepared the way for the French attempt to do what the Germans are attempting to do today—that is, to organize by force an international, or rather supernational, New Order in Europe; and more particularly, of the part played by the Capuchin monk Father Joseph, who had once been Baron de Maffliers, in those power politics. In this, the simplest part of the book, all Mr. Huxley's remarkable powers of narration and of lucid analysis of the 'determining conditions' of historical events come into play, and produce a historical work of a very high order, an order sometimes misleadingly called 'philosophical.' Some of his better-known gifts come also into play. The Aldous Huxley—or is it the old Adam?—who wrote *Antic Hay* can still describe the portraits of Queen Marie Médicis as revealing 'a large, fleshy, gorgeously bedizened barmaid.' The lover of paradox can still write of Father Joseph, 'combining in his own person the oddly assorted characters of Metternich and Savonarola, he could play the diplomatic game with twice the ordinary number of trump cards.' And the young modern whose learning was so delightfully, so scabrously, indecent is still able to turn that learning into satire—satire that, like much of Swift's, will be relished by some of his

337

poor, human readers as something rather less exalted than satire: witness, for instance, his description of the painting Rubens would have made of the miraculous cure of Cardinal Richelieu's piles by St. Fiacre, if only St. Fiacre's cure had worked.

But, as critics have noticed, something is happening to the bright young modern. The Voltaire of our Freudian age is turning mystic. *Grey Eminence* is in a part a discourse on mysticism, which, after a very brief account of the Hindu origins and early Christian development of the mystical tradition, dwells more at length on Father Joseph's teacher, Benet Fitch of Canfield, and on his contemporary, Pierre de Bérulle. Mr. Huxley, like his semantically innocent predecessors in the mystical tradition, who were unable to appeal to Professor Bridgman's *Logic of Modern Physics*, cannot break down entirely the wall which separates the mystical experience from the best and noblest and simplest of words.[1] Reduced to words, Mr. Huxley frequently uses Father Benet's phrase, 'active annihilation,' and his own 'one-pointedness' to attempt to describe the mystical experience of oneness with God.

That experience, he insists, is a fact, and subject therefore to what Professor Bridgman calls an operational test. The metaphysical and theological theories which mystics have often used to explain this experience (and sometimes to conceal from themselves the fact that they have not really achieved it in fullness) are not for him facts, but meaningless theories. Here, he maintains, Father Joseph went astray, so far astray that he could try to combine power politics with the mystic life; for under the influence of Father Benet's aberrant acceptance of certain Catholic dogmas as a part of the mystic life, he could identify the glory of France with the will of God. For the psychic goings-on, from miracles to plain catalepsy, which are frequently manifested in the behavior of the apprentice mystic, Mr. Huxley has almost as little regard as for metaphysical or theological theories; to these curiosities of the psychophysical mechanism 'the wiser mystics pay as little attention as possible.' There remains the long hard way to 'active annihilation' which the gifted few must learn by practice under the teaching of a master, as those gifted in the less important worldly skills, like painting or tennis-playing, must learn. Mere reading, even reading great works with high emotion, will no more make a mystic than such reading will make a tennis player.

---

[1] Percy Williams Bridgman (1882–1961), U.S. physicist who, in his *Logic of Modern Physics*, supported the operational point of view that it is meaningless to interpret physical concepts except as they are capable of observation.

A persistent hangover from his eighteenth-century upbringing tempts this reviewer to object to Mr. Huxley's use of Bridgman, that, although everybody, given the proper scientific education, can make the necessary operational test to determine whether what a physicist says is 'true,' very few people can make the necessary operational test to determine whether what a mystic says is 'true.' It is, however, plain that in fact ordinary people can no more be educated at present to perform such a test on the work of Professor Bridgman, who is a very good physicist, than they can be educated to perform such a test on the work of Swedenborg, who seems to have been a somewhat muddled mystic. Modern physics is at least as far from common sense experience as is mysticism. There seems indeed to be more agreement among physicists than among mystics. The systems of these latter seem almost as varied and clashing as the systems of philosophers. But according to Mr. Huxley, this is only because unwise mystics have been led to formulate systems. On the central core of their experience they are in discernible agreement. We shall probably have to grant Mr. Huxley his operational test, even though we cannot possibly make it ourselves. Certainly his is the most lucid exposition of mysticism available to the general reader.

Finally, *Grey Eminence*, like so much else that appears in print today, is concerned to find a way out of our present difficulties. Mr. Huxley despairs completely of politics. The road trod by Father Joseph's bare feet has led straight to totalitarian society, which Mr. Huxley apparently thinks as inevitable for the democracies as for the rest of the world. Our only hope is in small groups 'on the margin,' which, under the leadership of a few 'theocentric saints' will practise 'goodness politics' instead of power politics. Only small groups can practise such politics, since 'the quality of moral behaviour varies in inverse ratio to the number of human beings involved.' The immediate outlook is thus very dark. At most, such small groups can perform a certain antiseptic and antidotal function in our society, and preserve it from total ruin. 'Society can never be greatly improved, until such time as most of its members choose to become theocentric saints.' And cease to write books?

105. Richard V. Chase in *Partisan Review*

May–June 1942, ix, pp. 262–4

Richard Volney Chase, b. 1914, professor of English at Columbia University and widely published critic of American literature, has written books on Melville (1949), Dickinson (1951), and Whitman (1955), as well as *The American Novel and Its Tradition* (1957). See Introduction, p. 24.

The review is entitled 'Yogi-Bogey.'

Ostensibly *Grey Eminence* is a biography of Father Joseph, the aristocrat who became a Capuchin friar and later an agent and collaborator of Richelieu. By lending his sinister talents to the promotion of the Thirty Years War and the preparation of France for the tyrannical nationalism of Louis XIV, Father Joseph became one of the forgers of 'the long chain of crime and madness which binds the present world to its past.' As a biography the book is an only partly successful product of Huxley's now rather flaccid and uncritical intellectualism. But it is not meant to be primarily a biography. It is a piece of propaganda for the religious mysticism which Huxley and Gerald Heard have transplanted from the quagmires of British pacifism to the propitious atmosphere of Southern California. Heard's eight or nine volumes on the subject constitute the official historiography and teleology of the sect. Huxley, since the appearance of *Eyeless in Gaza* (1936), has functioned largely as a publicist for the new religion. In this latest book, the life and character of Father Joseph symbolize what Huxley and Heard take to be the dilemma of civilized man.

[Briefly recounts Heard's beliefs]

Huxley's Father Joseph symbolizes the fissured psyche of mankind in general. On the one hand he is the heir of the vaguely orientalized tradition of Christian mysticism. He has learned the method of self-annihilation and the affective reunion with God. He carries on the pacific philanthropy of the dedicated saint. But on the other hand he is the individualized man of action, the cynical manipulator who bribed the Swedish Protestants to fight the German Protestants and who was otherwise instrumental in furthering the war which killed one-third of the population of Germany. Father Joseph, to put it mildly, is a split personality.

The absurdity of this purely psychoanalytic explanation of history and human behavior becomes apparent when Huxley ascribes Father Joseph's antisocial conduct to a flaw in the technique of mysticism by the time it had come down to the early seventeenth century. Father Joseph has hallucinations of Christ on the cross in his moments of mystic trance (which seem, by the way, to border on a state of catalepsy). But since the purpose of the mystic experience is the annihilation not only of the self but also of all worldly imagery, Father Joseph's reunion with Ultimate Reality is never completely accomplished. In other words, Father Joseph's psyche remains 'fissured,' and *he* remains both a benevolent mystic and an immoral politician.

The lesson of *Grey Eminence* is that Father Joseph should have refused to have anything to do with political or military action. His true destiny was to be a 'theocentric saint,' detached from the criminalities of his time. Huxley proceeds to urge all those who are capable of the mystic experience to form a caste of saints (Heard calls them neo-Brahmins) who will have an 'antiseptic and antidotal function' in present-day society. The saints are to begin their religious teaching in small groups, finally, as their teaching and good works become accepted, bringing about the decentralization of government and industry into 'federated . . . local and functional' autonomies.

The most curious thing about this book is that it might have been written, in slightly different terms, by, let us say, a Buddhist who had only recently become acquainted with the social problems of Western culture and whose knowledge thereof consisted largely of a few epigrams. Why, for example, should we believe that even a 'well-intentioned' plan of political action 'must be pursued for its own sake, as an end in itself'? There is no evidence that political planning must degenerate into bureaucratic atrophy because it is the nature of political planning to do so. Huxley's use of his favorite scare-word 'political' is highly arbitrary: 'the great paradox of politics,' he says, is 'that political action is necessary and at the same time incapable of satisfying the needs which called it into existence.' But surely not many social thinkers are still psychologically narrow enough to maintain that purely political action, except perhaps in isolated cases, is capable of satisfying the diversity of human needs. And are we supposed to believe that the 'quality of moral behaviour varies in inverse ratio to the number of human beings involved'? That kind of catch-phrase ought to have expired along with the dogmatisms of the 'crowd psychology' books which came out of the first World War.

The altruistic morality and the social affection of the mystics are admirable; but from the time of the Buddhist heresy down to the Quakers, this altruism has been accompanied by various unsavory anti-speculative and anti-intellectual tendencies. Huxley follows the pattern, for he rejects not only power politics but *all* kinds of rationally-conceived social action. He attacks not only the grosser kinds of pragmatic thought but *all* 'analytic thinking and imagination,' for these prevent 'enlightenment.'

Huxley's early satirical novels had a fine strain of biological irony and a kind of materialist wit in them. We need a novelist of that sort to deal with some of the current aberrations of the bourgeois mind, such as religious mysticism, for instance.

106. William Somerset Maugham on Huxley

1944

(William) Somerset Maugham (1874–1965), a widely known novelist, playwright, and man of letters, was author of *Of Human Bondage* (1915) and *Cakes and Ale* (1930), among others. See Introduction, p. 4.

Excerpt from Maugham's *Introduction to Modern English and American Literature* (Philadelphia: Blakiston, 1944), pp. 335–6.

Aldous Huxley is an essayist whom I would be ready to rank with Hazlitt. The essay such as it was written in its great days has fallen into decay. Though essays are written still, they are either technical pieces on literary or other subjects, interesting chiefly to experts, or tittle-tattle about any subject upon which an author thinks he can write a couple of thousand words to fill the column of a newspaper or a page or two in a magazine. They bear reading in book form with difficulty.

If Charles Lamb, Hazlitt, Macaulay or Bagehot were writing now they would find it hard to get a hearing. The essayist needs character to begin with, then he needs an encyclopedic knowledge, he needs humour, ease of manner so that the ordinary person can read him without labour, and he must know how to combine entertainment with instruction. These qualifications are not easy to find. Aldous Huxley has them; so, in a much smaller way, had Virginia Woolf. To my mind both these writers have been more successful in this particular style than in the novel. It is singular that this should be so, for both seem to be possessed of many of the gifts necessary to write fiction. I hazard the suggestion that if Virginia Woolf did not write it so successfully as might have been expected, seeing how keen her observation was and how subtle her sense of character, it is because she had an inadequate acquaintance with life.

Aldous Huxley has greater gifts than she had, a vigour, and a versatility that were beyond her, and if he has never quite acquired the great position as a novelist that his talent seems to authorize, I think it is because of his deficient sympathy with human beings. The novelist must be able to get into the skin of the creatures of his invention, see with their eyes and feel with their fingers; but Aldous Huxley sees them like an anatomist. He dissects out their nerves, uncovers their arteries with precision, and peers into the ventricles of their hearts. The process gives rise in the reader to a certain discomfort. In saying this I do not wish to disparage Aldous Huxley's fiction; he has the priceless gift of readability, so that even though you balk at his attitude, you are held by his narrative skill and stimulated by his originality.

TIME MUST HAVE A STOP

August 1944

---

107. Thomas Mann, letter to Agnes E. Meyer

11 October 1944

Thomas Mann (1875–1955), famous German novelist and recipient of a Nobel Prize for Literature in 1929, had met Huxley in France in the 1930s (see *B*, I, pp. 275 ff.) and would renew the acquaintance in California during and after World War II. Mann had high praise for the writing of the earlier Huxley (Introduction, p. 17).

Extract from Mann's *Letters*, 1937–47 (Frankfurt, Germany: S. Fischer, 1963), pp. 392–4. The translation is by Ursula Bender. For another remark by Mann on this novel, see Introduction, p. 23.

Pacific Palisades, California
1550 San Remo Drive

Little or nothing can be said against your Huxley criticism, sharp as it is, and I am glad that I too have decidedly sought distance from the spirit and sentiment of the book—and even of the man in general. This spirit is extremely western European, mellow, decadent, as you quite correctly say. In Russia he would be quickly brought to reason, and the fact that America rejects him can only be applauded. It would not be desirable for this mystical defeatism to find acceptance here. I, who have a certain weakness for the decadent and am also at home in morbidity, with a kind of knowing pride—I am irritated by the complete insensitivity of the reviews which I saw to the charms of the book *as a novel*, charms which you cannot deny either. The telephone scene with the former mistress who reads to him from old letters at the one end, and at the other the present girl friend in the room; the death of the uncle; the entire intrigue with the desired evening suit, and the moralistic entanglements from which the boy can no longer free himself—all that and still more is new, daring, interesting, [full] of grating liveliness. One must be a very convinced moralist simply to reject it. And yet, I do not deny that my morality was offended with every step. Even the fact that the author exploits his hate of all fleshly life, so that through the very presentation of the pleasures of the flesh he seeks to make himself attractive as a novelist, is somewhat annoying. But his cold attitude toward everything that burns under our skin, the things we hate and love, is truly deplorable. An Italian professor who leaves his oppressed country and goes into exile must not necessarily be presented as a fool; there must be something to him. And the way in which the exhaustion and disappointment of a social fighter is narrated does not show bitter pessimism, it is no indictment of a world so difficult to improve, but is a barking ridicule of the fool who would not rather think of the salvation of his own soul.

It is not at all the book of a present day Englishman, but it appears rather to have been written ten years ago, when the world did not and would not yet understand the events in Italy and Germany. The first supposition of the book is that a rich British family in Mussolini's Italy, completely indifferent to everything going on there, leads its aesthetically decorative parasitic existence. The expelled anti-fascist must live in England, and the English in turn live in beautiful Italy. One misses any feeling for the dullness which lies therein, and with which no highly ascetic superiority over the world can be reconciled.

But I am using up paper and time to tell you things which you anyhow know and have felt as I did. The book is exciting because it is talented and, from the literary point of view, it is an engagingly advanced accomplishment. But it is reprehensible, you are right in that. Only, I myself do not have a very good conscience as far as the subject of morbidity and decadence is concerned. I have in this matter clearly several points on my score board ever since the *Buddenbrooks*; *Death in Venice* is not altogether pure either, and now *Dr. Faustus* concerns itself with matters which again are not entirely healthy in content. . . .

108. Edmund Wilson, review in *New Yorker*

2 September 1944, xx, pp. 64–6

Edmund Wilson (1895–1972), influential American critic and essayist, was awarded America's Presidential Medal of Freedom in 1963. Among his many books are *Axel's Castle* (1931), *Patriotic Gore* (1962), and *The Dead Sea Scrolls* (1947–69).

The review was reprinted under the title 'Aldous Huxley in the World Beyond Time' in Wilson's *Classics and Commercials: A Literary Chronicle of the Forties* (New York: Farrar, Straus, 1950), pp. 209–14. See Introduction, p. 23.

Aldous Huxley's new novel, *Time Must Have a Stop*, is a good deal better than his last one, *After Many a Summer Dies the Swan*. For one thing, he has returned to Europe for his characters and his settings, and he is much more successful with the English intellectuals in the London and Florence of the twenties than he was, in the earlier book, with an American millionaire and his hangers-on. His people, in many cases, are still conventional figures of satire: the disgusting voluptuary who lives in Italy and talks about the art of life, the rude old rich lady who has a pet Pomeranian and raps out imperious orders, and an up-to-date version of the hard Gradgrind[1] parent, who is a socialist instead of a utilitarian; but Huxley does not run here the same risk of an obvious and purely external caricature that he did in his California fantasia. Here there is much more that is piquant in the social observation, much more wit in the talk and the unspoken thoughts of the characters, much more novelty of invention in the action. And along with this there goes an improvement in his handling of the religious element which has lately come to figure in his fiction. Huxley's peculiar version of the life of contemplation and revelation was expounded in *After Many a Summer* by a boring non-satirical character who read homilies to the other

[1] Thomas Gradgrind in Dickens's *Hard Times*.

347

characters with an insufferable air of quiet authority and who constantly made the reader feel that it would have been better if he, too, had been satirically treated as a typical California crank. But in this new novel these matters have been dramatized and incorporated in the story on the same level as the other material. The voluptuary dies of a stroke, and we follow him into the non-sensual world. We see him drift about the fringes of the Divine within its gravitational field; return at moments to communicate with his friends through the agency of an extremely stupid medium, who garbles what he is trying to say; and finally, shrinking from absorption in God, get himself born back into humanity in the body of a baby expected by the wife of one of the other characters. Now, one may not be prepared to accept Huxley's views about spiritualistic phenomena and the Platonic rebirth of souls, but the whole thing has been given plausibility—though queer, it is never creepy—by treating the disembodied vicissitudes of Eustace Barnack's soul in the same dry or droll way as the adventures of his consciousness while still in the flesh. The result of threading this in with the doings of the characters who are still alive is an effect which must be new in fiction. In its essentially rather dismal and dark-brown way, *Time Must Have a Stop* is quite a brilliant performance.

It is difficult, however, for Huxley to celebrate convincingly in a novel his present ideals of abnegation and withdrawal from the things of the world, just as it was for T. S. Eliot, in *Murder in the Cathedral*, to celebrate the ideal of humility. These are virtues which—unlike some others: courage and brotherly love, for example—do not lend themselves to being illustrated in public by clever and accomplished writers, long admired and much in view. Just as Eliot's Thomas Becket becomes superior to the verge of snobbery in his perfect achievement of meekness, so Bruno Rontini, the contemporary saint of Huxley's latest novel, seems sometimes attainted by the smart virtuosity of so many of Huxley's other characters in his insight into other people's states of mind, his power to forecast what they are going to do and an ability to outmaneuver them morally which gives almost the impression of scoring off them—all talents that have something in common with those of the infallible detective that figures in so much mystery fiction. Aldous Huxley sharply criticizes Dante for carrying up into Heaven his partisan antagonisms and his pride, but the danger with Huxley himself is that he will turn Buddha, Pascal and St. John of the Cross into another neat performance for the salon. It must, however, be said that his descriptions of the dissociated trancelike states in which his characters sometimes feel or seem about to feel a super-corporeal union with God have a certain sound of authenticity and convince one that they are based on experience.

One's objection to what, at this point in his career, can only be called the moral teaching of Huxley is not that it is not derived from real states of exaltation, but that these states of exaltation themselves imply an incomplete experience of the earthly possibilities of human life. Huxley's satire has always been founded not only upon a distaste for humanity but also upon a real incapacity for understanding most of the things that seemed to other people important and exciting. It used to be fashionable to call him 'intelligent,' but he was never particularly intelligent. His habit of reading the *Encyclopedia Britannica* gives the quality of his appetite for facts and ideas; his interest in the great intellectual movements that were bringing most light in his own time was on exactly the same level as his interest in a twelfth-century heresy, a queer species of carnivorous plant, a special variety of Romanesque architecture or a Greek poet surviving in fragments. Freud, Lenin, Einstein, Joyce—he sometimes expressed about them, in his casual essays, opinions as obtuse and philistine as those of the ordinary Fleet Street journalist. The new paths that they opened, the new hopes that they woke, were not opened or awakened for Huxley. For Huxley, in his satirical novels, the man whose imagination was aroused by, say, the quantum theory did not appear any more interesting than the old-fashioned pre-quantum mechanist, or the connoisseur of abstract painting than the fancier of Victorian bric-a-brac.

For the satirist, of course, this attitude may provide a basis for valid work. The Lilliputians of Swift seem too little, no matter what they do; the Bouvard and Pécuchet of Flaubert (invoked by one of the characters of *Time Must Have a Stop*) remain numskulls no matter what sciences or arts they think they are experimenting with. But Huxley is not, like Swift or Flaubert, complete and self-sufficient as a satirist. He has not even had the real love of writing, the power to express himself through art, of Evelyn Waugh or Ronald Firbank, the novels of both of whom may very well last longer than Huxley's. Merely a manipulator of Punch-and-Judy figures, he has inevitably to shake them off his hands and to use these hands in pulpit gestures as he comes forward to preach his way of life; and in this role his defects of intelligence again become fatally clear. We realize that his readiness to reject the world is due to his not knowing what is in it. That mixed and immature humanity which has been handled by the great thinkers of his time—Huxley was not impressed by what they had been able to create from it because he had never had the full sense of what humanity was like and, hence, of what it might become. His whole ascetic system, for example, is arrived at by way of the conclusion that 'the flesh,' though theoretically to be tolerated as a device for perpetuating the species, can never, through sexual selection or through the idealizations of love, become a part of our higher activities. In this novel, sex is never represented as anything but cold or perverse. There is nothing beyond momentary pleasure in any of the amorous relations of *Time Must Have a Stop*. Of the fact that the relations between men and women are involved in everything humanity builds—in the forms of art, in the structure of thought, in the incitement to achievement and leadership—you will get no inkling from Huxley. This would be perfectly all right in a satire which did not purport to be anything else—the satirist has always the license to turn down the flame of life in order to let us take account more grimly of the mechanical aspect of the fixtures and the sordidness of the surrounding room; but it is very misleading in a fable which pretends to bring us solemnly to consider the fundamental problems of human behavior and destiny.

Aldous Huxley would probably say, in reply to the objection above, that it does not really matter what we build on this earth. Our retort would be: How does he know? since he has taken little part in the building. His inability to build solidly in his novels is itself an evidence of this. You cannot live in them; the author himself has not lived in them. He has always found it easy to drop them in order to report on his spiritual progress. The epilogue to *Time Must Have a Stop* consists mostly of a series of *pensées*,[1] the journal of the central character, a poet, who is schooling himself in the discipline of self-renunciation. These last pages have a terseness of writing and an accent of moral sincerity that one has hardly found before in Huxley. But what sort of general validity can be expected of a set of principles derived from the diminished and distorted world invented by the author of this novel? Since the story is admittedly a satire, it should follow that a religious system deduced from the conduct of its characters is either not wholly serious or not susceptible of wide application.

[1] 'Reflections.'

109. Orville Prescott, review in *Yale Review*

Autumn 1944, xxxiv [n.s.], p. 189

Orville Prescott, b. 1906, was co-editor of the *New York Times Book of the Times* (1942–66) and has written such books as *The Undying Past* (1961) and *History as Literature* (1971).

Prescott discusses Huxley's book and Thomas Mann's *Joseph the Provider* as examples of the declining talent of each novelist.

. . . Mr. Huxley was for many years the ablest literary representative of the post-war disillusionment, the scientific materialism and moral cynicism which between wars were so intellectually fashionable. With impressive scholarship and brilliant satire he ridiculed a decadent and dying world, often not so much with the story-telling or character-creating purpose of a novelist as with the rage and scorn of a moralist. Yet since Mr. Huxley accepted the a-moral standards of his characters he really had no grounds for his fury. But in recent years Mr. Huxley has seen visions and become a convert to a private mystic faith. His last three or four books have been contrite attempts to live down his earlier ones. Unfortunately, though spiritually elevated, they have been dull and mediocre.

In *Time Must Have a Stop* Mr. Huxley has provided a case history of himself. It is a novel about a gay old dog, a selfish sensualist and aesthete, who represents the earlier Huxley, and about a youthful poet, a saintly Italian anti-fascist, and the ghost of the cynical reprobate in heaven, who stand for the reformed Huxley. They all have learned to believe in the baffling mystical abstractions of Mr. Huxley's new faith. But, ironically enough, it is the sinner who is amusing and likable and the reformed characters who are dull and irritating. So *Time Must Have a Stop* is a clumsy failure as fiction; and much of its mystic message is incomprehensible and even a little bit silly. Aldous Huxley has found his own peculiar path to paradise, but most readers who may try to follow him will be certain to lose their way.

110. Theodore Spencer, review in *Atlantic Monthly*

September 1944, clxxiv, p. 129

Theodore Spencer (1902–49), poet, editor, critic, taught English at Harvard University from 1927 to 1949 and wrote, among others, *Shakespeare and the Nature of Man* (1942). See Introduction, p. 23.

Readers of Aldous Huxley's last two novels will not be greatly surprised by this one; to borrow a phrase from Somerset Maugham, it is 'the mixture as before.' There is the familiar Huxley hero, who, in the words of Ovid, sees and understands the better, but follows the worse; there are the epicurean sensualist and the disillusioned siren, the background of a superficially cultured but futile society, the hatred and irony expended on lust and old age; and—most important of all for Mr. Huxley—there is the sage, the man with a vision of universal truth, to whose precepts the previously weak hero is converted at the end.

[Summarizes the role of Sebastian]

No more than in *Eyeless in Gaza* and in *After Many a Summer Dies the Swan* has Mr. Huxley in this book discovered how to fuse the form of the novel with the material of the didactic essay. The narrative, to be sure, is never dull: some of the characters, especially Uncle Eustace, are very well done, and the sequence of events concerning Sebastian is cleverly manipulated; but for the most part, the people move on strings, against a backdrop we can hardly believe in.

The major weakness of the book, as a novel, is that Mr. Huxley has neglected to write the essential part of it. If we are to be convinced that the maimed and reformed Sebastian of 1944 is the same person as the self-centered adolescent of 1928, and that the change from the one to the other is inevitable, we need a great deal more than the brief flashbacks over those sixteen years which are all that Mr. Huxley gives us.

Mr. Huxley has never seriously attempted the novelist's most difficult task, the presentation of a slow development in a chief character; his people have nearly always been fixed types, almost 'humors' in the Jonsonian sense. Here we feel that his solution of his problem is perfunctory—as perfunctory as his use, three times in the course of the story, of the rubber arm of coincidence stretched to the limit.

The exposition of Mr. Huxley's religious philosophy, presented in Sebastian's notebooks but insufficiently related to his character, thus comes as a postscript to the novel, not as part of the novel itself. But earlier in the story Mr. Huxley does try to relate his philosophy to character, and what he does is the most original and ambitious thing in the book. When the self-indulgent Uncle Eustace dies in the W.C. we have a description of his state of mind after death. But even this part of the book lacks intensity, and the apparent hell of Uncle Eustace—which is not very hellish after all, since he does not seem to be unhappy in it—is in the long run no more convincing than the conversion of Sebastian to his vision of heaven.

It would appear from this book that the world he now sees about him is unavailable to Mr. Huxley as a novelist; the placing of his main action in 1928 is as significant as his refusal to deal with events of more recent date. Indeed his philosophic emphasis on eternity, which allows him to look at the human level of 'time and craving' only as something to flee from, makes an impossible basis for novel-writing; and as long as he insists upon it—as his conviction tells him he must—his novels, like this one, can only describe a set of futile mechanisms writhing on sand.

111. Anne Fremantle, review in *Commonweal*

15 September 1944, xl, pp. 519–20

Anne Fremantle served as associate editor of *Commonweal* 1947–52, has done considerable work for the United Nations, and has often reviewed books for the *New York Times*.

The opening paragraphs, here omitted, discuss Eustace's post-mortem experiences as 'very touching' accounts of Huxley's personal thought.

. . . But moving and articulate from the spiritual viewpoint as they may be, from the purely technical, writer's angle, Mr. Huxley is ill-advised in attempting to describe what goes on when Uncle Eustace meets the Trinity. . . . By describing as the experiences of Eustace Barnack after death what are much more likely those of Aldous Huxley very much alive, the latter detracts from their verisimilitude, and by thus deliberately paraphrasing his own experiences, he needlessly denigrates them. Technically again, he should not draw his moral from Sebastian's note-book nor from Bruno's sayings. Wilfred Owen said, once for all, that 'the poetry is in the pity'—or should be. The pity should *not* be in the poetry. Thus this is a bad novel, because the moral, which stems magnificently out of the story of the Degas drawing, is rubbed through a hair-sieve both in the middle and at the end of the tale. Sebastian's dinner-jackets would have made a superb short story, *à la hauteur*[1] of de Maupassant or even Dostoyevsky, if only Mr. Huxley could have let well alone and allowed the story itself to point its own ghastly truth, which is made amply clear by the inevitable sequence which follows on the boy's heartless, selfish, but unthinking act. The impossibility of reparation would then have stood out most clearly, and the novel would not only have been a great story but also a tremendous piece of apologetics. For the difficulty is always to make the sequence significant. And that Mr. Huxley's genius had done. But what his

[1] 'On the level.'

genius created, his moralizing overlaid. This is a mistake the New Testament never makes. In the parables, Christ is not reported as having rubbed in the moral. He asks His disciples, do you understand? And sometimes begins or ends by saying, 'The Kingdom is like this,' or by questioning, 'Which do you think. . . ?' But He never labors His point. Mr. Huxley, who has absorbed so many of the moral lessons of the Gospels, needs to pay closer attention to their consummate artistry. He has made great strides toward understanding something of the Divine compassion; is it too much to suggest he should also try to comprehend something of the Divine wit? 'If the blind lead the blind, shall they not both fall into the ditch?' was surely not said without irony.

The average reader, wading through much unnecessary nastiness and muck, finds it impossible also not to wish that Mr. Huxley had got one stage further. After loving human beings—and all other creatures— for God; after loving God in His creatures, human and other; it is necessary to come to love those creatures—even oneself—in God. (This is the knowledge Bernanos's Country Priest arrives at on his deathbed.) If only Mr. Huxley could do this, he would be less tangled in the terrible love-hate of repulsion-attraction that would be comic if it were not so nauseating. All the oldest Freudian gambits are in his new novel, from the ' "goats" pills of excrement' to the Eliot-esque tart's rubber corset, and even to *Fräulein* with the *töpfchen* (chamberpot).

355

112. Unsigned review in *TLS*

24 March 1945, p. 137

The review is entitled 'Time's Fool.' See Introduction, p. 23.

He who rides on a tiger, runs the Chinese proverb, can never dismount. So, unhappily, it seems to be with Mr. Huxley since he took to a ravening philosophy of the non-human, of more than mortal knowledge and blessedness. There was a time, before he was fully aware that time could stand still, when Mr. Huxley as a novelist had some patience with human nature's daily food; up to *Those Barren Leaves* he had not yet exhausted a novelist's interest, admittedly never very warm and sympathetic in his case, in the ordinary run of mankind. But from *Point Counter Point* onwards disgust with mere humanity, springing in some measure perhaps from physical disgust, seemed to take ever stronger possession of him, and the bleak cerebral pessimism which it evidently bred has grown chillier and chillier in successive volumes of fiction. At the same time, however, some compensatory instinct in Mr. Huxley, it would appear, has sought the impersonal assurance of the absolute. This assurance he has discovered in the mystical apprehension of eternity. With it all, in his progress Mr. Huxley as novelist has proved unwilling to forgo the youthful pleasure of cynicism. There is, if one may say so, something a little ghoulish in the imaginative use he makes of the doctrine of non-attachment.

His latest novel has neither the intellectual range nor the comic scope of its predecessor, *After Many a Summer*. In its light and sometimes not too cruel amusement, in its aestheticism and piquant curiosity of mind, the book has something of the quality of his earliest novels of all. It exhibits Mr. Huxley's learning, his gift for limericks, an acute sense of the craft of poetry and a genuine power of modern poetic phrase, a flow of ribald expression and more than a feast of dark and desperate conclusions about sex. The characters are ingeniously posed, though there is not a great deal in the way of the creation of character, which has never been one of Mr. Huxley's strong points; with a single exception

356

only, the people in his story have all been encountered in his previous novels, some of them more than once. They argue less on this occasion, however, and are more embroiled in familiar circumstance, and that is all to the good. Altogether *Time Must Have a Stop*, in which the ease, flexibility and finish of Mr. Huxley's prose style are much to be admired, is a work of impressively light and various accomplishment. Light and various, that is, in its tenebrous and single-minded horror of human existence.

[Summarizes the plot and describes the roles of the characters]

And the conclusion of it all? Religion and politics—politics especially —are silliness and murder. Education is stupidity and destruction. Science produces lies and imbecility. Art alone saves life in our common state of spiritual ignorance and squalor from complete meaninglessness, and art dissolves into nothingness in awareness of the Intelligible Light and unity with the divine Ground. All this is, for Mr. Huxley, the consummation of a deal of cynical japing and gibing in his latest novel. It seems a little odd that so incommunicable a sense of indwelling superiority should lead him to write a novel about human beings at all.

113. Cyril Connolly, review in *New Statesman and Nation*

7 April 1945, xxxix [n.s.], pp. 228–9

For a biographical note see No. 47. The review is entitled 'Onward Christian Brahmins!' See Introduction, p. 23.

This is Mr. Huxley's best novel for a very long time. He has recaptured the gaiety, the conciseness, the passionate interest in human beings, in fact the novelist's attitude which seemed to have eluded him. *Time Must Have a Stop* is admirably constructed; character after character is introduced with casual informality, their repercussions on each other follow with the intricacy of a chess opening. The scene is Florence, and all Huxley's youthful love and knowledge of Italy reappear. The book is bright and sunpierced and there is a happiness such as is seldom found in his later work in descriptions like that of the young poet's arrival at the villa in a car by night, or his morning meditation in the garden. And an unfailing sense of comedy. Except for too many flashes of the old vulgarity in style Mr. Huxley seems to have been born again.

[Gives a brief summary of the plot]

All the usual Huxleyan characters are here (including a particularly well-drawn rich old woman, Eustace's mother-in-law) but spring-cleaned, freshened up, recreated through a firmer satiric draughtsman-ship, a wiser intuition, a deeper moral sense. The social comedy is magnificently reinforced by the spiritual tragedy. Heaven now exists as well as earth. Uncle Eustace dies of heart failure in the lavatory, but in chapter 13 his sensations after death are described in a remarkable piece of writing, an experiment which aims at indicating a completely depersonalised experience in appropriate language. By a most ingenious use of the séance a relationship is maintained between Uncle Eustace and the living. The conflict goes on.

The only technical flaw in the novel is the introduction into the epilogue of Sebastian's note-book, which is the inevitably Huxleyan device for releasing his didactic essayist vein. Deeply interesting though these reflections are they spoil the objectiveness of the rest of the novel and slow down its tempo.

As a work of propaganda *Time Must Have a Stop* is much more than a novel. It is a religious tract. The doctrines of the Hollywood com-munity of mystics are now bearing fruit, and the Sacred Books are appearing. They include the recent works of Gerald Heard, Isherwood's translation of the Gita, Maugham's *Razor's Edge* and Huxley's *Grey Eminence*.

[Discusses 'the new California religion']

The new faith produces good books. So does Existentialism, the Devil's Brew which Central Europe has served up. In Huxley's tract the good triumph, at least in inward happiness, and the wicked are punished. Uncle Eustace in fact literally goes to Hell. On what grounds? He dies at 53 because he is a frivolous and self-indulgent sensualist; but because he refuses to let his personality be liquidated after death and rejects absorption in the Divine Ground he is condemned to eternal remorse and the repetition of inane blasphemies and sensualities with reincarnation as the only alternative. Rarely does a modern novelist condemn a character to Hell and describe his torment. Let us look closer at the wicked Eustace, and anatomise his sins. We will take a typical vice and follow it through the tractarian treatment.

[Cites several examples of Eustace's sensual love of brandy and cigars]

. . . The onslaught on Eustace is almost neurotic. Three brandies and two glasses of champagne will not kill a man of 53, even with a Romeo and Juliet thrown in—and the abstemious Eustace avoids cocktails, whiskey, port, beer and aperitives. A solid breakfast—yes—but a two-course lunch and a three-course dinner. Perhaps a little too much cream, but let anyone who can truly say that they would refuse such a day's rations cast the first stone!

Why is Eustace really punished? Because he is immensely dangerous. Beauty is very dangerous to God. Jehovah in the Talmud forbade the Jews to look at a tree. Aesthetics are offensive to mysticism, hedonism to Christianity. Art is its own religion, which gradually develops in its worshippers a system of ethics and a set of beliefs; one cannot love art and not be changed. Huxley has known this and makes Eustace not a Flaubert but a rich dilettante who collects bric-à-brac, can't finish a book, jumbles up masterpieces with clothes and cooking, a Mr. Norris in the *train-de-luxe*. The caricaturing of him, the faith of Lucretius and Montaigne, behind which he shelters, is caricatured also. And in the end Eustace is punished by the Light for something very like blasphemy, and a Ground which punishes for that is all too human! Huxley is manifesting the intolerance which is often the first visible consequence of a religious conversion.

'The habit of sensuality and pure aestheticism,' writes Sebastian in his notebook, 'is a process of God-proofing. To indulge in it is to become a spiritual mackintosh, shielding the little corner of time, of which one was the centre, from the last drop of eternal reality.'

But they are not one habit but two habits, and to ignore the connection between the pure love of beauty and the apprehension of eternal reality is to deny the whole contribution of Art, of Greece, and Chartres and Rome and Byzantium. A denial which reflects itself in many dreadful phrases, in Uncle Eustace in Hell, 'the iron teeth combing and carding the very substance of his being. For ever and ever, excruciatingly'.

As a moralist Huxley uses characters to illustrate vices. Mrs. Ockham with her mother-love, Mrs. Thwale with her lust, the mother-in-law clinging selfishly to life, Walter Barnack to left-wing publicity, Mr. Weil to art-dealing—they are one-dimensional, and their pleasures but serve to illustrate their retribution. The warm air of healthy instinct, of affectionate kindness, of famous hope and unconscious delight in existence which makes up the human climate is something which Mr. Huxley has always disliked and ignored. Hence his overestimate of the extent of human misery. Yet for its sake people go on living. Mr. Huxley may damn them for it, but we have no evidence that the Divine Ground will. Mr. Huxley puts Sensuality as his besetting sin, but he suffers from one which is far more dangerous in a Reformer— Dyspepsia.

THE PERENNIAL PHILOSOPHY

September 1945

---

114. Signe Toksvig, review in *NYTBR*

30 September 1945, p. 3

Signe Kirstine Toksvig, b. 1891, has written books on Hans Christian Andersen (1934) and Emanuel Swedenborg (1948), and has edited *American Rainbow* (1970).

The review is entitled 'Aldous Huxley's Prescriptions for Spiritual Myopia.'

A young American who had had a close look at what this war was like, wrote home that, in regard to his plans for the future, he considered it at least as important to try to find out about God as to go into the insurance business. He also told his startled parents that he might carry on his search in a community of Quakers, a Franciscan monastery, a neo-Buddhistic monastery and the Chicago Divinity School.

If his object were to see what the best of the higher religions have to offer intelligent, literate—and desperate—inquirers, he could now find it out with fewer transportation problems by reading Aldous Huxley's *The Perennial Philosophy*. . . .

. . . [I]t is important to say that even an agnostic, even a behaviorist-materialist, model 1925, can read this book with joy. It is the masterpiece of all anthologies.

As Mr. Huxley has proved before, he can find and frame rare beauty in literature, and here, long before Freud, writers are quoted who combine beauty with profound psychology. Take Fénelon on simplicity:

[Quotes Chapter VI, pp. 130–1]

This anthology is above all a masterpiece of discrimination. Without it we might have missed this subtle clarity, or the vigor of Eckhart, the morning freshness of Traherne, or most of the writers both of East and West whom Mr. Huxley has brought together, men and women who are able to present goodness without inducing reverent stupor.

But Aldous Huxley is there, too. In what he calls the 'connective tissue' between the citations he has really written a book, perhaps a third of the big volume. It is the peak of his pilgrimage. While the old whip of scorn cracks now and then at 'ordinary nice unregenerate people,' the 'slime' of their too personal loves, and their daydreaming on the sofa after tea instead of making more of an effort, yet the Huxley that emerges is himself a sublimated man, in deadly earnest about saving values.

[Summarizes in detail several aspects of Huxley's position]

. . . The young American who wanted to ask different religions what they could tell him about God was on the right track. As we most awesomely are what we believe, it is not too much to say that 'theological imperialism is a menace to world peace.' There is still, Mr. Huxley says, 'a certain blandly bumptious provincialism' even among learned Christians, which makes them feel and write as if nobody else had ever thought about these subjects. For this there is no excuse now that translations are available of the sacred books of the East. The reign of violence will never come to an end 'until the adherents of every religion renounce the idolatrous time-philosophies with which, in their own particular faiths, the Perennial Philosophy of Eternity has been overlaid,' and 'until political pseudo-religions which are ready to commit every iniquity in the present for the sake of the future' have been rejected.

In *The Art of Seeing* Mr. Huxley told how to cure physical myopia. Since spiritual myopia is no less common, perhaps Mr. Huxley in *The Perennial Philosophy* has, at this time, written the most needed book in the world.

115. C. E. M. Joad, review in
New Statesman and Nation

5 October 1946, xxxii [n.s.], pp. 249–50

Cyril Edwin Mitchinson Joad (1891–1953), author of several books on religion and moral philosophy, was Head of the Department of Philosophy at Birkbeck College, University of London, 1930–53.

The review is entitled 'Huxley Gone Sour.' See Introduction, p. 24.

The Perennial Philosophy is a mine of curious and erudite learning. The running commentary is clear and vivid and there are a number of first-rate discussions of such topics as time, eternity, prayer, spiritual exercises, psychic influences, charity, solitude and so on. Nobody who reads the commentary can fail to recognize that he is in the presence of a mind both profound and acute, although he may find it hard not to raise the eyebrows of a mild surprise at finding Huxley believing apparently in the curative power of relics and idols, in spiritual presences incarnated in sacramental objects and in the objectification of ideas and memories.

The critic of this philosophy is placed in an invidious position, since if its conclusions are correct, nobody is in a position to assess its value who has not enjoyed the experiences on which it is based. In this sense all criticism by non-initiates is a form of question begging.

There is, nevertheless, one point which, without begging too many questions, one may, I think, legitimately raise. What, precisely, does the position in its most moderate statement assert? On the logical side, that this, the natural order, does not provide the principles of its own interpretation; that, in fact, the explanation of this world must be sought elsewhere; on the moral and aesthetic, that what is good and beautiful has its origin and derives its significance from an order of absolute reality which is other than the beautiful things and good actions in which it is manifested, with the corollary that, as poets and saints have sensed, the beauty of the sunset always means more than its beauty and the worth of the selfless act more than its worth; on the metaphysical, that there is a reality which lies beyond the changing show of facts on which our minds feed and the stimuli which evoke our senses and our feelings; psychologically, that this reality is immanent in ourselves, so that it is in our moments of spiritual activity that we both become most completely ourselves and approach most closely to the reality which is beyond ourselves.

I have stated all this as moderately as I can, stated it in a form in which many, I think, would be prepared to subscribe to it, and in which it may well be true . . . [sic] But it is not thus that Huxley states it. There is a 'thus saith the Lord' air about this book which tends to put up even the sympathetic back. It never seems to occur to the author that he may be mistaken. Hence, I find it difficult to refrain from making the charges of dogmatism, and intolerance. Huxley is dogmatic because, the universe being after all unknown, he supplies the place of knowledge by converting other people's conjectures into dogmas. The sole justification of existence, he seems to imply, is the glorification of God; while to be good is to annihilate oneself in the 'Divine Ground'. Perhaps; perhaps not. But even if this is true, isn't he altogether too hard on the frailties of our ordinary mortal flesh? Huxley praises the virtue of love but he shows little signs of practising it. Throughout the book the ordinary, sensual unthinking man is castigated and condemned. His pleasures are those of the pig, his thoughts, those of the imbecile, his ways of behaving 'generally silly', 'often insane', 'sometimes criminal'. He is accused of eating too much, eating the wrong things, worrying about money, craving for excitement and stimulation, wanting to succeed, liking gorgeous architecture, elaborate ornaments, rich colours, and so on . . . [sic] It is, perhaps, otiose to point out that this attitude does not endear the religion which it purports to illustrate; irrelevant to inquire whether this isn't after all a very odd and maybe a rather cruel universe in which the right life, the intended life, the prescribed life can be had by only a very few people—even the animals, it seems, have gone astray—and in which pretty well everything we want to do is wrong. Huxley is entitled not to care whether *The Perennial Philosophy* attracts ordinary men or whether his mode of exposition is calculated to commend it, and the universe may well be both odd and cruel. Nevertheless, I find it difficult to deny myself the pleasure of asking him who he is that he should feel entitled to bear so hardly and to speak so contemptuously of the great mass of his fellow creatures, or what it is he knows that he should be so blind to the fun, the sunlight, the treats, the jolly coarseness and warm-hearted insufficiencies of ordinary life. . . .

I hope he won't mind my mixing my metaphors to the extent of taking the words out of his own mouth to hit him below his own belt. 'The art of life consisted for the Greeks in giving every god his due . . . no god must be cheated and none overpaid.' Thus, we 'make the best of the world and its loveliness while we can—at any rate during the years of youth and strength'. That is what Huxley wrote in *Do What You Will* in 1929, as a 'worshipper of life who accepts all the conflicting facts of existence'. And *how* he went for Plato, for making Socrates say that the philosopher won't value sex or eating or drinking or the 'business of looking after the body'. On Socrates' phrase, 'the soul withdraws itself as far as it can from all association and contact with the body and reaches out after truth by itself', he comments, 'With what results? Deprived of its nourishment, the soul grows thin and mangy, like the starved lion. . . .' 'Poor brutes!' he goes on, 'we cry at the sight of such extraordinary and lamentable souls as those of Kant, of Newton, of Descartes, "Why aren't they given enough to eat?" '

I remember being rather shocked at this at the time on the ground that it seemed to me to set too much store by the earthy Paradise, to value too highly the tripe and the hogwash. Yet if a choice must be made, the unregenerate Huxley of sixteen years ago seems to be infinitely preferable to the sour-faced moralist of to-day. The trouble with Huxley is and always has been intellectual whole-hoggery. Ideas will go to his head. He should read Aristotle on moderation.

116. W. R. Inge on Huxley's perennial philosophy

Philosophy, April 1947, xxii, pp. 66–70

The Very Reverend William Ralph Inge (1860–1954), extensively published philosopher, theologian, and essayist, was Dean of St Paul's, 1911–34. He wrote some widely popular articles as regular contributor to the *Evening Standard* (1921–46) and authored several books, such as *The Church in the World* (1927) and *God and the Astronomers* (1933). See Introduction, p. 24.

Inge's agreement with Huxley on several essential points indicates the respect Huxley's position commanded from some important philosophers (see Jacques Maritain, Introduction, p. 36). Several opening paragraphs on 'syncretistic religion' and Wilbur Urban's *The Intelligible World* are omitted.

And now we have a book by Aldous Huxley, duly labelled *The Perennial Philosophy*. The development in the thought of this brilliant writer towards a spiritual religion was already apparent in his *Ends and Means* (1937). He is now quite definitely a mystical philosopher. The same tendency is manifest in other independent thinkers. To myself, as is natural, it appears as one of the very few encouraging signs in the dismal age in which our lot is cast. But the perennial philosophy, for Huxley, goes much further back than Thomas Aquinas, further than Origen and Plotinus, further than St. Paul and the Fourth Gospel. It is the philosophy of India, and of the whole mystical tradition, which is fundamentally the same in all countries and behind all creeds. So at least our author thinks.

[Discusses the history of 'the higher religion' and concludes that one fact is well established: 'The flowering times of humanity follow the fusion of two cultures.']

. . . There is no give and take now between Moslems and Hindus in India, nor even between separated branches of the Christian Church. And yet it may not be too late, if both sides realize that their unwillingness to learn is doing them both harm. It has been said that Christianity and Buddhism are both suffering from their refusal to respect each other. Radhakrishnan's stimulating book on Eastern and Western thought gives a long list of European and American writers who have acknowledged great obligations to Indian philosophy, and this writer himself, like Rabindranath Tagore, has not studied European philosophy in vain. Much, however, remains to be done, and, as Huxley sees clearly, the rapprochement must be through mystical religion, the communion of the soul with God, which is religion in its essential foundation.

[Summarizes some leading points of the book]

This book, enriched by copious and well chosen quotations from the masters of the spiritual life, is probably the most important treatise on mysticism that we have had for many years. But many will think that it is more Buddhist than Christian. Crucial questions suggest themselves. Was the Christian revelation a mere disclosure of timeless truths, or do happenings in time affect supertemporal reality? Is the conflict with evil a real battle, still undecided? Is the growth of soul into spirit rightly described as self-noughting—*ich bin entworden*, as the German mystics said?[1] Many of the Christian mystics have used this language. 'Leave nothing of myself in me,' Crashaw makes St. Teresa pray. But surely personality is enlarged, not transcended as we advance in the spiritual life. Personality must be preserved, Plotinus says. . . . In the spiritual world, as he pictures it, we are transparent to each other, because there is no longer anything that separates us. But this does not mean that we are no longer ourselves.

The question comes to a head when we consider our relations to our 'even-Christian', as Julian of Norwich puts it. 'Until we put an end to particular attachments,' Huxley says in p. 122, 'there can be no love of God with the whole heart.' Is this true? There is, we remember, a text in the Gospels in which Christ bids us 'hate' even our parents as the condition of being his disciples. If Christ ever said this, it is an example of the hyperbolical language which he permitted himself, like other popular preachers, to use without fearing that his words might be misunderstood. A cloistered contemplative might be free from particular

[1] 'I am dis-become,' i.e., annihilated.

attachments; but is this a counsel for persons living in the world? Can we love God without loving our brother also? And do not many of us arrive at the love of God through the purification and intensification of family and conjugal affection? What do we mean by the love of God? For myself, it means homage to the attributes of Love or Goodness, Truth and Beauty, in which the divine nature has been revealed to us, and gratitude for the response to private prayer, of which I have sometimes, less often than I could wish, been conscious. But the kind of isolation which some of the extreme mystics seem to recommend would be for me a fatal impoverishment of my spiritual life. . . . The spiritual life, as lived on earth, must be a double movement of withdrawal and return.

There is one other curious feature in this book which may or may not have a vital connexion with Huxley's philosophy. He has studied psychical research, and believes that 'laboratory tests' have established the reality of some beliefs which fifty years ago would have been stigmatized as foolish superstitions. He now believes not only in telepathy but in clairvoyance or second sight, miraculous cures, the power of predicting the future, and even in levitation. These 'mystical phenomena', as they used to be called, are in his opinion on a lower level than spiritual religion, and are therefore, I suppose, irrelevant to the philosophy of mysticism, but on the material and psychical plane he believes them to be real. He speaks as a man of science, and would regard my incredulity as mere obstinacy; but though I try to keep an open mind about telepathy, of which I am still quite unconvinced, I do not believe a word of all the rest. Either Christina Mirabilis and Home, the medium, flew without wings, or they did not. If they did, the law of gravitation is unreliable. If they did not, no doubt seeing is believing, but intelligent people may sometimes see things that are not there. I know of a case when two detectives flew howling from a ghost which was, literally, only moonshine. Crookes[1] was an honest man and a real man of science, but he was not necessarily exempt from hallucinations. He chose as the motto for his coat of arms, *Ubi crux ibi lux*.[2] His friends amended it to *Ubi Crookes ibi Spooks*.

I think Thomas Huxley would have spoken severely to his grandson.

[1] Sir William Crookes (1832–1919), English chemist and physicist, developed a theory of 'radiant matter' or matter in a 'fourth state.'

[2] 'Where a problem [is seen as such], there [is] light.'

APE AND ESSENCE

August 1948

---

117. Anthony Bower, review in *Nation* (New York)

21 August 1948, clxvii, p. 210

The review is entitled 'Huxley Was Here Before.'

The contemporary satirist is in the unfortunate position of being almost forced to go too far. Buchenwald and Hiroshima, Belsen and Nagasaki make the vilest individual human actions seem almost like acts of compassion—every debutante implies an Irma Kraus and wide-eyed innocence the baby-face killer. Evelyn Waugh has recently been driven to embalming and the funeral parlor, and now we have Aldous Huxley back in a new world far less brave and far more bestial than the one he gave up sixteen years ago. Malthusian belts have been replaced by raw-hide whips, the 'feelies' and the most enjoyable unbridled license by five days of orgy and three hundred and sixty of unadulterated hell.

[Summarizes the story]

It is absurd to attempt to deny that Mr. Huxley's message is anything but pertinent, urgent, and true—rampant nationalism is obviously the enemy of progress, humanity has recently displayed the ape within with a vengeance, and moreover seems firmly bent on self-destruction. One does begin to wonder, however, whether a statement of such obvious fact, no matter how wittily and trenchantly made, does not tend to enter the realm of platitude unless it implies a solution—a means of escape—more convincing than a blend of Eastern mysticism and Western technology. The world has been dying since its inception, and

369

nuclear fission only gives man the means to speed the process—it does not present any new philosophical problem. Splitting the atom could as well be a cause for optimism as for pessimism: the greater the knowledge of science, the greater the chance of scientific thought presenting an irrefutable and universal logic governing every field of activity and leading to the establishment of a sane world order.

The reiteration in this book of Huxley's deeply pessimistic views leads one to believe that in withdrawing, as he has done, to the periphery, he has put himself outside any real compassion for humanity —which always implies a certain optimism—without having gained any particularly enlightening insight in compensation.

118. Alice S. Morris, review in *NYTBR*

22 August 1948, p. 5

Alice S. Morris was literary editor of *Harper's Bazaar* and taught in the mid-1960s at Columbia University.

The first part of the review, which summarizes the novel, is omitted. The title of the review is 'Mr. Huxley Holds That Man Is As Yet Many Monkeys.'

This timely message of doom and exhortation, Mr. Huxley (after a brief contemporary-Hollywood introduction) has cast in the form of a free-hand movie scenario with flashbacks, 'mood' shots, soundtrack indications, and the interpolations of a 'Narrator' who comments on the action and its implications. If roomy, it is a somewhat claptrap vehicle. Mr. Huxley's arguments on the side of humanity (as they are voiced by the Narrator and the Arch-Vicar) are responsible, opportune and logical; the satire which carries them is arbitrary, opportunistic, and proceeds without logic. The story of Poole and Loola thus appears to unfold not as an organic growth but as a manipulation to permit introduction of the arguments. Form and content maintain a separate existence; the catalysis which would fuse them never takes place—perhaps because Mr. Huxley was more possessed by his reformer's urgency than by his artist's austerity. Beyond this, the distinction of language, the ironic wit, the *mots justes*[1] that gave flavor and brilliance to *Antic Hay*, *Point Counter Point*, and *Eyeless in Gaza*, are sporadic and alien in *Ape and Essence*. Only the skeletal outlines of the superb Huxley manner are distinct.

However, if in *Ape and Essence* Mr. Huxley seems to have a flawed satiric novel, he has a potentially brilliant and penetrating satiric essay. And I wish he had written it.

119. Charles J. Rolo, review in *Atlantic Monthly*

September 1948, clxxxii, pp. 102–3

Charles James Rolo, b. 1916, has edited *The World of Aldous Huxley* (1947) and *The World of Evelyn Waugh* (1958), and he contributed regularly to the *Atlantic Monthly* at the time of this review.

When Huxley wrote *Brave New World* in 1932, it seemed to him that mankind was headed toward the soulless, mass-produced contentment of a scientific Utopia. His fable dramatized the choice between this 'death-without-tears' and a return to 'noble Savagery' which was both squalid and ignoble—a choice between 'insanity on the one hand and lunacy on the other.' Mr. Huxley has since sought to show that there exists—in the precept and practice of the mystics—a way to sanity. The

1 'Precise words, apt expressions.'

source of man's madness, he avers, is that the unregenerate Adam is an angry ape; he can cease to be one only through awareness of his Essence—of the spiritual reality underlying the world. Whence Huxley's new title, *Ape and Essence*. *Brave New World* envisaged the *painless* triumph of standardization, which Huxley then considered the logical end product of a science controlled by soulless rationalists. 'Our Ford' was the prophet. *Ape and Essence* depicts the *miserable* triumph of animal bestiality, which Huxley now suggests will be the logical end product of a science controlled by war-minded ape man. The prophet is Belial.

[Summarizes the story]

At first reading, *Ape and Essence* struck me as an extremely puzzling performance. Why the script form? And what of the 'moral'? Poole has the special knowledge which he might use to save the community from starvation. Instead of which he elopes with his lascivious Loola to catch up on his arrested Kinsey rating. Is this the final triumph of Belial? Or is it the case of the world well lost for Romance, which would amount to much the same thing—the triumph of Hollywood over Huxley? The fact that these and a good many other questions arise shows that Mr. Huxley, who here as always has something important to say and says it entertainingly, has registered a miss with *Ape and Essence*. That still leaves it in the upper bracket of the year's fiction.

The script form is not suited to Huxley's satiric talent. I am told he tried the idea out as a 'straight' novel and found it 'too heavy'—he was aiming at pure fantasy (and perhaps wider appeal).[1] The use of the Narrator in place of the customary Huxleyan sage, marginally involved in the plot, is also designed to avoid realism and weightiness. It is, I feel, rather unsuccessful, though the blank verse does give a lyrical quality to the counterpoint—the Essence—which is opposed to the harsh point— the Ape.

The 'moral' of the fable, as I interpret it, is twofold. First, the idea that love is progress toward Essence. Is there not a hint, asks the Narrator, that there is, 'beyond *Adonais*, the wordless doctrine of the Pure in Heart'? Second, the conviction (previously expressed by Huxley) that our society—of which Belial's is a sardonic extension—is irretrievably polluted and salvation is possible only on the periphery— in refugee communities of free spirits. *One must cultivate one's oasis.*[2]

---

[1] *L*, p. 600, confirms this.
[2] Cf. the conclusion to Voltaire's *Candide*: 'One must cultivate one's garden.'

120. Anthony West, review in
New Statesman and Nation

5 March 1949, xxxvii [n.s.], pp. 232–3

For a biographical note see No. 97.

The review is entitled 'Post-Atomic Sex.' Ellipses in the text are West's.

Mr. Huxley's gift horse gives the uncritical rider such a blood-curdling ride through the Californian Yahoo country that the critic hesitates, and hesitates, before forcing the beast's jaws apart. Let us say that it is a first-class pseudo-scientific shocker—something like M. P. Shiels' *Purple Cloud*—and let us then hasten away. There is a clearly recognised literary field in which people produce stories about mad scientists who do rum things, but literary critics have no business with what goes on there—that is the affair of the Watch Committees, the Chief Constables, and such robust moralists as the late Lord Brentford, and Mr. George Orwell. Let us therefore . . . but it is Mr. Huxley himself who makes the claim to be talking seriously about matters of importance and who thus forfeits the shocker writer's immunity. He begins his excursions into the possibilities of what may be called post-atomic sex on the highest possible plane: 'It was the day of Gandhi's assassination . . .', line two refers discreetly to Jesus, and the rest of the page is as thickly studded with 'good' names as a well-conducted gossip column. One nods to Ptolemy, Beddoes, Byron, Keats, Shelley before passing on to page two where one immediately encounters Martin Luther speaking— as one might expect—German. It is plain that this is serious business, and no shocker, and that we are getting on to serious topics, guilt, ethics, moral responsibility, and all that. 'It was the day of Gandhi's assassination . . . but across the desk in his office, across the lunch table in the Commissary, Bob Briggs was concerned to talk only about himself. . . .' The familiar Huxley approach to the familiar Huxley

373

theme: one settles back expectantly . . . but something comes over Mr. Huxley when Bob Briggs is on the scene.

[Quotes narrator's reflections on Briggs, p. 1]

Bob Briggs has been, it is quite obvious, filched entire from a back number of one of the sillier women's papers, from his absurd name down to his all-girls-together manner.

Bob took my arm and squeezed it.
'You've been enormously helpful,' he assured me again.
'I wish I could believe it, Bob.'
'But it's true, it's true.'

Bob may think so, but at least one reader can't. Poor Bob is a Hollywood script-writer on the slide, they are rude to him at the studio when he asks them for money, his wife has taken all his property and money from him by a smart legal trick, his hair is going white, and his mistress is taking what is known in civil service circles as the appropriate action about his failing sexual powers. And all Huxley can do for the poor chap is to knock the tar out of him for not feeling guilty about the assassination of Gandhi. Mr. Huxley hasn't taken much trouble with poor Bob because his only function is to introduce another character called Tallis, who elbows him aside after a few pages. Tallis has the considerable advantage, from a Huxley character's point of view, of being dead and beyond further suffering. He earned his peace, though, the hard, Huxley way. His first wife was a frigid German, his second a hot American bitch, and his declining years were clouded by a suspicion amounting to a certainty that his daughter by the first marriage was existing in Germany by trading you-know-what for Hershey Bars with the army of occupation. We come to know him posthumously through the film script he wrote to raise enough money to save the poor girl from her life of shame. Now we know more or less what Hollywood is, and we know pretty well what Hollywood does; what are we to think of Tallis, after giving him credit for his entirely laudable motive, for turning in for consideration by a Hollywood studio a script of which this is a typical sample:

[Quotes thirteen lines beginning 'Surely it's obvious,' p. 11]

Could anyone but an idiot send this second-rate parody of Auden at his quainte olde alliterative Saxony worste in to Hollywood as a possible money-spinner? And if Tallis is an idiot who can make such an absurd assessment of Hollywood, what value are his speculations about the more complex aspects of reality? These speculations are the substance of the book.

Tallis's script—one's admiration for the Huxley of the Twenties compels one to put it that way—describes the arrival of a research expedition from an untouched New Zealand on the coast of a California which has been sliding back into barbarism for two generations after an atomic world war. The war destroyed everything in the Americas that sustained elaborate social organization, and the Californians have sunk to the most primitive kind of tribal life. The New Zealander who incautiously lags behind a landing party is carried off into, oh, the strangest world. It has to be confessed that Tallis has originality of a kind; no one else has suggested that dilettante eclecticism in religious matters is likely to be a by-product of atomic fission. Nor does Tallis in so many words, but nothing else can explain his Californian developments. The New Zealander encounters a theocracy of castrated priests who worship Belial with a ritual based on *Salammbô*,[1] and patchily enriched by material from the works of Dr. Harrison, Sir James Frazer, and one or two others. That these Californian castrati should be able to undo four thousand years of religious development in fifty to sixty years is unlikely enough; that they should complicate their task of enthroning a god of evil by giving him the horns and tail which have made Old Nick an absurdity for two or three hundred years puts the thing into the realm of the impossible. The history of religions, so far as it is known, affords no instance of a devil or recognised god of evil ousting a god of light—the movement is always the other way, and once an obsolete God has been kicked downstairs he remains in the realms of darkness until he emerges into the daylight as a comic figure.

Gods are like old prize-fighters, They Never Come Back. As if uneasily aware that the religious side of the story is so much poppy-cock, Tallis has boosted up the 'factual' side to justify it. What these people have been through! Gamma ray poisoning has played old harry with their sexual make-up to a point that makes swallowing Old Harry himself a trifling matter. As many monstrous births take place as normal ones (even pretty little Loola, the heroine, has an extra pair of nipples), and men and women come into season for a five-week heat period in the spring during which they enjoy sexual relations publicly and promiscuously. A rogue ten per cent. who are born into this nightmare are sexually pre-atomic and so crave love and permanent relationships: their

[1] Flaubert's historical novel (1862) of revolt in ancient Carthage.

ALDOUS HUXLEY

society calls them 'hots' and buries them alive or castrates them and enrolls them in the priesthood. . . . Tallis's skill with scientific patter makes all this nonsense seem more convincing than the religious guff, but not even a towering genius could get away with the thesis that is his real concern. It is, quite incredibly, that this hasty set-up corresponds with the realities of human nature and that the atomic bomb has merely stripped California of its pretences. Own up, says Tallis, isn't sex just a degrading and traumatic experience, the penalty at the end of the otherwise pleasant business of courtship? Isn't the horror and shame of the loathsome act fatal to any really dignified relationship? And then look at the revolting consequences—the nightmare of birth, the defiling indignity of breast feeding . . . of napkins. . . . There is a good deal in the early part of the book, for which Mr. Huxley takes direct responsibility, about diapers, but there is no apparent realisation either on his part or Tallis's that there are two ends of a baby and that the end where the brains are is the interesting one. A writer must inevitably deal with his own experience when he gets to grips with reality; but individual experience as limited, and as unusual, as this should not be offered as truth of universal validity. Tallis's script quite irrationally equates the atomic bomb with virility and goes off into a screaming fit in which he describes the consequences of its use in language identical with that normally employed by the type of neurotic who rejects his virility with fear and loathing. It is difficult to feel that the book does more than that, or that it is of more than clinical interest.

121. John Armstrong, letter in reply to Anthony West

New Statesman and Nation, 12 March 1949, xxxvii [n.s.], p. 253

Mr. Anthony West demolishes the Ape and ignores the Essence in Mr. Huxley's book, which is as sensible as an attack on the logical structure of a fairy story.

Mr. Huxley writes tracts in which the inevitable powder is disguised by varying qualities of jam. If, in this instance, the jam happens to be plum and apple and Mr. Huxley dresses himself up in horns and piebald fur to administer the dose, it does not mean that the powder is the less purgative; it is merely less pleasant to take. 'Conquerors of Nature, indeed! . . . they had merely upset the equilibrium of nature and were about to suffer the consequences. . . . An orgy of criminal imbecility. And they called it Progress.' The equivalent of such remarks ought to be blazoned round the new House of Commons and every other place of human assembly. That would save us, at any rate, some of our hypocrisies—such as printing Mr. Walter Elliot's pious reproof of Mr. Huxley in the *News Chronicle* side by side with a leading article casting doubt on the adequacy of our preparations for atomic war. God and the devil never share the same page.

122. Stephen Spender on *Themes and Variations*

NYTBR, 30 April 1950, pp. 5, 36

Stephen (Harold) Spender, b. 1909, poet, critic, and editor, has been a professor of English at University College, London, since 1970. With Auden and Day-Lewis, he was a leading poet of the new social consciousness of the 1930s. Among his many works are *Collected Poems* (1954), *The Struggle of the Modern* (1963), and *English and American Sensibilities* (1972).

The review is entitled 'Credo of the Last-Ditch Individualist.'

Only the first essay on the philosopher Maine de Biran and his *Journal Intime* can really be described as a theme with variations. The rest of these essays—on art and religion, a baroque tomb, El Greco, and Piranesi's engravings of prisons—are meditations in a manner certainly owing much to the musical form with which Aldous Huxley has already made us familiar.

The essay on Biran is in Mr. Huxley's happiest manner of mixing the themes of the biographer and essayist with something of the sermonizer thrown in. With pleasing if self-conscious artistry owing something to the movies, he gives us a 'shot' of Biran in 1816 established as quaestor of the Chamber of Deputies taking a cure in the Pyrenees. We are made to see Biran vividly through a 'close-up' of the philosopher in the act of 'energetically pressing the tips of his extended and unseparated fingers against his chest in order no doubt more effectively to assert the fact of his personality' whenever he explains the ego (*Le Moi*), which was the center of his philosophy.

History is seen through the eyes of *Le Moi*, *Le Moi* from the point of view of history—his inmost thoughts, his relations with his family and circle of friends, the system of his egocentric philosophy, his physiology and psychology. With shifting lights and changing points of view, Mr. Huxley turns Maine de Biran round and round, back and front, exhibits him from inside and out as isolated ego and social phenomenon.

This is an exquisitely skillful, intelligent and delightful performance, both gay and serious. Occasionally some of Mr. Huxley's King
Charles' heads crop up—'cerebro-tonic,' 'psycho-somatic' jargon for a
paragraph or so and Vedanta; but this is at worst rather endearing, and
at best it is a means of conveying Mr. Huxley's purpose. Just as buildings
have to be constructed with the aid of scaffolding, so Mr. Huxley's
reconstruction in its various stages needs strong scaffolding of scientific,
psychological or mystical jargon. All the same, the building goes up,
the elevation is magnificent and behind the framework the lines are
pure and clear.

What is the intensely serious single theme which binds these sets of
variations together? It is really several purposes, or rather one purpose
existing on several levels. On one level there is political-moral intent—
to challenge authoritarianism and to state in the most definite way that
politics should renounce the aim of creating the Social Man who is a
functioning unit within the state which proclaims itself the be-all and
end-all of human happiness.

Politics, Mr. Huxley insists in a desperately important essay, 'The
Double Crisis,' should renounce abstractions and have practical aims in
the service of mankind, aims such as the simple one of preventing the
starvation of an overpopulated world within the next generation.

At a deeper level, Mr. Huxley is concerned to assert the fundamental
and basic individualism of human existence. He is what one might call
a last-ditch individualist, and in this he joins hands with writers like
George Orwell and Albert Camus who have attempted to state the
rights of the individualist not in terms of privilege but as the reality of
the minimal naked consciousness of existence. Perhaps last-ditch individualism is the only tenable position for the individualist today.

Occasionally Mr. Huxley may be charged with false historicity.
Critics have already been getting at him for comparing Piranesi with
modern Cubist painters. Certainly his interest in the timelessness of
certain contemporary problems floods his preoccupation with particular past times and places. As a historian he is more fascinated and fascinating than correct. He is really a seeker after parables—and the lesson
of the parable is always the same. It is that we should think about fundamental nature and the purpose of living and act out of a deeper realization of what these are in order to save our civilization from disaster
before it is too late. The disaster-like crisis is a double one: of complete
submission to the state on one hand, of total destruction on the other.
In thirty years (he is precise about time) it will be too late.

THE DEVILS OF LOUDUN

October 1952

123. E. M. Forster, review in *Listener*

9 October 1952, pp. 595, 597

Edward Morgan Forster (1879–1970), famous British novelist and essayist, intimate associate of the original Bloomsbury Group, wrote among others *A Passage to India* (1924) and *Two Cheers for Democracy* (1952).

Several opening paragraphs summarizing the book and comparing it with *Grey Eminence* are omitted.

The review is entitled 'The Possessed'.

The Loudun case fascinated the whole of western Europe. Tourists came to hear the nuns scream, the town grew rich, the Prioress' chemise, after she had been exorcised, was laid upon Anne of Austria when she was giving birth to the future Louis XIV. We are amazed. We are disgusted. Those people must have been mad! How could they have believed in devils? And then, remorselessly, Mr. Huxley relates them to ourselves.

[Quotes some passages on the invention of devil-substitutes for purposes of persecution by authoritarian powers, Chapter V, pp. 140–2]

This is a formidable indictment. If anyone cares to test its validity, he can easily do so by saying a sentence containing the word 'Moscow' in mixed company. No one will bat an eyelid if he says 'Hell', for Hell no longer exists. But Moscow—!

The book has other aspects. Even more than its predecessor[1] does it

[1] *Grey Eminence*.

bring out Mr. Huxley's peculiar attitude to life. It is an attitude which some will condemn, others approve, but it is in any case valuable, because it is so rarely held. He is a humanist who dislikes humanity. Ordinary people bore him, extraordinary people impress him as wicked or unhappy or both. He has a typical humanist's equipment—integrity, intelligence, sensitiveness, curiosity, erudition, tolerance—but he is denied the humanist's reward of earthly warmth. Montaigne enjoyed himself and also enjoyed his Self so far as he knew that he had one. Mr. Huxley may sometimes enjoy himself, but he loathes his Self; it 'insulates' him, it prevents him from reaching the spiritual life which transcends the immemorial madness of life on earth. And he loathes the Self in others. And everyone has one. He seeks a path of escape, and he sympathises most with a person like Surin who also seeks it. To many readers of *The Devils of Loudun* Surin will be a most trying exorcist—superstitious, silly, uninterestingly introspective, and physically diseased; we are told that his *Catechism Spirituel* is comparable to Augustine Baker's *Holy Wisdom*[1] and it may be, but who will read either of them? Still, Surin searches, he struggles to get free from the Self. Hence his importance. And he has the guidance of Authority, which Mr. Huxley, being a humanist, must lack. He can belong to a church. He has been trained how to pray. Prayer is characteristic of the darkling religious scenery of Loudun. All else is overshadowed by it. The importance of prayer, the comparative unimportance of praise.

> Praise to the Holiest in the height
> And in the depth be praise?

Perhaps; but the normal need is for prayer, for striving. Strive to be where you aren't, to get what you haven't, and to throw away what you have. Mr. Huxley is not much interested in the facilities provided by religion for thankfulness. As a humanist who dislikes humanity, how should he be?

The Devils of Loudun is the product of a fearless and a fertile mind. At the very end, for instance, Mr. Huxley throws in a fascinating appendix on the subjects of alcohol, sex, and crowd-mentality. All three are devices which the individual has adopted in the hope of forgetting himself and transcending his Self. The first two have been recognised by the state as potential dangers, and have usually been controlled. The last—crowd-mentality—though equally dangerous has not yet been

[1] Augustine Baker (1575–1641), monk of the English Benedictine congregation, important and controversial writer on ascetic and mystical theology.

controlled, and perhaps never will be: it may destroy us all in the end. In any case, neither it nor the other two are the Way; only the mystics know that.

There is one defect in the book to be noted—a defect common indeed to all readable histories. Every now and then the author invents and pads, in order to ease the jolting that comes from the unmitigated use of documents. When he does this over trifles, the device is pardonable. For instance, in the first chapter Grandier 'rode slowly' into Loudun, while later on there are some horses that 'trotted'. It is unlikely that authorities can be quoted for the speed of the horses in either case, but who cares? We do care when it comes to psychology. Are the earlier ravings of the Prioress taken from the memoirs she subsequently wrote? Or has Mr. Huxley made them up for her? We are not sure, but we are sure that he makes up the thoughts and the talk of the plotters in the apothecary's shop. This engenders mistrust. In a book dealing with the interior life we have the right to know whose interior we are viewing.

124. Angus Wilson, review in *New Statesman and Nation*

1 November 1952, xliv [n.s.], pp. 516, 518

Angus Frank Johnstone Wilson, b. 1913, is a well-known novelist and has been a professor of English Literature at the University of East Anglia since 1966.

The review is entitled 'Mr. Huxley's Split Mind.'

Mr. Huxley's study of the supposed possession of the Ursuline nuns at Loudun in the 1630s contains numerous digressions. In one of them the writer recapitulates the classic split personality case of Miss Beauchamp. Why Mr. Huxley should have made so many excursions into rather hackneyed historical phenomena is difficult to explain, but his preoccupation with split personality is intelligible enough if only on purely subjective lines.

Throughout *The Devils of Loudun* the reader is constantly reminded of the strange existence within Mr. Huxley of two or more hardly reconciled—indeed hardly reconcilable—personalities. There is the popular historian, the closest descendant of the great satirical novelist of the Twenties—a competent though often a little absurdly dogmatic retailer of broad historical pictures derived from more 'stodgy' secondary sources, at his worst when pretending to historical scholarship, at his best when looking at the past as a satirical observer of personages. There is the Aubrey-like lover of past scandal.[1] There is the Swiftian hater of the flesh, obsessed by a powerful love-hate of the human body, fascinated by a vision of great gentlemen and ladies, proud lovers and famed beauties swimming for an eternity of damnation in lakes of ordure and suppuration. There is the convincing and powerful teacher of religious truth, the man possessed by the vision of the Good, beside whose contemplation all other exercises, whether of artistic pursuit of beauty or saintlike devotion to good works, are as chaff before the wind. Finally, there is the acute political student of the human will in pursuit of power, the stern moralist who detects the moment of damnation when noble ends are destroyed by the use of ignoble means. As with Miss Beauchamp, there are moments when the 'finer' Mr. Huxleys seem to glimpse momentarily and with disgust the lesser Mr. Huxleys. Unlike Miss Beauchamp, the various personalities of Mr. Huxley often combine to produce even stranger forms.

At his most disturbing, the popular historian combines with the man obsessed by human filth and the scandal-lover to produce a sort of 'modern' sixth-form history master, whose sweeping generalities liberally besprinkled with 'blue' revelations about the past are calculated to command the attention of even those 'foul' boys at the back who are normally employed in searching for the 'hot' bits in the Bible. Then, again, his horror of the flesh with its inevitable view of the world as the realm of the Prince of Darkness seeks an impossible reconciliation with what seems to me the essence of his religious belief—'by thinking primarily of evil we tend, however excellent our intentions, to create occasions for evil to manifest itself' and again 'the effects which follow too constant and intense a concentration upon evil are always disastrous'. To reconcile this belief in All Pervasive Good with the Manichaean dualism to which his *Schadenfreude*[2] leads him, he reasonably

[1] John Aubrey (1626–97) wrote pen portraits of his contemporaries. [2] 'Malice.'

rejects poverty and sickness as the external symbols of inward grace, but illogically implies a sort of connection between physical health and holiness, which is as absurd as the Christian Science doctrines he so often mocks. At his highest, however, Mr. Huxley's vision of the Good is so intense that it banishes his obsessions and unites with his masterly sense of human motive to produce analyses of religious experience with an intellectual sympathy rare in such studies.

As may be well imagined, these warring and powerful forces find their literary expression in books that are both uneven and unconnected. *The Devils of Loudun* has in full degree its depths and its heights, and from start to finish the central theme of the book is never constant. The work opens with a description of seventeenth-century France at Mr. Huxley's sixth-form worst, and passes to an account of the Abbé Grandier at his satirical novelist's best. The story of this *homme moyen sensuel*[1] who gradually built around him, in his arrogance, a ring of outraged enemies, has something of the dramatic effect of the assembly of Elvira, Anna and Ottavio; if this narrative came as the direct prelude to the vengeance that falls upon him, the drama might be as telling as Don Giovanni's. Before the terrible end of Grandier, however, we are given a very complete account of the supposed demonic possession of the Ursuline nuns which was eventually used by Grandier's enemies to secure his ruin. Since this diabolic visitation was even viewed by most contemporaries as fraudulent, it has not the intrinsic interest as a parapsychological phenomenon to justify the length at which Mr. Huxley treats it. Other and more genuine phenomena, after all, are at hand for investigation. The numerous digressions, too, on seventeenth-century science, witchcraft and medicine are based upon such well-thumbed sources that it is difficult to know for what audience they are intended; while others, like that upon antimony as a popular contemporary purgative, are marked by that obsessive interest in the sordid already described as so disturbing.

When the narrative returns to the gradual spinning of the web around Grandier which leads to the horrors of his torture and public burning, Mr. Huxley's dramatic powers are masterly. The focus here, however, is not upon religious phenomena, real or spurious, but upon the Reichstag fire methods by which Richelieu and the Grey Eminence pursued and destroyed their victim. No one can analyse such a vile confusion of ends and means as brilliantly as Mr. Huxley, nor, I think, is there anything so heartening as the absolute liberalism of his defence

[1] 'Average sensual man.'

of the rights of individual human beings, when he is so clearly repelled by humanity as a whole. Yet the force of this section is weakened by the obscurity in which he leaves the motives of Richelieu's interest in so apparently local a proceeding. In any case, the story is a political and not a religious one. The final section is concerned with the hysteric infection which passes from the nuns to the last of their exorcists, the Jesuit Surin. This is both the most moving and the most significant episode, for Surin is of a spiritual calibre far above the other actors in the story and the long agony of his invasion by evil is genuine tragedy. Not the least among the paradoxes of Mr. Huxley's exposition is his emphasis, in this part of the book, upon the healing powers of the Natural World which rises at times to almost Wordsworthian heights. Such emphasis seems once again a strange divergence from true contemplation.

All these contradictions and disturbing shifts of emphasis only illustrate the fascinating range of Mr. Huxley's powers. It is because he still remains so entirely stimulating a writer that he could so easily eschew the obsessive, the sensational and the popular and demand from his readers the difficult discipline that the remarkable intensity of his vision of pervasive Good should claim.

125. Robert Richman, review in *New Republic*

27 October 1952, cxxvii, pp. 18–19

Richman's was that rare perspicacity in a reviewer which discerned Huxley's essential aim in writing *The Devils of Loudun*. Huxley had written to Harold Raymond of his hope for the Biran essay in *Themes and Variations*, a hope which he clearly cherished for *The Devils of Loudun*: 'If the thing comes off as I hope, it will be an example of what I think is a new literary form, in which philosophical discussion is enlivened and given reality by the fact of its being particularized within a biography' (*L*, p. 608n).

The review is entitled 'The Discarnate Spirits.' See Introduction, p. 27.

Certainly the success of any satire in prose fiction depends upon the matching of a fine prose style (that can hold up its proud head) with a well-wrought indignation. And such a match is delightfully present in nearly all of *The Devils of Loudun*. Aldous Huxley's *Point Counter Point* immediately suggests itself; and I do not mean that the latter is an imitation of the former, nor cast in the exact manner, nor indeed is it of a like cloth of theme. I think rather of these two: of the musical structures of *Point Counter Point* and of Huxley's hand and mind experimenting with the Form of fiction.

The extraordinary value of the use of a musical structure in literature is that the writer is able to announce one theme, to vary it; then to state another and vary each; to repeat the themes with their variations; and then with the full license of the contrapuntal method to blend all themes into still another theme with a set of variations following in its organic turn. The writer is permitted a large complex of ideas which when brought under the controls of art gives intricate pleasure.

[Discusses via plot summary several themes, especially 'love-celibacy,' and their variations]

The trial and the burning at the stake of Father Urban Grandier, some of the most dramatic scenes in modern fiction and comparable to

St. Joan's in Shaw's drama, show the excellence of the elaborate contrapuntal structure of these main themes and variations—and of the
many not mentioned—and remind us of the method of music. The
many ideas of this novel become doubly and trebly meaningful by such
an elaboration, in his mastery of narration, characterization, dramatic
moment. But more than this: I believe Huxley was attempting to
develop or evolve further a new form for fiction—the 'essay' novel. I
mean that he used the essay in the service of his fiction as Samuel
Richardson had used the 'letter' in the service of his fiction which we
call the epistolary novel. Huxley uses his materials and sources and
documents differently from those which Sterne in *Tristram Shandy* had
ventured to use; and equally as different from Scott; and it differs also
from the writers of the naturalistic 'novel of ideas'; or from the pastoral
novel—the name William Empson called the proletarian novel. Nor
can we say Gide has done it before.

Although Huxley is the omnipresent central authority in the work,
he bestows a similar power on the reader who can weave in and out of
the sources and the characters, the conflicts and concepts, being at one
and the same moment in the center of this musical network of themes
set in 1625 in time, and placed in France, and identified now with
Father Grandier, or Soeur Jeanne, or Father Surin; and being at the
next moment in 1952 seated in one's own home. In such masterful use
of aesthetic distance, even the third chapter, which as a discussion of
perennial philosophy is an *essay*, has earned its right to be in this fiction.
And whether we agree with this philosophy or not does not matter.

It is true we have every reason to assume that the serious reader and
the qualified critic would have accepted upon the publication of T. S.
Eliot's *Ash Wednesday* the fact that for contemporary literature (as it is
for any age) religious thought and experience was one subject proper
to a poem; and that it did not matter, or make it art, or prevent its art.
Those who hailed the experimental Huxley of *Point Counter Point* and
have deplored a softness which they thought was appearing in his art
at the hour of his turning to mysticism, and those who think that
Huxley, with Eliot and Auden, has forsaken the mantle of art for the
shirt of hair may be assured that Mr. Huxley has left his hair-shirt
hanging in the closet of his library when he wrote *The Devils of Loudun*.
He dares to seek the rare company of prose artists—Thomas Browne,
William Congreve, Laurence Sterne—who held style and the graceful
control of the English sentence to be the highest achievement in the art
of prose.

126. Carlyle King on the later work

1954

Dean Carlyle Albert King, b. 1907, educator, critic, editor, is Vice-Principal of the University of Saskatchewan, Saskatoon, Canada. He was chairman of Saskatchewan's English Department 1950–64, has edited *Saskatchewan Harvest* (1955) and *A Book of Canadian Poems* (1963), and has written *Saskatchewan: the Making of a University* (1959) and *Extending the Boundaries* (1967).

King's article, entitled 'Aldous Huxley's Way to God,' is from the *Queen's Quarterly*, Spring 1954, lxi, pp. 80–100. As an introductory note to the original article points out, the argument 'challenges the fashionable academic view that Huxley was at his best in the earlier negative and cynical work.'

Several opening paragraphs, where King reviews the 'sad-sacks' and cynics of the early novels, are here omitted. See Introduction, p. 29.

Now while these characters certainly reflect some part of the mind of their creator—what may be called 'the small devil of happy malice' within him—Huxley steadily represents them as repulsive and life-denying. He himself has never been a cynic; he has always been a seeker. All his work is a quest for values. He has been in despair, he has been horrified by the squalor of 'The Human Vomedy,' as his typewriter one day in accidental but felicitous slip proclaimed it; but from the beginning he has also been a passionately serious thinker, eager to discern some pattern of meaning in things and some clue to the good life. His early books show the impact of World War One upon a sensitive mind. Nineteenth century values in religion, morals, and politics have gone to pieces; they were blown into bits by the catastrophe of 1914. Indeed, nineteenth century values in religion, morals, and politics led to that catastrophe. What, then, shall we put in their place? What can a man believe? How shall we face the dilemma of our time? That has always been Huxley's subject.

[Describes several attitudes Huxley takes toward the problem of meaning in his early books]

That anyone could ever have missed Huxley's seriousness of purpose is surprising in the light of the clear statements of his views in the books of essays and travel notes which he was publishing concurrently with his novels and short stories. *On the Margin* (1923) proclaims his horror of the pursuit of pleasure, his distaste for the sensualist and the aesthete, and his inability to understand 'the outlook on life of a man who lives for sensations rather than for ideas and emotions.' He points out that there is a range of mind, like that of Dostoevski or Blake or Beethoven, that the sceptical ironist like Lytton Strachey cannot possibly understand. He even sounds like Matthew Arnold or T. H. Huxley when he says in *Along the Road* (1925) that there is 'an absolute standard of artistic merit . . . and the standard is in the last resort a moral one,' or in *Jesting Pilate* (1926) that he learned from his travels round the world 'that the established spiritual values are fundamentally correct and should be maintained.'

[Traces Huxley's work to the early 1930s and comments on the influence of Lawrence]

In the year after *Brave New World* Huxley began to qualify the primitive-paganism or pagan-primitivism which he had developed under the influence of Lawrence. A world-wide economic depression and the spreading cloud of war on the international horizon made the Life-Worshipper's creed look as silly as it is, and the reasonable man in Huxley must soon have been amused at the psychological double-jointedness and the triple-plated intestines needed by one who would be excessive in all directions. In 1933 Huxley visited that splendidly savage society of Lawrence's *The Plumed Serpent* where civilized women gladly 'drowned in the grand sea of the living blood.' He travelled to Mexico and other parts of Central America and came back shaking his head; the un-self-conscious life in the blood is not the answer to our need. . . .

Beyond the Mexique Bay (1934) is the watershed in the Huxley canon, for the tone of the books he has written since then is quite different from that of the earlier work. The change can be stated simply: Huxley became fully adult. Writing to Lady Ottoline Morrell in 1929 D. H. Lawrence had said of his friend: 'I feel only half a man writes the books —a sort of precocious adolescent. There is surely much more of a man in the real Aldous' [See No. 53]. Lawrence's faith was justified; in *Eyeless in Gaza* (1936) the real Aldous arrived—and has stayed in twelve subsequent books. *Eyeless in Gaza*, the longest, most subtly contrived, and most thoughtful of Huxley's novels, is 'the objective correlative' of what was happening in the author's soul in 1934 and 1935. The fictional life of Anthony Beavis is a parable of the mental life of Aldous Huxley.

What happened? First, there was Huxley's growing concern at the steamroller approach of war. Even in *Beyond the Mexique Bay* he was worried about this menace to human values; many of the best sections in the book are discussions of the causes of war and of ways of keeping the peace. In the late twenties Huxley had lightly assumed that the world would last his time; he had said that a dislike of cruelty was steadily growing, that men were less obsessed with power and more reluctant 'to carry authority to its logical conclusion in brute force.' The virulent revival of nationalism and militarism in the early thirties gave the lie to that easy optimism, and by 1934 Huxley found himself looking straight at the ugly fact that nation-states and the people who lead them and the people who comprise them are greedy, stupid, and bloodthirsty.

The next step for Huxley was to ask himself the question he was later to use as the title for a famous pamphlet: What are *you* going to do about it? Are you going to continue to be like a college professor, detached, superior, uninvolved, or are you going to get your hands dirty trying to clean out the human pigpen? Are you going to be, all your life, the privileged spectator and judicious commentator, or are you going to be a participant in the human struggle for the human cause? Something like that Huxley began to ask himself. Anthony Beavis in the novel is a sociologist—a so-called social scientist—but he might just as well be a professor of chemistry or a professor of English. He has always evaded social responsibility; he has played the part of the detached philosopher; he has taken care to avoid emotional evolvement. He is what universities call a fine scholar: he compiles comprehensive bibliographies, he sedulously turns out learned papers and books, and whenever real life closes in on him he ducks into his card file, pulls down the lid, and pretends that he is leading the Higher Life.

[Quotes Beavis on the pleasures of intellectual work, in *Eyeless in Gaza*, Chapter XIII, pp. 171–2]

Anthony Beavis strikes off the shackles of the Higher Shirker. It tears the sinews of his soul to do it, but he gives up the display of erudition and the pursuit of the bubble reputation that are the scholar's death-substitutes. He finds the enormous courage, like that of an early Christian martyr, to cease being smart and to begin being sensible. In so doing he ceases to be an intellectual and becomes a human being.

Something like that happened to Aldous Huxley. There is a significant passage in *Grey Eminence* (1941) where Huxley is describing the conversion of François Leclerc, who was to become Father Joseph. The young man had been leading the so-called normal life of innocent triviality when suddenly, without apparent cause, at a party he became aware of the complete futility of what he had been doing. Huxley makes this comment:

Most of us, I suppose, have had a similar experience—have woken up all of a sudden from the sleep of everyday living into momentary awareness of the nature of ourselves and our surroundings.

> It is a party in a parlour
> Crammed just as they on earth were crammed,
> Some sipping punch, some sipping tea,
> And all as silent as could be,
> All silent and all damned.

Suddenly to realize that one is sitting, damned, among the other damned—it is a most disquieting experience; so disquieting that most of us react to it by immediately plunging more deeply into our particular damnation in the hope, generally realized, that we may be able, at least for the time, to stifle our revolutionary knowledge.

François Leclerc was not one to follow that course, nor was Aldous Huxley. The final factor in his conversion—the catalytic agent, as it were—was his meeting and subsequent friendship with Gerald Heard and Dick Sheppard.

[Discusses Heard's writing and the advent of the Peace Pledge Union in 1935]

All of his work since then is his answer to the two related problems which his friends Heard and Sheppard had tackled, namely (1) How shall men behave if they are to live in peace in our age of triumphant technology and moral savagery? (2) What attitude to the universe can produce that behavior, and how does one secure and maintain that attitude? As we have seen, *Eyeless in Gaza* (1936) tells the story of a man in painful process of becoming a rational idealist; *Ends and Means* (1937), a companion work, expounds the creed of a rational idealist. This, the most rewarding of all Huxley's books, is subtitled 'An Enquiry into the Nature of Ideals and into the Methods employed for their Realization.' That phrase describes the theme of all his recent work, in fiction, biography, history, and philosophy.

[Recounts the doctrines of *Ends and Means* and *The Perennial Philosophy*]

The doctrine of *Ends and Means* and *The Perennial Philosophy* is preached in the novels *After Many a Summer* (1939) and *Time Must Have a Stop* (1944). Essentially these are morality tales, like Tolstoi's fiction after his conversion to Christianity. In *After Many a Summer* there is a scholar pervert, a Ford pervert, a Newton pervert, a sexuality pervert, and a politics pervert, each living in his or her private hell. Mr. Propter, the religious man (who sounds like Gerald Heard), by example and by precept tries to lift them out of 'the stinking slough of personality' and make them participants in timeless good. Understanding and compassion are the two virtues that matter, he tells them, and the 'most characteristic features of an enlightened person's experience are serenity and disinterestedness. In other words absence of excitement and absence of craving.' *Time Must Have a Stop* could properly be called 'The Redemption of Sebastian Barnack.' Sebastian is a gifted young poet; in competition for his soul are sexuality perverts, science perverts, gentle-Jesus perverts, aesthetic perverts, and politics perverts. After twenty years he is saved by Bruno Rontini, who teaches him 'the sacrifice of self-will to make room for the knowledge of God' and who himself sacrificially gives his life for his young friend.

Likewise *Ape and Essence* (1948), Huxley's latest fiction, is really the scenario of a morality movie which warns men to flee from the wrath to come. It is also a footnote to *Brave New World*. Here is a horrific picture of what American society will be like in the 22nd century if we continue to misuse the gifts of science and technology as we appear to be hell-bent upon doing. In a little book, *Science, Liberty and Peace* (1946), published two years before *Ape and Essence*, Huxley had urged in sober prose that science should be used for man instead of man being used by science, and had exhorted research scientists to stop their pandering to the passions and prejudices of capitalists and politicians, bureaucrats and soldiers, and start working for the individual men and women who make up what we call 'society.' Huxley wants scientists, like professors, to give up the pretence of being Higher Lifers, to crawl out of their test tubes, and have the courage to cease being lickspittles for big business, big government, and big armies.

This certainly shows that Huxley, while believing that 'actual good is outside time,' has not ceased to be interested in expedients for improving the life of men in time. Academic smart alecks like to represent Huxley today as sitting out in the California desert, contemplating his navel, and thinking about the identity of Atman with Brahman. Huxley may be meditating all right, but the point is that he is meditating about you and me. His doctrine is not passive or quietistic; the main problem for him continues to be how to live with love and compassion in time and still be devoted to timeless good, or, as he put in the mouth of Anthony Beavis, how to be 'serene like an old man and active like a young one.' Three of his recent books have been devoted to studying this problem through the lives of actual people, all of them Frenchmen.

[Discusses *Grey Eminence*, the Biran essay in *Themes and Variations*, and *The Devils of Loudun*]

The careers of Grandier and Surin lead Huxley to acute reflection on how men do in fact escape from the horror of their selfhood, the stinking slough of their personality. He starts from the observation that men are just about as anxious to get out of themselves as they are to express themselves; the human record shows that 'an urge to self-transcendence is almost as widespread and, at times, quite as powerful as the urge to self-assertion.' John Steinbeck said the same thing in a novel many years ago when he pointed out that man's self-love is neatly balanced by his self-hatred. That is why the efforts of the educational psychologist to develop the child's personality are forever in vain; the poor little kid will grow up to hate himself anyway! As every thoughtful person comes to see, hell is being condemned to be himself forever, and the beginning of wisdom is the nauseated recognition of what a dung-beetle he is. So men always seek self-transcendence. Most do it through booze or sexuality or crowd delirium or rhythmic sound—this Huxley calls downward self-transcendence; many seek it through identification of themselves with some cause wider than their immediate interests, such as art, science, philosophy, or politics—this is horizontal self-transcendence; but the salt of the earth are those who attempt upward self-transcendence into the universal life of the Spirit.

Painfully Aldous Huxley has been working his way forward to this position from the days of his youth when he saw himself as a boy rattling his noisy cleverness to scare the bird of quiet reflection from his mind. The way has been rough and roundabout and sometimes down-hill. It is a hard thing to humble the mind to quiet. Perhaps all that Huxley would claim for himself was said 320 years ago by a great poet, who also began as a satirist:

> On a huge hill,
> Cragged, and steep, Truth stands, and he that will
> Reach her, about must, and about must go;
> And what the hill's suddenness resists, win so . . .

[Donne, 'Satire III']

127. Thomas Mann on *The Doors of Perception*

1954

Letter to Ida Herz, 21 March 1954, from Mann's *Letters* 1948–1955 (Frankfurt, Germany: Fischer, 1965), p. 332. See Introduction, p. 28. The translation is by Ursula Bender.

For a biographical note see No. 107.

I thank you for *The Doors of Perception*, but I fear I cannot generate the enthusiasm which this book provoked in you. It demonstrates the last, and I would almost insist, the most audacious form of Huxley's escapism, which I could never appreciate in this author. Mysticism as a means to that escapism was, nonetheless, reasonably honorable. But that he now has arrived at drugs I find rather scandalous. I get already a guilty conscience because I take a little seconal or phanodorm in the evenings in order to sleep better. But to put myself during the day in a position in which everything human becomes indifferent to me and I should succumb to unscrupulous aesthetic self-indulgence, would be repulsive to me. This, however, is what he recommends to the whole world, because otherwise stupidity at best and suffering at worst would become the lot of worldly existence. What a use of 'best' and 'worst'! His mystics should have taught him that 'suffering is the fastest animal which will bring us to perfection,' which one cannot say of *doping*; and meditating over the awesome existence of a chair and on various delightful color illusions has more to do with stupidity than he thinks.

Dr. Frederking of Hamburg[1] warns that the state of excitement from mescalin intoxication could be handled only by someone with extensive experience in psychotherapy. (And Huxley is not an experienced man, but a dilettante.) The indication for mescalin intake should be limited, as the doctor points out, and one surely could not predict whether the results of a mescalin experiment would be at all worthwhile. Well, encouraged by the persuasive recommendation of the famous author many young Englishmen and especially Americans will try the experiment. For the book sells like hot cakes. It is, however, a completely—I don't want to say immoral, but one must say irresponsible book, which can only contribute to the stupefaction of the world and to its inability to meet the deadly serious questions of the time with intelligence.

[1] Walter Frederking (1891–1964) experimented with the use of mescalin and LSD in psychotherapy.

128. A critical symposium on Huxley

London Magazine, August 1955, ii, pp. 51-64

Five contributions by various writers under the title 'A Critical Symposium on Aldous Huxley.' The original sub-titles are retained in text. The contributors are:

(a) Evelyn Arthur St John Waugh (1903-66), widely known satirical novelist often compared with Huxley (as in Sean O'Faolain's *The Vanishing Hero*), author of *Decline and Fall* (1928), *A Handful of Dust* (1934), *Brideshead Revisited* (1945), and many others.

(b) Angus Frank Johnstone Wilson—for a biographical note see No. 124.

(c) Francis Wyndham, b. 1924, journalist and critic who since 1964 has been an assistant editor for the *Sunday Times Magazine*.

(d) John Barrington Wain, b. 1925, formerly lecturer in English at the University of Reading (1947-55); a free-lance novelist and critic, known especially for *Hurry on Down* (1953).

(e) Peter Quennell, b. 1905, author, critic, editor, writer of several books on British literature, such as *Byron in Italy* (1941) and *Romantic England* (1970).

(a) Evelyn Waugh on *Antic Hay*: 'Youth at the Helm and Pleasure at the Prow'

Not everyone in 1923, not I for one, knew without recourse to the dictionary that a 'hey' or 'hay' was a country jig. As we sped from Blackwell's with our eagerly awaited copies of Mr. Aldous Huxley's second novel, its title suggested a neglected stable and, strange to recall, as we read it in that fragrant age, the tale did smack a little sour. To be quite accurate in reminiscence I got my own copy second-hand from the present literary critic of the *Daily Mail*—a young man already plainly destined for high position—and he passed it to me (for a financial consideration) saying I should find it 'dreary'. *Dreary!* Re-read now after all that has happened, after all that has been written, after all Mr. Huxley has written, the book has the lilt of Old Vienna.

It is placed in London in springtime. The weather, page after page, is warm and airy and brilliant. Did we ever enjoy quite such a delightful climate? We certainly do not find it in modern fiction. And London is still in 1923 eminently habitable, a city of private houses and private lives, leisurely, not too full even in the season, all leafy squares and stucco façades and Piranesan mewses. The pavements of Bond Street are 'perfumed', the shops are full of desirable goods. All one needs is a little money—not much; £300 a year is a competence, £5,000 is wealth—and that little is easily acquired by some whimsical invention such as a pair of pneumatic trousers. Regent Street is doomed but Verrey's is still open, open after luncheon until it is time to go out to tea. A few miles out in Surrey and Sussex an arcadian countryside is opening to the never-failing sun. Although all the inhabitants of this delicious city have been everywhere and speak every language they are thoroughly English, at home in their own capital. No character in *Antic Hay* ever uses the telephone. They write letters, they telegraph, they call, and there are always suitable servants to say 'not at home' to bores. It is Henry James's London possessed by carnival. A chain of brilliant young people linked and interlaced winds past the burnished front-doors in pursuit of happiness. Happiness is growing wild for anyone to pick, only the perverse miss it. There has been the single unpredictable, inexplicable, unrepeatable calamity of 'the Great War'. It has left broken hearts—Mrs. Viveash's among them—but the other characters are newly liberated from their comfortable refuges of Conscientious Objection, to run wild through the streets.

The central theme of the book is the study of two falterers 'more or less in' their 'great task of happiness', Mrs. Viveash and Theodore Gumbril. Everyone else, if young, has a good time. Two clowns, Lypiatt and Shearwater, get knocked about, but that is the clown's *metier*.[1] Rosie is happy in her pink underclothes and her daze of romantic fantasy, picked up, rolled over, passed on, giving and gaining pleasure and all the time astutely learning the *nuances* of cultural advancement. Coleman is happy, uproariously blaspheming. Men rather like him turn up later in Mr. Huxley's works, miserable men, haunted and damned. Coleman is boisterously happy, a sort of diabolic Belloc.[2] And

[1] 'Craft, trade.'
[2] Hilaire Belloc (1870–1953), French-born poet, essayist, and historian.

Mercaptan is happy, unambitious, sensual, accomplished, radiantly second-rate. He is a period piece, still in his twenties with the taste and pretentions of ripe middle-age. They do not come like that today. Today one knows quite certainly that a young bachelor with a *penchant*[1] for white satin sofas and *bibelots*[2] would not be running after girls and, moreover, that though he might drop into idiomatic French, he would be quite incapable of writing grammatical English.

Mrs. Viveash and Gumbril are the falterers in the Great Task and their situation is not quite desperate. She has her classic, dignified bereavement. Promiscuous sexual relations bore her. But she has, we are told, almost limitless power, power which, I must confess, has never much impressed me. She was 25 when I was 20. She seemed then appallingly mature. The girls I knew did not whisper in 'expiring' voices and 'smile agonizingly' from their 'death beds'. They grinned from ear to ear and yelled one's head off. And now thirty years on, when women of 25 seem to me moody children, I still cannot weep for Mrs. Viveash's tragic emptiness.

Gumbril rejects the chance of a *Happy Hypocrite* idyll,[3] of love, literally, in a cottage. But it would never have done. He is a clever, zestful cad. He would have been hideously bored in a week. He is off abroad to a wide, smiling continent full of wine and pictures and loose young women. He will be all right.

The story is told richly and elegantly with few of the interruptions which, despite their intrinsic interest, mar so much of Mr. Huxley's story-telling. The disquisition on Wren's London should be in a book of essays but the parody of the night-club play is so funny that one welcomes its intrusion. The 'novel of ideas' raises its ugly head twice only, in the scenes with the tailor and the financier, crashing bores both of them but mere spectators at the dance. They do not hold up the fun for long.

And there is another delicious quality. The city is not always James's London. Sometimes it becomes Mediterranean, central to the live tradition. The dance winds through piazzas and alleys, under arches, round fountains and everywhere are the embellishments of the old religion. An ancient pagan feast, long christianized in name, is being celebrated in a christian city. The story begins in a school chapel, Domenichino's *Jerome* hangs by Rosie's bed, Coleman quotes the Fathers. There is an

---

[1] 'Leaning, fondness.'
[2] 'Knick-knacks, trifles.'
[3] A story by Max Beerbohm.

insistent undertone, audible through the carnival music, saying all the time, not in Mrs. Viveash's 'expiring' voice, that happiness is a reality.

Since 1923 Mr. Huxley has travelled far. He has done more than change climate and diet. I miss that undertone in his later work. It was because he was then so near the essentials of the human condition that he could write a book that is frivolous and sentimental and perennially delightful.

(b) Angus Wilson on *Crome Yellow* and *Those Barren Leaves*: 'The House Party Novels'

Aldous Huxley was already a considerable name to me when I was thirteen. My sophisticated, literary inclined elder brothers spoke of him with what they intended for familiarity. All that came over to me was the underlying awe. He alone, I imagined, could free me from the prison of family Philistinism and, at that time, I already felt like one born in the Bastille. On August 11, 1929, my fifteenth birthday, I was given *Antic Hay*. The revolutionary forces that released me were all and more than all that I expected. It seemed a revelation of emancipation and intellectual richness. To be precociously sophisticated, then, was indeed 'very heaven'. For many years *Antic Hay* and *Point Counter Point* were my favourites. Smart, intellectual and artistic London was after all just outside my door. The inmates of the Kensington hotels where I lived might talk as they would, but in every bus and tube on which I travelled to and from school there were brilliant, twisted Spandrells, blaspheming Colemans, or perhaps even 'civilized' Mr. Mercaptan going home to read Crebillon fils's *Sofa*. A few years more and I, too, would be a Gumbril.

I read *Crome Yellow* and *Those Barren Leaves*, of course, but at that time they seemed less exciting—the world of country house weekend parties and of Italian villas lay too far away to give me the same thrill. In any case, like most adolescents, I was looking for a certain loucherie, a life of 'fast' tempo. The strange, idyllic pastoral mood of *Crome Yellow* and *Those Barren Leaves* passed me by, or, if I noticed it, it rather bored me. Nevertheless, they ate deeper into my imagination than I realized. Nearly twenty years later when I wrote my first story, *Raspberry Jam*, I added to what came from the heat of my own fancy a character designated to give an element of wit and worldliness. I was proud of my creation. It was only afterwards that I realized that the addition was pure pastiche of Mr. Scogan or Mr. Cardan. Whatever our final verdict on Aldous Huxley's work, the debt of so many later authors to his work is extraordinary.

The appearance of *Decline and Fall* soon removed the creation of *Antic Hay* into another sphere. But the house party novels, *Crome Yellow* and *Those Barren Leaves*, remained alone. There were countless imitators, of course, in the late 'twenties and 'thirties, but only the novels of Richard Oke and a forgotten book, *They Winter Abroad*, can be called estimable. It was only when I had read more picaresque novels, and, above all, when I had read Peacock that I began to appreciate *Crome Yellow* and *Those Barren Leaves*. The influences were obvious, but the creation remained unique.

Those Barren Leaves (1925) follows exactly upon *Crome Yellow* (1921) though other books were to intervene. In his first novel, the pattern is a simple one: the young intellectually aspiring Denis visits the Wimbush household—a world of rich, witty, sophisticated, talkative people. He makes a fool of himself in word and in love. The destruction of youth's pretensions and illusions, particularly sexual ones, is a favourite theme of Aldous Huxley, but in these early novels the note is less shrill, more pleasing than in, for example, *Time Must Have a Stop*. The 'philosophy' of sexual hedonism and the ideal of romantic love are mocked, but there is none of the pathological wallowing in physical disgust that began to darken the picture in *Point Counter Point* and *Eyeless in Gaza*, and has now become so tedious. Denis's intellectual aspirations are soon made absurd by contrast with Mr. Scogan's more mature cleverness, his love-making ends in farce when Ivor, with his genuine Byronic dash and his true sexual fervour, appears on the scene. Yet the author stands apart and mocks these mentors, too, with a nice irony, in which Denis's innocence plays a considerable part as a touchstone. In *Those Barren Leaves* the sexually competent, romantic Ivor returns in two roles: his speed, youth and energy, his 'dashing' motor car appear in Lord Hovenden, a rare combination of absurdity and excellence in Huxley's work; his romantic prowess and heroic looks go to Calamy, the equivalent of Denis, the picaresque visitor hero with far more intellectual powers than either Denis or Ivor. Cynical, comfortable, sad, hedonistic old Mr. Scogan reappears in Mr. Cardan and is equally a mocked mentor. Most of the other characters reappear, but they are more formidable targets for Mr. Huxley's satire—the talk is better, the intellectual fireworks more astonishing, perhaps a little too much so.

At the end of the novel Calamy retires to the mountains to meditate, whereas Denis just went back to London to his own social and intellectual uncertainty. The ending of *Those Barren Leaves*, in fact, brings us to that point of rejection of all material creeds, whether high or low minded, that search for spiritual truth to which all the author's later work is a coda. Whatever the validity of Mr. Huxley's religious creed, it has to be said at once that Calamy's spiritual doubts are artistically far more satisfying than the increasing dogma of the later novels.

Irony, wit, well described 'humours', rejection of inadequate materialism and of spurious, popular spirituality—Mr. Barbecue-Smith of *Crome Yellow* is kin to the more sophisticated Burlap of *Point Counter Point*—are all there in as full measure as in the later, more ambitious works. Most of what was to be added later has not enriched Huxley's work. It is not, however, only a negative virtue that *Crome Yellow* and *Those Barren Leaves* possess; something that was in them has been lost. It is this quality, which I can only describe as the power to delight, that has made me value these two books with increasing affection. It is not, to my mind, present in *Antic Hay*, excellent though that is. The quality, I believe, is therefore connected with their country setting—the English country house, the farmyard of *Crome Yellow*, the Italian scene of *Those Barren Leaves*. Mr. Huxley has always made great sport of pantheism, nature worship or the transcendentalism of Daddy Wordsworth; yet there is in these two books an exultation, a sense of material pleasure in the natural world that irradiates the scene. They are, in a unique manner, idyllic, pastoral, bucolic, This does not mean that the satire is 'kindly' or the approach sentimental, but only that, despite himself and his rejection of the world, Mr. Huxley communicates a satisfying acceptant quality which enchants. It shows itself most particularly, of course, in those two inserted episodes—the brilliant tale of the dwarf Sir Hercules in *Crome Yellow* and the touching story of Mr. Cardan's rescue of the feeble-minded Miss Elver in *Those Barren Leaves*. It is present directly in the remarkable descriptive scenes. Its presence, however, is felt more subtly throughout both novels, and is not to be found anywhere else in modern literature.

(c) Francis Wyndham on *Point Counter Point* and *Eyeless in Gaza*: 'The Teacher Emerges'

Reading a book by Aldous Huxley is like being entertained by a host who is determined that one should not suffer a moment's boredom and works perhaps a bit too hard to ensure one's continual amusement. The fruit of his considerable erudition is lavished on his readers in flattering profusion: quotation from literature, references to art, history and science—if one takes the allusion, it is with a pleasant sense of sharing the author's culture, and if not one is privileged to learn a new fact or to hear an unusual and provocative point of view. For this reason Mr. Huxley is an ideal novelist for young men: remarkably intelligent, genuinely sophisticated, he takes for granted these enviable qualities in his readers. His first three novels, *Crome Yellow*, *Antic Hay* and *Those Barren Leaves*, and the stories, essays and poems of that period, represent a perfect form of undergraduate literature: elegant, informed, irreverent, ironic, as it seems amoral yet serious, they appeared at a time— the early 1920s—when the scene was set for brilliant young men and when to be a brilliant young man was the most rewarding thing to be. But brilliant young men must grow into brilliant middle-aged men; the undergraduate, though he may be sent down from one university, eventually becomes a don at another. Mr. Huxley could not for ever maintain a position of gay and destructive criticism; a constructive remedy had to be proposed and the entertainer had to make room for the teacher. In his later novels, the feast of diversion spread before his readers is no less rich than before, but it has become slightly indigestible.

Point Counter Point, which was first published in 1928, brings his earlier manner to a point of culmination and contains the germ of his later development. Formidably long, it introduces a host of representative characters (several of whom are clearly derived from real people) and sets them talking at each other. A complexity of design resulting from the large dramatis personae gives the novel's construction a superficial resemblance to that of Gide's *Les Faux-Monnayeurs*, which had appeared three years earlier; but neither *Point Counter Point* nor *Eyeless in Gaza*, in which Mr. Huxley later exploited a confusing time sequence, can lay claim to technical innovations. Mr. Huxley has never been an experimental writer; he is rather an accomplished popularizer of experiments recently made by others. *Point Counter Point* would be more amusing if it were less exhaustive, if its gallery of rogues and fools were less definitive; and *Eyeless in Gaza* might be easier to reread if its episodes were arranged in simple chronological order. The ideas of D. H. Lawrence dominate *Point Counter Point*, expounded at second-hand through the medium of a character called Mark Rampion. Rampion and his wife are possibly the first figures in Mr. Huxley's novels to be treated with a minimum of irony; yet the author's ironic attitude is infectious and his readers catch it by mistake; Rampion emerges, unintentionally, as a pretentious bore. However sympathetic to D. H. Lawrence as an artist Mr. Huxley may be, his own talent is naturally resistant to Lawrence's influence; an impression is given by *Point Counter Point* that the follies and vices of the time have been condemned from a position that is not truly the author's own.

Brave New World may well prove to be Mr. Huxley's most lasting book. Purely satirical and brilliantly prophetic, it is the last destructive work by an essentially destructive writer. By the time *Eyeless in Gaza* was published in 1936 Mr. Huxley had become a disciple of Gerald Heard; and Anthony Beavis, the hero, hopes to find balm for his disgust with life in the teachings of the mysterious Miller. From now on, an increasing concern with mysticism was to take control of Mr. Huxley's life and work, and the final pages of *Eyeless in Gaza*, which contain Anthony's spiritual meditation, point the way to all his future writing, including his last book about mescalin. Why does this development, so boldly constructive and apparently so consistent, not entirely satisfy? A certain element in his treatment of what he thinks disgusting weakens, in his novels, the force of his striving towards what he thinks pure. In spite of the case made out for withdrawal Mr. Huxley, it seems, relishes life, and not at all in the way of which Mark Rampion would approve. In an early collection of slight but elegant stories, *Mortal Coils*, there is one about a nun whose lover rapes and abandons her, stealing her false teeth which he hopes to sell. This story, according to the blurb, has been described by Jocelyn Brooke as 'admirably written in his best comic vein'. Among the incidents in *Eyeless in Gaza* which drive Anthony to Miller's contemplative comfort are three, also written in Mr. Huxley's best comic vein, which are well known: a dead dog is dropped from an aeroplane to burst over Anthony while he makes love on a roof; a schoolboy is interrupted while masturbating by his friends who jeer and throw things at him; a young girl pointlessly steals raw meat from a butcher's shop. All these episodes *are* comic, but not straightforwardly so; one laughs less with the author than at him for having invented them, and one suspects that he (a witty but humourless writer) only thinks them funny to the extent that, in various ways, they are potentially shocking. He seems, in fact, to be perpetually trying to shock himself by emphasizing the inadequacies of physical life, by pointing out that lovers look ridiculous when copulating, that the food we enjoy eating is revolting when raw and makes us belch and so on, but the shock results in titillation rather than rejection and disgust. As the writer of pornography pays, in his fashion, a compliment to sex, so Mr. Huxley obliquely honours the sensual life; but this is done in a series of highly cerebral *divertissements*[1] advocating discipline, control and meditation as the means towards spiritual peace and transcendent illumination. Yes, he is an excellent host; there is something here for everybody. The quality is high, the menu varied, but it is not, in the last analysis, a sustaining diet.

(d) John Wain on *Brave New World* and *After Many a Summer*: 'Tracts against Materialism'

Aldous Huxley, like George Orwell, W. H. Mallock, G. K. Chesterton and Charles Williams, is a pseudo-novelist; I use the expression not harshly, but merely to describe an author who finds himself using the form of the novel for some alien purpose. Mr. Huxley's purpose is to write tracts. Both these books are tracts against materialism.

As *Brave New World* is complicated by its special form, let me take the later book first. *After Many a Summer* concerns itself with a group of characters who typify, in one way or another, the confusions and miseries of the materialistic outlook. This outlook is so fruitful of confusions and miseries that Mr. Huxley can give us a very large gallery of characters, ranging from Dr. Obispo, whose personal character (as distinct, perhaps, from his work as a scientist) is utterly repulsive, up to Pete, his laboratory assistant, who is just a nice mixed-up kid. In between these two points on the graph lie Mr. Stoyte, Jeremy Pordage, Virginia Maunciple, in all of whom the author takes a protective interest, half tender and half repelled, as one might in an idiot child.

These figures are not 'characters', of course; they are Humours. As such they would be more successful if they were not all facets of the same Humour—highbrow Bloomsbury materialism, lowbrow Hollywood materialism, clean-limbed bewildered materialism, and so on. Over against them is set the figure of Mr. Propter (a most significant name—he is 'proper' and a 'prompter' and also *post hoc, ergo propter hoc*[2]) who knows all the answers, and is able to tell the other characters why materialism is wrong. He it is who makes the remark which sums up the effect on the reader of himself and his fellow-characters.

[1] 'Amusements.'
[2] 'After which, therefore because of which.'

They stand for certain things on the human level. But the things the writers force them to stand for when they describe events on the level of eternity are quite different. Hence the use of them merely confuses the issue. They just make it all but impossible for anyone to know what's being talked about.

He is actually referring, it will be remembered, to certain words in philosophical terminology, but his words apply startlingly well to this arid thesis untidily shovelled into the framework of a novel.

Apart from this artistic malaise, *After Many a Summer* is seriously damaging to its own cause. Its thesis is that materialism is to be abandoned and a version of mysticism ('on the level of eternity', as Mr. Propter is fond of saying) to be put in its place. But those who preach views of this kind should guard against giving the impression that to them, all human life is disgusting and wearisome, and all normal human emotions in themselves to be suspected. If the reader thinks that the book has been written by someone who just doesn't see the point of being human, the message will bounce off him. This impression has been enough to neutralize some of the very greatest satires, such as *Gulliver*, and it certainly neutralizes *After Many a Summer*. To turn to this book after reading, say, Chaucer, is to be struck by the difference between a wise and tolerant (however ironic) view of the human condition, and a mere foaming attack on it. In his eagerness to demonstrate that normal human pleasures are worthless and degrading, Mr. Huxley even repeats a situation he had already handled in an earlier novel; the scene in *Antic Hay* (chap. 20) where Coleman, preparatory to raping Rosie, tells her that it's a pity she is an agnostic, because she will miss half the fun of it by having no sense of sin, is a remarkable anticipation of the relationship between Obispo and Virginia:

[Quotes Part I, Chapter XIII, p. 178]

But Obispo, like Coleman, enjoys making his victim feel that they are 'honeying and making love over the nasty sty'. And the only other sexual relationship described in the book (if we exclude Pordage's fortnightly visit to Maida Vale, where he apparently engages two women at once) is the monstrous sadism of the eighteenth-century nobleman, who keeps himself alive by swallowing fishes' guts, and is discovered at the end of the story, two or three centuries old and still finding his sole pleasure in inflicting pain on his mate, who 'whimpers apprehensively' at his approach—recalling Virginia's 'moaning and gibbering' under the attentions of the skilled sex-mechanic Obispo. . . . What on earth has this got to do with the life of a normally poised human being? Of course, it touches the life of a normally poised person at this or that point; but my submission is that the old mistake has, once again, been made; if you set out to sermonize on the World, the Flesh and the Devil, and reveal clearly by your writings that for you, personally, the ordinary and attainable human joys are as tempting as a thumb in the eye, the reader will simply shrug it off. We can all refuse to adopt the methods of Coleman and Obispo without necessarily following the example of Origen.

Brave New World is also an anti-materialist tract. It is a well-understood convention that the Utopian kind of pseudo-novel, though set in a remote position as to period or place, is always a criticism of the author's own society. *Brave New World* is a criticism of Western society in 1932, as *1984* is of the same society in the closing months of the Second World War; any discussion of such books that sets out to assess their plausibility as *predictions* seems to me hopelessly off-centre. The citizens of the Brave New World are entirely conditioned to a life which ignores the possibility of any values except those of pleasure and material well-being; they live in great physical comfort which is paid for in terms of an appalling spiritual dryness. As a criticism of the more prosperous Western countries in the late 'twenties it could not be bettered; the 'prophetic' framework is valuable largely because it allows free play to the author's marvellous wit (the jokes about Ford, etc.).

The thrust against materialism had point in 1932, and has point now; but in the actual future, I doubt if it will have any. People who live very primitive and physically exhausting lives are never materialistic; on the contrary, they are always deeply religious. And it will, of course, be a primitive and laborious life that human beings will live in a hundred years' time and indefinitely thereafter; even if there are no World Wars, the increase of population, coupled with the exhaustion of natural resources, will usher in an era of famine and shortage. Our great-grandchildren will listen open-mouthed to stories of the 1950's, when even quite ordinary people had motor cars of their own, to go more or less where they liked, and could buy petrol without a police permit; people who lived in houses which could be warmed by merely switching on an electric fire, and where hot water gushed out of the taps! I think, in short, that humanity has already reached the most highly urbanized and gadget-ridden state it is ever likely to reach; anyone who wants to know how the peoples of the Western countries will be living in a century's time could find out more from a tour of South-East Asia than anything else: that swarming, half-starved proletariat—

that is our future, not a world in which ordinary citizens take trips by helicopter from London to New York.

It was the brave *old* world that Mr. Huxley was describing: the world with a tremendous material ascendancy, whose natural danger was sceptical materialism. In the world we are actually going to inhabit, the dangers will be devil-worship and witch-burning. But this fact does not, of course, diminish the value of Mr. Huxley's works.

(e) Peter Quennell on *Music at Night* and *Beyond the Mexique Bay*: 'Electrifying the Audience'

One of Mr. Aldous Huxley's Oxford contemporaries, who sometimes attended the same tutorials and heard him read his essays aloud, has described to me the admiration—the stupefaction almost—that they were apt to produce among his fellow undergraduates. His style was already fully fledged; he already displayed that breadth of reading, that gift of ranging rapidly to and fro across the fields of literature, art and science, discovering unexpected analogies between apparently diverse subjects, which he has since revealed in a long series of novels, stories and critical essays. Few writers of the present age have combined greater facility with a larger share of erudition. But so much facility (as Mr. Huxley himself is well aware) has obvious disadvantages; and twenty-five years ago he published an admirable pamphlet entitled *Vulgarity in Literature*, which contains some incisive criticisms of the critic's own method. He is discussing the novels of Flaubert:

[Quotes passage on Flaubert's ability to resist the temptation to digress, *Music at Night*, pp. 295–6]

The pamphlet was published in 1930. It was followed in 1931 by *Music at Night*, a book of miscellaneous essays, and three years later by a collection of travel-sketches, which he called *Beyond the Mexique Bay*. To re-read them is an interesting experience. Again one marvels at the writer's dexterity; each of these essays and sketches is the kind of production for which the editor of a weekly or monthly journal is constantly looking and usually looks in vain—adequately serious, sufficiently light, neatly fitted into the prescribed space, flavoured here and there with a paradoxical sense of fun. They belong, of course, to that unregenerate period when Mr. Huxley was still prepared to make irreverent jokes about 'mysticism' and 'misty schism'. The Literature of mysticism, he then assured us, 'which is literature about the inexpressible, is for the most part misty indeed—a London fog, but coloured pink'. But he had felt the heady influence of D. H. Lawrence, whose genius is hailed, though not without some shrewd reservations, in the last chapter of *Beyond the Mexique Bay*; and the sceptical astringency of his early novels and stories, of *Crome Yellow* and *Mortal Coils*, was slowly disappearing as the sceptic advanced on middle age.

Yet, despite a gradual change in the author's outlook, he retained many of his youthful foibles—his love of coining an effective phrase and, regardless of the literary consequences, following up an irrelevant train of ideas. The result is diverting, but at times unsatisfying. Many of the articles printed in *Music at Night* are surely a little too slight to deserve republication? 'The Beauty Industry', for example, merely exhibits a number of ingenious variations on the familiar journalistic problem as to whether feminine beauty is, or is not, skin-deep; while others have the charm, but also the impermanence, of entertaining table-talk. The essayist is repeatedly scoring points; but the points he scores, and the flourish with which he advertises them, are apt to seem more important than the convictions out of which they rise. He is customarily on the side of the angels—'Foreheads Villainous Low' and 'The New Romanticism' are timely exposures of current literary fallacies; but by his glib manner of presentation he frequently weakens the angelic case.

More troublesome is what may perhaps best be described as the lack of any *unifying* quality. It has often struck me that, while writing fiction and analysing the behaviour of his fictitious characters, Mr. Huxley shows a strange inability to appreciate any type of experience that is not either ecstatic and spiritual or grossly and repulsively sensual. There is no intermediate stage. His characters must either be exploring the heavens, opened by the great artists and the great composers, or wallowing in the slime—which the novelist describes with some relish—of their lowest physical appetites. There is never a hint of a marriage between Heaven and Hell: never a suggestion that there might exist a whole range of experiences, available to the ordinary human being, which never raise him to spiritual ecstasy yet, equally, never plunge him into the depths of moral squalor. A similar limitation seems to afflict the essayist. If he is not—as in 'Music at Night' and 'Meditation on El Greco'—writing of a subject by which he is deeply stirred and which inspires him to pro-

duce his best prose, he is inclined to adopt an attitude of flippant distaste, the flippancy sometimes degenerating into journalistic cleverness.
How marked the contrast with D. H. Lawrence, who, both as a novelist
and an essayist, often wrote very badly but, even at his silliest and most
perverse, seldom wrote insignificantly: whose peculiar vision of life
pervaded all that he did and said, enlightening the confusion and soften-
ing the contradictions! Lawrence was an intensely serious writer; and
so, without a doubt, is Aldous Huxley. But Mr. Huxley's work occasionally produces the impression that he will only condescend to be
serious upon the topics he has himself selected.

Elsewhere he is content to display his virtuosity—a brilliant trick-
cyclist of the intellect, calculated to electrify the audience at any literary
music-hall. There are moments, indeed, when he simply can't be
bothered. Thus his travel-book consists of a series of essays in which
genuine feats of observation are interspersed with brisk explosions of
journalistic back-chat: 'Jamaica (he informs us) is the Pearl of the
Caribbean—or it is the Clapham Junction of the West? I can never
remember.' And Jamaica is thereupon dismissed in three smart and
skimpy paragraphs. Odd that he should have failed to admire the
island's exuberant natural beauty! But then, the essayist's mind is more
readily excited by ideas encountered than by things seen—and, among
the things he sees and describes, he is generally less susceptible to Nature
than to works of art. Sights, sounds and scents leave his imagination
comparatively unmoved; and, since travel is primarily a *sensuous*
experience, the effect made by his travel-sketches is often rather bleak
and arid. Like his essays, they may instruct and entertain; but they
arouse no sense of mystery, open up no new perspectives, as did Lawrence in *Sea and Sardinia* or in his book about the ancient Etruscans. The
man who composed them, we feel, was always the prisoner of his own
intelligence; and that intelligence, whether by accident or design,
although it is splendidly equipped, in some of its essential features has
remained severely circumscribed.

THE GENIUS AND THE GODDESS

June 1955

---

129. V. S. Pritchett, review in *NYTBR*

26 August 1955, pp. 4, 12

Victor Sawdon Pritchett, b. 1900, author, critic, director of *New Statesman and Nation*, has been visiting professor at several British and American universities, and has written, for example, *The Living Novel* (1946), *Collected Stories* (1956), and *Balzac* (1973).

The review is entitled 'Drug of Reminiscence.'

This short novel, once more, shows Aldous Huxley, in all lucidity, treating human beings as a mixture of moral and scientific phenomena.

[Summarizes the action of the book, concluding with the accident]

A tragedy? No, the tale is a moralist's melodrama.

The theme is an old one of Mr. Huxley's: the conflict between puritanical science and the harmony of the happy sensual life or the beauties of the spirit. The virgin young prig, Rivers, may be saved by committing the sin of adultery. The wife's infidelity may enable her to save her husband's life. Good very often comes out of evil. We must beware of having rigid views. But science will intervene with a lot of ugly words and will insist on the 'physiological correlates' of emotion. A young girl of 14 is after all a zoological specimen as well as a funny thing writing macabre poetry and posing as a wounded soul or a *femme fatale*.[1]

It has always been a delicate matter to know where the encyclopedic curiosity ends and horror of the flesh begins; where Mr. Huxley is the

[1] 'Vamp.'

410

humane and unshockable inquirer and where he is the *voyeur*,[1] shocking himself, in the manner of the Genius of this story. There is no reconciliation. The result is that we get (as we so often do in a Huxley novel) disastrous lapses into vulgarity which afflict the puritan mind when it jokes about an unbearable truth.

In their conversational narrative the two old men of this story blunt the delicate edge of experience by treating life and people not as comedy or tragedy but as the guesswork of reminiscence, and one of Mr. Huxley's many epigrams is that reminiscence is a drug as powerful as gin or sodium amytal.

One has to make these harsh criticisms of the cleverest writer of an exceptionally brilliant generation, who was molded by a period when the art of conversation was revived. This copious and original novelist tends now to the journalistic rewrite of his former self. His savagery, his horror, his misanthropy and his satire belong to literature; the mellower pages of his later work, I think, do not. He remains, as the present novel shows, a master of observation and of scene where it is a question of thinking of people in terms of their conditioning by ideas or biological facts; the portrait of the adolescent girl in this story is brusque but sympathetic. He has caught the atmosphere of the great scientist's old-fashioned American home wonderfully well and he has mastery of invention and surprise. The talk is never boring. Mr. Huxley has, in short, all the gifts except that fine single voice of the artist who does not argue or discuss because he knows, limits, feels and tells.

[1] 'Peeping Tom.'

130. Thomas E. Cooney, review in *Saturday Review* (New York)

27 August 1955, xxxviii, pp. 9–11

Extract from a substantial review-article entitled 'The Intellect vs. The Spirit.'

Aldous Leonard Huxley has published ten novels in the last thirty-four years. Without exception, from *Crome Yellow* in 1921 to *The Genius and the Goddess* in 1955, these novels have been in some degree about intellectuals, and have been filled with their talk on the dizzily inter-secting planes of esthetics, psychology, history, science, and mysticism. If Emerson's scholar is Man Thinking, then Huxley's intellectual has often seemed to be Man Talking. But despite their ceaseless clacking of tongues and ping-pong of ideas, these intellectuals have also acted out the amusing and terrifying fables of Huxley's satirical invention, and have thus traced the journey of a brilliant critical intellect through the jungle of twentieth-century life toward his declared goal of 'individual psychological freedom.'

[Presents a synopsis of Huxley's career]

For in spite of the insistence of most critics that *Point Counter Point* is his best novel, it is as the sardonic prophet of *Brave New World* that he has had the greatest impact on the general public. In 1932 that novel could be dismissed by the unwary as a delightful jape, perhaps even as mere science-fiction; but in this day of helicopters, standardized amuse-ments, standardized sex, standardized opinions, and the frantic standard-ized production and destruction of consumer goods, we can see that the fetus of Brave New World is straining to be born. There is today even a counterpart to the island on which the discontented intellectuals Bernard Marx and Helmholtz Watson were isolated: we read of the Soviet Siberian prison community of Vorkuta, where hundreds of political unreliables have been transported, and where they enjoy complete freedom of thought and discussion within the bounds of their prison.

Where does *The Genius and the Goddess* stand in the stream of Huxley's work? In that part which is devoted to diagnosing man's slavery to his ego, or in that part which tries, rather coldly and unappealingly, to show him how to subdue that ego for his soul's good? Apparently Huxley is back at diagnosis again, but not with the old vigor. One can easily imagine the whole story of Henry Maartens, with his brilliant facade of intellect and his craven dependent psyche, woven into the fabric of *Point Counter Point* or *Eyeless in Gaza*. And one can also see Maartens as a microcosm of Huxley's whole criticism of man: the intellect dutifully assisting the ego in its idiot efforts to kill the soul.

Whenever Huxley has suffered at the hands of critics it has been because they decry his insistence on making his characters talk out and act out his ideas; realism and esthetic unity are thereby doomed, they say. But Huxley has clearly committed himself to the novel of ideas, convinced that the literary species is most viable in the bracing climate of satire. He has demonstrated that beauty can be found not only in harmony of form, but in the relevancy of ideas to man's eternal struggle with himself. Like his brother satirists of the eighteenth century, he is notable more for valor in the war of ideas than for ability to depict human personality. After all, Voltaire too was a destructive critic, a humorist, and even something of a science-fiction writer.

131. Sidney Alexander, review in *Reporter*

8 September 1955, xiii, pp. 46–8

Sidney Alexander, b. 1912, novelist, poet, dramatist, author of
The Man in the Queue (1941) and *Michelangelo the Florentine* (1957),
is also a translator and writer for film and radio.

The review is entitled 'Huxley: The Infant in the Powerhouse.'
Descriptive sub-headings have been omitted.

The phases of Aldous Huxley, like those of the moon, are luminous
dialogues between the powers of light and the powers of darkness.
Darkness is human bondage, the flesh; light is nonattachment, an
apprehension of the Highest Common Denominator, the metaphysical
Ground. Over a long and prolific writing career Huxley has stressed
first one and then the other of these terms: sense and spirit, flesh and
soul—back and forth his erudite, witty, and abstract mind has shuttled
as if between two ancestors: his Darwinian grandfather, T. H. Huxley,
and his pedagogical great-grandfather, Dr. Thomas Arnold.

Although the author is much a child of this century, his central concern has been a Victorian one—the relative claims of science and
religion. Like another famous kinsman,[1] he has been at Dover Beach
reflecting on the waning and the waxing of the sea of faith. Nor is he a
pasteboard moon either; the quality of his intelligence is spherical. In
the light we are always aware of the dark; ape and essence are ironically
and agonizingly yoked.

Huxley's latest novel continues the dialogue. But there is a difference
in tonality that, to the best of my knowledge, sets this slight and neatly
wrought take off from all the other conversation pieces. We are still on
the quest; we are still trying to find meaning in a Brave New World of
monkey monsters, hydrogen bombs, and lovers blissfully sweating
palm to palm. But into this brittle, cerebrally glittering universe of
Huxley something tremulous, humble, and human has crept—as if an
infant had wandered into a powerhouse.

[1] Matthew Arnold.

414

In terms of novel writing *The Genius and the Goddess* must be considered a minor work by comparison with the cunning montage of
Point Counter Point or *Those Barren Leaves* or the comic energy of *Antic
Hay*. Lovely and fluent though the prose texture may be, brilliant with
familiar patches of paradox, irony, and aphorism, the tale is told rather
than evoked, reflected upon rather than lived, and the characters are
more ideal than individual. Huxley has been after transcendence of
personality for a long time, and he thinks he has found it for the most
part in Hindu and Chinese philosophy and religion. Might this not be
one important reason why the Orient has failed to develop that most
personal of arts—the novel? What is more perilous than for a novelist
to deprive his characters of their uniqueness? And only a tired Huxley
would kill off his goddess so conveniently in an auto accident—*a dea ex
Cadillac*,[1] one is tempted to say.

The story is simple, almost classical in its proportions. The traditional
triangle: old husband, young wife, young lover. Two children have
been thrown in, with a sub-theme of an adolescent girl's love for her
mother's lover, but this doesn't matter. Indeed, the whole French-farce
situation is so ridden with cliché that the novelist is released to deal with
what genuinely concerns him: diabolic science and beatific love. The
clockwork monster this time is named Henry Maartens, Nobel Prize
atomic physicist, a man with enough intellectual equipment for six
men, but withal 'the psychological equivalent of a fetus.' He represents
the inorganic mind, the abstract tendency that must lead to war and
destruction. Yet the Henry Maartens who has read all the books on
child psychology and yet cannot establish a living relationship with his
own children—the Henry Maartens with the immense learning in the
head and pornography in the safe—really doesn't interest us. Huxley
has demolished him too many times before.

Who does interest us is Katy. For Katy, the goddess, the incredibly
lovely young wife of the half-insane genius, is something new, I think,
in Huxley's portrait gallery. She is new less for what she is herself than
for the author's attitude toward her. She is one of those perfect females
who exist only in fiction, lovely evidence of the dreams of male authors.
But whereas the earlier Huxley would have mocked at his own adoration, this Huxley does not. What is new in this novel is the complete
absence of irony in the treatment of love.

And what opportunities for irony there are! For the love affair
between Katy and her husband's research assistant, a minister's son,

[1] Cf. *deus ex machina*, the use of a contrived incident to resolve a difficulty in the plot.

twenty-eight years old and innocent, occurs just after the death of Katy's mother and while her husband is seemingly on his deathbed. At such a moment, temporarily broken, the goddess instinctively does what she must—she finds her way '. . . home to Olympus by the road of sensuality.' The young man's passage on that road (in the telling he is sixty, Huxley's age, looking back through the wrong end of a telescope) is described in terms of pentecosts, visitations, doves descending. What has happened to the zoology? What has transformed Huxley's lifelong trance of fascinated horror before the fact of love into this sob of adoration?

Of course, the young man is tormented by the woodpeckers of remorse. 'In silence, an act is an act is an act. Verbalized and discussed, it becomes an ethical problem, a *casus belli*,[1] the source of a neurosis. . . . Goddesses are all of one piece. There's no internal conflict in them. Whereas the lives of people like you and me are one long argument. . . . The point . . . was her experience of the creative otherness of love and sleep. The point was finding herself once again in a state of grace.'

Animal grace—that is Katy. By love she is made whole again, and of her wholeness her husband survives. That the love is one which society considers illicit, that the genius's survival rests upon a shaky reed of ethics—this might appear familiar Huxleyan irony. But there is scarcely a trace of the old flippancy. Now, beneath the irony, the agony: All of Huxley's champagne talk, some forty frothy volumes' worth, has been leading to this. An act is an act is an act. And let's keep our traps shut.

In other words, we are back in the bosky intuitional mystery lands of D. H. Lawrence. For a long time that Messiah of Impulse exercised a powerful gravitational pull upon Aldous Huxley. The juxtaposition of Mark Rampion against Lucy Tantamount in *Point Counter Point* was the Whole Man against the Part Man, Being versus Equal To. But Huxley turned against Lawrence's religion of sex; by the middle 1940's the flesh had become Ape and the task was to rise by meditative exercises to the apprehension of Essence.

But now, one hazards the guess, Huxley is not so certain that the flesh is Ape. With what warmth does he write of his Katy, of her immersion in animal being! She is the most embodied (as one might expect) person in this curiously abstract novel. She is Nature, an 'is-ness', and 'Some of her isness spills over and impregnates the entire universe.' Goethe was mistaken; all that passes is not a symbol. 'At every instant

---

[1] 'Cause of war.'

every transcience is eternally that transcience. What it signifies is its own being. . . .'

In other passages the author is at pains to remind us that animal grace is only one of three paths, all equally valid, all 'aspects of the same underlying mystery.' For there is also spiritual grace, the Clear Light of the Void, and there is human grace—the divine made human, 'what St. Paul called "Christ" . . . ideally all of us should be open to all of them. And yet . . . a third of a loaf is better than no bread.'

It is easy to be scornful. But I find a humility here, a tenderness in this late Huxley that was entirely absent in the *enfant terrible*[1] of the 1920's or in the West Coast mystic of recent years. Huxley's mysticism was never convincing on several counts. For one thing there was the gritted-teeth intellectualism of its approach. Love toward the human, or toward the more-than-human, is a yielding, not a willing. Watching Huxley at his meditative exercises was like watching a spiritual athlete. We may have admired the discipline and the muscle flexing but we certainly were not stirred to emulation.

Secondly, there has always seemed to be an air of meretriciousness when westerners drink their deepest draughts from Oriental wells. One wonders how much of the cosmic jag results from the exoticism of the liquor. The Huxley residing in California with its Bahai temples and musical cemeteries and kidney-shaped swimming pools, the Huxley at the corner of Hollywood and Heard—somehow it was difficult not to wonder whether his flights into Nirvana weren't really rope tricks. Philosophy may be perennial, and the metaphysic Ground may know no East or West. Nevertheless an Englishman in a loincloth is ridiculous.

Now, for the moment at any rate, he is out of his loincloth. The *enfant terrible* has become the *enfant* vulnerable. Naked on the earth he lies and terribly defenseless. For the first time we feel that Aldous Huxley has not tried to be clever; for the first time he bows his head and is as mired as the rest of us in the human condition.

[1] 'Problem child.'

417

132. Cashenden Cass, review in *New Republic*

12 September 1955, cxxxiii, pp. 16–17

The review is entitled 'Irascibility in Love with Love.'

A long silence is hard to break. The greater the silence the harder it gets. And Aldous Huxley's long silence felt like a great one. This time no Grey Eminence emerges, and it may be with a feeling of disappointment that one reaches the last sentence of Mr. Huxley's new book. For me the disappointment had been growing throughout this short moral story, lifting here and there at some recognition of the author's fine vision; but at the end, the disappointment increased as the author closed with a comment on Christian society that would go down better at one of those religious meetings held in football stadiums where crowds stand to convert their own goal. But this is a failure that calls for preferential treatment. The reader, stranded among the debris of the contemporary novel's self-consciousness, is likely to have put more upon a new book by this writer than mere expectations. On it, he may well have pinned his faith; and however much of a let down there may be, the faith is still justified. For Mr. Huxley is not one to enjoy the cream of a religious conversion under the pretext of a penitential dose of sour milk. For him it is yogurt without sugar, the real thing, and good for you. Nor does he lobby away at some doctrinal issue to boost a literary reputation. His is the work of a wonderfully intelligent mind at fair odds with itself, a spectacle worth attention.

Here the spectacle has been stripped of its trimmings, the extraneous litter of novel writing ignored. Unfortunately with this economic presentation of his novel Mr. Huxley has left out more than he has put in. He is determined to show only essentials and the main essential is the belief in one roughly defined theology, or what for want of a better word I will call God, and its adjunct, the at least theoretical possibility of man's achieving this. An extraordinary primitive statement when one remembers, as one *does*, the novels of the young Mr. Huxley, and a

transition almost remarkable enough in itself to confirm the precept by
his own example. In fact the author's own history would do more to
soften one up to his persuasion than this rather skimpy novel which
tends to default his very good faith. There is little in Mr. Huxley's
words here to restore our optimism, for although he is firm on a love
of God he floors this by an inability to love man, and one is no good
without the other.

He gives us a scientist-genius villain, a goddess wife, and a young
scientist substitute-hero. Plots do not worry me much, provided the
novelist can render them unimportant by the fascination of his creatures
and their interplay. But this is as typed a trio as ever came out of a far,
far worse best-selling novel than it should be possible for Mr. Huxley
to write.

[Recounts the plot of the book]

. . . The author, appearing to be quite out of patience with his
characters even in this short time of their being, dismisses the genius
as a gibbering old bit of folly, kills off the son in Korea, and finds the
good scientist a suitable wife in the fresher air of the Lebanon. Thus
none of the problems are truly resolved, and by not resolving them, or
by dispersing them by these connivances, Mr. Huxley protests that he
is bettering fiction with reality. His reality is as naïve as the fiction he is
displacing, and coming from such a well-read and well-written man
this naïveté rather leaves one wordless. How can we be surprised by the
revelation that a genius may in many ways be despicable? We may be
considerably more surprised that a mature confident woman could
suddenly become so unnerved by her child's nagging as to drive smash
into a lorry.

The curious thing in this novel is the hatred the scientist-genius is
supposed to provoke and does provoke in the author. This is the only
character who smudges his copy with a little common humanity, an
attribute for which in this novel there is no regard. It is only the children
in the story who are treated with care, and here the prose, which too
often favors an ironic use of psychiatric aphorisms, breaks away from
an imposed detachment—the authenticity of which is added to by the
young man telling the story as an old man—and is all the better for the
sympathy let slip by the author.

There is a brilliant entry made in the style of *Point Counter Point* and
held for a few moments of scorching effect, by a youngish married
couple, and when one sees how easily he can enchant us with his

disenchantment it is perhaps no wonder that a novelist of this ability should tire of that game. The conversational telling of the story throws out a generous array of ideas and propositions. If they fall not to be picked up there is never a moment's doubt that the man knows what he is talking about and could well take them up if he chose. As it is, he prefers a direct reference to the correct authorities, and one judgment on this book could be praise of its high standard of intellectual references, but although these are always acknowledged, not stolen, they leave a sensation of the reader having been somewhere cheated.

It is the book of a man who puts a good question, who believes that the answer cannot be adequately phrased, but that the answer is with us, although most of us spoil it with our crude imperfections. It is '. . . a situation with which only a thoroughgoing Christian or Buddhist could adequately deal,' as the storyteller remarks about the state of affairs in the book. This goes for our affairs too, and Mr. Huxley is angry that we are not all top level Christians or Buddhists; but he also knows that anger is not what he really should feel, nor can he keep it up for long, or this book would have run into many more pages. There's nothing that fails like trying again but, angry or not, it's good to be reminded that there is an Aldous Huxley around the place.

133. Isabel Quigly, review in *Spectator*

8 July 1955, cxcv, pp. 69–70

Isabel Madeleine Quigly, b. 1926, has been film critic for the *Spectator* since 1956 and has written for many British papers, e.g., *Observer*, *Sunday Times*, *Daily Telegraph*, *Guardian*, and *Encounter*.

Some introductory remarks on 'that old reviewer's problem of how to differentiate between those two incomparables, success and scale,' are omitted.

The Genius and the Goddess, being neither successful nor (one hopes at least) ambitious, hardly raises the problem at all, except in so far as one opens it with a certain hope and excitement. But there is only the spectacle of a slicked-up Mr. Huxley managing adroitly that cumbersome form the interrupted soliloquy, with two old cronies, or rather one and an echo, talking through the evening about an old love affair. With the first words Mr. Huxley sticks his neck out, for he lays down a law and promptly breaks it. 'The trouble with fiction,' said John Rivers, 'is that it makes too much sense. Reality never makes sense.' 'The criterion of reality,' he goes on to say, 'is its intrinsic irrelevance.' After that anti-fictional blast you expect at least a whiff of intrinsic irrelevance, some escape from a routine plot and hackneyed fictional characters. But no: Mr. Huxley gives us a situation as contrived and almost as stately as a minuet, a dance of force and counterforce exactly matched, action, reaction, and finally an accident as opportunely placed to kill off unwanted characters as galloping consumption used to be, or, more recently, angina pectoris. The genius is that old fictional favourite the half-wit intellectual, the absent-minded professor so brilliant he cannot tie his own bootlaces, the goddess that other fictional standby, the earth-mother-barmaid, beautiful and amused and sensual and unexacting; and the pattern of their behaviour is mapped out by every fictional precedent till the car accident, relevant with a vengeance, sorts their destinies neatly out. The whole thing is far more readable, far more amusing even, if that is what you want from a novel, than many of his earlier works; but Mr. Huxley looks to be just freewheeling on a well-oiled technique.

134. Richard Lister, review in *New Statesman and Nation*

16 July 1955, l[n.s.], p. 76

Richard Percival Lister, b. 1914, has written several books and contributes to *Punch*, *Atlantic Monthly*, *New Yorker*, and others.

Mr. Huxley's brilliant new short story—*The Genius and the Goddess* runs to only 120-odd pages—is a most characteristic piece of work, witty, expert, erudite, and just a little, as they say of game, 'high'.

[Quotes passage on existence, p. 1, as an accurate reflection of Huxley's views]

In his imagination flesh and philosophy, God and the glands do lie side by side and each cancels out the satisfaction that the other by itself might offer. As a novelist, Mr. Huxley's aim might be defined as the attempt to bring Beauty and the Beast into as simultaneous an existence as it is possible for arrangement to bring them, and, since the sense of sin is stronger in him than the sense of enjoyment, the desirable is always only the filling sandwiched between two slices of the nasty.

[Summarizes the story and comments on Katy as 'a pagan Goddess figure']

. . . The love of the senses is for a brief span displayed as health-giving. But then—and this is too predictable—Mr. Huxley cannot resist paying everyone out with a whack from the stinking fish of puritanism all round. But the defect is easily swallowed for the other pleasures which Mr. Huxley offers. The story is told with ease, gusto and vividness, and it is decorated with his lively idiosyncratic observations on life and behaviour. Above all, how wittily Mr. Huxley writes; one moves through his tale on a continual ripple of smile and laugh. . . .

[Closes with an example, Rivers's comment on his mother, p. 14]

135. V. S. Pritchett on the collected short stories

New Statesman and Nation, 22 June 1957, liii [n.s.], p. 814

For a biographical note see No. 129. The review is entitled 'Mellifluous Educator.'

The attraction of the early Huxley was—as I recall—that of a young fashionable preacher: he was brilliant, worldly, flashing with culture. He was profane and yet soothing, destructive but—inevitable in the Huxleys—a mellifluous educator. The pleasure of his novels came not very much from his people (who were indeed thin transcripts from educated society between London and the Mediterranean) but from the non-stop talk by which he drove them into exhaustion and nagged them into nothingness. Talk was the cult of the Twenties and he was its exploiter. With him it was not table talk; he talked the clothes and souls off his people, he talked them out of life into limbo and, since he was astute enough to know what he was doing, *Limbo* was the title of his first book of short stories. They are the hors d'oeuvre of a prolonged cannibal feast.

It is thirty-seven years since the publication of *Limbo* and now we have the *Collected Stories* of his lifetime. They belong mainly to a period now remote: the last age of rich old hedonists, businessmen (vulgar), intellectuals (incompetent in love), savage hostesses, grumpy artists. The old educated class is seen breaking with Victorian commitment as it loses its sons or its property, and ascending into that captious island of Laputa which floated in sunny detachment above Western Europe between the wars. As a writer Mr. Huxley has always been proficient in every genre he undertook, but it would not be just to judge him by these shorter pieces. He needed space for the great scoldings, for if you hate life it is best to hate it in a big way. He needed more room for the horrors, the savageries; more room for the kinder and learned comedies. In the very short stories—I exclude his *nouvelles*—his intellect turns out people like skinned rabbits. They are either not worth his trouble or one resents that his brain has reduced their worth. In general his stories are not about people and situations; they are talk about people in relation to ideas that appear to have been set up in order to snub them. It's when the people seem equal to the ideas that the good stories emerge; in the bizarre and tragic 'Sir Hercules', in the sinister 'Gioconda Smile', in a sharp light thing like 'Half Holiday', the geniality of 'Little Mexican', one of the rare life-loving tales, in 'The Rest Cure', a triumph over the talker, and in the pitying tale of 'Young Archimedes'. Here the driving voice abates and the preacher's chastisements are softened. A very good book.

In the other satires one is sooner or later aware of Mr. Huxley's weariness of his own brain. We cannot separate ideas and people; and there is a disagreeable disparity between the cleverness of the commentary and the banality of his realism. No one drops so surprisingly into cliché when describing the ordinary run of feeling. His lovers speak out of the pages of magazines. Mr. Huxley is self-conscious enough to be uncomfortable about the clichés. After all, are not all the valued human feelings clichés and are they the worse for that? The answer surely is that, to the artist, they are not clichés. It looks as though Mr. Huxley was frantic for novelty when he was tired. In the end it has been the accumulation of novel ideas, once so golden, that have now become heavy as lead in these comedies of displeasure.

One excellent story—'Chawdron'—stands out as a remarkable example of a writer's ability to use all his powers. It is at once a story of emotional nausea and a story of talking about it. The influence of Lawrence can be felt here. Lawrence was a master of magnetism in the short story. He forced his characters and their situations to a standstill, while he whipped them by repetitive phrases into greater intensity. Without passion or the poetic imagination, the method becomes merely frenzied and that is Mr. Huxley's case; but the genial, broken-down writer who has talked his talents away redeems him. 'Hogwash' is his word for the emotions of the tycoon he is describing. Hogwash, hogwash, hogwash, he repeats throughout, in all varieties of scorn known to a clever man. The effect is funny, cruel, devastating, indignant and dismissive. And the fact that the talker himself, who knows all the beauties and delinquencies of talk, is the prisoner of an old housekeeper who comes in and out contemptuously, without saying a word, adds the final macabre commentary. I have mentioned this Jamesian masterpiece also because it is an example of a story which could hardly now be written. The subject is good enough; the financial chimpanzee who at fifty falls in love with a pious baby-bitch who calls him Nunky and is herself called Fairy by him—that is irresistible. By embedding this in a lot of clever theorising, by working in the usual art notes on St. Catherine of Siena, Carlo Dolci, Rowlandson, Podsnap, Othello and Jesus, the characters are properly snubbed and we are skilfully given an intellectual comedy—but not the *comédie humaine*.[1] This is the kind of tale which is now dealt with directly. We write the dialogue, describe the moves; and being up against the characters themselves and not a sexual theory, we find the situation richer and more alarming. We would see Chawdron corrupting the educated writer. We would see Fairy hating him. We would laugh more or be more terrified. We would have lost educated explanation and its clever footpaths along the precipices of life; we would have lost talk and gained the explicit. But there it is: for better or worse, Mr. Huxley has always been the artist-educator, the preaching connoisseur who finds his stern text in our spiritual bric à brac, the illusions and novelties of belief.

[1] 'Human comedy.'

136. C. P. Snow on *Brave New World* and *Brave New World Revisited*

New Republic, 12 January 1959, cxl, pp. 18–19

Sir Charles Percy Snow, b. 1905, novelist, playwright, essayist, author of the eleven-volume novel sequence *Strangers and Brothers* (1935–71), *The Two Cultures and the Scientific Revolution* (1959), and others. The review is entitled 'Aldous Huxley—Romantic Pessimist.'

It is always wrong to deny or forget one's gratitude, as a wise radical friend of mine said, warning himself as well as me, just after we had listened to one of Churchill's speeches in 1940. It would be wrong for any Englishman of my age, ten years or so younger than Aldous Huxley, to deny the gratitude we owed him in the twenties. No one has set us thinking about so many different things: no one sharpened our wits or widened our sensibilities so much. That happened, and it's on the literary record for good and all.

Having said that, I now want to say that I am profoundly out of sympathy with *Brave New World Revisited* and with *Brave New World* and, I fancy, with any further attempts of his to rationalize his views on the social condition of men. I never liked literary Utopians much: I like literary anti-Utopians even less. Both Orwell's *1984* and Huxley's two *Brave New Worlds* seem to me likely to do much more harm than good. They are neither art nor life, but essays at just that kind of abstraction which most distorts the truth. They are quite different in kind and intention from books which Huxley refers to with approval, such as *The Power Elite* and *The Organization Man*. Those admirable works are written within the grain of society; they are part of the real social world just as a direct realistic novel is; we can learn from them some of the price we have to pay for advanced industrial security, without losing contact with its immense gains. Immense gains, I said, for the sooner intellectuals in the US and Western Europe realize that industrialization is the one hope of the poor, the sooner we shall get hold of a social purpose again.

In both of Huxley's anti-Utopias there is one basic fact. It is that in organized societies men can be deprived of their free minds: the power-bosses in Communist countries, the concealed power-bosses in capitalist societies, can use various kinds of technique, sheer force, propaganda, subliminal advertising, drugs, and so on, to make the 'masses' go contentedly, unresistantly and even happily to whatever actions the power-bosses decide on for them. The trouble with statements of that kind—and it is the trouble with two thirds of this new book—is they are neither true nor untrue. Of course, in advanced industrial society (let's call it 'a.i.s.') a very large amount of power seems to be concentrated in a few hands and sometimes is. Of course, by the nature of a.i.s. and the scientific revolution which brought it about new sorts of persuasion, manipulation, coercion and control can be used on a larger proportion of the population more immediately than ever in the past. So far, so bad.

But that this is transforming the texture of individual life now or in the foreseeable future seems an entirely romantic view. In fact, one is left wondering what romantic conception of the free mind is hallucinating Huxley—how does he imagine it operating in, say, a peasant in mediaeval England or in Tsarist Russia? And in what ways are these operations preferable to those of an unfree mind in a factory in Lancaster, Pennsylvania, which has been exposed to subliminal advertising or even tranquillizers? And in what senses does he imagine the unfree mind in Lancaster really demonstrates its individual unfreedom, as opposed to a similar mind about 20 years ago before a.i.s. got fully into its swing? How long is it since he talked disinterestedly and intelligently to people fully within the grip of a.i.s. not seeing it, as he is bound to see it, from outside and with distaste?

He appears to have become—perhaps he was always so—more pessimistic about the individual condition. Probably the combination of social pessimism and individual romanticism is more common than we think. It is a serious disqualification for social thinking for a rather curious reason. It means that one is constantly trying to think, or idealize, the individual into a non-social context. Huxley has always been tempted to this. He has never had any feeling for the social plasma in which we, as human beings, really live our lives. The social plasma is incomparably more important to our destinies than tranquillizers, mescalin, hidden persuaders, the whole bag of sophisticated horrors.

137. Frank Baldanza on Huxley's human fugue

South Atlantic Quarterly, Spring 1959, lviii, pp. 248–57

Frank Baldanza, b. 1924, has been a professor of English at Bowling Green State University since 1957. He has written books on Mark Twain (1961) and Ivy Compton-Burnett (1964), and over two dozen articles for critical and scholarly journals.

Baldanza's article, entitled '*Point Counter Point*: Aldous Huxley on "The Human Fugue," ' is a sustained analysis of the musical analogy in the novel. The essay heralds the small but serious body of academic attention which was beginning to be paid to Huxley's work, especially in America, toward the end of his lifetime. See Introduction, p. 31.

The British intelligentsia of the twenties and thirties took their music seriously; Virginia Woolf records in her diary funeral services, like that of Roger Fry, at which not a word was spoken, the entire service consisting in music. She herself composed much of *The Waves* during sessions with the later works of Beethoven on the gramophone, works to which T. S. Eliot's *Four Quartets* owe more than their title; and the passage on the Beethoven sonata in *Room with a View* and the magnificent concert performance of the Fifth in *Howards End* provide only a hint of E. M. Forster's devotion to music and musicoliterary analogy, which he expands a bit in *Aspects of the Novel*.

But we have learned from earlier romantic theorizing on such analogies that they are highly untrustworthy unless considered either very skeptically or else very metaphorically. Aldous Huxley, in 'Music at Night,' summarizes the perils involved: 'Music "says" things about the world, but in specifically musical terms. Any attempt to reproduce these musical statements "in our own words" is necessarily doomed to failure.' But if the 'statements' of music can be conveyed only in terms of music, nevertheless, Huxley apparently found that the structure of music provided, in the 'theme and variation' form, an analogy that could successfully be applied to literary material. And it is in his novel *Point Counter Point* that he worked out this analogy for all its fictional worth. Early in the book, during a performance of Bach's Suite in B minor for flute and strings, he comments: 'In the human fugue there are eighteen hundred million parts. The resultant noise means something perhaps to the statistician, nothing to the artist. It is only by considering one or two parts at a time that the artist can understand anything.'

In *Point Counter Point* the vehicle for Huxley's method and the embodiment of his introspective activity is the novelist Philip Quarles, at once a portrait of himself and an outlet for his preoccupations. And it is in the journal of Quarles, quoted sporadically in the novel, that we find Huxley's speculations on the suitability of musical structure for the novel of ideas.

The first thing Huxley saw was that if one or the other of the two elements of the novel of ideas—the ideas themselves or the depiction of humanity—had to be sacrificed, then humanity would have to go: 'The chief defect of the novel of ideas is that you must write about people who have ideas to express—which excludes all but about .01 per cent of the human race.' But it is out of such a dilemma that his most brilliant inspiration came, one that enabled him not only to preserve both elements, but to make them mutually complementary and functional. It was in the example of music that he found a structural analogy which retained intellectual order and complexity without sacrificing emotional connotation. And, like Virginia Woolf, T. S. Eliot, and E. M. Forster, it is to Beethoven he turns for all his illustrations. Although the soirée in the opening passages of the novel is dominated by a performance of Bach's Suite in B minor, it is Beethoven's A minor Quartet which motivates Spandrell's suicide at the end, and it is Beethoven's B flat major and C sharp minor Quartets and the Diabelli variations that Huxley invokes for illustrations on how fiction might be 'musicalized.'

Abrupt transitions and subtle modulations from one mood to another are two of the basic devices he discusses. He means to reproduce, in the sequence of scenes in a novel, 'majesty alternating with a joke' as in the first movement of the B flat major Quartet. Translated into literary terms, 'While Jones is murdering a wife, Smith is wheeling the perambulator in the park.' And toward the end of this novel, a lover arriving for a tryst is cracked on the head by an Indian club; as one of his murderers peruses the advertisements in a copy of *Vogue*, Burlap seduces Beatrice Gilray, Philip goes to a Satie concert, and Elinor rushes to the country to the bedside of her dying son. As the boy dies, Arkwright frets because the father is thus prevented from writing a preface to a new illustrated pornographic book he is publishing. But Huxley considered the modulations and subtle variations to be at once more 'interesting' and more 'difficult' than the abrupt transitions. The latter effect he hoped to gain by either having similar characters performing dissimilar acts, or having dissimilar characters caught in parallel situations. Obviously in order to gain all these effects, he needed a large and varied gallery of types, which he apparently drew from his own experience, since this novel is often treated as a *roman à clef*.[1]

The basic theme of the novel is provided by the outlook of Mark Rampion, a figure modeled after Huxley's admired friend, D. H. Lawrence. All the other characters of the novel are ranged about Rampion and his situation; perhaps the surest sign of this arrangement is Rampion's detachment from all the rest, who are related to each other by complicated ties of blood, intimacy, and friendship. In fact, although the novel has little enough plot in the conventional sense, Rampion simply appears at Sbisa's restaurant where he pontificates on his theories, but he takes no direct hand in any significant action in the book.

In a whole range of sexual frenzy, only Rampion and his wife Mary are satisfactorily adjusted, although their bickering relationship is a kind of contrapuntal balance of opposites. The theory that summarizes Mark's appeal to Mary, and which also stands as the basic theme for which all else in the book is a variation, is:

'Civilization is harmony and completeness. Reason, feeling, instinct, the life of the body—Blake managed to include and harmonize everything. Barbarism is being lop-sided. You can be a barbarian of the intellect as well as of the body. A barbarian of the soul and the feelings as well as of sensuality. Christianity made us barbarians of the soul and now science is making us barbarians of the intellect.'

Certainly the theory has a recognizable relation to the ideas of D. H. Lawrence, who fascinated Huxley as a person.

What interests us at the moment is the suitability of this philosophy as a basic structural theme on which to work variations. In commenting on the theme of the Diabelli variations, Huxley says: 'The whole range

[1] A novel in which actual persons and events are presented under the guise of fiction.

of thought and feeling, yet all in organic relation to a ridiculous little waltz tune. Get this into a novel.' If one needs only 'a ridiculous little waltz tune,' then we should not be perturbed at either the inadequacy or the triteness of the philosophy because it is the number and variety of the variations, and the range of thought and feeling which the variations embrace, that constitute the artist's aim. Let us take the catalogue in the order in which it is presented in Rampion's speech ('reason, feeling, instinct, the life of the body') and note the ways in which Huxley varies each of these qualities in the lives of his characters.

Philip's interest in biology symbolizes the overdevelopment of his intellect and the consequent neglect of instinct and feeling in his relations with his wife. Frustrated by years of attempting to maintain an intimate relation with a nearly ghostly abstraction of a man (and even having failed to interest him in extramarital affairs as a therapeutic measure), she turns in revulsion to Everard Webley, the exact opposite of her husband. Webley's green-shirt fascist organization is a perfect channel for his blustering emotionalism: in contrast to Philip's orderly deductions, Webley's speech in Hyde Park represents the quintessence of antirational *non sequitur*. Elinor, however, finds herself incapable of surrendering to Webley: although she is thrillingly moved by the spectacle of his speech, her reason interrupts again and again to remind her that he really considers love to be 'just an occasional brief violence in the intervals of business,' and not a wholehearted passion that integrally informs one's entire life. Elinor stands as a kind of bridge between the two men and although she incorporates a wholesome balance of the elements that Rampion finds in Blake, she is foiled by the lopsidedness of the people she associates with. Thus the three characters represent a kind of triadic variation on the reason-emotion theme.

While the contrasts offered by these three characters sufficiently illustrate the theme of the balance of reason and emotion, we rely more on the author's word as far as instinct is concerned. Suffice it to say that instinct is a quality which blends in a harmonious balance with the other qualities in the well-integrated characters like Mark Rampion and Elinor Quarles, and it also goes along with the more lovable traits of those who live almost entirely in their emotions, like John Bidlake. But instinct is found less and less frequently in the intellectually obsessed and unbalanced characters, until it disappears totally with such a person as Philip or Illidge, the Communist, who has overdeveloped his reasoning faculties.

It is when sensual indulgence enters as a factor that the real complexity of the interrelation of these qualities is evident. Where the body is totally incapacitated, as is the case with Lord Gattenden, one passes his time seeking out mathematical proofs for the existence of God. Together with Lord Edward, he is as lifeless as it is possible to be without actually dying. Old John Bidlake, the sybaritic painter who is widely known for his fleshy and voluptuous nudes, makes his love 'straightforwardly, naturally, with the good animal gusto of a child of nature.' But when this same child of nature approaches death toward the end of the book, his panic fear of doctors and the elaborately circumscribed net of superstitions that controls his emotions show him to be a spiritual and rational savage.

However, his conversation with his former mistress, Lady Edward, at least reveals that he is capable of emotional attachments; when he turns to address her daughter, Lucy Tantamount, he faces a purer sensualist than even he could have conceived. Lucy, while she represents a kind of debauched jazz-age youth, also stands in Huxley's schematic arrangement as the extreme in dedication to nervous titillation, at the opposite pole from Lord Gattenden and Lord Edward, her father. She surrounds herself obsessively with company, regardless of its quality, and refuses to break up any party until dawn. 'She could pursue her pleasure as a man pursues his, remorselessly, single-mindedly, without allowing her thoughts and feelings to be in the least involved.' She takes Walter Bidlake as a lover only after her maddening regime of all-night table- and club-hopping drives him to several desperate and passionate attempts at physical attack. Surprised and delighted, she indulges him until his true character as a mawkish and ineffectual sentimentalist manifests itself. Lucy, who began going to the theater at the age of six, and who finds all balls uniformly dull, has exhausted all other sensations except those centering around cruelty. If she is not the victim of violence and capriciousness (as it at first appeared she would be with Walter) then she must inflict it on others, as in her fiendishly detailed description to the distraught Walter of her street encounter in Paris with the violent and olive-skinned Neapolitan.

Walter's attraction to Lucy was coincidental with his abandonment of Marjorie Carling, a timid and whey-faced woman very like himself, without the spiritual resources to use her intelligence effectively, and without the will to follow out her commitment to a life of sensual indulgence. Both Marjorie and Walter consequently get the worst of the four realms—intellectually frustrated, emotionally riddled by feelings of inferiority and guilt, instinctually hesitant and bungling, and physically discomfited, Marjorie by her unwelcome pregnancy and Walter by his bitter longing for the perverse and elusive Lucy.

An even subtler variation is attained in the depiction of Maurice Spandrell and Denis Burlap, both of whom are harried by pseudo-religious convictions but in different directions. They are distinguished from the preceding characters in that they indulge in reason, feeling, instinct, and the life of the body in a fairly balanced manner; neither of them concentrates exclusively on one of the faculties at the expense of the others. Subconsciously or not, both Burlap and Spandrell are committed to a quest for spiritual experience, deriving directly in Spandrell's case from Oedipean sources, and it becomes clear enough in the course of the novel that this drive is the one that vitiates and distorts their sensual lives and makes them such monsters of hypocrisy. Although it is clear, too, that Huxley has not always looked this dourly on man's need for God, the position fits well in the D. H. Lawrence–Rampion code that dominates this particular novel.

For a variation on both Burlap and Spandrell, Huxley manages to have the latter run into Carling, Marjorie's estranged husband, at a pub. Although deserted by his wife for drunken brutality, he drowns his sorrows in alcohol while he lectures the barmaid (who has the temerity, after his fifth whiskey, to call him 'young Sacramento') on the inviolability of the sacrament of marriage.

But such a schematization of Huxley's method obscures the major effect he was seeking, the sense of progression and suspension as the themes work themselves out. To gain a sense of this buoyant plasticity as it manifests itself in the novel, we shall have to turn to the second of the devices we mentioned earlier, having similar characters doing dissimilar things and having dissimilar characters caught in similar situations. It is by the multiple ironies involved in these complex contrasts that the most subtle and elegant counterpoint is attained in the novel.

Thus Walter Bidlake's affair with Marjorie Carling, a high-minded and spiritual relation, contrasts with his frenzied pursuit of Lucy Tantamount, an affair that only the very late Roman empire could appreciate. The attraction and repulsion he feels for both women simultaneously symbolizes the split in his nature between allegiance to spiritual and physical values. And Illidge's humanitarian love of mankind expresses itself as surely in his biological researches as his hatred for the upper classes does in his high-principled murder of Everard

Webley. Another purposefully muddled person, Denis Burlap, works at his major opus on St. Francis, but takes time out for childlike romps in the bathtub with his secretary.

However, the basic structural unit of this novel is the 'scene,' an afternoon or an evening during which a group of contrasting characters gather for conversation. And it is in playing one scene off against another, or in breaking up one scene by interspersed passages from other scenes, that Huxley gains his major ironic variations and shows dissimilar persons performing similar acts.

A miniature example of contrast in scenes is in Elinor's return from her first meeting with Webley after the Quarles's trip to India. She has determined to tell Philip about Webley's attraction for her in order to stimulate him to jealousy and, perhaps, to love; he, however, is so deeply immersed in a manual of biology that he hardly hears what she says. Later in the book, he attempts to seduce the talkative Comtesse d'Exergillod, but learns in the process that she only flirts in order to be able to talk about—but never to do anything about—love. When he returns home, humiliated and angry with himself, Elinor retaliates, unconscious of the total irony of the situation, by immersing herself in a book and refusing to listen to his confidences. But behind the irony of situation is a more complex irony of meaning; Elinor is attracted by the real brutality of Webley, and just as effectually repelled by it when he attempts to actually embrace her; Philip, the over-civilized intellectual, attempts to fake out brutality in his advances to Molly d'Exergillod, but she perversely proves herself even more civilized in her shocked panegyric on Platonic love.

Of greater importance in terms of the total work are the grand 'units' of scenes, such as the one that opens the novel. During the musicale, various contrasts occur; Illidge, the Communist, is introduced not only to reactionary military gentlemen, but even to the fascist Webley. Later, he expatiates on his bitter hatred of the rich to Walter Bidlake, who was harried during his ride on the tube to Tantamount House by *his* hatred of the poor. Just as Bidlake on the tube thought back to the disgusting charity visits he made as a child to poor tenants' cottages with his mother, so Illidge now thinks back over the life of the poor as exemplified in his own childhood.

Then come in swift alternations a series of fragmentary conversations at Sbisa's, each of which is interrupted by a 'going home' scene as one character after another comes home from the Tantamount musicale. In the same manner that Virginia Woolf organized *Mrs. Dalloway* a few years earlier, Huxley uses general contemporaneity as the means to shift from one group of characters to another and to embroider his ironic and thematic meanings. But in contrast with Mrs. Woolf's, Huxley's art is predominantly objective, and he embodies his meaning in conversation to such a degree that he simply uses the listings and turnings of the talk at Tantamount House or at Sbisa's to dictate the content of the intermezzi.

And of course there is a subtler and more detailed counterpoint of ideas running through the novel which does not find expression in major scenes. Illidge, the Communist, detests the virtues of wealth and good breeding—'disinterestedness, spirituality, incorruptibility, refinement of feeling, and exquisiteness of taste.' Later, and for totally different reasons, Lucy Tantamount, the compulsive aristocratic slummer, mutters about her mother's 'bear garden' soirées, in perfect accidental agreement with Illidge: 'There's nothing I hate more than the noise of cultured, respectable, eminent people, like these creatures.'

In addition to all of these fairly obvious correspondences and variations, all of which center about specific ideas, Huxley also repeats abstract behavior patterns from scene to scene. For example, Marjorie, in the opening scene, pleads with Walter to stay at home with her; he offers all sorts of excuses and rationalizations, but finishes by acquiescing in her demand; however, by this time, Marjorie has begun to feel guilty about her insistence, and now they argue on opposite sides of the issue, she insisting he go and he adamantly determined to stay. The same pattern occurs between Walter and Burlap when Walter asks for a raise in salary; the interview ends with Walter elaborately rejecting the proffered raise and Burlap magnanimously bestowing it. Thus Huxley has twice reproduced the 'hourglass' pattern in which each character at the end of the scene holds the position occupied by the opposing character at the opening of the scene.

The opposite pattern for a scene is one in which both characters hold the same position simultaneously but for different reasons: after Elinor and Philip have quarreled in Chapter XXIV about the proper way to rear their child, each has misgivings and each suppresses an impulse to apologize to the other.

In addition to these structural devices, Huxley employs, again as did Virginia Woolf in *Mrs. Dalloway*, flashbacks which taken together form counterpoints played off against present developments in the novel. A series of eight recollections, for example, explores the courtships of various couples.

The end of the novel, initiated with Chapter XXXII, consists of a series of variations on the theme of death. We saw earlier that the first symposium in Sbisa's gave Rampion the opportunity to expose his philosophy, which we took as the basic theme of the book; the second symposium was devoted to predestination and to determining to what degree an individual shapes events to resemble his own character. Now the third of the great symposia which state philosophical possibilities that events in the novel bear out occurs again at Sbisa's; and again Rampion has the rostrum, with death as his subject. While this unit is composed of more scattered and discrete scenes than the opening unit that centered around the musicale at Tantamount House, it is richer in meaning and fuller in complexity, depending as it does on all kinds of pre-established orientations on the part of the reader which Huxley could not avail himself of at the opening of the novel.

It is in Rampion's final philippic that we have the definitive statement of his humanistic values, and as we read it, we need to keep in mind what Huxley said earlier about art as a way of presenting 'the human fugue':

'After all, the only truth that can be of any interest to us, or that we can know, is a human truth. And to discover that, you must look for it with the whole being, not with a specialized part of it. What the scientists are trying to get at is non-human truth. . . . By torturing their brains they can get a faint notion of the universe as it would seem if looked at through non-human eyes. What with their quantum theory, wave mechanics, relativity, and all the rest of it, they do really seem to have got a little way outside humanity. Well, what the devil's the good of that?'

It is, by implication, only the completely balanced artist (Rampion draws and paints in addition to writing) who has a full view of life from a human point of view; any distortion or perversion leads inevitably to death.

The inevitability of death is at the same time in the process of being demonstrated as the novel closes. As little Phil suffers excruciatingly, Huxley contrasts the attitudes of old John Bidlake who is apparently dying of intestinal cancer and of the querulous elder Quarles who convinces himself with a flurry of self-pity that he is dying in order not to have to face the rages of Gladys Helmsley, his abandoned Cockney mistress. The death of young Philip comes as a kind of senseless and unmerited horror, accompanied by gruesome suffering, hopeful rallyings, and final despair. The murder of Webley, as he eagerly arrives at the Quarles home, gives Huxley a major opportunity for a disquisition on death. When Beatrice Gilray's ascent in the office of the *Literary World* is finally climaxed by her surrender to Burlap's caresses (aptly compared, given the preoccupation with death, to an inflated rubber glove used at seances to represent caresses from The Beyond), Ethel Cobbett is dismissed. Her consequent suicide is a kind of bitter and backhanded assertion of her idealism, as is the suicide of Spandrell to the closing strains of the Beethoven piece. His tentative prodding of the dead Webley's eye with his heel was a final attempt, like his premeditated seductions, to prove that there was a final horror that would assert its opposite, the existence of God. Having been foiled in this search all along, and knowing that, as Rampion had just said, he would be rejected from heaven at the ending of the Beethoven ersatz heaven, he took the only logical step left.

COLLECTED ESSAYS

August 1959

---

138. Martin Green, review in *Commentary*

8 December 1959, xxviii, pp. 551-2

Martin Burgess Green, b. 1927, teaches English at Tufts University in Medford, Massachusetts, and has written, among others, *Reappraisals: Some Commonsense Readings in American Literature* (1965) and *Cities of Light and Sons of the Morning: A Cultural Psychology for an Age of Revolution* (1972).

The review is entitled 'More Than a Clever Man.'

When people told me I was clever to console me when I was growing up, I would add, *sotto voce*,[1] to myself, sourly, 'Like Aldous Huxley, I suppose.' He somehow summed up the word clever for me, filled it out in more directions than one could imagine, almost than one could believe, and yet did not overflow it. And nobody, I thought, wanted to be like that.

And I have discovered since that he fills this same role, of 'the clever man,' for lots of other people. It is not only that he knows such a lot, about painting and music, art and nature, statistics and philosophies, mysticism and mescalin. It is not only that he writes about all these things so unfailingly well; the challenging first sentence, the clarity of construction, the richness and precision of the diction, the brilliant pacing of paragraph and essay. The really dazzling thing is that he has felt everything, experienced everything, and can give you a quick rundown on the act of love with a great courtesan, or the opening of a rose at dawn when your best friend died last night.

[1] 'Under one's breath.'

438

At the same time one cannot escape, while reading him, the recurrent, quite spontaneous reflection, 'This is all *mentally* known, purely *mental*; there should be so much more to life than this.' One has a sense, constantly, of running aground, quite grittily, on the conscious analysis and conscious assimilation of whatever experience it may be. This is of course most drastically and damagingly true of his creative writing (he is now the author of forty-five books, including ten novels and six volumes of short stories) but it mars even this collection of essays, which represents him at his best. You get an almost physical sense of power and speed and scope as you pass from 'In a Tunisian Oasis' to 'Variations on a Baroque Tomb' to 'Landscape Painting as a Vision-Inducing Art' to 'Drugs that Shape Men's Minds'; forty-seven brilliant pieces of writing, truly intelligent and incredibly well informed. But every other time you turn a page you say, 'But it's so limitedly mental.'

Why should we feel this so much more with him than we do with, say, his grandfather, T. H. Huxley, or his brother, Julian Huxley, or even Lytton Strachey or Bertrand Russell, people who have limited themselves much more completely? Partly, I suppose, because Aldous has not accepted his limitations, because he has exposed his sensibility to every possible mode of experience. In fact, he has deliberately sought out those modes of experience to dwell on longest which most resist rational assimilation, the religious, the aesthetic, the sexual. And he has done this not with any ambition of extending the empire of pure mind, but rather with the desire to see it defeated and humiliated. D. H. Lawrence once wrote to Richard Aldington that he, Aldington, and Huxley, were alike in that what they both most deeply wanted was to be raped; I think one can see what he meant reflected in this active seeking out of, but passive self-presentation to, self-subjugation to, 'experience.'

Could one perhaps say, in fuller answer, that he has chosen the philosophies most fatally unadapted to his temperament? He has most consistently been, throughout his changing career, an irrationalist. In 1929, 'It is life itself; and I, for one, have more confidence in the rightness of life than in that of any individual man, even if the man be Pascal.' And in 1956, 'For, after all, Love is the last word'; this feeling we have when reading him, that mentality is not enough, that mental experience is not real experience, is an irrationalist's feeling. In other words, it is Huxley himself who is inciting us all the time to that spontaneous and deadly criticism.

It is possible, I suppose, to dismiss this as masochism, as a desire to aggravate his own humiliation. But I wonder if it isn't as much the result of his strength, of a stubborn fidelity to the best as he saw it. He grew up, after all, through the Great War and after, when, especially in England, the life-worshippers were completely routed. From 1880 on, with Whitman, Bergson, Nietzsche, the deification of multifarious, amoral Life had been a powerful international movement; in the pre-1914 novels of E. M. Forster and H. G. Wells, and the acclaim that greeted *Sons and Lovers*, you can see the general expectation of more life, more freedom, more beauty, more passion, more sunlight, for everyone in England. But with 1918 and *Eminent Victorians*, and 1919 and *The Economic Consequences of the Peace*, a much more ironic, self-conscious, selective, 'civilized' mode of sensibility took over. A much more limited expectation of happiness, a much less enthusiastic approach to experience; life-worship became unfashionable. Aldous Huxley obviously fitted in, by personal temperament, with that new cynical self-consciousness, but he continued to believe in the earlier, more enthusiastic attitude as the theoretical best.

This comes out most strikingly in his relationship to D. H. Lawrence. 'Of most other eminent men I have met I feel that at any rate I belong to the same species as they do. But this man has something different and superior in kind, not degree.' His whole essay on Lawrence is not only one of the finest things in the book, it is one of the finest things on Lawrence there is. And not, let us note, primarily for its intellectual power, but for its dignity and generosity and fullness of response. Writing about Lawrence, by people who had known him personally, is almost universally marred, at one level or another, by a quite ugly effort at self-defense, or revenge, or sheer destruction. Huxley almost alone records the impact and challenge with humility, with enthusiasm, with generosity. Not so much with intellectual understanding; what he says of their arguments about science seems to show Lawrence dancing ahead, out of Huxley's reach. But Huxley almost alone gave a moved and moving *human* response to the total human phenomenon.

The others, Bertrand Russell, Lytton Strachey, Virginia Woolf, excluded Lawrence from consideration, because he could not be fitted into the scheme of life which they had constructed for their comfort. Huxley has constructed no such schemes. In consequence, he has known very little comfort. But he has achieved a movingly naked purity, within his limits, and he has moments of a humanity which transcend not only his own limitations but theirs too.

139. Frank Kermode, review in *Spectator*

4 November 1960, ccv, p. 696

John Frank Kermode, b. 1919, critic, editor, essayist, has been Lord Northcliffe Professor of Modern English Literature at University College, London, since 1967. Among his many studies are *The Romantic Image* (1957) and *Modern Essays* (1971), as well as books on Donne (1957), Milton (1960), Wallace Stevens (1960), and others.

The review is entitled 'Amphibians.'

One of these essays, written without the least attempt to disguise the author's encyclopædic cast of mind, is about psychology, and reproaches modern practitioners for their neglect of the body. Doctors are getting used to the psychosomatic; it's time psychologists paid attention to the somatopsychic. Everybody has a body, and all bodies are different, but psychologists don't care. Mr. Huxley deplores their 'voluntary ignorance'. This is a fault most of his readers will detect in themselves. He makes knowing everything seem so easy that ignorance must be due to an absurd, sullen exercise of the will. We are all dimly and contentedly aware that the world is full of a number of things; only Mr. Huxley requires to know exactly what each of them is.

This selection of essays shows that from early to late Mr. Huxley has, in some important respects, changed little. He himself observes that the 'philosophy of meaninglessness' appropriate to his youth has vanished— he is now concerned with understanding as distinguished from knowing. But this is a less radical change than appears. Knowledge, of which he has so much, supplied evidences of meaninglessness and now ministers to understanding; at first it showed that the things of the world were so diverse and yet so concrete and unique that the intellect could produce no 'laws' to explain them; and at last it serves only to prove its own irrelevance to the purely intuitive processes of understanding. But without knowledge you can't know that there is really nothing to

441

know; and equally you can't know that you don't need to know. When sampling mescalin, which will set a crown upon your life-time's effort to see things as they *really* are, have a tape-recorder handy; arrange, as you prepare to glimpse eternal bliss, to be asked questions about Time.

It is a notable experience to read through this book and observe Mr. Huxley's fidelity to a doctrine expressed in the very first essay reprinted, 'Wordsworth in the Tropics'. (By the way, more of *Do What You Will* would have been welcome; and it is a great pity that only a fragment of the Pascal essay survives.) This doctrine is one that Wordsworth is held to have neglected, namely that 'our immediate intuitions are of diversity'. This is basic to the early Huxley: 'Matter is incomparably subtler and more intricate than mind.' But the older Huxley, now much more in sympathy with Wordsworth, delighting in the *Istigkeit*[1] of Meister Eckhart (at present enjoying a fortuitous celebrity as Mr. A. Waugh's 'Is-ness business') and in the inscape of Hopkins, merely has these intuitions more strongly, though he can now speak of 'a bunch of flowers . . . that was yet eternal life.' He has always been in the Is-ness business.

And these *intuitions* of diversity are, of course, supported by his great *knowledge* of diversity. Among the matters treated in this book are olives, drugs, churches, poetry (an essay on Famagusta turns into a study, full of pure pleasure, of Mallarmé), flowers, cicadas, mesmerism, *coitus reservatus*, painting, dung, D. H. Lawrence and Baroque art. He does not deny himself the right to generalise; Indian villagers scramble for the dung of young Mr. Huxley's elephant; what a strange animal Man is, using as well as producing dung! And so to our neglect of the body in studying spiritual experience; to Lawrence, whose awareness of 'otherness' never excluded the body; and to Baroque, which has a special power over Mr. Huxley. The ecstasies of Baroque certainly do not forget the body; indeed Bernini overdid it in 'the posture of the ecstatics, their expression and the exuberance of the tripe-like drapery which surrounds them and . . . overflows in a kind of peritoneal cataract onto the altar below'. Baroque is the outcome of thoroughly somatic meditative techniques; it reminds us that, 'floundering between time and eternity, we are amphibians and must accept the fact'. The artists of Baroque, like the manufacturers of mescalin, know that to get outside the body you have to use it.

One has only to read the Pascal essay of 1929 to see that in Mr. Huxley's development there are no radical changes, only shifts of

[1] 'Quiddity.'

emphasis; and this applies not only to speculations on ecstasy but to the literary method employed, which is fundamentally similar in 'Pascal' and in 'Maine de Biran', published in 1950. There are, however, changes in the texture of the writing: most of the early essayistic exuberance, the poses of early twentieth-century essayism, disappear; American usage has left its mark, sometimes surprisingly, as when *ca[c]care non poterat*[1] is archly rendered 'could never go to the bathroom'. But the collection is all of a piece, and the fruit of a remarkable, if exhausting, mind. We all know the proper, disabling things to say about Huxley if one wants to recover self-esteem; but an honest man would surely acknowledge his voluntary ignorance and call this book a valuable as well as a chastening experience.

140. Herbert Read on *On Art and Artists*

Saturday Review, 19 November 1960, xliii, p. 44

Sir Herbert Read (1893–1968), well-known essayist, critic, poet, and novelist, wrote many books on art and letters, such as *Reason and Romanticism* (1928) and *The Philosophy of Modern Art* (1952).

The review is entitled 'A Culture out of Chaos.'

The essayist is out of fashion: the magazines that used to publish his elegant effusions have disappeared. And yet here is Mr. Huxley, who has practised the art for the past forty years and can now, from the contents of several volumes characterized by their variety (as volumes of essays should be), select another characterized by its unity. That, at least, is the excuse for this anthology, but Mr. Huxley remains as various as ever, for he never had the ability, which is again a virtue in the essayist, to keep to his subject. The subject of this volume is art, but the reader must be prepared for divagations on the sexual taboos of the

[1] Literally, 'could not defecate.'

Eskimos, the dangers of over-population, or the pathological effects of an overdose of mescalin. For Mr. Huxley has a curiosity that ranges haphazardly over the whole universe, and his favourite reading (and reading is his only recreation) is the encyclopedia.

I remember how he came one day in the early 20s to a tea party in Edith Sitwell's and drew a volume of Buffon's *Histoire Naturelle*[1] from his pocket, from which he proceeded to read with great gusto a passage he had just discovered on the amorous activities of elephants. The essay is a record of such discoveries, linked together by the author's zest. If the zest is apparent in the writing, the reader does not ask for consistency (for consistency, as Mr. Huxley remarks in one of these essays, is a verbal criterion and cannot be applied to the phenomena of life).

Since the contents of this volume have been deliberately selected and its subject is art, we must ask nevertheless if any consistent philosophy of the subject emerges. What, according to Mr. Huxley, is art? The answer, as we might expect, is that it can be almost anything provided the artist has talent. The artist himself is an accident, the chance product of [a] random assortment of chromosomes, and it cannot be shown that either society ('a vast roulette table'), or environment, or religion, has the slightest effect on his development. Art is a logic of formal relations, an individual's attempt to reduce the chaos of appearances to some comprehensible unity. This attempt is rarely successful—most art is bad or indifferent, at all periods. And what we call a tradition is at best a partial substitute for personal talent; it enables people with little talent to produce good work because it relieves them of the necessity of using their own second-rate, or tenth-rate, imaginations. A good tradition may be defined as 'the ghosts of the dead artists dictating to bad living artists'.

It follows from such a philosophy of art that little good can be said of the art of our own time, which is basically vulgar. It is vulgar because it must be addressed to a vastly increased population of semi-educated people agglomerated 'in cities of interminable monotonies, of hopeless dreariness, and suffocating oppression'. Such urbanization of the population becomes automatically sub-urbanization, an environment deadly to all creative life.

[Summarizes Huxley's view that 'Fordism,' a 'dreadful religion of the machine,' will destroy the human race]

A gloomy prospect, therefore. Perhaps the wisest thing to do, con-

[1] 'Natural History.'

cludes Mr. Huxley, is to abandon the popular arts, which can never be good, 'to their inevitable vulgarity and ineptitude and concentrate all available resources on the training of a minority that shall be capable of appreciating the higher attributes of the spirit'—what might be called an oasis culture. But who, in this world of diasporic tourism, who is to protect the oases?

Mr. Huxley offers no adequate solution of the problem he poses with such eloquence and urgency. In the end he retreats to his ivory tower and like Montaigne, whom of all authors of the past he most resembles, cultivates his own radiant and ambling spirit. The second part of this volume is entitled 'Criticism' but it should have been called 'Appreciations'. Here, to read once again, or with what joy to read for the first time, are the essays on Chaucer, Ben Jonson, Crebillon, Swift, Baudelaire, Piero della Francesca, Goya, Breughel, El Greco, Lautrec, and Gesualdo. No better appreciations of such artists have been written by anyone since Pater, and their virtue lies in their lack of pretension, in their sensuous sensibility (the choice of artists is indicative of that quality), in their tolerance and wit. We may perhaps object that occasionally the moralist (for the anti-puritan is also a moralist) displaces the hedonist: for example, so many pages to reprove Baudelaire for being a satanist, and only a line or two to admit that he is, nevertheless, a very great poet. The art, we might insist, is somehow related to the artist (that surely is implicit in Mr. Huxley's philosophy) and it is the business of the critic to reveal the mystery of that connection. But Mr. Huxley is not a critic with 'a business'. We are made to realize once more that the best writing about art is not academic, nor even professional, but the product of curiosity and leisure, and that its only law is sympathy.

ISLAND

March 1962

---

141. Cyril Connolly, review in *Sunday Times*

1 April 1962, magazine section, p. 31

For a biographical note see No. 47. The review is entitled 'Storm-clouds over Utopia.' See Introduction, p. 30.

This is Mr. Huxley's most important novel since *Time Must Have a Stop*. He has been working on it for a long time and when he spoke to me about it several years ago,[1] he gave me the impression that it formed a companion piece to *Brave New World*, that the earlier novel depicted the horrors of a scientifically planned society, organised to obtain maximum efficiency, and that the new one was to expose a purely humanistic society selfishly centred upon the pursuit of happiness. This was a misconception. The islanders of Mr. Huxley's new novel are not wrong in a different way to the Brave New Worldlings; they are right. That is to say as right as Mr. Huxley can make them and because right, virtually defenceless against the inevitable take-over from East or West.

To write a philosophic, even a didactic novel about an imaginary Utopia is a most difficult thing. Too often the characters in Utopias are unreal while their opinions are cloaked in the dust of the lecture room. *Brave New World* is an exception because of the ferocious energy of the satire. Mr. Huxley is the outstanding example of the novelist who has mastered the 'two cultures', but his absorption of science and humanism did not lead him in the path of Wells and Butler but into mysticism and religious meditation. So he is set the even harder problem of writing a novel which is alive in its own form, about a religious Utopia and a

[1] See Connolly's interview with Huxley, *Sunday Times*, 19 October 1958, p. 10.

446

religion with which neither Christians nor agnostics, in fact the bulk of his readers, will sympathise.

He has solved the problem brilliantly, first by choosing as décor an island very similar to Bali, beautiful in itself and inhabited by a beautiful race, a paradise with which most of us are familiar even though we have never been there, even as we are familiar with the story of the Brooke family in Sarawak which supplies a plausible historical background for an English-speaking English-educated Indonesian community. Indonesians are people we all find lovable and attractive. They solve Mr. Huxley's first problem: they are Utopians with sex-appeal. Moreover, some islands are Buddhist and Buddhism stems from Brahminism like Mr. Huxley's own religion as put forward in *The Perennial Philosophy* and *Time Must Have a Stop*. He is not inventing a Utopia, but simply coming home.

His hero or rather his experimental guinea-pig is a particularly unpleasant type of the Huxleyan Anglo-Saxon male investigator, an aggressive special correspondent of a corrupt newspaper engaged on the side in oil deals for his proprietor and bearing the usual Huxleyan burden of private guilt and harrowing personal memories. He is however unhappy enough to be open to conversion, and well-educated enough to spout scientific or theological data with the best of them. The plot is simple but effective and carries one firmly through the many dissertations, for any inhabitant of the island of Pala is capable of holding forth on extra-sensory perception, artificial insemination, Sheldonian typology, *coitus reservatus*, and other burning topics.

But Mr. Huxley is primarily a novelist, and I think he has succeeded in infusing life into what might otherwise prove a succession of short essays and sermons; he is moreover an exceptionally adult novelist and his technique is at the service of his lucid intelligence. The more convincingly attractive his islanders are, the more deadly is his indictment of modern civilisation, of the worship of money and power, mass consumption and totalitarian strength. 'Two-thirds of all sorrow is homemade,' wrote the whimsical Rajah of Pala, 'and so far as the universe is concerned, unnecessary.'

The beauty of Mr. Huxley's island is that it combines the charming pagan *pietas* of Buddhism in Ceylon, of the child offering flowers to the wayside shrine, with the mystical 'Divine Ground' or 'Clear Light of the Void' which are Mr. Huxley's terms for Infinity. But Pala is not Tibet. Although it refuses to develop its oil resources, it pays its way in the modern community of nations by mining a little gold, developing its agricultural methods and practising birth control. Everyone has enough to eat. Education is completely up to date. Delinquents are spotted almost before they can talk, and taken gently in hand. Aggression is canalised, the most recent psychological techniques are put into practice, hypnotism ensures painless childbirth, and quick recuperation. Neurosis is almost unknown: family situations are not allowed to develop. The wonder-mushroom permits a short-cut to the mystical experience, to compassion, non-attachment. 'Knowledgeless understanding.' Such a community is bound to be pacifist and therefore, since it possesses oil, bound to be invaded.

Mr. Huxley can put up no defence, for this is not science fiction and the islanders have no magic. They convert the troublesome journalist; they cannot take on the nearest dictator. The conclusion implies that, while the world is so wicked and wrong-headed, such an isolated community of perfectionists in living is bound to be swamped, yet somehow the good will triumph in some other place or century. 'The work of a hundred years destroyed in a single night. And yet the fact remained—the fact of the ending of sorrow as well as the fact of sorrow.'

Here I think we come up against a major difficulty. Buddhism, for all its compassion, is a pessimistic religion and non-attachment is somewhat chilly. It is hard to love those for whom love itself is an illusion and so we cannot be as concerned with the fate of the Palanese as we should be.

Island ends with one of the best descriptions of the effect of mescalin (or possibly the wonder mushroom) which I have ever read and Mr. Huxley clearly believes that what it gives us is a revelation of the true nature of reality, when the morning stars sing together and mind is 'luminous bliss'. The cactus and the mushroom admit infinity; they do not merely liberate memory. And so their employment, as a climax to this novel, is justified. Another temptation of Utopia-writers is to fall in love with their denizens and make them a little too cosily virtuous like prefects in a girls' school. There is more than a hint of this and the wicked Western narrator and the reader too are expected to wag their tails whenever any of those relentlessly edifying creatures make their appearance.

All readers of Mr. Huxley's novels are by now used to being lectured, with mounting enthusiasm, by superior monomaniacs, and *Island* has its fill of them. But unlike D. H. Lawrence's Utopias, or indeed anybody else's, Mr. Huxley's makes sense. It deserves to rank among the true philosophical novels where real people act and are acted upon and discuss at the same time problems which engross us all and which they know more about than we do. 'You're assuming that the brain *produces* consciousness. I'm assuming that the brain transmits consciousness. And my explanation is no more far-fetched than yours.' We have come a long way from *Crome Yellow*.

142. P. N. Furbank, review in *Spectator*

30 March 1962, ccvii, pp. 420–1

Philip Nicholas Furbank, b. 1920, critic and translator, has written books on Samuel Butler (1948), Italo Svevo (1966), and *Reflections on the Word Image* (1970).

The review is entitled 'Thanks to MAC.'

'But if theology and theosophy, then why not theography and theo-metry, why not theognomy, theotrophy, theotomy, theogamy? Why not theophysics and theochemistry?' So meditates Gumbril in *Antic Hay*, just before the invention of the Patent Smallclothes, and so Huxley has constantly meditated. His major subject was always the split between mind and body, and he has ransacked life, literature and zoology for horrifying and delicious instances of it. But side by side with this there went a favourite project, that by some ecumenical science or system of sciences the split could be closed. Huxley's science was always Victorian and utilitarian in flavour. He saw science as the study of labour-saving, and his cherished aim was to find a mechanical short-cut to spiritual advantages. But then the science in his earlier writings was more than half *jeu d'esprit*.[1] He adumbrated the 'ultimate science' in much the same spirit as Gumbril the inflatable trousers. It was all part of a high-spirited and debonair satirical poise. Huxley was never in the

[1] 'Witticism—in jest.'

least a misanthrope, and the quest for the ultimate science went with delight in and alarmed affection for the atavistic human muddle.

It is when he wants us to take his science literally that his writing goes wrong, and his new novel is a case in point. *Island* presents, without satire, his ideal society. The scheme of the book is simple.

[Summarizes the story]

The move away from satire turns out, sadly, to be a move away from humaneness. In *Brave New World*, though the Wellsian Huxley is obviously delighted with the vistas of bokanovskification and neo-Pavlovian conditioning, these remain a gleeful but admonitory fiction, and sympathy is still with the atavistic Savage. In *Island*, since the ends of this supposedly libertarian Utopia are ones he approves of, Huxley ceases to scruple about the means of enforcing them, and loses all sympathy with non-conformity. As children his islanders are systematically indoctrinated and brainwashed, as adults they are kept happy and politically quiescent by the sex-yoga (so much like the *soma* of *Brave New World*). And, revealingly, when the islanders propound their views, they use the very salesman's language of the Western society they condemn. 'Thanks to MAC', they are fond of exclaiming; they explain that they give their children an 'up-to-date version of Aesop's Fables. Not the old anthropomorphic fictions, but true ecological fables with built-in, cosmic morals.'

Huxley makes the worst of the islanders' case, because he doesn't at heart believe in it himself. He makes them priggish and arch, sententious, censorious and smug. They are some of the most disagreeable Utopians I have met. The only one I felt any sympathy with was the old Raja, who could not be cured of buttering the family lingam; it was of black basalt, it had been in the family 800 years; and though the Raja knew this to be intellectual weakness, for all island opinion was against symbols and ritual as obstacles to 'pure experimental mysticism,' he could not desist from the habit of pouring melted butter over it from 'an extremely ornate silver sauce-boat'. An excellent old man. And what a butterer of lingams we have lost in Huxley himself!

143. Wayne C. Booth, review in *Yale Review*

June 1962, li, pp. 630–2

Wayne Clayson Booth, b. 1921, author of *The Rhetoric of Fiction* (1961) and *Now Don't Try to Reason with Me* (1970), has been George M. Pullman Professor of English at the University of Chicago since 1962.

Booth's review, entitled 'Yes, But Are They Really Novels,' includes five books besides *Island*, among them Katherine Anne Porter's *Ship of Fools* and Alan Sillitoe's *Key to the Door*. See Introduction, p. 29.

Professor Leavis recently accused C. P. Snow of not having the slightest idea of what the novel is. Facing this batch of new novels, I find myself envying Leavis his confidence. All of them are called novels on their jackets, yet they are about as different from each other as six works could possibly be. It would be easy to move down through the lot, ruling one after another out of the circle where only true novels dwell. In fact the chorus of 'not a true novel' has already been sung, in public, for at least two of these works, and we can be quite sure that sooner or later it will be sung for the rest.

Perhaps the author most likely to suffer from readers' preconceptions about *the* novel is Huxley. *Island* is 'late Huxley,' another amalgam of narrative and undisguised ideas; it will be easy to show, once more, that he hasn't written a true novel since *Antic Hay*—or has he, in fact, *ever* written one? And that takes care of Huxley. Only here is *Island* still, calling itself a novel, and to refuse it the title hardly takes care of the critical task.

Properly placed within that other, non-Leavisonian 'great tradition'—works like *Gulliver's Travels*, *Candide*, *Rasselas*, *Erewhon*, using fictional devices to provoke thought—*Island* can command full attention and respect, though it might more appropriately be reviewed along with works of philosophy or political science. Within its tradition, it is one of those very rare birds, an affirmative Utopia—not a projection into the future of how bad things are now, but a discovery in the present of how good they might be. Huxley has asked: Given what we now know about the virtues and vices of modern civilization, and about man's nature, and about the various philosophical and religious programs that have been offered by East and West, what would be an ideal social pattern?

Fictional accounts of such patterns are almost inevitably less vivid than negative Utopias (what some people are calling dystopias these days). An attack is always more lively than a defense, sin is more interesting than virtue, the horrors of *Brave New World* are more vivid than the peace and joy of Pala, Huxley's imaginary island. But the effort to portray a good society, however difficult, is a useful supplement to the effort to show how bad things now are; we could see how much Huxley has done to overcome the inherent problems if we compared his happy world with the simple-minded Utopia of Skinner's *Walden II*.

The society of Pala is a synthesis of the virtues of East and West. The details of how the fusion came about are not important; one says nothing significant about this novel when he says that Huxley handles many of the novelistic details perfunctorily. It matters not in the least that his two philosopher kings who establish the society—the tough-minded Scottish doctor, refugee from Calvinism, and the Buddhist Raja—are improbable stereotypes, or that 'too much' time is spent in a sociological tour of the island's advantages. Like the details about the reactions of the visitor from outside, in this case, a corrupt English journalist who finds spiritual salvation in the new society, these are conventions of the form, necessary, but to be handled by both author and reader lightly, even playfully. Standards of verisimilitude appropriate to many novels would destroy *Island* from page one.

What does matter in this form is the synthesis of ideas. Such a work should do two things: make me think in fresh ways about my own society and what might be done to improve it, and convince me that the author's ideas are not only provocative but sound. *Island* succeeds admirably in the first of these. I am provoked, in the best sense, from beginning to end; I am unable to skip even the long conversations about the ills of Western society and the social and spiritual health of Pala—conversations which would be judged disruptive if viewed in 'the novel' convention.

The second standard is not so successfully met. The synthesis of West and East, of medicine, genetics, electricity, and literature with a spirituality-cum-sexuality adapted from Mahayana Buddhism, is often fascinating in detail but unconvincing as a whole. The happiness of the Palanese, the happiness to which the Englishman is converted (with the help of the vision-producing drugs used in Pala) is engaging enough. One feels suitable regrets as the island is destroyed, at the end of the book, by oil-seeking invaders. But somehow one never feels convinced of the viability of this society, or even of Huxley's seriousness about the ideas on which it is based.

On its own terms then: a qualified success. Perhaps somebody will someday give as much thought to the artistic problems raised by this nameless and tricky genre—the term Utopia conceals more than it clarifies—as has been given to the James–Leavis kind of thing. Until then, lacking for myself any clear standard of how to relate my notions of overall weakness with my experience of particular strengths, I can only report that *this* one carried me through to the end, arguing with Huxley all the way.

144. Frank Kermode, review in *Partisan Review*

Summer 1962, xxix, pp. 472–3

For a biographical note see No. 139. The review is a section from the magazine's 'Fiction Chronicle.' See Introduction, p. 29.

. . . Reviewers ought to watch their superlatives, but *Island*, it is reasonable to say, must be one of the worst novels ever written; there are Victorian fiction-tracts with exactly as much claim to serious attention, at any rate if one excludes the excellent little scene at the beginning of Huxley's book about corrupt lovemaking in a Charing Cross Road flat; ecstasy lit by neon signs, green for putrefaction, pink for passion. That passage recalls the considerable achievement of *Point Counter Point*, and reminds us that Huxley *studied* fiction, used his intelligence

to compensate his lack of a natural bent. Yet as a novelist he was perhaps always more or less consciously lowering himself (Wyndham
Lewis's rough handling of the opening page of *Point Counter Point* is
apposite) [No. 76] and here he makes the easiest and most perfunctory
gestures possible, without apology. *Island* invites, but then rejects, comparison with *Brave New World*. The *soma* which was once anathema-
tized as a cheap escape from the ardors of reality is now essential to
social health; as a result, Huxley's energizing disgust, which could be
good for fiction if not for the soul, is lost. A utopia in which nearly
everybody is sanely educated, happy and intelligent—*nice* they are,
really—is useless to Huxley the artist.

Island is about a community, soon to be swept away by the mad
greed of the rest of the world, in which there has grown up a way of
life based on the perennial philosophy, hallucinogenic plants, practical
hypnotherapy, maithuna (*coitus reservatus*) and other yogas which are
taught at school. A life-battered Englishman with a bad sexual history
is wrecked on the island, and is converted to its way of life, but not
quickly enough to prevent his helping the Oil Interests to destroy it.
There is a dreadful revivalist Ranee, to show that there is still fake
mysticism around, and a cynical Indian called Mr. Bahu, last of the long
line of Huxleyan *bons vivants*[1] or Scogans. But most of the characters
live without complexities, whether of irony or anything else, 'making
the best of the here and now,' coping intelligently with birth and sex
and death, with economics and visionary experience. The novel is an
extended study of such a society, made up mostly of conversations,
lectures, extracts from key educational books, and reports on mush-
room-visions. This kind of society has to get along without art, since
nobody is unhappy enough to make any, and the book reflects this
state of affairs. It is a kind of sterile hybrid, bred of a volume of sermons
and *She*. I have never felt free to join those who profess an easy contempt for this writer; anybody who can dispose of his amount of information does us a favor by showing how little we use our heads. And
if he is essentially *philosophe* rather than novelist, that makes his good
novels remarkable as testimony to what can be done by intelligence and
information in the absence of original talent. But he has obviously lost
interest in fiction. Much of *Island*, the sermonizing in fact, has great
interest, and so have his recent essays. One may look forward to many
more volumes from Huxley, but it is permissible to hope that this is his
last novel.

[1] 'Jolly people who enjoy good living.'

145. Arthur Herzog, review in *Nation* (New York)

25 August 1962, cxcv, pp. 74–5

Arthur Herzog, former magazine editor, novelist, and free-lance writer.

The review is entitled 'Who Enforces Utopia?'

The opening paragraphs, omitted here, discuss some problems in constructing Utopias and mention some of the anti-Utopian books which have emerged in the twentieth century.

But while the counter-utopists may have put a cautionary light on many contemporary ideals, they have provided nothing in their place. It is this job that Huxley attempts in *Island*. It is a curious book, more successful as a vehicle of ideas than as a novel. It is written heavily and without the incisiveness of *Brave New World*. The characters are weak and poorly drawn. The later Huxley flaws—the verbosity, the over-intellectuality—are much in evidence. Like a nervous lover, Huxley seems almost to talk himself out of the main chance. And yet, despite its defects, *Island* is a stimulating visit.

Like most utopias, *Island* is a study of ends, but Huxley is also aware of the difficulties of means. He quotes Aristotle as saying, 'In framing an ideal we may assume what we wish, but we should avoid impossibilities.' Huxley's utopia is what he calls 'near-in'—that is, the ideas are presumably susceptible to being put into practice.

[Describes Pala's origins and Farnaby's arrival]

. . . Pala is called the Forbidden Island because progress-carrying Westerners are not welcome, but the islanders prove hospitable and proceed to demonstrate and explain their social system. The discussions are in English—in keeping with the fusion scheme, the islanders use English for science and business, Palanese for religion and love—and they are of interminable length and determinedly impressive erudition. In fact, the Palanese are some of the longest-winded people around.

[Recounts Pala's attempt to combine the best aspects of East and West]

One gathers that Huxley agrees with Koestler that Eastern thought is a shambles, and the islanders have swept most of it away. They have retained, though, a variety of Zen Buddhism. Roaming wild on Pala are mynah birds that cry 'Attention!'—meaning, I gather, attention to the self of selves, or, as Huxley puts it, 'If I only knew who in fact I am, I should cease to behave as what I think I am; and if I stopped behaving as I think I am, I should be what I am.' The islanders are immersed in the yoga of everything, which Huxley attempts to dramatize in a scene where Farnaby takes Palanese perception mushrooms and has a visionary experience. They are keen on the yoga of love—it is not clear whether the Palanese are promiscuous, but they are certainly not inhibited—and reach total fulfillment in sex. They believe, in short, in living deep.

Farnaby, obsessive and guilt-ridden, is set off against these supposedly calm and happy people as an example of Western man; and, always just, Huxley gives us some pretty unsavory non-Palanese Eastern types as well. But Farnaby falls in love with a Palanese and decides to stay. In the meantime, the greedy, overpopulated world closes in. It wants the oil and can't stand the existence of a truly sane society. But Huxley suggests that the world can still learn from Pala.

Will it? I think not. For one thing, life there seems a little dull—at times the Palanese are uncomfortably close to grazing in Chesterton's fields of veal cutlets, curry-style. It is a regrettable truth that the wicked utopia makes better reading than the good, and one sympathizes with Huxley's efforts to make Pala interesting. (He might have done so with a little more plain Palanese fun.) And then, it seems unlikely that Zen and perception mushrooms are going to be used by any large number of people. Huxley suggests, in fact, that the Pala-model might be something for under-developed rather than developed countries.

[Quotes Chapter XIII, pp. 210–11]

Focusing as it does on the inner and not merely the material life, *Island* is a new departure for utopia. Impractical as much of it may be, it is still more provocative than the usual reports of commissions on national goals. Perhaps we need less pragmatic thinking; need instead, a few of Ruskin's locomotives dressed up like dragons, more imagination, more utopian ideals. This, basically, is what *Island* says, and it is worth repeating.

146. Chad Walsh, review in *NYTBR*

1 April 1962, pp. 4, 46

Chad Walsh, b. 1914, author, educator, clergyman, has taught English at Beloit College, Wisconsin, since 1945. He has written several books on religion and poetry, as well as *From Utopia to Nightmare* (1962).

The opening paragraphs of the review, here omitted, discuss the relation of *Island* to the 1946 foreword to *Brave New World* and trace Farnaby's conversion to Pala's way of life. See Introduction, p. 30.

The review is entitled 'Can Man Save Himself?'

It is a happy marriage of Mahayana Buddhism and science. The religion is not world-denying; it teaches that everything, from food to sex, can be a road to enlightenment and liberation. Science is devoted to such practical tasks as improving tropical crops and devising psychological methods for reducing dangerous aggressions in society. In contrast to *Brave New World* the family flourishes, but in a broader form. Fifteen to twenty-five households combine into an extended family. Any child fed up with his own parents can take a refreshing vacation in another home. Artificial insemination is frequent, but voluntary. It is often employed by couples who want more variety in their children and a better genetic heritage for them.

The Brave New World and Pala both have rather related patterns of sexual behavior—Pala even commissions certain mature ladies to give practical instruction to young male virgins. But to the Brave New Worlder sex is merely fun; to the Palanese it is one of the most useful roads to enlightenment. Most striking resemblance of all, the *soma* of Brave New World is matched by the *moksha*-medicine of Pala, a mushroom derivative to induce mystical vision. But again, it is the purpose that differs. Brave New World takes *soma* for a release or a harmless binge. The Palanese use the mushroom extract as an opening wedge into ultimate consciousness.

Throughout the book one senses the outer world—hungry, greedy, breeding itself into nightmare, armed to do murder, falsely spiritual and crassly materialistic—closing in on Pala. How the story ends it is not fair to say here. Nor can anyone really discuss *Island* as though it were merely a story. In this book Mr. Huxley has said, for the moment, his final word about the human condition and the possibility of the good society. *Island* challenges the political scientist, the psychologist, the philosopher and the theologian. The reader's reaction will depend on his own postulates—in particular, whether he considers the human predicament curable by growth in awareness, or whether he finds man's condition so deeply poisoned at the roots of being that both spiritual surgery and spiritual growth are required. In short, can man save himself?

It is the achievement of the book that it vividly dramatizes these very questions. In recent decades the supply of new Utopias has dwindled in both quantity and quality. *Island* is a welcome and in many ways unique addition to the select company of books—from Plato to now—that have presented, in imaginary terms, a coherent view of what society is not but might be.

147. Two obituaries

December 1963

(a) V. S. Pritchett in *New Statesman*, 6 December 1963, lxvi, p. 834

For a biographical note see No. 129.

Almost the last time I saw Aldous Huxley was at the Kokoschka exhibition. A tall, thin man paled by Californian sun, who had cleverly mastered the calamity of extremely bad sight, he bent to look at small areas of the pictures, his eyes hardly more than a couple of inches from the surface. But not with the despair of those who see little. On the contrary, with the alertness of one who sees much, who is making new discoveries of texture under a microscope. Art and science—the so-called 'two cultures'—were the pursuit. He had the passion of the two kinds of seeing.

In the Twenties, reading his first poems and the Peacockian novels, one had thought him an assertive and alarming figure. He was immediately an enormous success, a young man packed with brains, modish, the perfect embodiment of the new American word, 'highbrow'; so assured at once in scientific outlook and in his enormous knowledge of music, painting, architecture, history and most of the famous sites and museums of the world; more important to us, a ribald innovator in the modernities, blasphemies and iconoclasms of the period. One was overwhelmed. There was no need to be. Huxley was the most considerate, gentle, most softly and brilliantly conversable of men, in the simplest terms. Arnold, Mrs. Humphrey Ward and his famous grandfather were formidably behind him, and perhaps this was why he was that rare being—the prodigy, the educable young man, the perennial asker of unusual questions.

For the artist in him this compulsion must have been a burden as well as an inborn exhilaration. Like Bacon's jesting Pilate, from whom he borrowed a title, he asked and did not stay for an answer. He moved on. Nothing short of universal knowledge was his aim. No traveller through cultures, no connoisseur of human habits, no asker had lapped

459

up so much. As a writer, he became a mellifluous but active, ever-extending, ever-dramatising encyclopedia and he had the gaiety and melancholy of mind to put it out in novels, essays, plays and works of speculation and criticism. Endlessly educable, he was, in the family tradition, a hybrid—the artist-educator; an extraordinary filler-in of the huge gaps in one's mind. To the very young in the Twenties, this was inestimable. One might clap a label on him 10 years later but, in the meantime, the next decade had found him new. So it went on, until pretty well the present day. His range and his manner were irresistible to youth. The spell continued: to the latest appetites he offered the devils of Loudun; to the curious the merits of mescalin; to the pragmatic a therapy for blindness; to the terrified the possibility that man's survival was related to the non-human 'otherness' he shared with Nature.

Aldous Huxley's spell was the old Arnold-Huxley spell of an education, disseminated with wit from above. It was imposed by his mastery of the art of conversation. He was a daring assimilator rather than an original creative mind; but if it is true to say that the exquisite *Crome Yellow* was a pastiche of Peacock, how brilliant to have spotted that Peacock was just the author for disordered times and that whole passages could be adapted for today. The other good novel, *Brave New World*, which time has caught up on, is a work of disgust. It suffers ultimately from a sort of horrific complicity on the part of the author. Swift believed in ordinary men; Huxley believed in reason and that can lead to intellectual self-indulgence. Huxley was not a novelist in the sense of being interested in how people live and what they are wholly like. He turned for inspiration to Gide, that other master of conversation and contemporary morbidities, and wrote *Eyeless in Gaza* and *Point Counter Point*. They were amusing *romans à clef* but were both too newsy and too stilted compared with *Les Faux-Monnayeurs*. The characters were simply the faces on a pack of cards, good for a rubber or two of talk and scandal, but too flat and crude when asked to be human beings. They were too brittle to stand up to the preposterous things he offered them.

There was, I have said, a touch of complicity in Huxley's disgust with human beings, in his eye for the grotesque, the vulgar and libidinous. They became less ribald and more savage as he moved skyward from the Twenties into his Californian Laputa where scientific rationalism and the perennial philosophy disputed for possession of the facts of Nature and the soul's perceptions.

Huxley's conversation still dazzled because he pursued the strange facts the sciences offer to anyone with a dramatic instinct. One got from him a stereoscopic view of the world. One can call his method popularisation; but really the attraction lay not only in the new facts, but in the opportunity for more speculation. Perhaps, after all, the sexual practices of the dotty Oneida community were better than our own? Was not the classical view of the 'eternal Mediterranean' a fraud? The olive groves of Cézanne and Renoir represent a benign pause in man's war against landscape. The mulberries were being replaced by the peach tree in the Rhône valley because of the invention of artificial silk. Might not the peanut replace the olive just as the ilex and the scrub, destroyed by sheep and goats, had given way to the coarse grass of the *garrique*—itself to be effaced by the poisonous asphodel? The solitude of the desert had been a favourite place for experiencing the immanence of the divine being; but did not the lives of the hermits, after a little psychological examination, suggest that the solitude was populated by devils?

Whether such juxtapositions—and Huxley was expert in making them—are tenable, they are vivid, and more than vivid. They awaken. They disturb our settled superstitions. But even when we recognize this, we must inquire why superstitions exist, why they last and what estimable impulses of the human imagination they have both protected and perverted. Huxley enjoyed the follies of the human mind even as he stoically stood out against them.

His mind had, of course, the tricks of the man who knew too much and too well how to express it. He was one of the last of the Victorian liberals. He was totally pacifist. Logically he refused to be implicated. His manner had a lot of the old Bloomsbury in it. 'Significant. But significant of what?' 'Possibly. But possibly not.' The bomb explodes. One has not time to make the distinction. All the same these phrases were designed to drop us simple readers into a void where, defenceless, we were exposed to shock. Shock was one of the luxuries of the Twenties. But, for Huxley, perhaps the most accomplished educator of his generation, to shock was to ensure the course of intellectual freedom.

(b) Jocelyn Brooke in *Listener*, 12 December 1963, lxx, p. 991

Jocelyn Brooke, b. 1908, novelist, poet, critic, was the author of a pamphlet on Huxley for the *British Book News* supplements on 'Writers and Their Work' (1954), and has written studies on Ronald Firbank (1951) and Elizabeth Bowen (1952).

The essay is entitled 'The Wicked Uncle: An Appreciation of Aldous Huxley.'

I never met Aldous Huxley, yet the news of his death filled me with a sense of personal loss. This, I know, is the conventional language of the posthumous *éloge*,[1] but in this case it happens to be the truth. Huxley, in my youth, had a profound influence upon me, and I think of him to this day as a kind of literary uncle. His influence was not merely literary but moral and intellectual as well; it would hardly, indeed, be an exaggeration to say that if I hadn't discovered Huxley when I did, I should have been someone quite other than I am. At the age of fifteen or sixteen I was introduced, through his early novels and stories, to worlds hitherto unknown to me: exciting and seductive territories whose very existence, until then, had remained unsuspected. Huxley, in fact, was (though the analogy is a decidedly shaky one, in both its aspects) a kind of Huysmans to my Dorian Gray.

To a younger generation this may well seem strange; but I believe that no one under fifty can quite realize how exciting Huxley seemed to us who were schoolboys or undergraduates in the 'twenties. What Wells had been to the young men of twenty years before, Huxley was to us: like Wells, he was a popularizer of what, at that time, were 'advanced' ideas, though with Huxley the emphasis (at any rate in his earlier work) was upon art rather than science; like Wells, again, he was a liberator, who seemed to encourage us in our adolescent revolt against the standards of our parents. He was witty, immensely intelligent, unfailingly up to date, and occasionally (by the standards of those days) outrageously bawdy; as such, at the period of which I write, he was unique among English novelists.

To a schoolboy at that date—and to a majority of grown-ups, for that matter—the contemporary novel meant Bennett, Galsworthy, Wells,

[1] 'Praise, commendation.'

Hugh Walpole, and so forth; few of us had as yet discovered Lawrence, *Ulysses* was not easy of access, and E. M. Forster (apart from *A Passage to India*) was seldom to be found in libraries. No wonder that Huxley should seem exciting after *The Forsyte Saga* or *Clayhanger*. Quite apart from anything else, he was a kind of impresario for all those writers and artists whom we felt we ought to know about but didn't: he would refer, for example, casually and in passing, to Baudelaire, Brantôme, or Marie Laurencin, with the flattering implication that their works were as well known to the reader as to himself; with the result, of course, that one felt snobbishly impelled to find out more about them.

I remained under the Huxleyan enchantment well into my twenties. The magic began gradually to fail after *Point Counter Point* (1928); its failure was due partly to my discovery of other contemporary writers (Proust, Joyce, Lawrence), partly to the fact that Huxley himself had by that time lost something of his original sparkle. I felt little sympathy for his successive preoccupations with scientific utopias, pacifism, and Yoga; his writing, moreover, began to show signs of tiredness, and his characteristic mannerisms acquired, by compulsive repetition, an air almost of self-parody. Yet I continued to read him, admiring the lucidity of his arguments, even if I disagreed with his conclusions.

His stylistic weaknesses grew on him, and were painfully obvious in the novel, *Time Must Have a Stop* (1945), the first of his books which I found totally unreadable. Since then, I have preferred his essays to his fiction: the last few novels struck me as laboured and repetitive, with only occasional flashes of the old brilliance. Yet his intelligence never failed, and if one found his later ideas unsympathetic or even repellent, there could be no doubt of his intellectual integrity or of his genuine concern for the future of humanity.

He was a naturally religious man who was also by conviction (and, one is almost tempted to add, by heredity) a rationalist; many in his position have found a final refuge in Catholicism, but Huxley, as Lawrence once remarked, was not T. H. Huxley's grandson for nothing, and religion, to be acceptable to him, had to be of a kind which could be shown objectively true, or which, at any rate, required no blind act of faith on the part of the convert. The mystic's trance, in which the individual achieves a direct communion with Godhead, seemed to Huxley a demonstrable fact of human experience; one may or may not agree, and if one doesn't, the fact that Huxley's belief was largely based upon his experiments with hallucinogenic drugs does not make the argument any more convincing (nor, one feels, would

Huxley himself, in earlier days, have considered that mescalin or lysergic acid could be valid or permissible short cuts to the *tremendum mysterium*[1]). One suspects that he may at times have been tempted to surrender to the Church's authority; and one must deeply respect him for refusing, so scrupulously, to compound with his rationalist conscience.

For the reasons adumbrated above, I find it hard to be entirely objective about Huxley's *oeuvre*.[2] As a teacher, a philosopher, an exponent of the 'perennial philosophy', he seems to me ineffectual, for I am unable to believe that the major problems which confront mankind can be solved by quietism or the appeal to reason. As a novelist, his 'first period' seems to me unquestionably his best: I can still re-read *Crome Yellow*, *Those Barren Leaves*, *Limbo*, and *Little Mexican* with great pleasure, *Antic Hay* (which I used to think his masterpiece) with rather less; *Point Counter Point*, though beautifully constructed (on the pattern of *Les Faux-Monnayeurs*), already shows signs of fatigue, and, as Wyndham Lewis once pointed out, it does not survive the 'taxi-driver's test' [No. 76]. The title-story in *Two or Three Graces* (published a year or two previously) seems to me one of his best performances: a brilliant study of *bovarysme*[3] which also includes a malicious portrait of Lawrence, in sharp contrast with the flattering one in *Point Counter Point*. *Brief Candles* (1930) marks the end of this early period; 'The Claxtons' is certainly one of Huxley's funniest stories, though as a satire on arty-craftiness it seemed even at the time a little dated.

Then came *Brave New World* (1932), an entirely new departure, and not, I think, a very happy one: as Mr. Cyril Connolly put it, 'science had walked off with art', and a latent streak of vulgarity found expression in the ponderous jokes about 'Our Ford,' etc., which are both tasteless and unfunny. Thereafter, Huxley was at his best in his essays, a form in which he always excelled. I should like, also, to put in a word for his verse which, if derivative, is still agreeably readable.

Finally, a word about Huxley and sex. For my generation, his sexual frankness was one of the qualities which made him exciting: *Antic Hay* was banned by some of the libraries, though today the 'obscene' passages would hardly arouse comment if published in a school magazine. Huxley's attitude to sex is that of a man who, like Swift, is at once sensualist and ascetic: a dichotomy which was perhaps commoner in the

[1] 'Dreadful mystery.'
[2] 'Work.'
[3] Bovaryism—an exaggerated, glamorized concept of oneself, from Flaubert's *Madame Bovary*.

'twenties than it is today. I think that I was conscious, even at that period, of a temperamental affinity with Huxley in this respect; which is why, I suppose, he remains for me a kind of 'wicked uncle', whose earlier works haunt my mind with what he himself once described (referring to a sonnet of Mallarmé) as 'the inveterate persistency of an old remorse'.

148. Richard S. Kennedy on Huxley's final wisdom

Southwest Review, Winter 1965, 1, pp. 37–47

Richard Sylvester Kennedy, b. 1920, is a professor of English at Temple University, Philadelphia, and has written *The Window of Memory: The Literary Career of Thomas Wolfe* (1962), as well as articles on T. S. Eliot's plays (1965) and Edward Cummings (1966). He is co-editor of Wolfe's *Notebooks*, and is presently working on a critical biography of e. e. cummings.

Kennedy's article is entitled 'Aldous Huxley: The Final Wisdom.' See Introduction, p. 30.

Almost lost in the news during the unforgettable weekend of November 22, 1963, was the announcement of the death of Aldous Huxley. Those of us who grew up in the 1920's and 1930's experienced another feeling of loss. One by one the members of that brilliant generation of writers and artists have been passing from the scene, beginning with Wolfe in 1938 and Joyce in 1941, down to Hemingway, Faulkner, and Cummings of recent memory. Now a year has gone by since Huxley joined them, and we look about us and try to assess what he has left us and what he has meant to us.

We are struck, first of all, with the abundance and the variety of work from the typewriter of this tireless man of letters—novels, plays, scenarios, short stories, translations, personal essays, moral and philosophical essays, scientific and religious essays, biography, history, political journalism, travel sketches, and critical essays on literature, music, and art. We are aware that toward the end of his life he did not command the attention of critics as he did twenty-five years before. He had been with us as a keen critical eye and as an arranger of new perspectives for so long that we treated him like an old family retainer of the intellectual world. Critic and commentator had adopted a rather patronizing tone.

I suppose this did not matter to Mr. Huxley. He just continued to work, and to the end of his life at age sixty-nine he was still writing and publishing and altering the silhouette of his career, which had seen a great many shifts and changes over the years. In fact, in recent years he moved into a new period which deserves to be recognized and characterized. It was a period of harvesting, a period of synthesis, a period appropriate to the later part of a long and prolific life of letters.

[Reviews Huxley's career through the later 1950s, 'the period of synthesis']

If Huxley was wary of kinds of power such as might produce the dehumanizing dominance of the World State, what power opportunities seemed to him most threatening? First, he pointed to the problem of overpopulation, which can produce tremendous pressure because of the diminution of available resources of food and raw materials. This constitutes a temptation to power because, as Huxley put it, 'Whenever the economic life of a nation becomes precarious, the central government is forced to assume additional responsibilities for the general welfare.'

Second, he was aware that, with the increase of population and of technological advancement, society had become proportionately more complex. This led to a consequent need for more order in society, and thus social and political pressure built up to demand a standardization of human behavior, and to militate against any uniqueness of behavior.

Huxley was very much disturbed by the fact that in our time a great many devices had been developed or discovered which aid administrative forces in maintaining stability and help them in manipulating minds. He pointed to mass communication devices which can either distribute propaganda or create distractions to keep people from thinking about the important issues; chemical devices, such as tranquilizers, which reduce tension; and other methods of human engineering such as subliminal suggestion or sleep teaching. But warnings were not enough, Huxley felt:

[Quotes the passage on the values of freedom, love, and intelligence in *Brave New World Revisited*, p. 149]

Huxley answered his own call for something more positive by the publication of *Island* (1962), his first utopian novel. In this work, the new devices are used for good purposes—either for the enhancement of individual well-being or for the protection of individuals against abuses of power. More than this, *Island* represents best the synthesizing tendency of his last period, for it embraces what Huxley assumed was the best that both Western civilization and the culture of the East had to offer—biology, chemistry, technology, modern psychology from the West; and philosophy, religion, and ancient psychic practices from the East.

[Summarizes the background and story of *Island*]

The secret of the way to happiness possessed by the Palanese lies in their taking advantage of all the scientific discoveries of the West yet refusing to allow technological advancement to dominate their culture. In the application of psychology they have become more progressive than the West. Their aim in education is 'the training of the whole mind-body.' The principal of the elementary school describes it: 'What we give the children is simultaneously a training in perceiving and imagining, a training in applied physiology and psychology, a training in practical ethics and practical religion, a training in the proper use of language, and a training in self-knowledge. In a word, a training of the whole mind-body in all its aspects.'

Such a statement, and particularly one using a term like 'mind-body', implies an underlying philosophy of life. In Pala the philosophic outlook is drawn freely from Hinduism and Buddhism. Man is viewed as having both an individual self and a share in the Universal Self or Buddha-nature. Life is viewed as essentially all one. If a person has perception, he understands that his individual self is really only a part of the Oneness of all things; he understands too that all opposites are reconciled in this Oneness and that he must learn to accept everything that is natural and beyond his control, even if it is unpleasant, painful, or destructive. Thus he can face death as well as life, sorrow as well as the ending of sorrow. . . .

In Pala, the emphasis is on life here and now. This increases the importance of awareness. This also means that no concern about an afterlife is encouraged. Death is seen as a release of the self from a worn-out body; the union with the Universal Self ('The Clear Light', 'The Suchness of Things') then takes a different form. As a reminder of these things, the old Raja has trained all the mynah birds on the island to repeat some appropriate phrases. As they flutter around, they call, 'Here and now, boys', or they constantly repeat, 'Attention'. In case this sounds too tough-minded, they have been taught one more word too: *Karuna*, which means compassion.

Clearly, the religious philosophy of the Palanese is a refined and exquisite humanism.

[Discusses the application of William Sheldon's constitutional psychology to Palanese education]

One final detail in the Palanese way of life is associated with Huxley's continuing interest in mysticism. As a part of their religious practice, the Palanese take, from time to time, vision-inducing drugs which produce for them the mystical experience. These drugs, drawn from certain mushrooms, are referred to as the *moksha* medicine—*moksha*, a Hindu word meaning liberation—so called because the drugs both stimulate the visual cortex and open up areas of the mind that are seldom tapped except by practiced mystics. The experience has this kind of efficacy—the subject, after experiencing an intensification of all that is beautiful as well as of all that is fearful and horrible, feels that he has new understanding and a deeper compassion.

But the novel *Island* is not just a guided tour of ideas. A political and ideological conflict is developed with the outside world and with the dictator of Rendang, the neighboring island. The terrible irony is that the people of Pala are too happy. Such a situation cannot continue, warns the ambassador from Rendang:

'First, because it simply isn't possible for Pala to go on being different from the rest of the world. And, second, because it isn't *right* that it should be different.'

'Not right for people to be free and happy?' [asks Farnaby]. . . .

'Not right' [replies the ambassador]. 'Flaunting your blessedness in the face of so much misery—it's sheer *hubris*, it's a deliberate affront to the rest of humanity. It's even a kind of affront to God.'

Pala also has a vulnerable spot. Pala has rich, untapped resources in oil. In the end, through the treachery of the boy-Raja (who did not receive a Palanese education), Pala is invaded by the troops of the dictator, who will divide the oil royalties with the ruling family.

Huxley was hardheaded enough to bring about the fall of Pala in his novel, for its freedom and virtue were oversimplifications in a world of complexity. Many years ago, in *Proper Studies* (1927), he made this observation about utopian novels:

[Quotes passage on the 'inhabitants of Utopia', p. x]

Although Huxley created a utopia thirty years after writing these words, he still realized that idea and theory have to be blunted and shaped by the world of actuality.

But like other civilizations which were realer than Pala and which also fell, *Island* offers a provocative complex of ideas for our contemplation. Huxley has drawn together here the thought and experience of a lifetime. He has managed to synthesize religion and science, social order and individualism, and the cultural values of East and West. As a humanistic document, *Island* provides a worthy and fitting close to the career of a great intellectual of our time.

APPENDIX I

References for the Introduction

Sources not cited here are in the Bibliography, or they are fully documented in the text of the Introduction.

ACTON, HAROLD, *Memoirs of an Aesthete*. London: Methuen, 1948.

ADCOCK, ARTHUR ST JOHN, *The Glory That Was Grub Street: Impressions of Contemporary Authors*. New York: Stokes, 1928.

ALDINGTON, RICHARD, *Life for Life's Sake: A Book of Reminiscences*. New York: Viking, 1941.

ALDINGTON, RICHARD, *Portrait of a Genius, But. . . .* London: Heinemann, 1950.

ALLEN, WALTER, *The English Novel: A Short Critical History*. New York: Dutton, 1955.

ATKINS, JOHN, *Aldous Huxley: A Literary Study*. London: Calder, 1956.

BALD, R. C., 'Aldous Huxley as a Borrower', *College English*, January 1950, xi, pp. 183–7.

BARENSFELD, THOMAS, 'Aldous Huxley's Seven Years in America', *NYTBR*, 27 June 1943, p. 2.

BELL, JULIAN, *Julian Bell: Essays, Poems and Letters*, ed. Quentin Bell. London: Hogarth Press, 1938.

BENNETT, ARNOLD, *The Journal of Arnold Bennett*. New York: Literary Guild, 1933.

BENTLEY, JOSEPH, 'Semantic Gravitation: An Essay on Satiric Reduction', *Modern Language Quarterly*, March 1969, xxx, pp. 3–19.

BENTLEY, JOSEPH, 'The Later Novels of Aldous Huxley', *Yale Review*, Summer 1970, lix, pp. 507–19.

BIRNBAUM, MILTON, *Aldous Huxley's Quest for Values*. Knoxville: University of Tennessee Press, 1971.

BLOOMFIELD, PAUL, *Uncommon People: A Study of England's Elite*. London: Hamish Hamilton, 1955.

BOWERING, PETER, *Aldous Huxley: A Study of the Major Novels*. New York: Oxford University Press, 1969.

BRANDER, LAURENCE, *Aldous Huxley: A Critical Study*. London: Rupert Hart-Davis, 1969.

BROOKE, JOCELYN, *Aldous Huxley*. London: Published for the British Council by Longmans, 1954 (supplements to *British Book News* on 'Writers and Their Work', No. 55).

BUBER, MARTIN, *The Knowledge of Man*, ed. Maurice Friedman. New York: Harper & Row, 1955.

BUCK, PHILO M. Jr, 'Sight to the Blind: Aldous Huxley', *Directions in Contemporary Literature*. New York: Oxford University Press, 1942, pp. 169–91.

BURGUM, EDWIN BERRY, 'Aldous Huxley and His Dying Swan', *Antioch Review*, Spring 1942, ii, pp. 62–75. Reprinted in his *The Novel and the World's Dilemma* (New York: Oxford University Press, 1947).

CAMPBELL, ROY, *Light on a Dark Horse: An Autobiography (1901–1935)*. Chicago: Regnery, 1952.

CARRINGTON, DORA, *Carrington: Letters and Extracts from her Diaries*, ed. David Garnett. New York: Holt, Rinehart & Winston, 1970.

CHAMPNESS, H. M., 'Aldous Huxley at Sixty', *Spectator*, 23 July 1954, cxciii, p. 109.

CONNER, FREDERICK W., ' "Attention!" Aldous Huxley's Epistemological Route to Salvation', *Sewanee Review*, Spring 1973, lxxxi, pp. 282–308.

CONNOLLY, CYRIL, *The Condemned Playground: Essays 1927–1944*. New York: Macmillan, 1946.

CONNOLLY, CYRIL, *Enemies of Promise and Other Essays: An Autobiography of Ideas*. New York: Doubleday, 1960.

CONNOLLY, CYRIL, 'Told in Gath', *Parodies*, ed. Dwight MacDonald. New York: Random House, 1960, pp. 230–9.

CRAFT, ROBERT, 'With Aldous Huxley', *Encounter*, November 1965, xxv, pp. 10–16.

CRANE, HART, *The Letters of Hart Crane*, ed. Brom Weber. Berkeley: University of California Press, 1952.

DORAN, GEORGE, *Chronicles of Barabbas, 1884–1934*. New York: Harcourt Brace, 1935.

DYSON, A. E., 'Aldous Huxley and the Two Nothings', *Critical Quarterly*, Winter 1961, iii, pp. 293–309. Reprinted in his *The Crazy Fabric: Essays in Irony* (London: Macmillan, 1965).

EATON, GAI, 'Monk at Large: Aldous Huxley', *The Richest Vein*. London: Faber & Faber, 1949, pp. 166–82.

EDGAR, PELHAM, 'Aldous Huxley', *The Art of the Novel from 1700 to the Present Time*. New York: Macmillan, 1933, pp. 278–93.

ELIOT, T. S., *Thoughts After Lambeth*. London: Faber & Faber, 1931.

ELLMANN, RICHARD, *James Joyce*. New York: Oxford University Press, 1959.

FIRCHOW, PETER, *Aldous Huxley: Satirist and Novelist*. Minneapolis: University of Minnesota Press, 1972.

FOSTER, MALCOLM, *Joyce Cary: A Biography*. Boston: Houghton Mifflin, 1968.

GABOR, DENIS, *Inventing the Future*. New York: Knopf, 1964.

GILBERT, ARTHUR N., 'Pills and the Perfectibility of Man', *Virginia Quarterly Review*, Spring 1969, xlv, pp. 315–28.

GLICKSBERG, CHARLES I., 'The Intellectual Pilgrimage of Aldous Huxley', *Dalhousie Review*, July 1939, xxxii, pp. 165–78.

HACKER, ANDREW, 'Dostoevsky's Disciples: Man and Sheep in Political Theory', *Journal of Politics*, November 1955, xvii, pp. 590–613.

HANDLEY-JONES, W. S., 'The Modern Hamlet', *London Quarterly and Holborn Review*, July 1950, pp. 240–7.

HASSALL, CHRISTOPHER, *A Biography of Edward Marsh*. New York: Harcourt Brace Jovanovich, 1959.

HEARD, GERALD, 'The Poignant Prophet', *Kenyon Review*, Winter 1965, xxvii, pp. 49–70.

HODSON, JAMES LANSDALE, 'Julian and Aldous Huxley', *No Phantoms Here*. London: Faber & Faber, 1932, pp. 256–61.

HOFFMAN, FREDERICK J., 'Aldous Huxley and the Novel of Ideas', *College English*, December 1946, viii, pp. 129–37. Reprinted in *Forms of Modern Fiction*, ed. William Van O'Connor (Minneapolis: University of Minnesota, 1948), pp. 189–200.

HOLMES, CHARLES M., *Aldous Huxley and the Way to Reality*. Bloomington: Indiana University Press, 1970.

HOLROYD, MICHAEL, *Lytton Strachey: A Critical Biography*, Vol. II. New York: Holt, Rinehart & Winston, 1968.

HOUSTON, P. H., 'The Salvation of Aldous Huxley', *American Review*, December 1934, iv, pp. 209–32.

HUXLEY, LAURA ARCHERA, *This Timeless Moment: A Personal View of Aldous Huxley*. New York: Farrar, 1968.

Interview [by George Wickes and Ray Frazer], 'Aldous Huxley', *Writers at Work: The 'Paris Review' Interviews*, Second Series. New York: Viking, 1963, pp. 193–214.

JOAD, C. E. M., 'Aldous Huxley: The Man and His Work', *The Outline*

(*Supplement to John O'London's Weekly*), 25 July 1936, pp. 597–604.

KARL, FREDERICK R., 'The Play Within the Novel in *Antic Hay*', *Renascence*, Winter 1961, xiii, pp. 59–68.

KETTLE, ARNOLD, *An Introduction to the English Novel*, Vol. II. London: Hutchinson, 1953.

KOESTLER, ARTHUR, *The Ghost in the Machine*. New York: Macmillan, 1957.

KOHN-BRAMSTEDT, ERNST, 'The Intellectual as Ironist: Aldous Huxley and Thomas Mann', *Contemporary Review*, April 1939, clv, pp. 470–9.

LAWRENCE, D. H., *Phoenix: The Posthumous Papers of D. H. Lawrence*, ed. Edward McDonald. New York: Viking, 1936.

LAWRENCE, FRIEDA, *Frieda Lawrence: The Memoirs and Correspondence*, ed. E. W. Tedlock, Jr. New York: Knopf, 1964.

LEA, F. A., *The Life of John Middleton Murry*. New York: Oxford University Press, 1960.

LEHMANN, JOHN, *In My Own Time: Memoirs of a Literary Life*. Boston: Little, 1969.

LEWIS, SINCLAIR, *From Main Street to Stockholm: Letters of Sinclair Lewis, 1919–1930*, ed. Harrison Smith. New York: Harcourt Brace Jovanovich, 1952.

LEWIS, WYNDHAM, *The Letters of Wyndham Lewis*, ed. W. K. Rose. Norfolk, Connecticut: New Directions, 1963.

MCCORMICK, JOHN, *Catastrophe and Imagination*. London: Longmans, 1957.

MANN, THOMAS, *Briefe 1889–1936*. Frankfurt, Germany: Fischer, 1962.

MANN, THOMAS, *The Story of a Novel*, trans. Richard and Clara Winston. New York: Knopf, 1961.

MARAINI, YOI, 'A Talk With Aldous Huxley', *Bermondsey Book* (London), June 1926, iii, pp. 76–80.

MARITAIN, JACQUES, *The Range of Reason*. New York: Scribner's, 1952.

MAROVITZ, SANFORD E., 'Aldous Huxley's Intellectual Zoo', *Philological Quarterly*, October 1969, xlviii, pp. 495–507.

MATSON, FLOYD W., 'Aldous and Heaven Too: Religion Among the Intellectuals', *Antioch Review*, September 1954, xiv, pp. 293–309.

MAY, KEITH M., *Aldous Huxley*. London: Elek, 1972.

MECKIER, JEROME, *Aldous Huxley: Satire and Structure*. London: Chatto & Windus, 1969.

MECKIER, JEROME, 'Quarles Among the Monkeys: Huxley's Zoological Novels', *Modern Language Review*, April 1973, lxviii, pp. 268–82.

MILLGATE, MICHAEL, *The Achievement of William Faulkner*. London: Constable, 1966.

MIRSKY, DMITRI, *The Intelligentsia of Great Britain*. New York: Covici, 1935.

MUIR, EDWIN, 'Aldous Huxley', *Nation* (New York), 10 February 1926, cxxii, pp. 144–5. Reprinted in his *Transition: Essays on Contemporary Literature* (New York: Viking, 1926).

NEHLS, EDWARD, *D. H. Lawrence: A Composite Biography*, Vol. III, 1925–1930. Madison: University of Wisconsin Press, 1959.

NICHOLS, BEVERLEY, *Are They the Same at Home?* New York: Doran, 1927.

NICOLSON, HAROLD, *Diaries and Letters*, ed. Nigel Nicolson, Vol. II. New York: Athenaeum, 1967.

NIEBUHR, REINHOLD, 'An End to Illusions', *Nation* (New York), 29 June 1940, cl, pp. 778–9.

O'FAOLAIN, SEAN, *The Vanishing Hero: Studies of the Hero in the Modern Novel*. London: Eyre & Spottiswoode, 1956.

O'HARA, JOHN, *Sweet and Sour*. New York: Random House, 1953.

ORWELL, GEORGE, *Collected Essays, Journalism and Letters*, ed. Sonia Orwell and Ian Angus, Vol. IV. London: Secker & Warburg, 1968.

OSMOND, HUMPHREY, 'Peeping Tom and Doubting Thomas', *Twentieth Century*, June 1954, clv, pp. 521–6.

PARMENTER, ROSS, 'Huxley at Forty-Three', *Saturday Review of Literature*, 19 March 1938, xvii, pp. 10–11.

PATMORE, DEREK, *Private History: An Autobiography*. London: Jonathan Cape, 1960.

PORTEUS, HUGH GORDON, 'Aldous Huxley', *Twentieth Century*, August 1931, i, pp. 7–10.

POWYS, J. C., *Letters of John Cowper Powys to Louis Wilkinson 1935–1956*. London: Macdonald, 1958.

POWYS, LLEWELYN, *The Letters of Llewelyn Powys*, ed. Louis Wilkinson. London: Allen Lane, 1943.

PRIESTLEY, J. B., *Literature and Western Man*. New York: Harper & Row, 1960.

PROUST, MARCEL, *Cities of the Plain*, trans. of *Sodome et Gomorrhe* (1921) by C. K. Scott Moncrieff. New York: Modern Library, 1927.

QUENNELL, PETER, 'D. H. Lawrence and Aldous Huxley', *English Novelists: A Survey of the Novel by Twenty Contemporary Novelists*, ed. Derek Verschoyle. New York: Harcourt Brace, 1936, pp. 267–78.

QUENNELL, PETER, *The Sign of the Fish*. New York: Viking, 1960.

REID, RANDALL, *The Fiction of Nathanael West*. University of Chicago Press, 1967.

ROBERTS, JOHN HAWLEY, 'Huxley and Lawrence', *Virginia Quarterly Review*, Autumn 1937, xiii, pp. 546–57.

ROETHKE, THEODORE, *Selected Letters of Theodore Roethke*, ed. Ralph J. Mills, Jr. Seattle: University of Washington Press, 1968.

ROLO, CHARLES J., 'Aldous Huxley', *Atlantic Monthly*, August 1947, clxxx, pp. 109–15. Reprinted as the 'Introduction' to *The World of Aldous Huxley*, ed. Rolo (New York: Harper & Row, 1947).

SADLER, A. W., 'The Zaehner-Huxley Debate', *Journal of Religious Thought*, 1964–5, xxi, pp. 43–50.

SCALES, DEREK P., *Aldous Huxley and French Literature*. New South Wales, Australia: Sydney University Press, 1969.

SCHMERL, RUDOLF B., 'The Two Future Worlds of Aldous Huxley', *PMLA*, June 1962, lxxvii, pp. 328–34.

SPENDER, STEPHEN, 'An Open Letter to Aldous Huxley', *Left Review*, 1936–7, ii, pp. 539–41.

STEWART, D. H., 'Aldous Huxley's *Island*', *Queen's Quarterly*, Autumn 1963, lxx, pp. 326–35.

STOKES, SEWELL, 'Aldous Huxley in London', *Listener*, 12 December 1957, lviii, pp. 977–8.

STRONG, L. A. G., *Green Memory*. London: Methuen, 1961.

SULLIVAN, J. W. N., 'Interviews With Great Scientists: Aldous Huxley', *Observer* (London), 1 February 1931, pp. 15–16.

SUTHERLAND, ALASTAIR, 'Aldous Huxley's Mind at Large', *Twentieth Century*, May 1954, clv, pp. 441–9.

SUTHERLAND, JAMES, *English Satire*. Cambridge University Press, 1958.

SWINNERTON, FRANK, *The Georgian Scene*. New York: Farrar, 1934.

SWINNERTON, FRANK, *Swinnerton: An Autobiography*. New York: Doubleday, 1936.

SWINNERTON, FRANK, *Figures in the Foreground: Literary Reminiscences 1917–1940*. New York: Doubleday, 1964.

TEILHARD DE CHARDIN, PIERRE, *Letters to Two Friends 1926–1952*. New York: New American Library, 1968.

THODY, PHILIP, *Aldous Huxley*. London: Studio Vista, 1973.

TINDALL, WILLIAM YORK, 'The Trouble With Aldous Huxley', *American Scholar*, Autumn 1942, xi, pp. 452–64.

TUCK, DOROTHY, *Crowell's Handbook of Faulkner*. New York: Crowell, 1964.

WARD, ALFRED C., *The Nineteen-Twenties, Literature and Ideas in the Postwar Decade*. London: Methuen, 1930.

WATT, DONALD J., 'Vision and Symbol in Aldous Huxley's *Island*', *Twentieth Century Literature*, October 1968, xiv, pp. 149–60.

WATTS, HAROLD, *Aldous Huxley*. New York: Twayne, 1969.

WATTS, HAROLD, 'Introduction', *Point Counter Point*. New York: Harper & Row, 1947.

WAUGH, ALEC, 'The Neo-Georgians', *Fortnightly Review*, January 1924, cxv [n.s.], pp. 126–37.

WEBSTER, HARVEY CURTIS, 'Facing Futility: Aldous Huxley's Really Brave New World', *Sewanee Review*, April–June 1934, xlii, pp. 193–208.

WEBSTER, H. T., 'Aldous Huxley: Notes on a Moral Evolution', *South Atlantic Quarterly*, July 1946, xlv, pp. 372–83.

WILSON, ANGUS, 'The Naive Emancipator', *Encounter*, July 1955, v, pp. 73–6.

WOLFE, THOMAS, *The Notebooks of Thomas Wolfe*, ed. Richard S. Kennedy and Paschal Reeves, Vol. I. Chapel Hill: University of North Carolina Press, 1970.

WOODCOCK, GEORGE, 'Aldous Huxley: The Man and His Work', *World Review* (London), June 1949, iv [n.s.], pp. 52–4.

WOODCOCK, GEORGE, *Dawn and the Darkest Hour: A Study of Aldous Huxley*. London: Faber & Faber, 1972.

WOOLF, VIRGINIA, *A Writer's Diary*, ed. Leonard Woolf. London: Hogarth Press, 1953.

ZAEHNER, R. C., *Mysticism Sacred and Profane*. London: Oxford University Press, 1957.

Translations

Information on which the following table is based was generously provided by Huxley's British publishers, Chatto & Windus.

● = entire work   ★ = selection

Abbreviated title	Afrikaans	Catalan (Spain)	Chinese	Czech	Danish	Dutch	Finnish	French	German	Hebrew	Hungarian	Indian (Bengali)	Indian (Gujarati)	Indian (Hindi)	Indian (Ortya)	Italian	Japanese	Malayan	Norwegian	Polish	Portuguese (inc. Brazil)	Roumanian	Serbo-Croat (Yugoslavia)	Slovak (Czechoslovakia)	Slovene (Yugoslavia)	Spanish (inc. S. America)	Swedish	Turkish
Adonis				★				●								★										●		
AMSDS				●	●	●		●	●							●				●	●					●	●	
Along R								●								●	★									●	●	
Antic H				●		●		●			●					●				●	●					●	●	
Ape & E				●	●	●		●	●		●					●	●			●						●	●	
Art S	●			●	●	●		●								●	●									●	●	
Beyond								●												●	●					●		
BrNW	●	●		●	●	●		●	●	●	●	●				●	●		●	●	●		●	●	●	●	●	●
BrNWR				●	●	●		●	●							●	●		●	●	★	●				●	●	
Brief				★		●		●								●	★			★						●		
ColSS									●													★				●		
Crome	●			●	●	●		●								●	●			●						●	●	
Devils				●	●	●		●	●	●						●				●	●					●	●	
DWYW				★	●			●			★					●	★									●		
Doors	●				●	●		●								●	●		●	●	●					●	●	
Ends M				●	●	●		●	●		●			●		★				●	●					●	●	
EinG		●		●	●	●		●	●							●	●		●	●	●	●				●	●	
Genius				●	●	●		●	●							●	●			●						●	●	
GiocSm																●												
GreyE	●			●	●	●		●			●					●	●			●						●	●	
H & H	●			★	●	●		●	●							●	●			●						●	●	
Island	●			●	●	●		●								●	●		●	●	●		●			●	●	
JPil		●	★					●																				
Limbo		★	★			●		●												★						●	●	
Lit + Sc	●			★	●			●			●					●				●						●	●	
Lit Mex	●			★	★	●		●	★		★					●	★			★	★					●	●	
Mort C				★	★	●		●	★							●	★			★	★					●	●	
Music				★		●		●			●					●	★			★						●	●	
Olive								●								●	★									●		
OTMar																●										●		
Per Ph				●	●	●		●								●	●			●						●	●	
PCP		●	●		●	●		●	●	●						●	●		●	●	●	●	●	●	●	●	●	●
Pr St								●								●	★			●						●		
Sel Es				★																		●				●		
SLP				●	●	●		●	●		●								●	●		●				●	●	
T + V				★				●								●										●	●	
TBL				●	●	●		●								●				●						●	●	
TMHAS				●	●	●	●	●	●		●					●	●			●	●		●	●		●	●	
TTG	●			●	●			●	●		●					●	★		●	●	●		●	●		●	●	
Vulgar								●								●										●	●	
What Are				●				●								●												

APPENDIX III

Collected works sales

The following figures represent total sales of individual Huxley volumes in the British collected editions of his work. The totals combine sales in the Uniform Edition which began shortly after World War II, and the larger-format Collected Edition which was initiated in 1968. These figures represent hard-cover sales only, and are clearly more valuable in assessing the comparative popularity of individual titles than in indicating complete sales. Caution is advisable even in making comparative judgments, for the length of time in print varies noticeably for some of the books. Omitted titles have not yet appeared in the collected editions.

Title	First published in a collected edition	Copies sold to 31 December 1972
After Many a Summer	1950	12,510
Along the Road	1948	7,000
Antic Hay	1948	15,170
Ape and Essence*	1951	9,750
The Art of Seeing	1971	1,070
Beyond the Mexique Bay	1949	8,000
Brave New World	1950	55,620
Brave New World Revisited	1972	1,858
Brief Candles	1948	11,255
Collected Short Stories	1969	1,881
Crome Yellow	1949	16,470
The Devils of Loudun	1961	5,795
Doors of Perception/Heaven and Hell†	1960	5,225
Do What You Will	1949	8,355
Ends and Means*	1946	26,170
Eyeless in Gaza	1949	16,600
Grey Eminence	1956	4,800

Title	First published in a collected edition	Copies sold to 31 December 1972
Island	1972	590
Jesting Pilate	1948	10,070
Limbo	1946	16,170
Literature and Science/Science, Liberty and Peace†	1970	750
Little Mexican	1948	8,850
Mortal Coils	1949	8,330
Music at Night	1949	10,200
The Olive Tree	1947	5,750
On the Margin	1948	8,120
The Perennial Philosophy	1969	3,000
Point Counter Point	1947	35,800
Proper Studies	1949	7,510
Texts and Pretexts	1949	7,000
Themes and Variations	1954	3,150
Those Barren Leaves	1949	13,680
Time Must Have a Stop	1953	9,650
Two or Three Graces	1949	7,150
Verses and a Comedy	1946	10,000

* Sales of an extra printing of these two volumes not included.
† Both issued under single cover.

479

Bibliography

Other source materials are listed in Appendix I: References for the Introduction.

BEDFORD, SYBILLE, *Aldous Huxley: A Biography*, 2 vols, London: Chatto & Windus, Collins, 1973–4. The authorized biography, a most valuable portrait of Huxley the man.

CLARESON, THOMAS D., and ANDREWS, CAROLYN S. 'Aldous Huxley: A Bibliography 1960–1964', *Extrapolation*, 6, [1965], pp. 2–21. A helpful supplement to Eschelbach-Shober.

CLARK, RONALD W., *The Huxleys*. New York: McGraw-Hill, 1968. Chapters X, XIV, and XVII include considerable information on the critical response to Huxley's work.

ESCHELBACH, CLAIRE JOHN, and SHOBER, JOYCE LEE, *Aldous Huxley: A Bibliography 1916–1959*. Berkeley: University of California Press, 1961. The most complete list of works by and about Huxley yet to appear. Earlier bibliographies are cited by the compilers on p. 91.

HUXLEY, JULIAN, ed., *Aldous Huxley 1894–1963: A Memorial Volume*. New York: Harper & Row, 1965. Many recollections and assessments by friends, family, and associates—an important source book for personal views on Huxley's career.

KUEHN, ROBERT E., ed., *Aldous Huxley: A Collection of Critical Essays*. Englewood Cliffs, New Jersey: Prentice-Hall, 1974. Excerpts from books on Huxley by Birnbaum, Bowering, Firchow, Holmes, Meckier, and Watts, plus articles by Bentley, Hoffman, Marovitz, and Watt. The collection represents the revival of critical interest in Huxley since his death.

MECKIER, JEROME, 'Housebreaking Huxley: Saint Versus Satirist', *Mosaic*, Summer 1972, iv, pp. 165–77. A challenging review of several recent works on Huxley, concluding with a summary account of the current state of Huxley studies.

NAZARETH, PETER, 'Aldous Huxley and His Critics', *English Studies in*

Africa, March 1964, vii, pp. 65–81. Replies to Dyson's article and discusses several critical objections to Huxley's work.

SMITH, GROVER, ed., *Letters of Aldous Huxley*. London: Chatto & Windus, 1969. A valuable source of information for, among other things, Huxley's reactions to the reception of some of his work.

WEAVER, RAYMOND, *et al.*, *Aldous Huxley: A Collection of Critical and Biographical Studies*. New York: Doubleday [1929–30]. Essays done in the 1920s by Weaver, Carl and Mark Van Doren, Edwin Muir, Grant Overton, and Joseph Wood Krutch. Also a selection of 'personal sidelights' and 'critical comments from the press'.

Index

The index is divided into three sections: Huxley's works; periodicals and journals cited; and other names and titles. All references of significance, stated or implied, are included. References of the most casual sort have been omitted.

I HUXLEY'S WORKS

II PERIODICALS AND JOURNALS CITED

III OTHER NAMES AND TITLES